{ near National + Motor (w
Hu's

$5 to Jeanette
She paid 2.50
we all owe $5
she owes 2.50

I owe Tisha $5
she owes me $3
I owe her $2, ∴.

Darci gave me $5 (give to Tisha
Gretchen must pay still
Give Jeanette's 2.50 to Tisha.

LAW AND ECONOMICS

An Introductory Analysis

LAW AND ECONOMICS
An Introductory Analysis

WERNER Z. HIRSCH

Department of Economics
University of California, Los Angeles
Los Angeles, California

ACADEMIC PRESS

A Subsidiary of Harcourt Brace Jovanovich, Publishers

New York   London   Toronto   Sydney   San Francisco

ACADEMIC PRESS, INC.
111 Fifth Avenue, New York, New York 10003

United Kingdom Edition published by
ACADEMIC PRESS, INC. (LONDON) LTD.
24/28 Oval Road, London NW1 7DX

Library of Congress Cataloging in Publication Data

Hirsch, Werner Zvi, Date.
　　Law and economics.

　　Includes bibliographical references.
　　1. Law--United States. 2. Economics.
I. Title.
KF385.H55　　340'.0973　　79-51700
ISBN 0-12-349480-X

To Esther, Dan, Joel, and Lani

CONTENTS

zoning

III

ECONOMIC ANALYSIS OF LANDLORD–TENANT LAWS

IV

ECONOMIC ANALYSIS OF ZONING LAWS

V

CONTRACT LAW

VI

TORT LAW'S BASIC LEGAL PREMISES

VII

ECONOMIC ANALYSIS OF TORT LAW

VIII

CRIMINAL LAW

IX

ENVIRONMENTAL LAW

X

ANTIMONOPOLY LAW

PREFACE

"A lawyer who has not studied economics . . . is very apt to become a public enemy." Thus wrote Mr. Justice Brandeis in 1916 in his *Illinois Law Review* article, "The Living Law." At this distance, it is not clear what kind of economics, or how much of it, Justice Brandeis considered necessary. He could not have read Lord John Maynard Keynes's essay on Alfred Marshall in which Keynes described his vision of a polymath economist, who "must understand symbols and speak in words. He must contemplate the particular in terms of the general, and touch abstract and concrete in the same flight of thought. He must study the present in the light of the past for the purposes of the future." But Brandeis might well have been thinking about a similar facility to deal with economic matters—concepts and tools—that need to be applied to legal problems.

Today the merit of applying economic analysis to legal matters has been widely recognized, though not necessarily by all lawyers or economists. More and more scholars are actively engaged in discovering areas where legal and economic concerns interface. Many are seeking to marry approaches of both disciplines to gain a deeper understanding of legal problems that have an economic dimension.

Who would suspect that law and economics have much in common and can assist each other? At first glance, prospects for fruitful cooperation appear unusually remote. The law's overwhelming concern is justice. It focuses on the distribution among different parties of rights, entitlements, obligations, income, and the like, and therefore on how a pie of a given size is divided. Economics, on the other hand—particularly that part of microeconomics that has developed the most powerful paradigms—is largely

xi

normative. Its preoccupation is with the efficient use of resources to produce the largest pie possible. To look at it in a somewhat different manner,
underlying much of the law is the concept of the "reasonable" man. He is a
person who is not only protective of his own rights, but also has a fair
regard for the welfare of others. For example, the law holds that a person
whose acts deviate from the standard of the "reasonable" man can be found
negligent and held liable. Economics, on the other hand, is built around the
concept of the "rational" man, who in the extreme is totally self-serving,
seeking only to maximize his self-interest.

The antithesis of the two disciplines appears to go even further in
relation to their rigidity of conclusions, at least so it appears on the surface.
Law follows, by and large, a binary approach in its conclusions. Thus, a
court tends to find a defendant either liable or not liable. Not so economics,
which pursues an incremental approach. In negotiations between two parties to a transaction, the bargaining is about higher or lower prices and
higher or lower quantities to be supplied or demanded, and the outcomes
are also quantitatively different.

But before lawyers and economists conclude that there is a basic incom-
patibility between the two fields, they should look more closely. For there
are likely to be some surprises. What on first glance appear to be grave
fundamental differences in premises and approach turn out to be reconcil-
able and can often be brought into harmony. For example, it can be argued
that the "rational" man in seeking his self-interest takes into consideration
the effect of his decision on others to the extent that their reaction makes
an impression. In this manner, we can explain how a person can be rational
and at the same time altruistic. In the more technical language of the
economist, we would say that the effect of one person's decision on others
can enter as an argument into the first person's utility function.

In a similar manner, it can be shown that the binary approach used by
the court in reaching conclusions can at times become almost as flexible as
the overtly incremental approach of economists. First, many states have
adopted a comparative-negligence system for many personal injury
cases—compensation for losses is apportioned to the different parties to
the extent that each was found negligent. Second, in a criminal case, a
defendant charged with a particular crime may be found guilty of a crime
of lesser severity, and the court has the leeway to apply incrementalism in
sentencing. Thus, though the charge is murder, a court can find a defendant guilty of manslaughter; the penalty can be a prison sentence—which
may be suspended—of various lengths, a fine of lesser or greater severity,
or both.

Thus, what might appear to be fundamental differences in approach
between the two disciplines turn out, on inspection, not to be major obstacles to collaboration. What, then, are the major facets of the alliance

between law and economics? Where do lawyers and economists meet, and how do they join forces once they have agreed to meet?

Before offering this volume as a partial reply to these questions, I would like to pay my respects to the pioneers in the field of law and economics. Ronald Coase, Guido Calabresi, and Richard A. Posner, in particular, enabled the new field to take off in a fruitful and promising direction. As Posner has expressed it, "The new law and economics dates from the early 1960s, when Guido Calabresi's first article on torts and Ronald Coase's article on social cost were published." [1] Moreover, two journals have been particularly instrumental in advancing the new field of law and economics—the *Journal of Law and Economics*, which made its debut in 1960 under the able editorship of Ronald Coase, and the *Journal of Legal Studies*, which started publication in 1972 under its capable editor, Richard A. Posner. But it would be a mistake to underestimate the importance of various law reviews, which have published numerous outstanding contributions to the new field.

Those who have labored in vineyards of law and economics have sought to bring economics to bear on law in two distinctive ways. Posner is probably the foremost proponent of the first approach, the application of microeconomic theory to legal rule formulation. Here the focus has been on using microeconomic theory and paradigms to formulate new common-law rules and to interpret existing ones as consistent with efficiency considerations. The second approach has emphasized the application of microeconomic theory and econometric methods to the estimation of the effects of laws, both existing and proposed; this is the thrust of this volume. In the main it will be concerned with effect evaluation in the light of a rather deterministic view of the universe.

The emphasis on economic effect evaluation was selected for a number of reasons. The intellectual justification for assuming that the common law is predominantly efficiency-based and that microeconomic theory can be successfully used to formulate laws rests on rather shaky grounds. As will be argued in Chapter I, most of the essential assumptions underlying microeconomic theory are not met in real life. And why should judges, who in the first place do not know such theory, follow it and seek maximization of resource use, when their training and background seems to emphasize concern with justice and redistributional issues? But perhaps most persuasive is the fact that microeconomics and econometric techniques are particularly powerful and well suited for effect evaluation. From a theoretical point of view, such an effort looks upon the law as an important component of the environment within which transactions take place. The task, then, is

---

1. Richard A. Posner, *Economic Analysis of Law*, 2nd ed. (Boston: Little, Brown, 1977), p. 16.

to model the transactions in a changing legal environment and estimate the effects of these changes on the outcomes of transactions.

The world in which transactions take place is highly urbanized, industrialized, and mobile, and transactors interact continually. Thus, interdependencies abound and have to be reckoned with. In such a world, the entitlements and rights of some parties are frequently violated. And, although unwanted burdens are imposed on other parties, that is, as a result of violation of rights, compensation is often not forthcoming. Economists, as we shall see, then speak about the presence of externalities, and they have developed powerful theories for their analysis.

These theories are helpful in examining legal relations where entitlements and rights are freely and voluntarily exchanged—the province of property law and contract law. Following Calabresi's lead, we can also apply them when entitlements and rights are forcibly violated. When this happens, we find ourselves in the domain of tort law and criminal law. Whenever the collective wisdom and values of society permit such encroachments on entitlements or rights to be remedied through the payment of appropriate compensation, tort law becomes applicable. If, however, society determines not to tolerate certain violations of entitlements and rights, such as killings and robberies, criminal law comes into play.

Within this framework (developed in some detail in Chapter I), I first examine the basic legal premises of property law (Chapter II). Concepts and ideas so developed are then given economic content and placed within an effect-estimating framework. Thus, in Chapter III, certain landlord–tenant laws are presented and their effects on the welfare of landlords and tenants—especially indigent tenants—are analyzed. In Chapter IV, a similar effort is undertaken in relation to zoning laws.

The inquiry into property law is followed by a somewhat more limited effort with regard to contract law. One reason for the more limited scope is that contract law, rather than bringing forth side effects, is primarily supposed to facilitate transactions—a major concern of Chapter V. In Chapter VI, the major basic legal premises of tort law are presented. They are subjected to an economic analysis in the following chapter. Specifically, Chapter VII applies economic analysis to such pressing problems as malpractice, product liability, and accident law.

Chapter VIII looks at criminal law from the vantage point of protecting initial entitlements from criminal encroachment. Special attention is given to economic models that relate deterrence measures, including capital punishment, to the commission of crime. Thereafter, in Chapter IX, we come to the heart of the relations between law and economics in terms of the main theme of this volume—entitlements and externalities. Thus, environmental law seeks to define, allocate, and enforce environmental property rights and entitlements in a world replete with externalities. The response to this challenge of courts and legislatures is examined within an economic framework. Finally, in Chapter X, I turn to the most venerable area of cooperation between lawyer and economist—antimonopoly law.

By no means do I wish to suggest that this is a comprehensive treatment of the interface of law and economics. Legal and economic concerns interact in innumerable ways, and the number of aspects of this interaction that can benefit from a joint approach of both disciplines is great. I have merely offered some examples in the hope of stimulating among legal scholars an awareness of the contribution that economists might make to the law, and among economists an interest in applying their discipline to the lawyers' problems. An important area of mutual concern has been omitted—the field of taxation, which has long been studied by both disciplines; a voluminous literature already exists. Moreover, I intend to address myself to this field in the future.

There are many friends and colleagues who have been most helpful during the preparation of this volume. I would like to express special thanks to Guido Calabresi, who not only inspired me during extended conversations but also critically read Chapters I, VI, VII, and IX and offered many helpful suggestions, and to Gary Schwartz, who critically read the entire manuscript. Thanks are also due to Marvin Frankel, who read and commented on Chapter X, Donald Hagman (Chapter II), Neil Jacoby (Chapter X), Benjamin Klein (Chapter X), Mitchell Polinsky (Chapters II, VII, and IX), Arthur Rosett (Chapter V), and Denis Smallwood (Chapter VII).

During the preparation of the manuscript, library research was carried out effectively by Byde Clawson, Berry Yoch, and Kenneth Sweezy. Moreover, extended discussions with Joel Hirsch proved most useful. The manuscript was ably typed by Lorraine Grams, whose efficiency and cheerfulness were especially appreciated. However, by far my greatest gratitude is due my wife, Esther Hirsch, for her everlasting patience, encouragement, and assistance, without which this volume could never have been written.

Finally, I would like to express my sincere appreciation to the Rockefeller Foundation, under whose auspices I was able to complete major portions of the final manuscript as a resident scholar at the Villa Serbelloni in Bellagio. Its study and conference center provided a uniquely stimulating and intellectually invigorating environment.

LAW AND ECONOMICS

An Introductory Analysis

I

INTRODUCTION

NATURE AND ORIGIN OF LAWS

In the narrow sense, laws can be looked upon as commands backed up by the coercive power of the state.[1] A broader and perhaps more significant view is that laws are authoritative directives that impose costs and benefits on participants in a transaction and in the process alter incentives. They determine the environment within which transactions between two or more parties take place and as such can be made to contribute to overall efficiency and justice. In addition, laws as authoritative directives provide instruments by which questions of concern to different parties can be settled. Depending on the precision with which laws spell out the nature of the directive arrangements, laws provide a lower or higher degree of certainty about the law's implications for the performance of participants in a transaction. Transactions are thus facilitated or impeded; conflicts and court cases made more or less common; in turn, transactors' costs and returns are affected. Thus, laws can be looked upon as contracts—either voluntarily or involuntarily arrived at—adjudicated and enforced by government.

The making of laws is not costless. Their drafting and enforcement require real resources and involve the trading-off of costs and benefits to determine when to rely on written contracts and how detailed such contracts should be. We distinguish between *statutory* and *court-made* laws. The former include not only the statutes passed by the legislature but also the fundamental laws chiseled into the constitution.

1. Richard A. Posner, *Economic Analysis of Law* (Boston: Little, Brown, 1972), p. 393.

1

Increasingly, courts have made law by stepping in where, in their opinion, fundamental changes in social and technological conditions have not been reflected in legislation. Much of the debate among the more conservative and more liberal schools of jurisprudence centers around the issue of how far courts should go in assuming what is basically the responsibility of the legislature.

THE INTERFACE BETWEEN
LAW AND ECONOMICS

Where did lawyer and economist first meet professionally? No doubt it was in the lawyer's rose patch. It happened when the lawyer first thought it propitious to have expert witnesses, some of whom were economists. For example, my own professional association with lawyers began in the mid 1950s when I was asked to testify before the Interstate Commerce Commission in a freight rate case. Soon another law firm asked me to testify before a state public utility commission, and another one sought help with wage negotiations in the garment industry. I have also often joined lawyers in helping legislators formulate tax policy.

The most active area of cooperation for many economists has been the antitrust field. However, economists have gone beyond traditional areas to undertake research on criminal justice, pollution, poverty, racial discrimination, land use planning, accident prevention, landlord–tenant relations, and urban government, among others, where their interests often dovetail with those of lawyers.

But there is another point of contact. It relates to the criticism voiced by some that legal scholars view the law too much from within—too much in terms of the law's own logical structure. When law steps outside itself, these critics claim, it lacks a well-developed theoretical or empirical apparatus with which to explore the world around it. For example, Bruce Ackerman is disturbed that "lawyers are so little trained to consider in a sophisticated way the relationship between legal order and the ends of social life."[2] Yet as legal scholars look outside law, they find that economics has developed paradigms that seem to provide a powerful analytic framework for the study of the law. These paradigms, and economic theory in general, can be attractive to them. The economic model of self-interest, whose objective test relates to efficient allocation of resources, appears to offer a neat and uncluttered view of the world. Such a view is comforting to the lawyer who struggles in a complex world created in part by the diversity of values among people. If such an economic model serves merely as a first step for

2. Bruce Ackerman, "Law and the Modern Mind by Jerome Frank," Daedalus, 103 (Spring 1974): 119, 126.

legal analysis, its use has substantial merit. However, I must warn that if the model by itself is used to derive definitive legal insight and rules, results are likely to be erroneous. Efforts at reducing complexity for analytic purposes are commendable; however, merely streamlining assumptions and then pretending that simplicity has been achieved can be gravely misleading. More about models and their assumptions will be said in what follows.

First approach (Posners)

LEGAL RULE FORMULATION

Efforts of rule formulation are in the rational intellectual tradition of William Blackstone[3] on the legal side and Adam Smith[4] on the economic side. They can also be traced to Jeremy Bentham's utilitarianism, "in its aspect as a positive theory of human behavior, . . . another name for economic theory."[5]

A modern-day proponent is Posner. His view of the world of economics and to no small extent of law includes "the assumption that man is a rational maximizer of his ends in life . . . ,"[6] an assumption he correctly reminds us is "no stronger than that most people in most affairs of life are guided by what they conceive to be their self-interest and that they choose means reasonably (not perfectly) designed to promote it."[7] On the basis of this assumption, three major fundamental economic concepts emerge.[8] The first is the inverse relation between price and quantity; the second is the economist's view of cost as opportunity cost, that is, the price that the resources consumed in making (and selling) the seller's product would command in their next best use—the alternative price; and the third is the tendency of resources to gravitate toward their highest value uses if exchange is permitted. If voluntarily exchanged, resources are shifted to those uses in which the value to the consumer, as measured by the consumer's willingness to pay, is highest. When resources are being used where their value is greatest, they are being employed efficiently; they produce the largest possible output. On the basis of microeconomic arguments—those that allegedly reflect the behavior of firms and households—Posner, for example, is convinced that "it may be possible to deduce the basic formal characteristics of law itself from economic theory;"[9] consequently he argues that "the ultimate question for decision in many lawsuits is, what allocation of resources would maximize efficiency?"[10]

However, the application of microeconomic theory to legal rule formula-

3. William Blackstone, *Commentaries on the Law of England*, 4 vols. (n.p., 1765–1769).
4. Adam Smith, *An Inquiry into the Nature and Causes of the Wealth of Nations* (London, 1776).
5. Jeremy Bentham, *Theory of Legislation*, ed. R. Hildreth (n.p., 1864), pp. 325–326, 357.
6. Posner, *Economic Analysis of Law*, p. 1.
7. *Ibid.*, p. 5.
8. *Ibid.*, p. 6.
9. *Ibid.*, p. 393.
10. *Ibid.*, p. 320.

tion poses a number of serious problems. For example, microeconomic theory assumes that human beings are rational; whatever they do is in their best interest, given their tastes, market opportunities, and circumstances. This, in short, is the fundamental tenet of the *theory of revealed preferences.* By this theory, economists treat the actual behavior of consumers as faithfully reflecting preferences, and they consider preferences shown to be an extension of consumer behavior. Yet the theory is basically circular; it argues that since people are rationally self-interested, what they do shows what they value, and their willingness to pay for what they value is the ultimate proof of their rational self-interest. Some scholars have criticized the circularity of the argument; Leff, for example, points to the following difficulties:

> If human desire itself becomes normative (in the sense that it cannot be criticized), and if human desire is made definitionally identical with certain human acts, then those human acts are also beyond criticism in normative or efficiency terms; everyone is doing as best he can exactly what he set out to do which, by definition, is "good" for him. In those terms, it is not at all surprising that economic analyses have "considerable power in predicting how people in fact behave."[11]

The question has also been asked whether value is indeed determined by people's willingness to pay or whether it is not determined rather by people's ability to pay for a good or service. As Thurow sees it, "A market economy that starts with an unjust distribution of economic resources will yield an unjust distribution of goods and services, regardless of its efficiency."[12]

Additionally, there is an even more serious problem: The theory is best equipped to deal with resource-allocation efficiency, but justice and fairness which relate to distributional issues must also be considered. Our task would be so much easier if efficiency could be rigorously defended as the only and ultimate objective. Instead we face two all-too-often opposing objectives—efficiency and equity. It must be remembered that the ultimate goal is what economists like to call *social efficiency,* which requires trading off resource-allocation efficiency against distribution of income. Unfortunately, as all will agree, what is the most desirable distribution of income is a highly subjective decision. Nevertheless, legal rules must be concerned about both efficiency and income distribution. In a formal way there is a solution to this trade-off problem. Guidelines given by economic theory require two successive steps—first, income should be redistributed in the most desirable manner; second, resources should be allocated in the most

11. A. Leff, "Economic Analysis of Law: Some Realism about Nominalism," *Virginia Law Review* 60 (March 1974): 458.

12. L. Thurow, "Economic Justice and the Economist: A Reply," *Public Interest* 33 (Fall 1973): 120.

efficient manner, preferably in response to competitive forces. An effort must thus be made to agree on a subjectively preferred income distribution and it must be followed by an effort to attain allocative efficiency. The formulation of prudent legal rules would have to proceed by considering both goals, not just allocative efficiency—a formidable task.

Another problem is that efficiency must be related to a specific objective function. For example, if one were to assert that the purpose of criminal punishment is to deter criminal behavior, one therefore would like to see punishment commensurate with the committed crime. If, moreover, one were to find that the social costs of incarceration exceeded by far fines that might be imposed—because of the cost of running a prison, the loss of prisoners' productivity, and the prison's ill effects on prisoners—one would conclude that an efficient administration of justice should merely dispense fines. However, this conclusion results from the assumption of the existence of a single-valued objective function—deterrence. But what if society and therefore legislators and particularly law enforcement officers insist (as appears to be the case) not merely on deterrence but also on retribution through such punitive action as incarceration? Then the analyst will be forced to reach different efficiency conclusions about the criminal justice system, unless he turns preacher and calls to outlaw retribution. Furthermore, there are criminals who can neither be deterred by fines nor rehabilitated. Incarcerating them may be the only way to protect society. Altogether there is little evidence that economists or lawyers are particularly well qualified to select the most appropriate objective functions. As a matter of fact, many economists tend to have tunnel vision, since they find it so much more agreeable to engage in partial equilibrium, that is, piecemeal rather than general equilibrium analysis—not because they are intellectually lazy, but because the latter is so much more complex and often beyond their reach.

A final problem is that even for the determination of optimal allocative efficiency conditions, economists are forced to make a number of restrictive assumptions. At least three such assumptions are made in relation to Pareto efficiency: *zero transaction costs, zero redistribution costs,* and *convexity.* By transaction costs economists mean real resources employed in bargaining, getting information, and formalizing and enforcing agreements—costs that interfere with the working of competitive markets.[13] Thus, the assumption that all transactions are costless and that information about costs and prices is effortlessly available removes us very far from real life.

The second assumption relates to the cost of redistributing incomes

13. See Werner Z. Hirsch, "Reducing Law's Uncertainty and Complexity," *UCLA Law Review* 21 (1974): 1239, and K. J. Arrow, "The Organization of Economic Activity: Issues Pertinent to the Choice of Market versus Non-market Allocation," in *The Analysis and Evaluation of Public Expenditures: The PPB System,* a Compendium of Papers of the Joint Economic Committee (Washington, D.C.: U.S. Government Printing Office, 1969), pp. 47–63.

among consumers. Given that the initial endowment into which the population is born is considered inappropriate and redistribution is undertaken, virtually every redistribution scheme is costly in that it distorts incentives and behavior and imposes political as well as administrative costs. Thus, for example, efforts toward redistribution through an income tax that changes consumers' budgets, their spending habits, and their preferences for leisure are unlikely to be costless.[14]

The economic implications of the third assumption, convexity, circumscribe the structure of consumers' preferences and producers' technology. For example, with respect to households, convexity means, in the words of Arrow, that "if we consider two different bundles of consumption, a third bundle defined by averaging the first two commodity by commodity is not inferior in the household's preferences to both of the first two."[15] An example of nonconvexity would be the renter who has for years lived in the downtown area and then moves to the suburbs because of unchecked increases in downtown crime. Now a suburbanite, his interest in seeing crime combatted in the core city vanishes.[16] Nonconvexities are very common and lead to market failure, interfering with Pareto efficiency.

EFFECT EVALUATION

this dealt with in this book

Although economics, to a limited degree, can contribute to legal rule formulation, there exists a further, more promising area of contact. A contribution can be made by applying economic theory and econometrics to specify and quantify economic effects—direct and indirect—of legal rules and rulings, and the distribution of these effects. At a time when rule formulation involves normative economics, effect evaluation is basically an exercise in positive economics.

For the purpose of effect evaluation, it is necessary first to build a microeconomic model that represents as closely as possible the specific environment in which transactions take place and of which the law is an important part, a model that links the environment to various outcome dimensions. One of the great challenges is to model the specific law and its effects on important outcomes without doing too much violence to real-life conditions. Yet the model cannot be too complex, for complexity reduces the likelihood of its empirical implementation. The single most significant implementation step involves econometric techniques. When the modeling and the econometric work are successful, quantitative statements about the probable effects of the law, that is, statements within an inference setting, become possible.

14. T. C. Koopmans, *Three Essays on the State of Economic Science* (New York: McGraw-Hill, 1957).

15. Arrow, "Organization of Economic Activity," p. 49.

16. M. Polinsky, "Economic Analysis as a Potentially Defective Product: A Buyer's Guide to Posner's Economic Analysis of Law," *Harvard Law Review* 87 (June 1974): 1655–1681.

But, not infrequently, existing microeconomic theory and econometric methods and the availability of data limit the degree to which definitive quantitative statements about side effects can be made. In such instances we must be satisfied with deductive inquiries based on microeconomic models that can yield qualitative conclusions of major policy value.

Examples of the possible application of microeconomic theory and econometrics to the estimation of side effects are quite numerous. In relation to contract law, one might want to estimate the side effects of consumer-protection laws—those laws that reduce the rights of a seller under an installment plan to repossess cars, appliances, furniture, and other items. In relation to property law, the side effects of habitability laws are of interest. In relation to tort law, the potential costs and benefits of defensive medicine being practiced in the presence of *res ipsa loquitur* ("the thing speaks for itself") might be examined. Finally, in relation to criminal law, the costs and effects of crime prevention measures are of widespread concern.

WHERE LAW AND ECONOMICS
MIGHT NOT MEET

Although lawyer and economist have much in common, there are also some significant differences in their approaches. Only two fundamental differences will be taken up—the law's reference to a *reasonable* man versus the economist's assumption of a rational man, and the incrementalism of the economist versus the binary aspect of the court, which finds a defendant either liable or not liable.

The lawyer's concept of a reasonable man is quite distinct from the economist's rational man. The reasonable man, according to the traditional tort literature, will ordinarily behave in a reasonable, prudent manner. Thus, he will act with fair regard for the welfare of others. Negligent conduct, for example, which departs from the standard of the reasonable man, is in a real sense subnormal and deviant; this deviance helps to justify the imposition of liability rules on tortfeasors, about which more will be said subsequently.

The rational man, according to traditional economic theory, seeks to maximize his own self-interest; he shows only limited concern for the well-being of others.[17] This self-centered drive produces outcomes in which private and social costs diverge. These outcomes can conflict with the overall societal interest. Attaining private net benefit (e.g., profit) objectives is often inconsistent with the attainment of societal net benefit objectives.

17. This argument does not deny that economic theory can take into consideration the possibility that *Homo economicus* may include in his maximizing decisions some of the intangible benefits accruing to him from alleviating the suffering of the poor, the sick, or the aged.

Court rulings—except when comparative-negligence tort standards are applied—are usually much more rigid and as a result extreme in their effects. A court finds a defendant liable or not; insofar as the defendant's reputation, for example, is concerned, the effects of the two outcomes are grossly different. Once the defendant has been found liable, however, the court has some leeway and can apply incrementalism in sentencing, that is, in the kind and severity of punishment.

ENTITLEMENTS AND EXTERNALITIES AND THE ROLE OF THE LAW

The law, as was stated earlier, provides guidelines for transactions between parties. It does so by explicitly stipulating and allocating rights and entitlements, and responsibilities, and by providing remedial rights. By so doing the law can help minimize conflicts; moreover, it offers rules by which conflicts, should they arise, can be resolved fairly. From the economist's point of view, certain classes of conflict are closely related to externalities in that a conflict is the direct result of an externality. But before we look at externalities, let us consider rights and entitlements that are violated in the presence of externalities.

The *Restatement of Property* defines a right as "a legally enforceable claim of one person against another, that the other shall do a given act or shall not do a given act."[18] Therefore, property rights may be thought of in terms of the legal relationships—rights and duties—between a property owner and another person. One has a property right when one is able to compel another legally to do or not to do a given act. Thus, when a person's activity causes damage to a landowner, the landowner is endowed with a property right that can be invoked to force the person causing the damage to cease the activity and to compensate the landowner for the damage incurred.

An entitlement is akin to a property right. It is the legitimate claim a person has and prevails in case of conflict. There exist two major views on entitlements. One is a natural and historical view that looks at entitlements as exogenously determined. Accordingly, entitlements are policy instruments governments use in pursuing, for example, such goals as economic efficiency or income redistribution. In part this view is expressed by Ronald Dworkin, who states,

> Arguments of principle are arguments intended to establish an individual right; arguments of policy are arguments intended to establish a collective goal. Principles are propositions that describe rights; policies are propositions that describe goals . . . I shall make . . . a formal distinction that . . .

18. *Restatement of Property*, §1.

provides a guide for discovering which rights a particular political theory supposes men and women to have . . . a political theory which holds a right to freedom of speech as absolute will recognize no reason for not securing the liberty it requires for every individual.[19]

Dworkin goes on to argue that individuals have rights and entitlements that exist prior to any explicit legislation, and the most fundamental of these is a person's entitlement to equality.

Robert Nozick states that the "historical principles of justice hold that past circumstances or actions of people can create differential entitlements. . . . An injustice can be worked by moving from one distribution to another structurally identical one, for the second, in profile, the same, may violate people's entitlements."[20]

The second view looks upon entitlements as policy instruments that are endogenous. It is well expressed by Calabresi and Melamed, who maintain that

the state not only has to decide whom to entitle, but it must also simultaneously make a series of equally difficult second order decisions. These decisions go to the manner in which entitlements are protected and to whether an individual is allowed to sell or trade the entitlement. In any given dispute, for example, the state must decide not only which side wins but also the kind of protection to grant. It is . . . the latter decisions, . . . which shape the subsequent relationship between the winner and the loser.[21]

Now let us turn to externalities. E. J. Mishan considers concern with externalities as "a new field of specialization within the broader terrain of welfare economics."[22] But externalities are not a new concept. Alfred Marshall referred to what he called "external effects" as economies external to the firm but internal to the industry.[23] Arthur C. Pigou elaborated on the concept and pointed to it as a chief cause of divergencies between "private net product" and "social net product" and, therefore, as preventing optimality under conditions of perfect competition.[24]

Additional contributions to our understanding of externalities have been made by J. Meade, T. Scitovsky, and K. J. Arrow, who have helped clarify

19. Ronald Dworkin, *Taking Rights Seriously* (Cambridge: Harvard University Press, 1977), pp. 90–92. Similar views are taken by John Rawls, *A Theory of Justice* (Cambridge: Harvard University Press, 1971).

20. Robert Nozick, *Anarchy, State, and Utopia* (New York: Basic Books, 1974), p. 155.

21. G. Calabresi and A. D. Melamed, "Property Rules, Liability Rules, and Inalienability: One View of the Cathedral," *Harvard Law Review* 85 (April 1972): 1092. Copyright © 1972 by the Harvard Law Review Association. Similar views are held by R. Coase, H. Demsetz, and R. Posner.

22. E. J. Mishan, "The Postwar Literature on Externalities," *Journal of Economic Literature* 9 (March 1971): 1.

23. Alfred Marshall, *Principles of Economics,* 8th ed. (London: Macmillan, 1925).

24. Arthur C. Pigou, *The Economics of Welfare,* 4th ed. (London: Macmillan, 1946).

the concept.[25] However, there is no unanimity among economists as to the nature and definition of externalities. Perhaps the most all-inclusive view is that of J. M. Buchanan and W. C. Stubblebine, who talk about a "potentially Pareto-relevant externality," that is, an interdependency generating "desire on the part of the externally benefited (damaged) party (A) to modify the behavior of the party empowered to take action (B) through trade, persuasion, compromise, agreement, convention, collective action, etc."[26] A similar view can be attributed to Mishan.[27] He defines an externality as the dependence of someone's utility or output on an unpriced or improperly priced resource. If one of the resources is improperly priced, then gains from trade are possible.[28]

The difficulty with these definitions is not so much with their use of Pareto optimality as a benchmark—in theory any other social welfare function could be chosen—as with their implication that any inefficiency is an externality. As R. N. McKean points out, "any falling short of either the production-possibility boundary or the 'utility-possibility boundary' means that gains from trade are available—or, in Mishan's terms, that some resource is improperly priced."[29]

R. Turvey avoids this problem by defining externalities as "the impacts of the activities of households, public agencies, or enterprises upon the activities of other households, public agencies, or enterprises which are exerted otherwise than through the market. They are, in other words, relationships other than those between buyer and seller."[30]

Together with Turvey, Arrow, and Mishan, I propose that an externality exists whenever the decision of such economic actors as a household or firm directly affects, through nonmarket transactions, the utility or production functions of other economic actors.[31] An externality thus results as re-

---

25. J. Meade, "External Economies and Diseconomies in a Competitive Situation," *Economic Journal* 62 (March 1952): 54–67; T. Scitovsky, "Two Concepts of External Economies," *Journal of Political Economy* 64 (April 1954): 70–82; and Arrow, "Organization of Economic Activity," pp. 47–63.

26. J. M. Buchanan and W. C. Stubblebine, "Externality," *Economica* 29 (November 1962): 347–375.

27. Mishan, "Postwar Literature on Externalities": 1.

28. E. J. Mishan, "Reflections on Recent Developments in the Concept of External Effects," *Canadian Journal of Economics and Political Science* 31 (February 1965): 6.

29. R. N. McKean, "Appropriability and Externalities in Urban Government" (Paper prepared for the October 22, 1971, COUPE meeting in Cambridge, Mass.), p. 10.

30. R. Turvey, "Side Effects of Resource Use," in *Environmental Quality in a Growing Economy*, ed. Henry Jarrett (Baltimore: Johns Hopkins, 1966), p. 47.

31. The presence of externalities can be expressed by the following mathematical notations: $F^1(x_1^1, x_2^1, \ldots, x_m^1; x_n^2)$ represents an external effect generated by entity 2 on entity 1 where F^1 stands for the utility (or output) level of individual (or firm) 1; the x^1's are the amounts of goods $x_1, x_2, \ldots, x_m$ utilized by him (or it); and x_n^2 is the amount of some good x_n utilized by individual (or firm) 2. Mishan, "Postwar Literature on Externalities": 2.

sources are exchanged in nonmarket situations commonly involving involuntary exchange.

One individual's (or firm's) consumption can enter into another's utility (or production) function without proper market compensation because of imperfect appropriation of entitlements or rights.[32] *Imperfect appropriability of rights* means that because of a variety of reasons an individual, household, firm, or governmental unit is unable to appropriate (or capture) the full marginal value of the benefits each produces, or is unable to alleviate costs somebody else imposes.[33] Thus, even though from an economic perspective the holder of rights should be able to make decisions about resources and to claim the resulting rewards, there may be reasons why these rights cannot be asserted. Since these rights and entitlements help shape the household's, firm's, and governmental unit's set of opportunities and trade-offs, and therefore their behavior, the effectiveness with which these rights and entitlements are enforced will also affect behavior.

When there is imperfect appropriability of rights, then Musgrave's "exclusion principle" cannot work. This principle postulates that an individual should be "excluded from the enjoyment of any particular commodity or service unless he is willing to pay the stipulated price to the owner."[34] When there is joint consumption, as in Coase's lighthouse case,[35] and exclusion is impossible or requires considerable resources, then rights will be imperfectly appropriated. In short, appropriability can be made easy or difficult because of technological and other characteristics of the phenomenon under consideration. It is the high cost of effectively excluding individuals from partaking in joint consumption without proper payment, that is, the high transaction cost, that interferes with the existence of a market and brings about externalities.

This view of transactions requires a major modification of conventional microtheory, since most of that theory implicitly assumes discrete inputs and outputs with perfect appropriability of rewards and burdens. But this is an invalid assumption, particularly where externalities abound and inputs as well as utilities of individuals (and outputs of firms) cannot readily be identified and appropriated.[36]

Since an externality is generated by one or more decision units directly

32. McKean, "Appropriability and Externalities," p. 2.

33. Ethical and institutional reasons may reduce appropriability, though to a lesser extent than do technological conditions.

34. Richard A. Musgrave, *The Theory of Public Finance* (New York: McGraw-Hill, 1959), p. 9.

35. Ronald Coase, "The Problem of Social Cost," *Journal of Law and Economics* 3 (October 1960): 1–44.

36. Matters are further complicated by utilities and outputs being so frequently multidimensional. For example, a house provides not only shelter but also access to jobs, public services, and desirable neighbors.

affecting one or more units (often including the first unit) outside the marketplace, several important questions are raised. Which actors initiate the externality and which are affected by it? For example, in the case of congestion, many individuals participate in affecting others' utility functions, with virtually complete reciprocity. Thus they all contribute equally and are all equally affected. However, in the case of pollution, one or a few individuals (or firms) affect the utility (or production) functions of very many individuals without any reciprocity.

Is the externality spatial in character (that is, mainly a function of density) or is it the result of technology or affluence? If space is important, as in the case of neighborhood effects, "an individual's utility depends both on others' behavior (e.g., esthetic, criminal) and on their location."[37]

In the presence of externalities as well as high exclusion costs we find public goods. They can be rendered publicly or privately. For the latter case governments may provide financing (education), detailed controls (health codes), or legal arrangements to adjust for externalities by creating entitlements in third parties and by providing indemnity under a judicial forced-purchase procedure (tort law).

Whenever there are conflicting interests the law decides whose rights are entitled to prevail. As Calabresi and Melamed have pointed out, "the placement of entitlements has a fundamental effect on a society's distribution of wealth."[38] It is the country's constitution and its general values and mores that determine entitlements, such as to property, to free education, and to collective protection against crime and fire. Thus, private property can be looked upon as an entitlement that is permanently protected by a property rule. This rule involves a collective decision, based on the country's values, as to who is to be given an initial entitlement. The value of the property is determined not by the property rule, but by voluntary market transactions. These transactions are facilitated and enforced by property and contract laws.

Property rules stipulate and protect entitlements by ensuring that anyone wishing to remove an entitlement from its holder must buy it from him in a voluntary transaction in which the value of the entitlement and terms of the transaction are agreed upon by the relevant parties. Property law thus guides transactors of real property, that is, land and improvements, by providing rules that can help minimize conflicts among the transactors, and can help resolve conflicts that arise, whether they are settled out of court or by the court. Contract law provides guidelines in relation to similar issues faced with respect mainly to other than real property. It provides for enforcement mechanisms including rules on defenses and damages, in addition to procedures and institutions for enforcement. For example,

37. Arrow, "Organization of Economic Activity," p. 59.
38. Calabresi and Melamed, "Property Rules": 1098.

compensation is paid if an agreed-upon voluntary transfer of entitlements is not carried out in full.

From the economist's point of view, a major role of contract law and property law is to reduce transaction costs. Either law does so by providing prospective transactors with a set of normal exchange conditions. Moreover, the law provides useful information about contingencies—externalities in association with partially or totally aborted exchanges—and about how the courts seek to cure losses resulting from these contingencies. As transaction costs are reduced, more transactions result and can be carried out with enhanced efficiency; social welfare is thus increased. Examples of property law applications are violations of a warranty-of-habitability law; and examples of contract law applications are violations of implied merchantability.

We can also look upon the courts as applying the guidelines of property and contract law in order to protect owners of entitlements against adverse externalities. They do so by playing the role of externality adjusters. Historically the courts have been very jealous of this role. Although adversary proceedings could be reduced in number and transactions made more efficient if the parties were to agree in advance on specified liquidated damages in case of breach, courts have been reluctant to recognize liquidated damages. An overt stipulation could reduce uncertainties associated with a transaction. Each party could anticipate the gains and losses associated with a breach, rather than speculate what a jury would find to be an appropriate award.[39]

Although the initial entitlement is protected by property rules, its destruction is protected by liability rules; the party responsible (e.g., the tortfeasor) pays an objectively determined value. Under a liability rule, an external, objective standard of value is applied in relation to the transfer of entitlements. Thus, if in the presence of externalities entitlements are forcibly taken (e.g., if the government alters the laissez-faire distribution of property rights or a steel plant imposes externalities on neighbors), liability rules go into effect and guide the payment of damages. Damage awards are established by unilateral public assessment rather than by private negotiation, and enforcement is the responsibility of government. The reason why a liability rule is invoked and government intervenes is that tortious acts

39. During the 1977–1978 regular session the California legislature enacted a liquidated-damages bill (A.B. 570, 1977 Stats., ch. 198). This new law affects prospectively many contracts relating to transactions in real and personal property. It provides that as a general rule a contractual liquidated-damages provision is valid unless the party seeking to invalidate the provision establishes that it was unreasonable under the circumstances existing at the time the contract was made. Exceptions to the rule include some design to protect the person who is a victim of adhesion contracts, such as a party to a contract for retail purchase or rental of personal property or services primarily for the party's personal, family, or household purposes, and a party to a real-property lease for use as a dwelling.

would involve extremely high transaction costs if market valuation of entitlements were to be relied on. Examples are not only accidental damages, but government taking by eminent domain as well.

There are some special cases of entitlement transfers. For example, relative to crimes against persons or property, society refuses to convert property rules into liability rules and merely seek a compensation for the victim. Since society highly values respect for prevailing property rules, it opposes their violation by criminals. Therefore it imposes criminal sanctions in the hope of deterring future attempts to change property rules into liability rules.

Thus, society decides that certain entitlements are not freely transferable between willing buyers and sellers. The collective decision thus is that criminal conduct is not to be tolerated even though some individuals are willing to pay for the privilege of engaging in it. Society determines that the entitlement is inalienable and by so doing it limits or regulates the grant of the entitlement. Moreover, government may also establish mandatory minimum standards of conduct for permitted activities. For example, an inalienable entitlement might be for neighbors not to be disturbed by noisy bars and their drunken patrons after midnight. This in turn would mean that bars would have to meet a mandatory minimum standard of conduct, that is, they would have to close before midnight. The bar owner is prevented from undertaking a prohibited activity, even if he is willing to pay for its external costs. Mandatory minimum standards are based on collective directives in turn based on the community's values at the time. They can lead not only to orders to cease and desist but also to orders for affirmative action (e.g., a mandatory order included in a housing code).

In order to round out the discussion of the four law fields, we should point out that they also differ with regard to the conditions under which compensation is awarded to adjust for an externality. A contract or lease breaker is required to pay damages even if the breach results in an improved resource use. The same holds for trespassers, and the reasons are the same (i.e., more voluntary exchanges and greater efficiency of the exchange). Thus, parties are more likely to enter contracts if they are assured of legal protection in case of breach, and they are likely to own more real property if they are legally protected against unjustified impairment of the entitlement. Yet tortfeasors, who cause injury to a victim, are not liable to pay compensation if cost-justified precautions could not have prevented the accident, at least not under a negligence and contributory-negligence standard. This is because in accident cases compensation to victims of harm for which the injurer was not negligently responsible would raise transaction costs without producing benefits.

A further difference exists with regard to punitive damages, which, for example in California, are allowable in personal injury cases. Punitive damages, unlike compensatory damages, are designed to deter and prevent one person from harming another. In some respects, they resemble sanctions imposed under criminal law. Thus, under tort law compensatory damages and sometimes punitive damages are levied, whereas under property law and contract law virtually always the former only are applied.

In summary, the presence of externalities leads to conflicts in society as entitlements are impaired and violated. Legal thought and economic analysis can be joined in the hope of attaining a more insightful evaluation of laws and legal systems. These notions provide the intellectual underpinnings of much of the argument that is presented in the following chapters.

II

PROPERTY LAW'S BASIC
LEGAL PREMISES

INTRODUCTION

American property law has deep historical roots in English common law. From this beginning, property law has slowly changed to meet new conditions as they emerge in an increasingly urbanized and industrialized society. As we will see, the law has struggled to adjust itself to new circumstances.

In this chapter the basic legal premises of property law are examined.[1] First I discuss rights and entitlements to property, their permanent transfer, and their temporary transfer. Then I take up land use planning and development. Other chapters explore some of the economic aspects of certain property laws, especially habitability laws, just-cause eviction statutes, and zoning ordinances.

DEFINING RIGHTS AND ENTITLEMENTS
TO PROPERTY

Private property, under the American system of law, can be considered an entitlement protected by a property rule. Property law provides the rules with regard to the entitlement to land and improvements thereon.

---

1. American property law can be traced as far back as the Statute of Uses passed by Parliament in 1535. For a detailed treatment of property law see A. James Casner and W. Barton Leach, *Cases and Texts on Property* (Boston: Little, Brown, 1969).

These rules enhance the certainty of who owns a given property and under what circumstances. Moreover, they facilitate efficient transfer of title.

OWNERSHIP, POSSESSION, AND CONTROL

Of particular interest to lawyer and economist alike is the degree to which a given party has a right to a certain property under specified conditions. We can distinguish between ownership, possession, and control in an attempt to define the differing extent of a right to a particular property. An *ownership right* means that the enforcing party (e.g., the state) has determined that the holder of this entitlement has the benefit of the property for most uses. The owner will be able to transfer this right to others and accrue income from its use. However, there are certain restrictions on the owner's right to transfer. For example, an owner will not be allowed to limit the sale of his or her property to members of a certain racial group.

A *holder of possession* has more limited rights than an owner. He or she is temporarily entitled to the benefit of the asset or good while maintaining possession, but use is restricted, depending on whether the holder is a bailee or whether possession is constructive, adverse, involuntary, or unconscious. Although an owner is entitled to the property over a possessor, a possessor will be able to exclude one who merely *controls* a good, for example, a trespasser. An individual who is merely in control of a property has an extremely limited right.

THE ECONOMICS OF PROPERTY RIGHTS AND ENTITLEMENTS

The concept of property rights may be venerable, but that of entitlements is of much more recent vintage. As discussed in Chapter I, the latter concept is much broader than the first, referring to the legitimate claims possessed by a person. ⟸ENTITLEMENTS

Property Rights

The concept of property rights relates to the set of privileges and responsibilities accorded to a person in relation to the owning of property in general and real property in particular. These rights are determined by a long history of property laws, whether common laws or statutory laws. The right to property is the power to exclude others from or give them access to a benefit or use of the particular object. An elaborate system of property, liability, and inalienability rules exists to bolster an owner's claim to the property or good. Property rights to an unexplored area, such as the moon or the sea, are determined by international agreements entered into by bodies that have the power to enforce them. A mere individual without the coercive power of government could not hope to enforce a claim to, for example, the Atlantic Ocean.

The presence of property rights furnishes incentives to use resources efficiently. Given a legal system that enforces property rights, a holder can have confidence to obtain returns from the use of property.

Under what conditions is a system of property rights efficient? They include universality, exclusivity, and transferability. *Universality* implies that all resources should be owned by someone. *Exclusivity* is defined as the right to exclude people who might want to take part of the property. *Transferability* provides for voluntary exchanges that in general are value enhancing.

Universality is clearly preferred because the assignment of rights provides the maximum amount of economic incentive to use resources efficiently. The only exception is for goods so plentiful that everyone can consume them without reducing enjoyment by anyone else, and there are virtually no such goods.

The Coase Theorem. The existence of externalities limits the extent to which property rights are exclusive. According to the Coase theorem, in the absence of transaction costs, the Pareto-optimal resource allocation in the case of incompatible land uses will be obtained independent of the initial assignment of property rights.[2]

Let us consider the Coase theorem in some detail. It states that efficiency is unaffected regardless of which party is held liable, as long as transaction costs are zero. This is because both actors must consider the explicit cost of the activity itself as well as the implicit cost represented by the payment for not conducting the activity that the nonliable party could obtain. To demonstrate, suppose that A and B engage in incompatible land uses and A is given the right to pollute B's stream. This is worth $50 to A. However, B would pay $60 to A not to pollute. With no transaction costs, it is clear that both parties would agree not to pollute, even though the pollution is worth $50 to A. That is because the $60 payment he could receive from B represents a very real cost to A. Hence, he will bargain for a payment exceeding $50 from B. Similarly, if B was given the right to prevent the pollution, there would be no pollution, since A could offer B only $50 not to exercise his right and it is worth $60 to B to stop the pollution. Hence, the efficient result is reached in either case.

This result may be qualified depending on the initial distribution of wealth. Since A is richer in the first example and B in the second, such wealth distribution could alter demand for the pollution. Similarly, the initial assignment of the right could be determinative in an extreme case, for example where two men negotiate for a bottle of water necessary for survival in a desert.

Coase also mentions that, in determining a government solution to a

---

2. Ronald Coase, "The Problem of Social Cost," *Journal of Law and Economics* 3 (October 1960): 1–44.

market-system imperfection, the possible inefficiencies in the government solution should also be considered, and a cost–benefit analysis of the two systems should be undertaken.

Remember the crucial assumption of the Coase theorem: zero transaction costs. What can we say when these costs are not zero? When transactions are not costless, efficiency is advanced if the right is assigned to the party who would normally buy it, especially if transaction costs are so high that no exchange is likely. Then it is economically preferable to assign the initial property right to the party whose use is more valuable. Alternatively, liability could be imposed on the party whose use was less valuable, an assignment that would result in tort liability.

Often such a determination is hard to make and compromises are arrived at. Hence, a train that emits sparks that set fire to a farmer's crops may be fitted with a spark arrester to reduce sparks, the farmer may remove some of his crops from the neighboring tracks, or he may plant crops that are more fire resistant.

The ability to shift a resource from a less productive to a more productive use via exchange provides economic rationale for the free transferability of goods. When these transaction costs are high it is often necessary to make property rights less exclusive.

Entitlements

Rather than argue in terms of property rights, it might be advantageous to rely on the notion of entitlements, as suggested by Calabresi and Melamed.[3] As was indicated in Chapter I, there are two ways of looking at entitlements. On the one hand, they can be considered as policy instruments for government use in its pursuit of efficiency or income redistribution or both.[4] On the other hand, entitlements can be conceived of as bestowed on men and women in the form of natural or fundamental privileges that are to be protected by the state.[5]

Thus, we refer to entitlements as those privileges and responsibilities that accrue to an individual by virtue of his or her birth into a particular society at a given moment in time. These entitlements find their basis in the values and the mores and possibly in constitution of the society. They include any and all human rights that might be assigned to persons, whereas property rights emphasize specific and more lasting rights associated with physical property.

Or, to put it differently, in the presence of major interdependencies

3. G. Calabresi and A. D. Melamed, "Property Rules, Liability Rules, and Inalienability: One View of the Cathedral," *Harvard Law Review* 85 (April 1972): 1089–1128.

4. Ronald Dworkin, *Taking Rights Seriously* (Cambridge: Harvard Univ. Press, 1977), pp. 90–92; John Rawls, *A Theory of Justice* (Cambridge: Harvard University Press, 1971); Robert Nozick, *Anarchy, State, and Utopia* (New York: Basic Books, 1974), p. 155.

5. Calabresi and Melamed, "Property Rules," p. 1092.

among different persons' utilities, the values and mores of society determine entitlements in the light of externalities that come about. Just as these interdependencies can change over time, so can society's evaluation of the desirability and fairness of the externalities' impact. Consequently, human entitlements can and do change over time, whereas property rights tend to be much more stable. Thus, entitlements are used in a broader sense to indicate other rights that are not generally considered to be property rights. For example, the right to free education might be considered an entitlement rather than a property right, because education is not a physical object, nor are privileges of free public education venerable and immutable.

Occasionally there will be a conflict between the broader class of human entitlements and the narrower class of property rights. This might occur, for example, when a compromising picture of an individual is taken, with the photographer's right to dispose of his private property restricted by the other actor's entitlement to privacy. Hence, the property-right holder may be limited in his right by the extent of the entitlement granted. The right to privacy may so restrict the photographer's right to use the picture that at best only limited privileges to the exchange of the picture would be granted.

TYPES OF POSSESSION AND THEIR ECONOMIC RATIONALE

Let us next turn to the question of who has legal possession of a given property or good under various conditions. As we will see, some forms of possession (and ownership) are less obvious than others. In all six forms of possession that I will explore, I will seek to give economic content to the possession and ownership status.

Unconscious Possession. Possession is unconscious when one of three situations holds—when a person is unaware that a particular item is in his control, when a person is aware that some item is in his control but has no idea what it is, and when a person knows that an item is under his control and thinks it is one thing but in fact it is something else. Thus in *Hannah* v. *Peel*[6] Lance Corporal Duncan Hannah, serving during the early days of World War II in a battery of the Royal Artillery, was stationed in a house that had never been occupied by its owner, Major Peel. Major Peel had come into the ownership of the house late in 1938 and the house was requisitioned late in 1939 by the army. In August 1940 Hannah was adjusting the blackout curtains in a room when his hand touched something on the top of a window frame, loose in a crevice. Hannah thought it to be a piece of dirt or plaster and dropped it on the outside window ledge. The next morning he discovered it was a brooch covered with cobwebs and dirt. He informed his commanding officer, who advised him to hand it over

6. King's Bench Division (1945) 1 K.B. 509.

to the police. When after 2 years the owner had not been found, the police handed the brooch to Hannah, who sold it for £66.

In a subsequent lawsuit brought by Major Peel, the court stated

> There is no doubt that in this case the brooch was lost in the ordinary meaning of the term, and I should imagine it had been lost for a very considerable time . . . [Major Peel] was never physically in possession of these premises at any time. It is clear that the brooch was never his, in the ordinary acceptation of the term, in that he had the prior possession. He had no knowledge of it, until it was brought to his notice by the finder.[7]

The court ruled in favor of the finder Hannah.

Bailee. Quite often some property is left with a rather specialized agent so that he may perform certain services. During this period, the agent is the rightful possessor of an item but he is not the owner. He is a bailee. Examples include the railroad that is transporting freight, the watch repairman with whom a watch has been deposited, or the garage operator with whom a car has been left for repair. The bailee is absolutely liable for misdelivery and therefore can be looked upon as being the owner of the item as long as it is in his possession. Such rules give signals that can produce efficient resource use.

Yet the bailee is not liable when he could not reasonably have known that he was in possession of a valuable object. If you check a coat in a checkroom, for example, the bailee will not be liable for a missing unobserved ring. However, if the bailee is known to have seen the ring he will be held liable. This standard gives the owner incentives to inform the bailee of the object and its true worth, so that the latter can take cost-justified precautions.

Lost Articles. In the discussion of *Hannah* v. *Peel,* I mentioned that Hannah was advised by his commanding officer to hand a lost article over to the police. What are the ownership rights of those who are in possession of a lost article and how must they proceed to find the rightful owner? The law treats lost articles differently depending on where the loss occurs. If the article is lost in a public place and the owner is not found, it goes to the finder; if in a private place, it goes to the owner of the premise. The individual who lost the object in a private place will most likely look in that place for the object. Where there is no obvious owner, as when the item is lost in a public place, the finder has some incentive to report the loss since he has a good chance to become the legal owner, and the real owner has as good a chance to locate the finder as any other individual who might keep the find.

7. *Ibid.*: 509.

Involuntary Possession. Possession is involuntary when an individual is given a good that he does not want or accepts by mistake. The involuntary bailee is held liable if he exercises dominion by committing an overt act of interference with the real owner's possession. This offers the involuntary bailee the incentive to return the good immediately to the rightful owner before being held liable for conversion.

Constructive Possession. Constructive possession is essentially a legal assumption that an individual had possession, even if he did not have physical control over the property. Hence a bailor may constructively possess a chattel that is wrongfully converted while being transported by a bailee. This theory is more commonly used in the area of property law known as *constructive notice* or *constructive eviction,* and will be discussed later.

Adverse Possession. Finally, there is adverse possession, which can ripen into ownership if an individual has unopposed occupancy of land for a period of time such as 5 or 10 years. This rule provides incentives to make a higher valued use of land since the adverse possessor must occupy and improve the land for an extensive period of time while the dormant or nonexistent owner does nothing. More will be said about adverse possession later.

PERMANENT TRANSFER OF RIGHTS AND ENTITLEMENTS

At least four types of permanent transfers can be visualized—sale, taking by power of eminent domain, taking by police power, and adverse possession. They will be discussed next in some detail.

SALE

By far the most common method of transferring property in perpetuity is through sale. Therefore, it is little wonder that a large body of law has developed to provide guidelines for those who buy and sell property. Perhaps the most basic of all property laws is the Statute of Frauds of 1677.[8] It applies solely to real-property transactions and provides that any contract or sale of property has to be in writing to be enforceable. The purpose of the statute is to limit fraud and impress upon the parties the significance of their act. To the extent it provides useful information, the rule has some justification. The statute's application is limited today and is usually ineffective if the agreement has been partially performed.

Transferability of property by sale is normally efficient because it permits

---

8. Casner and Leach, *Cases and Texts on Property,* p. 679.

the reallocation of resources from lower- to higher-valued uses. However, some transfers may be restricted or at least complicated because of the existence of externalities, for example, a plant that pollutes an adjacent river.

Various forms of real-property transactions exist. A considerable body of ancient real-property law has evolved. The following concepts and forms of real-property transactions occupy distinguished positions in property law: contract for the sale of land, mortgages, deeds, recording acts, estates in land—common ownership, and classification of estates.

EMINENT DOMAIN

The exercise of the power of eminent domain involves a taking by a public authority for a public purpose with just compensation and in accordance with due process of law.[9] Many public authorities today freely exercise their power of eminent domain. However, an economic justification for the application of this power requires an investment or operation related to a public good, and/or a forestalling of a holdout monopoly.

Thus, government should be permitted to exercise its eminent-domain power only when it produces a good or service that has strong public-good characteristics, that is, in the presence of externalities and high exclusion costs.[10] The latter occur, for example, when it is costly to eliminate free riders. If government is to produce a public good, and since it is mandated to serve everyone anywhere in its jurisdiction, it may have to locate a physical facility in a particular location. Likewise, in order to fulfill a social objective, such as providing military defense, it may have to use the power of eminent domain. These considerations come into play in the locating of military defense installations, fire stations, and flood-control facilities.

Let us turn to the holdout monopoly. Whenever a major government installation requires the assembly of many lots, property owners may hike their prices when they know the location of the facility. Moreover, some owners might hold out to the very end and not want to sell. This does not deny that virtually everybody will sell once the price is high enough. However, holdouts not only raise prices to levels that can exceed prices that would otherwise prevail but also retard the completion of important projects. Both elements can lead to inefficiencies. An example in this connection is the construction of airports, highways, and sewer lines.

9. Under the Fifth Amendment, a person may not "be deprived of life, liberty, or property, without due process of law; nor shall private property be taken for public use, without just compensation." The Fourteenth Amendment provides, "nor shall any state deprive any person of life, liberty, or property, without due process of law; nor deny to any person within its jurisdiction the equal protection of the laws."

10. Werner Z. Hirsch, *Urban Economic Analysis* (New York: McGraw-Hill, 1973), pp. 297–298.

Exercising the power of eminent domain is only efficient when the expected collective valuation of benefits exceeds expected total social costs of the taking. By and large the taking should only be permitted when the market system fails to transfer real property for an important social purpose.

Compensation under eminent domain poses a number of interesting problems. The usual standard is to provide just compensation, basically in the form of fair market value. A more appropriate standard, however, would be to provide the person whose property was taken with compensation adequate to restore him to his previous position.[11] The difference between the first and second concept could in part be reconciled by adding relocation costs and a reimbursement for sentimental value to the fair market value. Since sentimental value is difficult to estimate, but the relocation costs are not, the solution might be to add some relocation allowance to the fair market value.

A major area in which eminent domain has been applied is the urban redevelopment of slum housing. In this scheme, it is claimed that, once houses are declared by public health officials as unfit for human habitation, the public interest warrants their condemnation and acquisition by eminent domain. But how strong is the public interest in this case? This is a significant, but rarely answered, question.

In fact there is great flexibility in the authorized exercise of the power of eminent domain with regard to redevelopment. Even private parties have been authorized by the legislature to bring condemnation actions. Generally, the legislature will declare a public use and the existence of a public necessity, and the private party will then select the particular property to be appropriated. The power of eminent domain is often given to universities, hospitals, other nonprofit institutions, and private corporations for redevelopment. However, usually the private entity must make a greater showing of right than a public entity.[12] The leading case in this area is *Berman* v. *Parker*.[13] The Washington D.C. Redevelopment Land Agency obtained nonslum property, and a department store was to be constructed on the land. After acquisition, the property was sold to another private party in accordance with a planning commission plan. A unanimous court held the plan valid.

The administration of acquisitions under the power of eminent domain differs among countries. For example, in the United Kingdom heavy reliance is placed on technical experts, with disputes going to a quasi-

---

11. F. Leary and E. D. Tucker, "The Injustice of Just Compensation to Fixed Income Recipients: Does Recent Relocation Legislation Fill the Void?" *Temple Law Quarterly* 48 (Fall 1974): 1–45.

12. *Linggi* v. *Garovatti*, 45 Cal. 2d 20, 286 P.2d 15 (1955).

13. *Berman* v. *Parker*, 348 U.S. 26 (1954). See D. Hagman, *Urban Planning and Land Development Control Law* (St. Paul, Minn.: West, 1975), p. 314.

administrative body—the Lands Tribunal. Courts can be appealed to only on a point of law—a most infrequent circumstance.[14]

In the United States, the eminent-domain process is initiated by the local government, usually a municipality, sending to residents notices of its intent to acquire certain property for certain public purposes. Usually these notices contain an offer to buy the property for fair market value, a value arrived at by city officials. (It often reflects a value more than the amount shown on tax assessment records, but less than the property would bring on an open market.) If the property owner rejects such an offer he can pursue administrative appeals, which are usually limited to the question of the value of the property. If informal administrative channels are not sufficient to produce an offer acceptable to the property owner, a complaint is usually filed by the governmental agency.

POLICE POWER

The police power is the right of the state to take action to protect the safety, health, and morals of the community. Under this power the expropriation or extinction of private property rights becomes legally possible. Unlike under eminent domain, compensation of the property owner is not mandatory and often is not granted at all. It may be argued that although the citizen, under certain laws and regulations enacted pursuant to the police power, is not financially compensated for the loss of his property rights, he benefits from the altruistic recognition that the just restraint is for the public good. This is admittedly a tenuous argument.

Under its police power, a public authority may take or destroy property in order to arrest the spread of fire, flood, or some other natural disaster; it may requisition property in time of war for national defense. In the latter case compensation on similar principles to those of eminent domain will normally be forthcoming.[15]

14. A public authority that seeks a compulsory purchase order applies to the minister concerned with the purpose of the acquisition, giving due notice to the property owner affected. A public inquiry is held under the authority of the minister by an inspector appointed by him. The case for compulsory acquisition and the objections, if any, of the property owners and of others having an interest in the purpose of the acquisition are heard. The procedures are judicial, the inspectors being trained and experienced in the matters before them, though the strict rules of evidence in judicial hearings do not apply. The inspector makes a report to the minister, who decides whether or not to issue the compulsory purchase order. He is in no way bound to follow the inspector's recommendation. If he issues an order, it may differ materially from that which was originally sought. Thus it may embody conditions intended to safeguard various interests. No appeal against the order can be made to the courts, except on the ground of procedural defect substantially prejudicious to an appellant. If there is a dispute on the question of compensation, the case goes to the Lands Tribunal, which is an expert body of professional valuers and lawyers. An appeal against the adjudication of the Lands Tribunal can go to the court only on a point of law and only within a short period after the tribunal's decision. Therefore, appeals to the court are rare.

15. Under the police power, the state may forbid use of property for the purposes of a

The exercise of police power ranges from cases close to those of eminent domain to those very remote from it. At the latter end of the spectrum, police power merges into a host of administrative, legislative, and even judicial powers affecting property rights positively or negatively. Compensation rarely takes place. The courts have the right, though they seldom use it, to declare certain contracts contrary to public policy and hence unenforceable. Moreover, many statutes, including corporation laws, antitrust laws, and zoning laws, distinctly affect property rights, often without compensation.

ADVERSE POSSESSION

An individual can gain title to property through adverse possession, a process designed to promote productive land use. The leading case is *Ewing* v. *Burnett*.[16] Both the plaintiff and the defendant claimed a parcel of property through a common grantor on the basis of written deeds. The defendant Burnett had lived next to the vacant lot for 31 years, paid taxes on the lot for 24 years, maintained trespass actions, and cultivated a gravel pit on the empty and contested property. The plaintiff and his predecessor in title had never occupied the property. Here the statutory period for adverse possession was 21 years. The Supreme Court held for Burnett, ruling that the substantive requirements were questions of fact for the jury to decide and were, unless clearly erroneous, not reversible by the trial court.

Generally, the claimant must show that he has some claim of right and actually possessed the land for an extended period of time. Such possession must be open, adverse, notorious, visible, and continuous for the duration of the statutory period. This period varies by states; it is 5 years, for example, in California. In addition, the land must have been cultivated or improved, in keeping with the purpose of promoting productive land use. Some states have further requirements, for example, that the adverse possessor pay the taxes assessed upon the land.[17] This is an almost impossible requirement since the tax assessment goes to the recorded owner of the property; but the court may "deem" that the taxes have been paid. For example, in *Duncan* v. *Peterson*[18] the contesting parties had lived on their respective properties separated by a fence for 42 years before a survey detected that the true dividing line of the properties was 104 feet east of the

---

gambling house or house of prostitution, or in a manner dangerous to public health. As a result the value of particular properties may decline. No compensation is awarded, but neither is there a physical invasion of the property. Instead the property remains physically intact in the hands of its owner. Although physical invasion almost always calls for compensation, its absence does not exclude compensation.

16. *Ewing* v. *Burnett*, 36 U.S. 41 (1837). Supp.
17. Cal. Code Civ. Proc. §325 (West 1976).
18. *Duncan* v. *Peterson*, 3 Cal. App. 3d 607 (1970).

fence. Since taxes were assessed based on section references, the plaintiff had not paid the taxes on the subject property as required by statute. However, the court held that "payment of taxes is not material as each coterminous owner is deemed to have paid the taxes according to his deed."[19] Since the parties had agreed to the fence as a boundary, the new boundary effectively attached to the prior deed and the plaintiff was deemed to have paid the taxes.

The adverse possessor may assert his alleged possession either as a defense against an owner or as a claim of right in an effort to prove his ownership. His claim of right and continuous possession are enough to evict a trespasser, even if the adverse possessor merely had an invalid deed and he controls part of the property described by the deed.

Often, however, the adverse possession occurs by mistake. Although not all of the normal rules may have been met—for example, the possession may have not been clearly notorious and adverse—the courts will usually transfer title from the owner to the adverse possessor. Since often the possessor has made a substantial investment in the property and the true owner did not care enough to challenge his ownership, the court is reluctant to transfer the property back to the recorded owner.

TEMPORARY TRANSFER OF RIGHTS AND ENTITLEMENTS

LEASES: LANDLORD–TENANT RELATIONS

One of the most interesting and dynamic aspects of property law covers landlord–tenant relations. In this relationship the landlord was historically favored over the tenant. Specifically, the doctrine of caveat emptor was applied to relieve the landlord of responsibility for warranting that a building rented for residential purposes was fit for that purpose at the inception of the tenancy. Likewise, the landlord had no responsibility to see that the building remained habitable during the term of tenancy. Repair of damage to existing facilities caused by ordinary wear and tear during tenancy was considered the tenant's responsibility.

In 1826, the doctrine of _constructive eviction_ was first recognized in the United States.[20] Grounds for constructive eviction, which permitted the tenant to surrender possession and vacate premises, were the _covenant of habitability_ and the _covenant of quiet enjoyment._ The covenant of habitability emphasized that premises were to be delivered in tenantable, fit, or suitable condition, where condition was assumed to be under the control of the

19. _Ibid.,_ p. 611.
20. _Dyett_ v. _Pendleton,_ 8 Cow. 727 (N.Y. 1826), and M. P. Rapacz, "Origin and Evolution of Constructive Eviction in the United States," _De Paul Law Review_ 1 (Autumn–Winter 1951): 69–90.

landlord; and the covenant of quiet enjoyment emphasized that the tenant was to be protected—to the extent that a landlord can provide such protection—in the quiet enjoyment of the premises, particularly from direct intrusion by the landlord.

Constructive eviction, although an improvement for the tenant, did not ensure him habitable premises. Fit and suitable conditions were not defined so as to ensure quality housing. Furthermore, the landlord had no duty to repair premises, since the covenant of quiet enjoyment could be breached by the landlord only by direct conduct and not by neglect to repair. Moreover, the only relief for the tenant was to vacate the premises within a reasonable time after the condition arose.

In the post–World War II period, some state statutes and court decisions modified and reinterpreted the doctrine of constructive eviction. The law began to make exceptions to the rule, first for short-term furnished apartments and then for defects reasonably discoverable by the landlord and not the tenant.[21]

Likewise, the early common-law rule that landlords were under no duty to repair and maintain residential premises leased to tenants had previously prevailed.[22] Moreover, since the rules of property law solidified

21. In the post–World War II period the doctrine of caveat emptor was reinterpreted in relation to property. The reinterpretation took into consideration the great complexity and interdependence of present-day society compared with that of sixteenth-century England, where most landlord–tenant relations involved a piece of land and simple dwelling facilities. Not only was the prospective tenant usually well acquainted with the particular dwelling, but it was uncomplicated, relatively simple to repair, and expected to be maintained by the technical skills of the tenant himself. Thus on first inspection the tenant knew reasonably well what the overall state of the dwelling was. This is quite different from the housing of both poor and rich in the second half of the twentieth century. Complicated electric wiring, heating, and plumbing all are inaccessible for inspection on first visitation, and a renter tends to have no qualifications to do so [*Reste Realty Corp.* v. *Cooper*, 53 N.J. 444, 452, 251 A.2d 268, 272 (1969)].

As a result, for example, the Supreme Court of Wisconsin held that

> The need and social desirability of adequate housing for people in this era of rapid population increases is too important to be rebuffed by the obnoxiously legal cliche, *caveat emptor*. Permitting landlords to rent "tumbledown" houses is at least a contributing cause of such problems as urban blight, juvenile delinquency, and high property taxes for conscientious landlords [*Pines* v. *Perssion*, 14 Wis. 2d 590, 595–596, 111 N.W.2d 409, 412–413 (1961)].

A 1968 Michigan statute [Mich. Comp. Laws Ann. 554.139 (Supp. 1970)] and a 1969 decision by the Supreme Court of Hawaii [*Lemle* v. *Breeden* 462 P.2d 470 (Hawaii 1969)] go in the same direction. This court ruling modifies the doctrine of caveat emptor by requiring the landlord to be responsible for "premises and all common areas [to be] fit for use" at commencement of tenancy.

22. A lease at common law was considered to be the purchase of an interest in property, subject to the doctrine of caveat emptor. Since the lease agreement was considered a conveyance of property for a term, the tenant was deemed to have assumed the obligations and liabilities of ownership.

before the development of mutually dependent covenants in contract law, a lessee's covenant to pay rent was considered independent of the lessor's covenant to provide housing. As a result, if a tenant's home became uninhabitable, even though it was through no fault of his own, he could neither demand that repairs be made by the landlord nor escape liability for the rent due for the remainder of the term. Thus, the tenant had to pay rent regardless of whether he received any benefits from the residential premises.

A major modification of this traditional common-law landlord–tenant relationship began to occur in the early postwar period. Basically, two approaches have been pursued, mainly through laws ensuring that tenants have habitable housing and, to a lesser extent, continued tenancy. Both approaches are discussed in the following sections.

1. Habitability Laws

By means of housing codes, many large American cities shifted to the landlord the responsibility for repairing leased premises and maintaining them in habitable condition. These codes impose the burden of repair and maintenance on the landlord and place the responsibility for the dwelling's cleanliness and for specified minor items of maintenance on the tenant.[23]

23. Still, the tenant is responsible for normal repairs and any waste or deterioration that he could have prevented. He may be excused from performance by commercial frustration, constructive eviction, abandonment, condemnation or retaliation by the landlord. To be excused by commercial frustration there must be a total destruction of the purpose of the transaction by an outside force. A material breach by the landlord can lead to constructive eviction, and an abandonment of the premises is effective if proper notice is given or the landlord accepts the surrender. Retaliation by eviction is prohibited by statute in many states. Money from a condemnation is usually apportioned between landlord and tenant, although in some instances the entire estate must be extinguished before the tenant can be excused from performance. The tenant may then get the money from the government.

When a lessee assigns or sublets his interest to another party he remains liable unless there was a novation. The lessor may be able to withhold consent to an assignment or subletting if his refusal is reasonable. Generally, an assignee must pay the rent, but a subtenant may not have to, depending on his agreement with the tenant and whether his covenant is deemed to "run with the land." An assignment generally relinquishes all of the lessee's interest in the land; but in a sublease the lessee retains some interest. Again, these agreements are basically contractual in nature and the results can be varied by the actors involved.

Tenants who stay over after the expiration of the lease are often liable for the entire next period of the lease. Therefore, if they had a 1-year lease, the tenants may be liable for a full year's rent if they stay over a couple of weeks. However, the landlord may have a statutory duty to mitigate damages by seeking out another tenant after the holdover leaves. In that case his damages might only be the difference in the rent obtained from the two parties, assuming he had to lease at a loss. This arrangement is efficient because it returns the property to the stream of commerce and equates the remedy with the true damage.

The tenant generally has the right to take removables with him when he leaves. Fixtures annexed to the land that are part of the building materials belong to the landlord.

Devices to ensure the performance of the tenant are usually strictly construed. Therefore, a rent acceleration clause may be void if it is a penalty or not reasonable, or if the damages are

Usually, the owner remains ultimately responsible for having housing code violations corrected. Parallel to these housing codes and in furthering their enforcement, courts and legislatures have created rights of actions of tenants. To this end, a number of legal remedies have been fashioned; they increase the property rights of tenants while reducing those retained by landlords. These remedies, designed to provide a minimum level of housing quality for tenants, include repair and rent deduction, rent withholding and abatement, and receivership. They are often supplemented by provisions that prohibit retaliatory eviction, facilitate return of the tenant's security deposit, and legalize rent strikes. Furthermore, courts have begun to rule that a warranty of habitability is implied in urban residential leases.[24]

These changes in landlord–tenant relations, by inferring and extending a warranty of habitability, revise the doctrine of caveat emptor. Since certainty about the law has declined, previously nonexistent legal risks have arisen, and the distribution of risks between landlord and tenant has been altered. For example, in the presence of caveat emptor, the landlord's obligations to repair and maintain premises are clear and he therefore faces few risks, regardless of how little repair and maintenance he provides. Under these conditions, tenants face many risks, all of which change when the doctrine of caveat emptor is modified.

Without a warranty of habitability, there is considerable potential for variation in the level of service delivered to the tenant. Thus, the tenant's lease agreement is, for him, a source of risk. There are two sources of this variability.

First, there is the risk that the tenant has not correctly assessed the attributes of the dwelling before leasing. Here the law would appear to economize on the cost of acquiring information, since the landlord is in the best position to evaluate his own property. Therefore, the law may be seen as requiring more complete disclosure of information, so that the tenant cannot claim that services he might reasonably have expected under the lease were not forthcoming.

Second, there is the risk that some damage to the dwelling will occur and reduce the flow of services during the period of the lease. When a habitability law is passed, the risk is transferred from tenant to landlord. In the absence of such a law, the tenant would be responsible for repair if he wished to derive the full benefits from his residence. To the extent that maintenance can vary, the tenant's consumption is subject to risk. Under a

---

readily ascertainable. Forfeiture clauses must give substantial notice. Self-help procedures by the landlord are not tolerated. He must use court proceedings to evict the tenant. The courts recognize the upheaval and waste of resources involved in moving on short notice, as well as the dangers of self-help and the misallocation engendered by penalty clauses.

24. Key cases are *Pines* v. *Perssion*, 14 Wis. 2d 590, 111 N.W.2d 404 (1961), and *Javins* v. *First National Realty Corp.*, 138 U.S. App. D.C. 369, 423 F.2d 1071, *cert. denied*, 400 U.S. 925, 91 S. Ct. 186, 27 L. Ed. 2d 185 (1970).

habitability law, risk is transferred to the landlord, whose profit is now subject to the variability of maintenance expenditures. The transfer of risk does raise serious questions as to who is the efficient risk bearer. Since the landlord may control many units, he may therefore have a smaller expected variation per unit. On the other hand, if the landlord's assets are specialized in housing, the total risk he bears may represent a relatively large part of his total wealth. The poor tenant may be less averse to risk than the wealthier landlord. Thus, there seems to be no clear a priori basis for determining whether landlord or tenant will have a larger evaluation of the cost of avoiding the risk associated with the rental dwelling unit. Let us next examine the major habitability laws.[25]

Repair-and-deduct laws offer tenants a self-help remedy by permitting them, on their own initiative, to repair defects in their premises and deduct repair charges from their rent.[26] By 1974, this remedy was available in 19 states. It is basically limited to relatively minor defects.[27] Wide application of this remedy in a large multiple-unit dwelling could be inefficient compared to repairs carried out by the landlord, who may benefit from scale economies.

A second form of remedy is _rent withholding_, through either _escrow_ or _rent abatement_. In the first case, the tenant pays rent into a court-created escrow account. Rental income is withheld from the landlord until violations are corrected. Illinois, Michigan, and New York even authorize rent withholding by the state welfare department or some other agency.[28] An alternative is rent abatement, which is more consistent with the application of contract rather than property law principles.[29] Rent abatement permits a tenant to remain in possession of the premises without paying rent or by paying a reduced amount until the housing defects are remedied. The condition of the premises constitutes a defense either to an action of eviction or to an action for rent. In most situations, the legal differences between withholding and abatement are very small. Even under abatement, rent is usually

25. This section draws heavily on Werner Z. Hirsch et al., "Regression Analysis of the Effects of Habitability Laws upon Rent: An Empirical Observation on the Ackerman–Komesar Debate," _California Law Review_ 63 (September 1975): 1098–1143.

26. The landlord must be notified after the fact, and only after he has failed to take action within an appropriate time period can the tenant contract for repair. In most states, the statute permits tenants to deduct no more than 1 month's rent to finance repairs.

27. Repair-and-deduct laws can be applied relatively easily by tenants, since the law can be invoked without a prior judicial determination. Should a judicial proceeding later determine that the tenant was not justified in taking action, he would merely be liable for the outstanding balance of the rent (the deducted repair bill).

28. As long as the violations continue, the welfare recipient is given a statutory defense to any action or summary proceeding for nonpayment of rent.

29. A tenant utilizing a rent-abatement scheme takes the risk that by refusing to pay rent a court may later determine that his actions were unjustified. If the court so decides, the tenant may have to pay rent due, moving expenses, attorney fees, court costs, and even statutory penalties.

placed into escrow, either as a good-faith gesture by the tenant or because courts so order pending a full investigation of the existence and correction of code violations. Therefore, we lump abatement and withholding together as withholding laws. By 1974, such laws were in existence in 25 states.

A third remedy is receivership, that is, appointment by the court of a receiver who takes control of buildings and corrects hazardous defects after the landlord has failed to act within a reasonable period. By 1974, this remedy had become available in 13 states. If large-scale repairs, which cannot be financed through rental payments, are needed, some statutes permit the receiver to seek additional loans. When this is done, old first liens are converted into new second liens, imposing particularly heavy costs on lenders and therefore ultimately on landlords. The initiation of receivership is usually preceded by a hearing in which the court determines whether the landlord has failed to provide essential services. If the court so rules, the rent is deposited with the court-appointed receiver until the violation is corrected. So long as the tenant continues to pay rent into escrow, his landlord cannot evict him for nonpayment.

Altogether, courts increasingly infer that warranties of fitness and habitability are implied in urban residential leases. This implied warranty of habitability may be used as a defense in both action of eviction and action for rent, if the tenant is able to show that a "substantial" violation of the housing code existed during the period rent was withheld. In addition, the tenant may take affirmative action against the landlord for breach of contract, though remaining liable for the reasonable value of the use of the premises.

Of the three remedies listed, receivership is potentially the most costly to the landlord. It results in a complete stoppage of rental income to him, since all tenants in the building, not only aggrieved ones, pay rents into escrow. Moreover, the landlord loses control over his building altogether. Instead, control is temporarily transferred to a receiver who may be enthusiastic about fixing up the building, possibly even above minimum standards established by housing codes. The repair decisions are thus made without due consideration of their potential profitability. Finally, contrary to most repair-and-deduct and withholding actions, receivership is usually initiated by government, which has vast resources behind it.

The three major remedies are often supplemented by laws that can reinforce them. For example, there are *anti-retaliatory-eviction* laws, which are designed to protect tenants from being penalized by landlords for complaining about housing code violations.[30] Such laws, which usually freeze rents for 90 days after compliance, existed in 1974 in 24 states.

---

30. Although initially designed to make habitability laws work by protecting tenants who complain about housing code violations, retaliatory eviction statutes can also be looked upon as devices to ensure that tenants will have continued tenancy during a specified period.

Furthermore, a number of states have laws that facilitate the return of the tenant's security deposit at the end of the tenancy. Finally, a few states, for example, New Jersey and New York, have legalized rent strikes by tenants against a particular landlord.

Laws that prohibit retaliatory eviction, facilitate the return of the tenant's security deposit, and legalize rent strikes, together with the other three remedies, impose costs on landlords. Parts of these costs may result from reduced flexibility, imposition of high repair and maintenance levels, and the possibility of legal costs. Of these remedies, anti-retaliatory-eviction laws resembling temporary rent controls tend to be the most costly to landlords.

2. *Just-Cause Eviction Laws* Stimulate rent controls.

In addition to the habitability laws, state legislatures have begun to pursue a second line of approach by ensuring a tenant's continued tenancy, mainly through just-cause eviction statutes. Under these statutes tenants can be evicted only for just cause, which is explicitly stipulated in the legislation. For example, such statutes in New Jersey delineate a limited number of legal grounds that constitute the sole basis for eviction:

1. Failure to pay rent
2. Disorderly conduct
3. Willful damage or injury to the premises
4. Breach of express covenants
5. Continued violation of landlord's rules and regulations
6. Landlord's wish to retire permanently
7. Landlord's wish to board up or demolish the premises because he has been cited for substandard housing violations and it is economically unfeasible for the owner to eliminate the violations[31]

A just-cause eviction law applying solely to senior citizens was passed by the California assembly in the 1973–1974 legislative session, but died in the senate.[32] It listed six grounds for evicting a tenant 60 years of age or older who has been in continuous possession of a dwelling for 5 years.

1. Nonpayment of rent and utility charges
2. Failure to comply with landlord's rules and regulations
3. Condemnation of the building
4. Failure to comply with statutorily imposed obligations
5. Intended use of the unit as landlord's residence
6. Intended use of unit for other than residential purposes

Like habitability laws, just-cause eviction statutes reduce the property

31. N.J. Stat. (1974).
32. A.B. 1202 (1973–1974 Regular Session) California Assembly.

rights of landlords, particularly the landlords' flexibility in renting out their apartments. Hence, such laws impose costs on landlords. These costs come about because tenants who are assured of continued tenancy can feel free to use all available legal remedies to obtain from landlords relatively high levels of repair and maintenance. Thus, just-cause eviction statutes reinforce the extension of the warranty of habitability and its enforcement and, as a result, further increase costs.

TIME-LIMITED RIGHTS

Patents and copyrights are rights that although otherwise exclusive are limited in duration. Therefore, although it is recognized that a property right in ideas provides incentives for their creation, there are time limits to the exclusivity of their ownership. Such time-limited rights are sometimes bestowed on real property. For example, in *United States* v. *Causby*,[33] military planes flew within 67 feet of the plaintiff's chicken farm, killing his chickens, reducing egg production, and damaging residential living. The court held that the government action could have constituted a taking, with the government becoming the owner of this easement of flight. Since it was a property interest, the easement had to be described accurately, and the court of claims awarded Causby $2000 for the taking of the easement. However, once the government flights ended, the easement could have reverted to Causby, since the United States no longer used that particular air base.

The time limitation of the property right is efficient for several reasons. First of all, a property right of infinite duration would be highly unfair to competitors who discovered the idea or produced the product immediately after the holder and are now forever foreclosed. The granting of this right also gives its owner a monopoly that may be inefficient if permanent. Furthermore, and most important, the law seeks to spread these valuable products as inducement to further advancement in technology and therefore in productivity.

Let us turn to time-limited easement, that is, a privilege without profit that one owner has in the estate of another owner, and its efficiency. For example, if a permanent easement were granted there might be no incentive for the easement owner to reduce an external cost, since the benefit would accrue to the owner for the rest of the time. This can be true, for example, of airplane noise easements. The time-limited easement produces some incentive to consider other possible internalizing measures particularly in the light of new technology. However, surrounding property owners would then have less incentive to reduce the impact of the easement holder's externality upon them.

---

33. *United States* v. *Causby*, 328 U.S. 256 (1946).

LAND USE PLANNING AND DEVELOPMENT

Government can take a number of direct actions that critically change the environment within which lasting changes in land use take place. I am referring to governmental zoning and regulation through various instruments by which transfer of land to new uses is restricted.

ZONING

The division of land into districts with different use regulations, usually in accordance with a comprehensive plan, is called *zoning*. It can take many forms, such as building and housing codes, permits, street ordinances, and architectural controls. As such regulation becomes more pervasive, the specific social policy it is designed to bring about becomes difficult to divine. Therefore, although an economic purpose of zoning might be to prevent external diseconomies, there may be other purposes, such as the exclusion of certain classes or groups, the maintenance of orderly development, fiscal advantage, the maintenance of property values, and the preservation of a neighborhood's character. Since zoning seeks to segregate uses and neighborhoods to reduce externalities, some of these results may be unavoidable. Still, the main objective is to prevent resource misallocation in the presence of major externalities associated with certain land uses.

We can distinguish between cumulative and exclusive zoning. A *cumulative zoning system* implies that externalities of activities are not limited to specified land uses and therefore permits activities in less-regulated areas up to a certain limit. The system is hierarchical in that any particular land use is prohibited in districts reserved for higher uses but permitted in its own district and in any district established for uses lower in the hierarchy. The typical ordinance places uses for single-family dwellings at the top, followed by various kinds of uses for multiple dwellings (e.g., two-family dwellings and walk-up apartments), followed in turn by various grades of commercial uses (e.g., neighborhood businesses, shopping centers, and central business districts), and ending finally with various grades of industrial use (e.g., light or heavy). From such an ordinance one infers that, in the opinion of its authors, any other use generates an external cost for owners of adjacent single-family dwellings, and so forth until at the bottom industrial uses generate an external cost for owners of all adjacent land not used for industry.

Exclusive zoning is based on the premise that in order to improve on the market's allocation of land, certain parcels must be set aside for particular uses. Not only must industry be excluded from residential zones but residences must also be excluded from industrial zones. Thus, exclusive zoning assigns a given district a single use and all other uses are excluded.

Both methods of zoning—cumulative and exclusive—involve grouping particular uses of land. But it is not clear to what degree this results in a modification of the market, since such grouping often occurs naturally as a consequence of positive externalities that are present in unregulated markets (e.g., warehouses are grouped near terminals). Zoning is meant to emphasize and reinforce this market tendency toward specialization of uses and to thwart another market tendency toward intermingling of uses. More will be said on this subject in a later chapter.

We can distinguish between three categories of zoning:

1. Zoning pertaining to the arrangement of activities within the community
2. Measures that exclude from the community certain nonresidential land uses
3. Measures that control the size and/or characteristics of the population of the community

Although these categories are conceptually separate, a particular legal measure may have components of each. For example, a measure that keeps low-cost multiple dwellings out of a jurisdiction (Category 1) may also affect the jurisdiction's population size and composition (Category 3). Alternatively, this indirect control of the population will affect the number and types of retail establishments in the community (Category 2).

Included in Category 1 are all of the most traditional zoning devices, which by definition have effects confined to the jurisdiction; for example, those that pertain to the control of nonconforming uses. Category 2 is also a form of control of externalities. If all resources were properly priced (i.e., if initial residents were given property rights in the environmental quality of the community), there would be no incentive to zone out any particular land use. The community could charge for any costs imposed. However, with normal constraints on local government behavior, a rational community will zone out economic activities that impose costs on the community (through pollution, congestion, etc.) greater than the benefits that they would yield (employment, property taxes, etc.). Category 2 measures will have their primary effect on those seeking to enter a community. For this reason, those affected will have little voice in determining policy. However, any systematic inefficiencies are unlikely, since firms can and do strike bargains with communities in order to be able to operate in them. So long as firms make payments in one form or another equal in value to the negative consequences of their activities, the community has no incentive to exclude them. Competition among communities would rule out extortion, except in those cases where the activity can only be located in one place, as in the case of oil drilling and certain recreational activities. Category 2 zoning activities then need not generally produce inefficient locational decisions. The problem is primarily one of providing the legal environment that allows communities to bargain openly with firms.

The third type of zoning measure, which places controls on community size, affects primarily those outside the community; these people have no voice in the decisions, and therefore inefficient behavior is likely. However, the distinction between the second and third categories is actually not all that clear-cut. If new entrants can be charged the net costs that they will impose on the community, the problem is solved. Communities will have no incentive to exclude, since newcomers impose no uncompensated costs. The primary distinctions are that arrangement for such compensation is difficult, and that the redistributive aspect of such compensation may appear to be unfair. There is no difficulty in asking a firm to pay for the new sewers that its presence makes necessary if normal revenues from the firm will not cover construction costs. But requesting the residents of a low-income housing project to pay for school construction seems somehow unfair. A number of devices currently employed by communities and considered by the courts can be viewed as means to collect compensation or alternatively zone out those who would impose costs that otherwise would go uncompensated.

Before going much further, let us briefly review the history of land use control in the United States. Zoning originated in the early days of the Industrial Revolution in Germany and Sweden. The first American zoning ordinance was enacted in New York City in 1916 to keep glue factories and other dirty, noisy, or bustling plants away from residential and shopping areas. Soon other American cities began passing ordinances to regulate land use and building heights. However, 1926 was the watershed because of the Supreme Court's approval of zoning.[34] Although zoning already had been enabled by a number of states, zoning rapidly became adopted by more and more states, who promptly delegated the zoning power to local jurisdictions. Moreover, in the same year the federal government issued zoning guidelines.[35] Soon the zoning goals of segregating inconsistent uses, preventing congestion, and contributing to economical public-service de-livery were extended into controversial areas: zoning out racial minorities, slowing the influx of urbanites to adjacent rural areas, and preserving open space. The new land use control techniques to slow down population growth included building moratoriums, population caps, open-space zon-ing ordinances, holding zones, and phased-growth ordinances. What started as an attempt to solve largely local problems of incompatible land uses and crowding became an effort to solve much larger regional prob-lems of population distribution and preservation of the environment.

In 1926, in the landmark case of *Euclid* v. *Ambler Realty Company*, the U.S. Supreme Court held that local zoning ordinances were clothed with a presumption of legal validity unless demonstrated to be "clearly arbitrary and unreasonable." At that time, Justice Sutherland indicated that the

34. *Euclid* v. *Ambler Realty Co.*, 272 U.S. 365 (1926).
35. U.S. Department of Commerce, 1926.

possibility should not be ruled out that in the future "the general public interest would so far outweigh the interest of the municipality that the municipality would not be allowed to stand in the way."[36] Since then, many aspects of life and many of the structural characteristics of cities have changed. Lower costs of transporting people first decentralized residence, then lower costs of surface transportation of goods decentralized employment. The megalopolis, a string of city suburbs extending even across state borders, now exists on the East Coast and is emerging elsewhere. Furthermore, increased specialization makes interregional migration a fairly common event.

On first blush, therefore, I would be inclined to conclude that the day foreseen by Justice Sutherland has arrived, and that today the general public interest need not correspond with that of the municipality. Yet the U.S. Supreme Court has retained the position taken initially in 1926. The Court has refused, as recently as 1974, to reexamine its scope of review of zoning cases.[37] When a district court, in *Construction Industry Association of Sonoma County* v. *City of Petaluma*,[38] took a different view and held that the desire of residents to retain the "small-town character" of Petaluma was not compelling and thus invalidated the Petaluma plan, it was overturned on appeal.[39]

Some state supreme courts have taken positions quite different from that of the U.S. Supreme Court. Most notable is the ruling of the New Jersey Supreme Court in *Southern County of Burlington NAACP* v. *Township of Mount Laurel*. It held that zoning must promote the general welfare. A municipality cannot only look to its own selfish and parochial interest and in effect build a wall around itself, "but must consider the needs of the region as a whole and offer an appropriate variety and choice of housing."[40] A similar position was taken by the Pennsylvania Supreme Court in *National Land Investment Company* v. *Kohn*,[41] and the New York Court of Appeals in *Berenson* v. *Town of New Castle*.[42]

The lack of clear guidance from the court stems directly from legislative inaction. The only statutory guidance is found in Massachusetts and California. The Massachusetts Zoning Appeals Law states that "local requirements and regulations shall be considered consistent with local needs if they are reasonable in view of the regional need for low and moderate

36. *Euclid* v. *Ambler Realty Co.*, 272 U.S. 390 (1926).

37. *Village of Belle Terre* v. *Borass*, 94 S. Ct. 1536 (1974).

38. *Construction Industry Association of Sonoma County* v. *City of Petaluma*, 375 F. Supp. 574 (N.D. Cal. 1974).

39. 522 F.2d 897 (1975).

40. *Southern County of Burlington NAACP* v. *Township of Mount Laurel*, 67 N.J. 151, 363, A.2d 713 (1975).

41. *National Land Investment Co.* v. *Kohn*, 419 Pa. 504, 532, 215 A.2d 597, 612 (1965).

42. *Berenson* v. *Town of New Castle*, No. 430, December 2, 1975.

income housing."[43] A quota system is set out that mandates that local requirements are consistent with local needs when (a) the number of low- or moderate-income housing units exceeds 10% of the total housing units in the community, (b) the amount of land used for low-income housing equals or exceeds 1.5% of the total land area of the community, or (c) the application would result in the construction of low-income housing on "sites comprising more than .3 of 1% of such land area or 10 acres whichever is larger."[44] If the quotas have not been reached, the committee presumably balances the factor of need for low-income housing against such factors as the need to protect health and safety, the need to preserve open space, and the need to promote better site and building design.

California has adopted legislation requiring general plans for municipalities and counties to contain within their housing element adequate provision for the housing needs of all economic classes of the community. State Housing Element Guidelines are promulgated by the Department of Housing and Community Development.[45] The state housing goal is to provide a decent home in a satisfying environment. That goal is reached by policy objectives giving all classes of persons a selection of housing with access to employment, community facilities, and services. Each locality is required to prepare a housing element for the improvement of housing, for the provision of adequate sites for all economic segments, and for those whose housing opportunities are affected by the locality. The housing element must be consistent with the locality's identified need and fair-share responsibilities. A good-faith, diligent effort is required and a course of action must be set forth. Emphasis should be on required changes in land use and development controls, regulatory concessions and incentives, and mitigation of other governmental restraints.

The department has the power to complete a fair-share allocation plan in the event of default. It reviews the adequacy of the housing element and can test its adequacy directly in court. Throughout California housing elements must be adopted no later than January 1, 1980, and in some specified areas as early as April 1, 1979.

Some authorities maintain that master planning and zoning are more costly than alternative control systems.[46] Administrative costs are high, changes difficult, and inefficient use-dispersal is common. The system may also be inequitable. Furthermore, zoning cannot generally restrict preexisting uses; therefore the greatest problems will often be unremedied. Land use controls may also redistribute income in unforeseen ways. Some of

---

43. *Mass. Gen. Law Ann.*, ch. 40B, §20 (1973).

44. *Ibid.*

45. 25 Cal. Adm. C. 6400, 6402, 6418, 6424, 6438, 6478.

46. See R. C. Ellickson, "Alternative to Zoning: Covenants, Nuisance Rules, and Fines as Land Use Controls," *Chicago Law Review* 40 (1973): 681–781.

these issues will be explored later, when certain side effects of exclusionary zoning are examined.

RESTRAINTS AND COVENANTS

A limitation placed on an owner's ability to transfer his land, called a *restraint upon alienation,* is not uncommon. However, to be valid the restraint must be reasonable. For example, a promise not to transfer property outside a small group for a limited period of time without allowing a member of the group to buy has been held valid. Therefore, in *Gale* v. *York Center Community Cooperative, Inc.,*[47] a cooperative was able to enforce restrictions against a member selling his interest in the community, where the association was given a year to buy out the member's interest at an impartially appraised or mutually agreed-upon price. The court compared the utility of the restraint with the possible consequences of the clause and concluded that since the member could liquidate his interest, the value of the restriction in a communal setting such as a cooperative exceeded the possible damage to the owner.

The rationale for the prohibition of many restraints upon alienation is that such restraints prohibit the free transfer and productive use of land. Such restrictions can be inefficient because even if they were optimal at the outset, they will not remain so as conditions change over time.

Let us next turn to covenants. Many deeds, leases, or contracts contain covenants with benefits and burdens running to the grantee and grantor. Legally these are enforceable only if the restrictions are deemed to run with the land and are not for the personal benefit of the original parties. Therefore the restrictions may or may not be enforceable, depending on the identity of the enforcing parties, notice by a later transferee, or the extent of the interest.

Some restrictions may be held invalid on constitutional grounds, especially if they discriminate against certain classes. Thus, the Supreme Court in *Shelley* v. *Kraemer*[48] prohibited enforcement of a covenant that precluded "occupance as owners or tenant . . . by people of the Negro or Mongolian race." The enforcement of the contract by state judicial proceeding was held violative of equal protection under the Constitution.

Under normal circumstances, however, property interests themselves are likely to be enforceable. Hence, an easement or license will be enforced, and an equitable servitude may be enforced in equity by way of an injunction. The restrictions can be ended by agreement of the parties, or if the conditions prevailing at the time the restrictions were formulated have changed substantially. Government action, such as condemnation, will also

47. *Gale* v. *York Center Community Cooperative,* 21 Ill. 2d 86, 171 N.E.2d. 30 (1960).
48. *Shelley* v. *Kraemer,* 334 U.S. 1 (1948).

terminate the restrictions. However, a change in zoning usually does not affect a prior use, unless the restriction comes under the changed-condition exception.

Covenants tend to be workable only where there are relatively few owners of the tracts of lands involved. Otherwise the transaction and information costs necessary to change or extend the restrictions are excessively high. Moreover, covenants can suffer from being inflexible at the very time that conditions tend to change. If an individual seeks to violate the restriction, thereby imposing external costs on the other covenantors in violation of the agreement, he may have to go to court or seek to transact a release with the other covenantors. Such a release will be difficult to negotiate because of possible holdout problems as well as high transaction costs. In addition, courts usually impose injunctive remedies rather than damages. This can be an inefficient solution since the violator will be stuck with the covenant, even where the benefit to him of breaching the covenant exceeds the cost to the owners of the other properties.

CONCLUSION

In summary, property law has developed some basic legal concepts and rules, many of which can readily be given economic content. Much of the analysis can be advanced by reference to property rights and, to a lesser extent, to entitlements. Since landlord–tenant relations and zoning ordinances lend themselves especially well to an analysis of their economic effects, these two areas are explored in particular detail. An effect evaluation of these two areas is undertaken in the next chapters.

III

ECONOMIC ANALYSIS OF LANDLORD – TENANT LAWS

INTRODUCTION

Economists have developed tools that can be applied to analyze some of the major economic effects of existing as well as proposed property laws. Such an analysis can be carried out on both a conceptual and an empirical level. In this chapter the focus is on landlord–tenant laws. In the hope of providing an illuminating illustration of the power and limitation of economic theory and econometric methods, habitability laws are examined in detail; also discussed are just-cause eviction, rent control, and housing subsidy laws.

Some of the discussion is quite technical, particularly the analysis of the welfare effects of habitability laws, which requires knowledge of both microeconomic theory and econometric methods. Some readers may therefore want to skip this section (pages 44–58). They may be satisfied with the conclusion of this analysis that the most powerful habitability law— receivership—appears to have led to greater rental expenditures by indigent tenants than benefits from improved housing quality. Therefore, to the extent that the law was enacted to improve the welfare of indigent tenants, it has failed and may even have been counterproductive.

HABITABILITY LAWS

In the preceding chapter, I reviewed the evolution and present status of landlord–tenant relations in general and habitability laws[1] in particular. I

1. For a fuller discussion of habitability laws see Werner Z. Hirsch *et al.*, "Regression

43

pointed to the interest of legislatures and courts in expanding the warranty of habitability and redefining the doctrine of caveat emptor in relation to landlord and tenant law. The reinterpretation has taken explicit note of the inferior bargaining power of tenants, particularly indigent tenants, in relation to that of landlords.[2] The landlord is now the party held ultimately responsible for the condition of the building.[3] If he should fail in his obligation, courts and legislatures, as mentioned in the previous chapter, have provided at least four types of remedy: (a) repair and deduct, (b) rent withholding, (c) receivership, and (d) anti-retaliatory-eviction laws. Not covered are those laws that regulate security deposits and legalize rent strikes. What has been the effect of these laws on the welfare of tenants, especially of indigent tenants?

A FRAMEWORK OF ANALYSIS

Rent, Housing Service Units, and Price

At the outset it must be made clear that rent is different from the price per unit of goods or services. Instead it is the price of a unit that we usually find difficult to define times the number of such units. Economists speak about an abstract concept of housing service units and the price per such housing service unit. It is useful to look upon a dwelling—a housing stock concept—as generating, over time, a flow of housing services. The quantity of housing services that is delivered by a dwelling during a certain period is difficult to measure, mainly because the flow of such services is not a well-defined, homogeneous commodity. For this reason a hedonic index of housing services has been developed.[4] It looks upon any particular aspect of the dwelling, be it paint, heat, size, or location, as a distinct economic commodity. Variations in these commodities are variations in the amount of goods being consumed by the individual occupying the dwelling. Aggregating over these commodities and summarizing all those characteristics, we arrive at the concept of housing services. Then a better dwelling, be it larger, in better condition, or both, is said simply to deliver more housing service units. Thus, it is of higher quality.

The hedonic index of housing is designed to capture the special features

---

Analysis of the Effects of Habitability Laws upon Rent: An Empirical Observation on the Ackerman–Komesar Debate," *California Law Review* 63 (September 1975): 1098–1143; Werner Z. Hirsch and S. Margolis, "Habitability Laws and Low-Cost Rental Housing," in *Residential Location and Urban Housing Markets,* ed. Gregory K. Ingram (Cambridge, Mass.: Ballinger, 1977), pp. 181–213; and Werner Z. Hirsch, *Habitability Laws and the Welfare of Indigent Tenants* (Los Angeles: University of California, 1978).

2. A. James Casner and W. Barton Leach, *Cases and Texts on Property* (Boston: Little, Brown, 1969).

3. The tenant is liable only for specific acts that affect health, safety, or some other aspect of maintaining the building.

4. For details see Hirsch, *Habitability Laws,* pp. 5–6.

of each dwelling and reduce them to a single value reflecting the consensus of the market about their relative importance. Construction of a hedonic housing price index involves empirical efforts at relating rent payments and specified dwelling characteristics.[5] If such quantification is carried out with the aid of regression analysis, then the regression coefficients can be interpreted as estimates of market prices that consumers are willing to pay for the individual characteristics. Such prices are weights that can be used to combine any set of measured attributes into a one-dimensional measure of the total flow of housing services from a given dwelling. The index thus permits the comparison of quantities of housing services yielded by different dwellings.

Short-Run Models versus Long-Run Models

Because housing is a highly durable commodity, the length of the period during which adjustments are permitted to occur is important, especially on the supply side. The length of the adjustment period bears on the distribution of housing costs between landlord and tenant. Thus, in the legal landlord–tenant literature two extreme assumptions have been made. B. A. Ackerman in the early parts of his paper employs a *short-run model*,[6] whereas N. K. Komesar has an extreme *long-run model*.[7]

A short-run model might be applied to certain housing pricing decisions, but it is less useful to an analysis of effects of habitability laws. Clearly, a short-run analysis that assumes no possible reaction by landlords will easily lead to the conclusion that landlords' reactions will not lead to higher rents. Yet in fact there *are* likely to be varying reactions by landlords to habitability laws. For example, filtering up—that is, improving the housing stock—is often quite expensive, and the effect of habitability laws on filtering down will also be small, since a depreciation into lower categories is the consequence of construction and maintenance decisions made many years in the past and of environmental factors not under the control of landlords.

By using cross-sectional data across SMSAs, we can approximate the behavior of the housing market in the long run, permitting ample time for adjustment to the market forces. Rent levels in different areas reflect the impact of differences in city population, real income, cost of production, tax structure, and so on. However, a long-run setting does not necessarily imply a horizontal supply curve of housing services. In a long-run analysis,

5. From a theoretical point of view, the hedonic index approach assumes perfectly competitive market conditions. Such an equilibrium is at best only approximated.

6. B. A. Ackerman, "Regulating Slum Markets on Behalf of the Poor: Of Housing Codes, Housing Subsidies, and Income Distribution Policy," *Yale Law Journal* 80 (1971): 1093–1197, and "More on Slum Housing and Redistribution Policy: A Reply to Professor Komesar," *Yale Law Journal* 82 (1973): 1194–1207.

7. N. K. Komesar, "Return to Slumville: A Critique of the Ackerman Analysis of Housing Code Enforcement and the Poor," *Yale Law Journal* 82 (1973): 1175–1193.

a rising supply curve is possible under the influence of increasing long-run marginal cost. Thus, a rising curve is assumed by deLeeuw and Ekanem to result from internal diseconomies.[8] A shift of the supply function, for example, due to the imposition of a habitability law, will tend to change the production surplus as well as distribute the additional cost between tenant and landlord. For the competitive long-run case, the supply of housing is a horizontal or near-horizontal line at a price that equals the cost of providing housing services.[9] In this case, the distribution of additional cost associated with the law is unambiguous; the tenant pays all additional costs. The effect on rental price is then equal or approximately equal to the change in costs. Hence the competitive case requires only an evaluation of the benefits and costs with respect to the tenant, but for the former case the question of distribution of additional cost between the tenant and landlord is also relevant.

For the analysis of habitability laws, thus, a long-run model is needed to evaluate the effect of a change in legal environment on the housing market, particularly the low-cost rental housing market.

The allocation of housing services is complicated, since consumers must choose among heterogeneous commodities, especially with regard to location. Although location gives a landlord some monopoly power, there usually are many close substitutes. A landlord, it can be argued, tends to accept the highest bid for his dwelling unit, and chooses a package of housing attributes so as to maximize his profits. Like a perfectly discriminating monopolist, the landlord will provide additional services as long as a tenant's marginal evaluation exceeds the services' marginal cost. See Figure 3-1.

Demand

Households are given information on monthly rents which are neither market prices nor quantities of a housing commodity, so essential for demand analysis. We must therefore rely on estimates of implicit market prices (obtained through the hedonic approach) to play the role of direct observations of prices in the traditional theory.

The household consumption problem can be expressed as follows:

$$\max U(Q, Z) \qquad \text{subject to } Y = BZ + PQ, \tag{1}$$

where PQ is the value of housing services or total bid (or rent payment), Q is a measure of housing services, Z is all other goods in the market, that is,

---

8. F. de Leeuw and N. F. Ekanem, "The Supply of Rental Housing," *American Economic Review* 61 (December 1971): 806–817.

9. A supplier may vary the quantity of housing services to attain optimal-size operation. Scale economies are exhausted and profit is reduced to zero because of free entrance. The optimal-size firm is located where the long-run marginal cost curve is at its minimum. The supply of rental housing is varied by changing the number of firms in the industry.

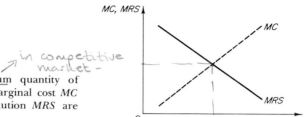

FIGURE 3-1 The equilibrium quantity of housing services Q where marginal cost MC and marginal rate of substitution MRS are equal.

nonhousing commodities, Y is household income, and B is the price of nonhousing commodities.

The bid-rent framework involves a production decision (which we assume here to be given) and a consumption decision process.[10] Given Eq. (1) the solution to the choice quantity of housing service Q is that point at which the household's marginal rate of substitution for housing and other expenditures is equal to the ratio of the bid value for an additional unit of housing services and the price of an additional unit of other commodities. If $P = \theta(Q; Y, u^*, \gamma)$ expresses the "willingness-to-pay" curves of a household, when income, utility level, and personal attributes are given, the optimal choice is where the household's marginal valuation equals the marginal cost of housing services Q, that is, A in Figure 3-2.

Note that in the willingness-to-pay function there is a set of personal attributes, γ. As γ varies, different θ curves emerge for such special groups as blacks or senior citizens. Such segmentation of households can be used to eliminate the assumption that all households have utility functions of the same form.

Supply

The supplier will be viewed as confronting a fixed price function $P(Q)$.[11]

10. Under the bid-rent approach, the household is regarded as if it were making an offer on every rental housing unit such that it would be equally well off if any one of the offers were accepted. This is consistent with the choice of a u^* in the θ function. Equilibrium is obtained when the values are such that every unit is occupied by the highest bidder and every household occupies no more than one unit. If an individual household bidder is the high bidder on more than one unit, he submits bids that are lower for all units, again such that he is indifferent as to which of the bids are accepted, thus obtaining a higher level of utility than obtained with the previous bids. The bidder who is high on no unit can reevaluate and submit a set of bids that are higher; that is, he bids along a lower indifference curve, each bid representing for him a choice of housing and nonhousing consumption.

Within this setting, we regard the process of a consumer trading off housing services for nonhousing consumption as moving along an indifference curve. Doing so, the household pays according to its marginal rate of substitution of housing for other expenditures for each successive unit of housing services.

11. This assumption of a fixed price function is equivalent to the assumption that competitive firms confront constant prices. Obviously the assumption cannot be literally true, but it probably reflects the supplier's perception that individually he has little influence on market price.

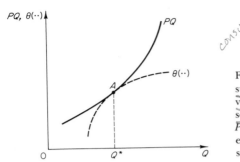

FIGURE 3-2 The optimum solution for consumers at A, where the household's marginal valuation equals the marginal cost of housing services. (Key: Q, quantity of housing services; PQ, market price function; $\theta(\cdot\cdot)$, consumer's equilibrium bid value; Q^*, optimum housing services quantity.)

The decision of the supplier can be formulated as follows:

$$\max \pi = PQ - C(Q, K, L),\tag{2}$$

where π is profit, $C(\cdot)$ is the total cost function, K is a vector of cost of production inputs, and L are legal activities relative to habitability laws.

In the supply setting, the bid curves represent equal willingness to supply. Thus for each supplier we can define the function that solves Eq. (2) for any specified π for values of the exogenous variables appropriate to the supplier. We define $P = \phi(Q; \pi, K, L)$ as representing points that provide equal profit for the landlord. As before, equilibrium is attained where the bid function is tangent to the implicit price function, since higher $\phi(\cdot)$ are obtained for higher values of π while holding all other variables constant (see Figure 3-3). Since $\phi(\cdot)$ represents points of constant profit, any particular $\phi(\cdot)$ is simply the total cost function, plus some constant. Therefore, at equilibrium, marginal cost equals the marginal price of Q. Equilibrium exists where the bid-rent function of a consumer is tangent to the supply function of a producer, whose slope equals that of the market clearing implicit price function.

Habitability laws can affect maintenance decisions, which in turn find their expression in the use of production inputs. The landlord increases maintenance up to the point where the marginal evaluation of additional

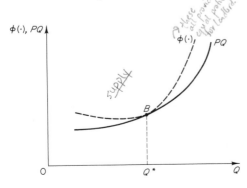

FIGURE 3-3 The optimum solution for producers at B, where marginal cost equals the marginal price of the quantity of housing services Q. Curve $\phi(\cdot)$ is the implicit price function; see key to Figure 3-2 for definitions of other variables.

housing services derived from a unit of maintenance plus the savings in depreciation equal the price of the maintenance input. However, I will not introduce the maintenance variable explicitly, since the vector of cost of production inputs will include resources used for maintenance and other production activities. We estimate the differential impact of habitability laws by distinguishing between populations according to the presence or absence of laws in each population. Landlords are expected to supply fewer housing services at a given price if they incur higher costs, whatever the nature of the cost increases. At the same time, the legal costs increase their incentives to provide services. Moreover, habitability laws affect landlords' maintenance expenditures, profitability, and life expectancy of dwellings.

EMPIRICAL FINDINGS

I will next briefly describe the data and then present the basic structural relationships of the model together with empirical findings.

Data

The data used to estimate the rent equation, that is, monthly gross rent and various rental housing characteristics, come from the SMSA Annual Housing Survey of 1974 and 1975.[12] The survey data were constrained and a subfile created of unfurnished rental household units in private nonsubsidized houses, apartments, or flats occupied by households with incomes in 1974 of $9000 or less. Monthly gross rent includes electricity, gas, oil, or coal bills.[13] Housing characteristics are grouped into quantity characteristics (QUANT)—number of rooms, age of building, number of bathrooms, presence of air conditioning, and use of rented parking; and four classes of quality characteristics—quality inside the dwelling (INDW), neighborhood quality that relates to the physical characteristics of the area (NEHDA), neighborhood quality that relates to public services provided in the area (NEHDB), and the quality of public space inside the building (PUBSP).[14] Variable definitions and sources are given in Table 3-1.

12. Personal interviews conducted by the Bureau of the Census under contract with the U.S. Department of Housing and Urban Development of about 15,000 households per area were carried out in the metropolitan areas of Boston, Massachusetts; Detroit, Michigan; Los Angeles–Long Beach, California; and Washington, D.C.–Maryland–Virginia between April 1974 and March 1975 and in Atlanta, Georgia; Chicago, Illinois; San Francisco–Oakland, California; and Philadelphia, Pennsylvania between April 1975 and March 1976. At the same time interviews of about 5000 households each were carried out in an additional 14 SMSAs in the 1974 survey, and in 17 SMSAs in the 1975 survey. Because of the interest in the effects of state laws, SMSAs covering more than one state and for which areas could not be assigned to one state were omitted.

13. Water cost is not included because few households pay for their water, for example, 5% of renters in Minneapolis, and this bill tends to be very small.

14. Of the 40 quality variables taken from the annual survey, some were dropped because (a) there was a high correlation with other more important variables, (b) formulation of the variable in the survey appeared questionable, or (c) there was little variation in the variable.

TABLE 3-1
Variable Descriptors

Variable name or number		
1974	1975	Description

Monthly gross rent including electricity, gas, oil, and/or coal (RENT)[a]

H001	H006	Age of building
H044	H033	Number of rooms
H059	H063	Number of bathrooms
H078	H081	Air conditioning
H121	H157	Rented parking

Inside dwelling quality (INDW)[a]

H045	H034	Working electrical wall outlets
H051	H053	Complete kitchen facility
H054	H058	Water breakdown
H058	H062	Complete plumbing facility
H071	H075	Additional heating equipment used
H073	H076[b]	Number of rooms without heat
H075	H078	Number of heating breakdowns
H076	H079	Rooms closed for warmth
H079	H082	Type of air conditioning
H083	H035	All wiring concealed
H087	H089	Basement in house

Physical neighborhood quality (NEHDA)[a]

H170	H207	Noise bothersome
H173	H218	Airplane noise bothersome
H176	H208[b]	Traffic bothersome
H179	H217	Odors bothersome
H182	H213[b]	Trash, litter bothersome
H184	H214	Abandoned structures
H187	H215	Rundown houses
H191	H216[b]	Industry bothersome
H193	H209	Streets need repair
H197	H211[b]	Street lighting bothersome
H214	H233	Deter housing on street

Public services neighborhood quality (NEHDB)[a]

H200	H212	Street crime bothersome
H202	H219	Inadequate public transportation
H204	H221	Inadequate schools
H206	H223	Inadequate shopping
H208	H225	Inadequate police
H210	H227	Inadequate fire protection

Public space quality (PUBSP)[a]

H043	H033	Passenger elevator
H215	H236	Light fixtures in hall

50

TABLE 3-1 (continued)
Variable Descriptors

Variable name or number		
1974	1975	Description
H216	H237	Light fixtures working ⎫
H217	H238	Bad stairways ⎬ quality
H219	H239	Railing attached firmly ⎭
OREUT[a]		Mean annual rent and utility payments as percentage of median family income
FAMINCO[a]		Median renter family income in thousands of dollars
PRICELEV[a]		Price level proxy
PERPTAX[c]		Per capita property tax in SMSA in thousands of dollars, 1974 and 1975
LAND[d]		Per square foot land value of dwellings in SMSA, 1974
CONWAGE[d]		Hourly average union rates of building helpers and laborers, 1974

[a] From SMSA Annual Housing Survey, 1974–1975, U.S. Department of Housing and Urban Development and U.S. Bureau of the Census.

[b] The 1975 survey modified the 1974 definitions of variables related to physical neighborhood characteristics. For example, the 1974 variables H169 (any street noise), H170 (noise bothersome), and H171 (noise objection move) were combined into a single 1975 variable, H207 (any street noise).

[c] From *Local Government Finances in Selected Metropolitan Areas and Large Counties*, U.S., Bureau of the Census, 1974–1975, 1975–1976.

[d] *From* Data for States and Selected Areas on Characteristics of FHA Operations under Section 203, *Handbook of Labor Statistics*, U.S. Bureau of Labor Statistics, 1977.

Using microdata of quality and quantity rental housing characteristics as right-hand variables, rental price and quantity indexes were estimated for 70 data points in the 34 metropolitan areas included in the SMSA Annual Housing Survey of 1974 and 1975. These indexes were then combined with additional area data to estimate demand and supply functions, respectively. The variables are of two types—conventional demand and supply determinants and data on the presence of habitability laws. For the conventional demand and supply variables, area data were used.

A special effort was made to obtain information on the status of specific habitability laws in the various states and the District of Columbia. A law file was established by searching statutes and court opinions as well as by making inquiries with legal aid organizations. (See Table 3-2.)

Rent Equations

The housing model described earlier requires, first, an estimation of household rent equations. This step is taken by using a hedonic price

TABLE 3-2

Presence of Habitability Laws, 1974[a]

	Repair-and-deduct laws	Withholding laws	Receivership laws	Anti-retaliatory-eviction laws
1. Arizona	1	1	0	1
2. California	1	1	0	1
3. Colorado	0	0	0	0
4. Connecticut	0	0	1	1
5. Florida	0	1	0	0
6. Georgia	1	1	0	0
7. Illinois	1	1	1	1
8. Kansas	0	1	0	0
9. Louisiana	1	0	0	0
10. Maryland	0	0	0	1
11. Massachusetts	1	1	1	1
12. Michigan	0	1	1	1
13. Minnesota	0	1	1	1
14. Missouri	0	1	1	0
15. New Jersey	1	1	1	1
16. New York	0	1	1	1
17. Ohio	1	1	1	1
18. Oregon	1	1	0	1
19. Pennsylvania	0	1	0	1
20. Tennessee	0	0	0	1
21. Texas	0	0	0	0
22. Utah	0	0	0	0
23. Virginia	1	0	0	0
24. Washington	1	1	0	1
25. Washington, D.C.	0	1	0	1
26. Wisconsin	0	1	1	1
Total	11	18	10	17

[a] 0 = absence of law; 1 = presence of law.

approach. The dependent variable—monthly gross rent including utilities (R)—is regressed against five quantity variables (QUANT) and four classes of quality variables,

$$R = f(\text{QUANT, INDW, NEHDA, NEHDB, PUBSP}). \qquad (3)$$

Thirty-three housing quality variables were combined to derive the four weighted quality classes. The weight of 1 was given to every variable in summing them to form each quality class. Serious consideration was given to employing factor analysis. I examined the simple correlation coefficients of the quality variable matrix, in search of groups of variables with high coefficients within the group but low ones across the groups. However, no consistent pattern was revealed. Since under such conditions factor analysis is unlikely to work, quality variables were grouped on the basis of theoretical and logical considerations. Rent was expected to have a positive relation with each of the five quantity variables, and a negative relation with each of the four quality variables, since the index number assigned to a dwelling increases with its shortcomings, that is, as its quality declines.

Rent equations were estimated for each of the 70 geographical areas in both semilog form and linear form. Since there was a slight improvement in $\bar{R}^2$ in the first functional form compared to the second and the semilog transformation rectified the heteroscedasticity that is common to most cross-section analysis, the semilog form was selected with the dependent variable in log form. Rent equations in semilog form for the 70 geographical areas, located in 25 states plus the District of Columbia, are presented in the Appendix Table. The statistical results can be summarized as follows: $\bar{R}^2$ ranged from 0.15 in Westmoreland County, Pennsylvania, to 0.73 in Montgomery County, Maryland. Among the quality groups, the inside dwelling quality (INDW) performed best in terms of both signs and statistical significance, followed by public space quality (PUBSP), physical neighborhood quality (NEHDA) and public services neighborhood quality (NEHDB). In a very few cases, the last two variables, although statistically significant, had a wrong sign.[15] Of the five quantity variables, number of rooms performed best, followed by age of building, number of bathrooms, presence of air conditioning, and renting of parking. The whole set of nine variables was found to be significantly different from zero at a 95% level (one-tailed test) for all regions except Kane County, Illinois. Altogether the magnitudes of the net regression coefficients were found to be consistent over all geographical areas.

Rental Housing Price and Quantity Index

From the 70 rent equations, rental housing price and quantity indexes were estimated by specifying a standard bundle of housing services and using hedonic values to calculate the cost of the standard bundle in each region. Similarly, I defined an average price vector for the entire sample size, and coupled that with the mean values of housing characteristics purchased by each region in order to obtain the quantity index.[16]

15. J. R. Follain, *Cross-Sectional Indexes of the Price of Housing* (Washington, D.C.: Urban Institute, 1978), also found that the price of housing is relatively insensitive to neighborhood characteristics.

16. The indexes were formulated as follows:

$$\bar{X}_k = \frac{\sum_{I=1}^{70} N_I \bar{X}_{Ik}}{\sum_{I=1}^{70} N_I},$$

where N_I is the sample size of geographical region I, $\sum_{I=1}^{70} N_I$ is the total sample size across the 70 geographical regions, that is, 28,753, $\bar{X}_{Ik}$ is the mean value of housing attribute k in geographical region I, and $\bar{X}_k$ is the mean value of housing attribute k weighted by the respective sample size in the 70 regions.

In matrix notation, the price index of region I, that is, P_I, can be formulated as the sum of

The Demand and Supply System

The functional form of the demand function can be expressed as

$$P_I = g(Q_I, L_I, Y_I, T_I, B_I),\tag{4}$$

where L_I are the law variables of region I, Y_I are the income variables of region I, T_I is the taste variable of region I and B_I is the price of the nonhousing commodities variable of region I.

In relation to the status of habitability laws, dummy variables were used to distinguish housing locations with active habitability laws from those without such laws—1 if an active law was present and 0 if not. The dummy variables reflect not only the presence or absence of a habitability law but also, wherever possible, status of enforcement. The issue of enforcement may have been less complicated than under most circumstances, since there exists great similarity in the case-filing pattern that emerged in a study in New York and that found by Mosier and Soble in Detroit.[17] In both instances, shortly after a habitability law appeared on the scene, many cases were filed during the first few years, reaching a peak after 5–6 years. By far

---

cross-product terms between the estimated hedonic values of region I and the fixed bundle of housing attributes

$$\underset{(\text{I} \times 1)}{P_I} = \underset{(\text{I} \times \text{k})}{\bar{X}} \; \underset{(\text{k} \times 1)}{\hat{r}_I},$$

where P_I is the price index of region I with respect to a fixed bundle of housing attributes $\bar{X}$, $\hat{r}_I$ are the ordinary least squares estimates (hedonic values) of the rent equation of region I, and $\bar{X}$ are the mean values of housing attributes, that is, a fixed bundle of housing attributes used to derive the price index.

Similarly, the hedonic value of housing attribute k of each region is weighted by their respective sample size to obtain an average price of k for the entire region.

$$\bar{r}_k = \frac{\sum_{I=1}^{70} N_I \hat{r}_{Ik}}{\sum_{I=1}^{70} N_I},$$

where $\hat{r}_{Ik}$ is the estimated hedonic value of housing attribute k of region I, and $\bar{r}_k$ is the mean hedonic value of housing attribute k weighted by the respective sample size of each region.

The quantity index of region I, Q_I, is formulated as the sum of the cross-product terms between the means of the estimated hedonic values of the entire sample size and the mean value of housing attributes purchased by a representative family in region I,

$$\underset{(\text{I} \times 1)}{Q_I} = \underset{(\text{I} \times \text{k})}{\bar{r}} \; \underset{(\text{k} \times 1)}{\bar{X}_I},$$

where Q_I is the quantity index of monthly flow of housing services purchased by a representative family in region I, $\bar{X}_I$ are the mean values of housing attributes purchased by a representative family in region I, and $\bar{r}$ are the mean hedonic values used as a weight to derive the quantity index of each region.

For further detail and estimated indexes see Hirsch, *Habitability Laws*.

17. M. M. Mosier and R. A. Soble, "Modern Legislation, Metropolitan Court Miniscule Results: A Study of Detroit's Landlord–Tenant Court," *University of Michigan Journal of Law Reform* 7 (Fall 1973): 8–70. Also see Hirsch *et al.*, "Regression Analysis," pp. 1135–1136.

the largest number of habitability laws studied by us relative to 1974–1975 had been passed in the preceding 4–6 years. Moreover, most states during those years had very active legal aid attorneys assisting indigent tenants. Therefore enforcement was uniformly stringent.

Thus, I introduced three law variables in the form of dummy variables:[18]

REPAIR   identifies states with repair-and-deduct laws in 1974.

EWHOLD   identifies states with both withholding laws and anti-retaliatory-eviction laws in 1974.

RECEIV   identifies states with receivership laws in 1974.

All three laws, if enforced, impose costs on landlords and should therefore be positively correlated with price. As an income variable, I used the median family income of renters in 1974–1975 (FAMINCO), expecting it to be positively correlated with price. As a taste variable I introduced mean annual rent payments by indigents as a percentage of median family SMSA income in 1974–1975 (OREUT), expecting a positive correlation with price. In the absence of data on nonhousing prices for the 34 SMSAs—the Bureau of Labor Statistics covers only 12 of them—I used, following DeLeeuw and Ekanem a price level proxy (PRICELEV).[19] Housing is an important item in consumers' budgets, and we do not know whether its price varies directly with the price level or inversely with it. In the former case, the correlation would be positive and in the latter case it would be negative.

The functional form of the supply function can be expressed as,[20]

$$P_I = h(Q_I, L_I, K_I), \tag{5}$$

where K_I is the vector of cost of production variables in region I; that is, PERPTAX, which is the per capita property tax in thousands of dollars in 1974–1975; LAND, which is the per-square-foot land value of dwellings in

18. Rather than introducing retaliatory eviction as a separate variable, I combined it with withholding laws. The reason is that since withholding remedies are tenant initiated and impose substantial costs on landlords, whereas repair-and-deduct remedies do not, tenants who withhold payment often require protection from retaliatory eviction. Since receivership is not tenant initiated, no such protection is needed.

Concerning the presence of habitability laws, I tested for a correlation with income or geographical location within the United States. Very low correlations were found. For example, such states as California, Louisiana, Texas, and Wisconsin and the District of Columbia did not have receivership laws.

19. DeLeeuw and Ekanem, "Supply of Rental Housing." I used the percentage of renters in an area with an annual family income of $5000 or more as a proxy. This proxy was found to be highly correlated with the area's median family income of all households and with the Consumer Price Index of select SMSAs ($r = 0.84$).

20. Since hourly wages of building helpers and laborers (CONWAGE) are basically the same throughout a given SMSA, they can be applied to the entire SMSA. However, property taxes and land values do vary over the SMSA. Although I would have preferred separate data for each data point, I had to use SMSA data.

1974; and CONWAGE, which is the hourly wages of building helpers and laborers in 1974. I expect the price, law, and production cost variables all to be positively correlated with price.

In order to estimate demand and supply functions, a two-stage ordinary least squares method was employed. The first stage was designed to find an instrumental variable that correlated with the dependent variable but had zero correlation with the disturbance term. Then the instrumental variables were used in the second stage to estimate supply and demand equations. Since the system was overidentified, I was not able to obtain one unique set of structural parameters from the reduced form parameters. Of the four possible sets of structural equations I have selected that which gives results consistent with my underlying hypotheses, that is, demand function $P = g(Q)$ and supply function $P = h(Q)$. Moreover, price (P) varies more than quantity (Q). Results are presented in Table 3-3.[21]

The demand function performed well. All variables, except REPAIR which were not statistically significant, had the right signs. Three variables —quantity (QUANT), income (FAMINCO), and taste (OREUT)—as well as the constant were found to be statistically significant at the 99% confidence level (one-tailed test); the receivership law variable (RECEIV) and the price level variable (PRICELEV) were statistically significant at the 95% confidence level (one-tailed test). The other habitability law variables were not statistically significant.

Also, the supply function performed well. All variables had the right signs. Four variables—quantity (QUANT), receivership law (RECEIV), tax (PERPTAX) and land value (LAND)—and the constant were found to be statistically significant at the 99% confidence level (one-tailed test). Two other variables—eviction-withholding law (EWHOLD) and wages (CON-WAGE)—were statistically significant at the 90% confidence level (one-tailed test). The other two habitability law variables—REPAIR AND EWHOLD —were not statistically significant.

Thus of the three laws, only receivership laws had statistically significant effects on the housing demand and supply functions of low-income renters.

I also estimated the double logarithmic formulation of the demand and supply functions, so that elasticities could be obtained directly. The price and income elasticities were −0.87 and 0.98, respectively. The price elasticity of supply was found to be 0.80, supporting my prior belief that supply of rental housing services to low-income groups is substantially less than perfectly elastic, even in the long run.

With the aid of the demand and supply functions thus estimated, specific habitability laws can be evaluated as to their welfare effects on demanders

21. Werner Z. Hirsch, "Habitability Laws and the Welfare of Indigent Tenants," *Review of Economics and Statistics, 58* (May 1981).

TABLE 3-3

Regression Results for Demand and Supply Functions for 70 Geographical Regions
(Inverse Semilog with Log Price as Dependent Variable)

	Demand		Supply	
	Coefficient	*t*-stat.	Coefficient	*t*-stat.
INTERCEPT	4.143	17.20*	3.118	6.57*
QUAN[b]	0.0069	4.87*	0.0079	3.25*
EWHOLD	0.022	0.98	0.072	1.43***
RECEIV	0.046	2.05**	0.156	3.27*
REPAIR	0.0026	0.14	0.019	0.43
PRICELEV	0.0093	1.96**	(a)	
FAMINCO	0.063	3.19*	(a)	
OREUT	0.0034	11.79*	(a)	
PERPTAX	(a)		0.561	2.40*
CONWAGE	(a)		0.035	1.28***
LAND	(a)		0.168	3.75*

 * Significant at 0.01 one-tailed test level ($t_{1.62} = 2.33$).
 ** Significant at 0.05 one-tailed test level ($t_{1.62} = 1.64$).
 *** Significant at 0.10 one-tailed test level ($t_{1.62} = 1.28$).
 (a) Variable not entered.
 (b) Estimated from first stage.

and suppliers of rental housing. For example, if tenants were unaffected by a habitability law, that is, if the net regression coefficient in the demand function relating price to the presence of a particular habitability law was statistically insignificant, no demand curve shift would have occurred. If, however, the net regression coefficient was statistically significant and positive, the presence of a habitability law would have increased the value tenants attached to their apartments. In a similar manner a statistically significant positive habitability law coefficient in the supply function would indicate that the presence of a law, on average, increased the cost of an apartment.

Welfare evaluation requires comparing the relative magnitudes of vertical shifts of demand and supply functions, respectively, in relation to the presence of a particular habitability law. If the upward shift in the demand function associated with the presence of a given habitability law is significantly larger than the shift in the supply function, the valuation by renters of improved housing exceeded the accompanying rent increase, and vice versa. Comparing the net regression coefficients that relate price and presence of habitability laws in the demand and supply function, respectively, we find that receivership laws raise the constant term of the supply equation by 27.1 price units and of the demand equation by 9.0 price units. The difference between the vertical shifts of the two equations is 18.1 units (see Table 3-3 and Figure 3-4).

These supply and demand function shifts can also be examined in terms of consumer's surplus with point C being the equilibrium in the presence of a receivership law and point E being the equilibrium in its absence. The

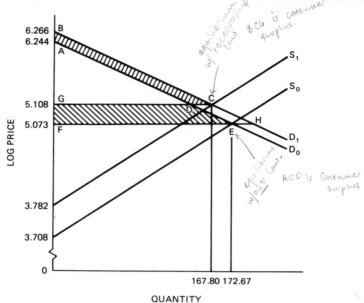

No Receivership Law

    Demand (D_0):   log PRICE $= 6.244 - .0069$QUAN

    Supply (S_0):   log PRICE $= 3.708 + .0079$QUAN

With Receivership Law

    Demand (D_1):   log PRICE $= 6.244 - .0069$QUAN $+ .046\overline{\text{RECEIV}}$
                                     $= 6.266 - .0069$QUAN

    Supply (S_1):   log PRICE $= 3.708 + .0079$QUAN $+ .156\overline{\text{RECEIV}}$
                                       $= 3.782 + .0079$QUAN

FIGURE 3-4 Comparison of consumer's surplus in the absence and presence of receivership laws.

consumer's surplus is the area under the demand equation, bounded by the equilibrium price level from below and the vertical axis on the left. In the absence of a receivership law, the consumer's surplus is area *AEF* in Figure 3-4; in its presence, area *BCG*. The change of consumer's surplus due to the law is the difference between areas *ABCD* and *DEFG*—a reduction of 10.1% of the consumer's surplus.

    In conclusion, of the three major types of habitability laws available to tenants, only receivership in 1974–1975 had a statistically significant effect on both demanders and suppliers of low-cost rental housing in 34 large SMSAs with more than one-fourth of the United States population. Its presence was found to be associated with a statistically significant increase in rental expenditures of indigent tenants, and with expenditures out-weighing benefits accruing to such tenants. To the extent that habitability laws are mainly designed to improve the welfare of indigent tenants, they have failed, at least in the sample studied. Receivership laws may even have been counterproductive.

JUST-CAUSE EVICTION STATUTES

Statutes designed to ensure continued tenancy for tenants are of very recent vintage. They can be viewed as constraining landlords from exercising all the prerogatives usually associated with ownership. Eviction, except for one of the causes specifically enumerated in a statute, is considered illegal. As a result, tenants are supposedly assured some degree of permanence, should they wish it.

For policy as well as analytical purposes, two types of just-cause eviction statutes may be distinguished:

1. Universal just-cause eviction laws that apply to all tenants, for example, the 1974 New Jersey law[22]
2. Discriminatory just-cause eviction laws that single out a particular group for "favored" treatment, for example, the 1973–1974 proposed California statute, which would have given just-cause protection only to tenants 60 years and older who had been in continuous possession of their dwelling for at least 5 years[23]

The effects of both types of statutes can be analyzed with the aid of a microeconomic model, with the second type of statute—that which extends coverage only to a particular group—the more complicated.

UNIVERSAL JUST-CAUSE EVICTION LAWS

A just-cause eviction law applicable to all tenants increases the security of tenancy. Within the hedonic price approach discussed earlier, security of tenancy is just another economic commodity traded between landlords and tenants. The demand function for apartments with just-cause eviction guarantees is higher, that is, further to the right, than that without such guarantees, *ceteris paribus*. Thus the law by protecting tenants provides benefits and enhances their utility.

Although just-cause eviction laws increase the welfare of tenants, they also impose costs on landlords. Specifically, such laws reduce landlords' rights and thereby their flexibility, and place greater risk upon them. For example, they reduce landlords' options to evict tenants in order to remodel their facilities for another class of tenants. Moreover, legal costs are likely to increase. As a consequence, the rental housing supply function shifts to the left in the presence of universal just-cause eviction laws, *ceteris paribus*.

In Figure 3-5, the effect of the imposition of a universal just-cause eviction law is illustrated. Rent, *R,* is on one axis and number of dwellings,

22. N. J. Stat. Ann. §2A, 18–53 (West Supp. 1974).
23. A. B. 1202 (1973–1974 Regular Session), California Assembly.

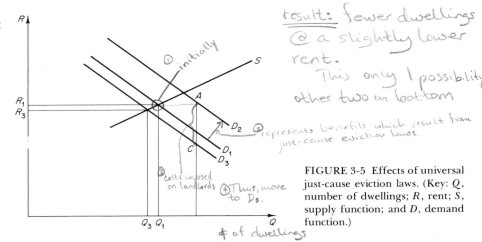

[handwritten annotations:] rent

① initially

result: fewer dwellings @ a slightly lower rent.
This only 1 possibility, other two on bottom

② represents benefits which result from just-cause eviction laws.

③ costs imposed on landlords

④ Thus, move to D_3.

# of dwellings

FIGURE 3-5 Effects of universal just-cause eviction laws. (Key: Q, number of dwellings; R, rent; S, supply function; and D, demand function.)

Q, is on the other. Prior to the imposition of the law, landlords face demand function D_1 and supply function S. They lease Q_1 dwellings at R_1 rent. The benefits that result from just-cause eviction laws can be represented in an upward shift of the demand function from D_1 to D_2, which for simplicity's sake is assumed to be parallel. Costs imposed by the law on landlords may be viewed as the insurance they can purchase against the hazards that ensue from the law. This insurance is assumed to amount to $A - C$, and accordingly the new demand function, reflecting both benefits to tenants and costs to landlords, will be D_3. (Note that in this case costs exceed benefits.)

As can be seen in Figure 3-5, the just-cause eviction law has a chilling effect on landlords who consequently supply fewer dwellings, $Q_1 - Q_3$, at a somewhat lower rent, $R_1 - R_3$. The decline in the number of dwellings supplied in the face of universal just-cause eviction laws can be explained in the following manner: The law forces landlords to supply an additional economic commodity, security of tenancy. Since rent increases to compensate for the additional costs are not permitted, landlords will seek to reduce costs by cutting back on other housing services, particularly repair and maintenance. As a consequence, buildings will deteriorate and sooner or later reach a stage where they are abandoned. Should habitability laws not permit reduced maintenance, financial considerations will stimulate conversion of apartment houses to condominiums, cooperatives, or perhaps convalescent homes, all steps that reduce the supply of low-cost rentals.

The case discussed so far and presented in Figure 3-5 is only one of three possible cases. In a second case, the cost to the landlord is smaller than the increased value to the tenant. The result usually will be more dwellings, but at a higher rent. In a third case, law-induced benefit and cost increases are about equal. As a consequence, all parties are left in the same welfare situation as before, with no change in either the number of dwellings or their rent.

A further side effect of universal just-cause eviction laws is their stimulus for rent controls. Clearly landlords working under just-cause eviction laws and incurring costs associated with such laws tend to raise rents. Rent increases will be contemplated for two reasons: to compensate for increased risk and cost, and to seek termination of tenancies of those who are protected by the law, since new tenants will pay higher rents. To counter such moves by landlords, government will be strongly tempted to institute rent controls, which will be examined subsequently.

DISCRIMINATORY JUST-CAUSE EVICTION LAWS

A just-cause eviction law, rather than protecting all tenants, can apply to a particular group of tenants. An example mentioned before is the bill that passed the California assembly (but not the senate) in 1974, singling out senior citizens for just-cause eviction protection.[24]

Thus, in the presence of a law that applies only to a particular group, landlords face two classes of renters: those who are protected by just-cause legislation and those who are not. Separation of these two groups is not difficult when they are identifiably defined, and enforcement is facilitated by the prohibition of subletting. For example, aged tenants are likely to have rental housing demand characteristics that are distinctly different from those of young tenants. The difference stems from the aged tenants' desire for relatively easy access to various private and public facilities, and their particular concern for a pollution-free environment and personal safety. These preferences are in part derived from the physical vulnerability of the aged, who by and large are risk-averse. As a consequence of these considerations the rental housing demand elasticity for aged tenants can be expected to be lower than that for young tenants, *ceteris paribus*.

In the light of these considerations and the assumption that landlords have only limited monopoly power, a short-run model can be constructed to show rent determination by landlords. In Figure 3-6, a landlord, having identified and separated aged from nonaged tenants, seeks to equate his marginal costs, MC, with the horizontally summed marginal revenues, that is, MR's from the two markets. He allocates Q_1^A housing units to elderly tenants at a rent of R_1^A, and Q_1^B housing units to the nonelderly at a rent of R_1^B. At this stage of the analysis, preceding the passage of a just-cause eviction law, rent paid by elderly and nonelderly need not be significantly different; but the number of dwellings for the elderly is unambiguously smaller than that for the nonelderly. This result stems from the different demand elasticities of the two groups. The less elastic the demand—and I

24. *Ibid.*

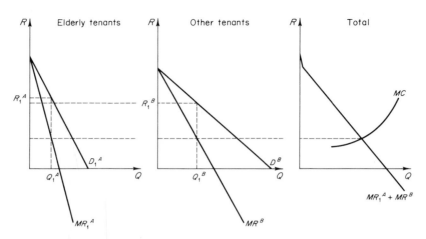

FIGURE 3-6 Short-run model of rent determination by landlords under market discrimination.

argued earlier that elderly tenants have relatively low demand elasticities—the greater the possibility for landlords to act as monopolists in the market.

After the enactment of discriminatory just-cause eviction laws singling out elderly tenants, their housing demand can be expected to increase. After awarding aged tenants increased property rights, their demand function will tend to shift upward. Housing has become more valuable to them, indicated in Figure 3-7, where the demand curve in the aged housing market shifts to the right, from D_1^A to D_2^A. (For simplicity, the shift is assumed to be parallel.) In the short run, the demand in the nonaged housing market remains unchanged, as this group is not directly affected by the law.

As discussed in connection with a universal just-cause eviction law, the cost of providing housing to those protected increases. Landlords, for example, may be viewed as purchasing insurance against the costs the new law is expected to impose on them, equal to the vertical difference between the two demand functions D_2^A and D_3^A. In effect, the difference between D_2^A and D_3^A is the additional cost to the landlord of delivering housing to aged rather than nonaged tenants. Here, D_3^A is the new average revenue curve confronting the landlord, with MR_3^A the associated marginal revenue curve. Landlords change the mix of dwellings offered to aged and nonaged tenants to the point where $MR_3^A + MR^B = MC$, supplying the elderly with Q_2^A at a rent of R_2^A, and the nonelderly Q_2^B at a rent of R_2^B.

As in the case of universal just-cause eviction laws, different cases are possible. Depending on the magnitude of the benefits conferred to elderly tenants compared to the costs imposed on landlords, three different cases emerge. In the first case, presented in Figure 3-7, the cost to landlords due

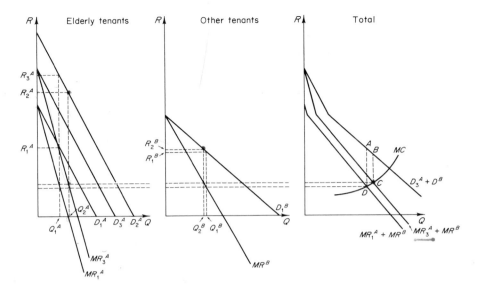

FIGURE 3-7 Effects of discriminatory just-cause eviction laws on rent determination by landlords.

to the law is less than the increased value to tenants. The elderly end up consuming more housing, but at a significant increase in rent ($R_2^A - R_1^A$). Rent to the nonelderly also rises, but by relatively less than does the number of dwellings; at the higher rent they demand less housing. The law produces a net welfare gain of area $ABCD$ in Figure 3-7, so that if the winners would compensate the losers, all would be better off.

In the second case, the cost to landlords due to the law is greater than the increased value to the tenants. If in this case D_3^A is the initial demand curve of elderly tenants, D_2^A is the increase in their demand due to the law, and $D_2^A - D_1^A$ is the cost to the landlord of buying insurance against the law, then the cost of delivering housing to the elderly is $D_2^A - D_1^A$ *more* than to the nonelderly. In this case, the elderly end up consuming less housing: Q_1^A as opposed to Q_2^A initially, at the higher price of R_3^A. The nonelderly actually receive *more housing* than they did before (Q_1^B as opposed to Q_2^A initially) at a *lower* rent (R_1^B as opposed to R_2^B initially). In this second case, a law designed to help the aged has ended up hurting them; it actually benefited the nonelderly at the elderly's expense. The nonelderly, as a result of the law, have benefited as the cost of delivering housing to them is lower than to the elderly; consequently landlords seek to rent additional units to the nonelderly. However, the nonelderly will only take the additional units at a lower price. In this case, there is a net welfare loss of area $ABCD$.

Finally, in a third case, law-induced benefit and cost increases are about equal, and the law leaves all parties' welfare situation unchanged.

∴, Law may be counterproductive.

From a policy point of view, just-cause eviction laws singling out the aged tend to induce landlords not to rent to senior citizens. As a matter of fact they may be inclined to refrain from renting to those who in 3 to 5 years would reach the age specified in the law as the lower limit of the protected class. Also, in the long run, landlords are likely to refrain from building apartment houses with characteristics that appeal particularly to the aged. Moreover, landlords will be reluctant to remodel apartments in a manner that makes them especially attractive to the elderly. Under these circumstances, greater segregation in the housing market will tend to result. With landlords increasingly reluctant to rent to older people, they will tend to end up in the least desirable places, and it is altogether likely that such laws will prove to be counterproductive.

MUNICIPAL RENT-CONTROL LAWS

A number of cities and states have experimented with rent-control laws.[25] In addition to New York City, which had rent controls for many years, starting with the end of World War II, more than 110 New Jersey municipalities adopted rent-control ordinances during the first half of the 1970s. In Massachusetts, the towns of Cambridge, Brooklyn, Summerville, and Lynn passed rent-control ordinances in the 1970s. During the same period Maryland had a rent-control law, which, however, expired on July 1, 1974. In June 1973, Maine adopted a local option law, and in November 1973, Congress passed a law authorizing the District of Columbia to adopt rent control. Pursuant to the federal act, the District of Columbia Council promulgated rent-control regulations in 1974.

Rent-control ordinances, designed to assist mainly low-income groups, can take various forms. However, they all reduce the freedom of landlords to set rent levels. Thus, although the actual cost of providing housing services is likely to increase, particularly during periods of inflation, rent-control ordinances can prevent landlords from passing on appropriate parts of these cost increases to tenants. The imposition of rent controls under such circumstances is presented in Figure 3-8. Specifically, the two axes are rent (R) and number of dwellings (Q). Before the imposition of rent control on low-cost apartments, at equilibrium the number of dwelling units were Q_1 and their rent was R_1. As a result of, for example, increases in the price of input factors (whether repair and maintenance costs, utilities, or property taxes), the supply function shifts to the left (S_2). Without a change in demand, a new equilibrium would be reached at Q_2 and R_2. Rent control would prohibit landlords from charging the rent that they would

---

25. Kenneth K. Baar, "Rent Control in the 1970s: The Case of the New Jersey Tenants' Movement," *Hastings Law Journal* 28 *(January 1977): 631.*

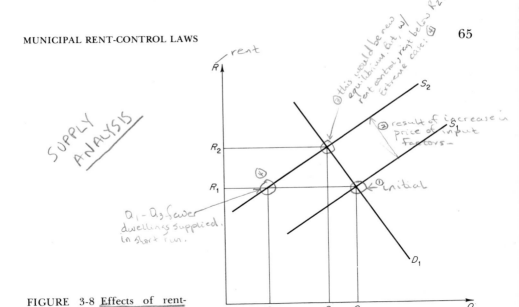

rent

SUPPLY ANALYSIS

③ this would be new equilibrium but w/ rent control, rent below ④ Extreme case.

② result of increase in price of input factors —

① initial

$Q_1 - Q_3$ fewer dwellings supplied. In short run.

FIGURE 3-8 Effects of rent-control laws-supply analysis.

otherwise have sought; that is, their rent will be below R_2. In the most extreme case where no rent increase is permitted, landlords would supply $Q_1 - Q_3$ fewer dwellings than would be demanded in the short run. In the long run, rent control is likely to have a chilling effect on investors and therefore curtail the supply of housing. Thus, cumulative declines in low-cost dwellings could be anticipated, accompanied by housing shortages.

Some empirical estimates of the likely side effects are possible. In an econometric study of 34 large metropolitan areas in the United States, the long-run price elasticity of housing supply related to land prices was found to be 0.20.[26] Thus, a 10% increase in the price of land per year would tend to increase rents by 6.5%. If no rent increases were permitted, supply would be reduced by 2.4% of low-cost housing units, and if only half of that increase were permitted the shortage would be 1.2%.

The effects of rent control can also be examined from the demand side. For example, because income in a given low-cost rental housing market increases over time, the demand function tends to shift to the right. If we assume that in the short run the supply of low-cost housing rental units cannot change, a new equilibrium would be reached at a rent of R_2 and number of dwelling units Q_2. (See Figure 3-9.) Rent control does not permit this new price for housing units to be obtained. For example, if no increases in rents are permitted, then a shortage of $Q_3 - Q_1$ dwelling units will result. Landlords not permitted to raise rents may reduce repair and mainte-nance, that is, the quality of housing. Or they may withdraw dwellings from the market. This can be done by converting apartments into con-dominiums, convalescent homes, homes for the aged, or cooperatives.

26. Hirsch, *Habitability Laws.*

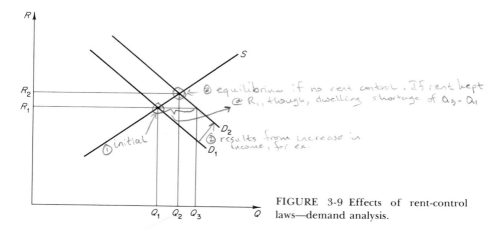

FIGURE 3-9 Effects of rent-control laws—demand analysis.

They may even be forced to abandon their properties because of the artificial imbalance between costs and rents.

Using the same econometric study of 34 large metropolitan areas, some empirical estimates can be offered. The income elasticity for low-cost housing was found to be +0.98 for 1974–1975. In an uncontrolled rental market, in the presence of an annual per capita income increase of 8%, for example, and on the assumption that the short-run supply of low-cost housing does not increase, annual rent increases of about 8.0% could be expected. If rent control were to be imposed and were to permit no increase whatsoever, an 8.0% shortage of low-cost rental units could be expected. If, on the other hand, rent increases were held to half the expected 8.0%, or 4.0% per annum, a shortage of about 4.0% would result. These shortages would be cumulative as long as income increases year by year.

There are other side-effects, of which only two will be explored in relation to local ordinances. Since rent-control ordinances induce landlords to skimp on repair and maintenance, tenants will find that their housing is deteriorating in quality. But the better-to-do and the affluent residents are willing to pay for good housing and are unlikely to put up with badly maintained dwellings. They will therefore tend to move to nearby communities that do not control rents. Thus, unless all cities impose rent controls, the city that has such an ordinance will lose middle- and upper-middle-income residents. It will be left with increasing percentages of low-income groups, who usually make disproportionate demands on fiscal resources. The result will be a deterioration of the city's fiscal health.

In addition to producing a shortage of rental units for low-income groups and providing a negative incentive for housing maintenance, rent control is likely to create difficult enforcement problems, which in all cases lead to a greatly enlarged bureaucracy. Moreover, as New York City as well as French and Italian cities have shown, rent controls once imposed are politically difficult to lift, and therefore generate many long-term ill effects—for example, on the tax base and on quantity and quality of housing stock.

For all these reasons, it is very likely that rent-control ordinances designed to aid low-income groups are often counterproductive. In the long run they are likely to hurt poor tenants rather than help them.

HOUSING SUBSIDY LAWS
alternative to rent control

Nevertheless, many low-income tenants cannot afford to pay rapidly rising rents, such as occurred at the end of World War II and again in 1977 in many parts of Southern California. If such low-income tenants cannot be helped by rent-control laws, what alternatives are available? Basically, income transfers are called for, and there exist various possibilities. Government income-transfer programs can be divided into those that provide subsidies to landlords and those that give payments directly to tenants. Moreover, tenants can be given general welfare payments or earmarked payments, as are provided for in Sections 501 and 504 of the Housing and Urban Development Act of 1970.

One of the differences between subsidies directed to landlords and those directed to tenants relates to the likelihood that the resulting benefits accrue to tenants in the form of improved housing. Clearly, subsidizing tenants' rents provides greater assurance of the benefits being reaped by them than by landlords.

However, even if tenants directly receive subsidies, not all of the monies will be used for housing, unless they are so earmarked. The housing allowance program with which the U.S. government has been experimenting seeks to make sure that the subsidy goes into improved housing. However, all earmarked subsidies, including rent subsidies, are less efficiently used by consumers than are general subsidies in the form of general welfare payments. Under the latter scheme, the poor are free to choose how they want to spend the subsidy and most likely will spend it more in line with their preferences, than if forced to spend the entire subsidy on housing.

Under a housing-allowance program, tenants who meet an income test are paid a rent subsidy as long as they do not live in substandard housing. The rent subsidy amounts to the difference between the rent payments and 25% of the tenant's income. Such an earmarked subsidy is very different from a general welfare payment that can be used by the recipient for whatever purpose he chooses.

Decision makers who must decide for or against earmarked subsidies are heavily influenced by the magnitude of the housing income elasticity. To the extent that the income elasticity of rental housing is smaller than 1, only parts of the subsidy will be applied by the tenant to housing.

There exists some evidence that the income elasticity of low-cost rental housing is less than 1.[27] Because of these considerations, earmarked subsidies appear to be preferable to general subsidies. As tenants receive such a rent subsidy, their housing demand function shifts to the right. Depending on the demand and supply elasticities and the nature of the demand function shift (i.e., whether it is parallel or not), part, none, or all of the subsidy will be shifted to landlords in the form of rent changes.

Tentative findings by I. S. Lowry in relation to the supply effects of some large-scale housing allowance experiments in Green Bay, Wisconsin, and South Bend, Indiana, are summarized as follows: "We have tracked rents in each place . . . , and find that they have risen less rapidly than in the midwest generally; moreover, virtually the entire increase during the first two years is attributable to rising fuel and utility prices."[28]

CONCLUSION

In summary, the rapid changes of landlord–tenant laws that have been witnessed can be subjected to an examination of their probable welfare effects. By building a powerful microeconomic model of the low-cost segment of the urban rental housing market, and applying econometric techniques to implement the model, much insight can be gained. Specifically, habitability laws that significantly extend the warranty of habitability are subjected to such economic analysis in order to estimate their welfare effects. Likewise, the economic effects of various just-cause eviction laws, rent-control ordinances, and subsidy laws are examined in a similar manner.

27. F. de Leeuw, "The Demand for Housing: A Review of Cross-Section Evidence," *Review of Economics and Statistics* 53 (February 1971): 1–10. The study of 34 large metropolitan areas referred to earlier revealed an income elasticity of +0.98 for 1974–1975.

28. I. S. Lowry, *Early Findings from the Housing Assistance Supply Experiment,* P-6075, (Santa Monica: RAND Corporation, January 1978), p. 4.

APPENDIX TABLE

Rent Equations for Seventy Geographical Areas, 1974–1975

Area	Constant	INDW	NEHDA	NEHDB	PUBSP	H001†–H006	H044 H033	H059 H063	H078 H081	H121 H157	$\bar{R}^2$	F	Sample size
Minneapolis (central city), MN	4.087	-0.030**	-0.001	0.022	-0.043	0.114***	0.150***	0.128***	0.127***	0.012	0.51	27.4	234
St. Paul (central city), MN	4.125	-0.005	0.003	-0.041**	0.028	0.106***	0.121***	0.124***	0.047	0.091**	0.35	10.5	160
Hennepin County (not central city), MN	4.568	-0.036**	0.001	-0.018	-0.025	0.096***	0.140***	-0.014	0.077**	-0.068†	0.33	12.9	219
Newark (central city in Essex County), NJ	4.666	0.012	0.006	-0.011	0.002	0.046**	0.088***	0.007	0.072**	-0.000	0.24	10.2	266
Essex County (not central city), NJ	4.468	-0.013*	-0.012**	0.042†	0.018	0.208***	0.112***	0.057	-0.003	0.028	0.41	19.7	217
Morris County, NJ	4.631	0.019	0.004	0.042	-0.025	0.147***	0.104***	0.041	0.012	-0.135	0.25	3.5	68
Union County, NJ	4.524	0.006	-0.007	0.026	0.008	0.137***	0.096***	0.067**	0.008	0.032	0.22	5.8	153
Orlando, FL	4.267	-0.027***	0.002	0.002	0.010	0.080***	0.090***	0.082***	0.192***	0.117**	0.48	46.0	447
Phoenix (central city), AZ	4.131	-0.015	-0.019**	0.037†	0.130	0.119***	0.134***	0.032*	0.175***	0.079	0.33	13.9	233
Phoenix (not central city), AZ	4.404	-0.045*	0.002	0.031	-0.029	0.049*	0.040*	0.111***	0.211**	0.159	0.42	10.6	122
Pittsburgh (central city in Allegheny County), PA	4.133	-0.050***	-0.004	-0.005	-0.010	0.209***	0.160***	0.030	0.060	-0.085	0.40	16.1	204
Allegheny County (not city of Pittsburgh), PA	4.125	-0.045***	-0.004	-0.051**	0.014	0.169***	0.139***	0.077***	0.064	0.019	0.45	21.1	221
Westmoreland County, PA	4.176	-0.018	0.003	0.011	0.080	0.203***	0.074***	0.075	-0.054	0.061	0.15	2.6	84
Boston (central city), MA	4.733	-0.020***	-0.003	0.006	0.018†	0.015	0.095***	0.090***	0.076***	0.033**	0.22	58.0	1866
Boston (not central city), MA	4.488	-0.023***	-0.001	0.017	0.011	0.095***	0.139***	0.086***	0.028	-0.001	0.33	60.3	982
Detroit (central city), MI	4.228	-0.010*	-0.003	0.002	-0.020	0.107***	0.107***	0.053***	0.072***	0.085***	0.27	46.5	1117
Macomb County, MI	3.896	0.001	0.016	-0.008	-0.057	0.160***	0.166***	0.083	0.104	0.116	0.53	8.5	61
Oakland County, MI	4.473	-0.030**	-0.005	-0.020	0.031	0.095***	0.145***	0.066***	0.091**	0.012	0.49	16.6	145
Wayne County (not central city), MI	4.142	-0.010	0.005	-0.018	0.045	0.149***	0.091***	0.119***	0.010	0.171***	0.41	15.1	184
Anaheim–Santa Ana–Garden Grove (city), CA	4.410	0.001	-0.009*	0.019	-0.063	0.089***	0.112***	0.059***	0.077**	-0.025	0.43	19.5	219
Anaheim–Santa Ana (not city), CA	4.378	-0.002	-0.008	0.022	-0.124***	0.107***	0.131***	0.051***	-0.015	0.030	0.41	30.8	380

(Continued)

APPENDIX TABLE (continued)

Area	Constant	INDW	NEHDA	NEHDB	PUBSP	H001[a] H006	H044 H033	H059 H063	H078 H081	H121 H157	$\bar{R}^2$	F	Sample size
Albany (central city), NY	4.398	−0.044***	−0.003	0.029†	−0.063**	0.106***	0.082***	0.099**	−0.015	0.040	0.22	11.1	333
Albany (not central city), NY	3.875	−0.004	0.015	−0.009	0.062	0.161***	0.116***	0.121***	0.083*	0.152***	0.44	17.5	190
Dallas (central city), TX	4.028	−0.040**	0.001	0.013	−0.100**	0.112***	0.097***	0.096***	0.130***	0.011	0.39	26.8	363
Dallas (not central city), TX	4.265	−0.060***	−0.004	0.013	−0.042	0.068*	0.072***	0.061***	0.091†	0.203	0.37	10.6	146
Fort Worth (central city), TX	3.914	−0.010	−0.003	−0.006	0.031	0.090***	0.120***	0.088***	0.167***	−0.001	0.35	20.8	292
Fort Worth (not central city), TX	3.630	−0.020*	0.001	0.033	−0.020	0.108***	0.154***	0.113***	0.140***	0.083	0.57	28.0	184
Memphis, TN	3.882	−0.019***	−0.007*	0.014	−0.022	0.116***	0.102***	0.097***	0.196***	0.082***	0.49	86.1	799
Salt Lake City, UT	3.945	−0.010*	−0.005	0.020†	0.000	0.142***	0.158***	0.006	0.074***	0.120***	0.45	54.0	591
Spokane, WA	4.195	−0.014*	−0.004	−0.002	−0.017	0.117***	0.128***	0.030*	−0.035	0.060*	0.33	27.4	472
Tacoma, WA	4.165	−0.009	−0.001	−0.001	−0.165***	0.119***	0.115***	0.055***	−0.096	0.115***	0.37	34.1	513
Wichita, KS	3.944	−0.030***	0.002	0.010	−0.100**	0.190***	0.143***	0.028*	0.047**	0.033	0.45	53.9	576
Los Angeles (central city), CA	4.144	0.001	−0.004*	0.009	−0.011	0.170***	0.121***	0.069***	0.086***	0.018	0.39	95.7	1342
Long Beach, CA	3.944	0.002	−0.009	0.020	0.003	0.175***	0.159***	0.083***	0.236***	0.052*	0.52	20.1	161
Los Angeles (not central city), CA	4.142	0.002	−0.003	−0.001	0.017	0.132***	0.129***	0.076***	0.033**	0.075	0.34	70.3	1194
Washington, D.C.	4.351	−0.027***	0.006†	−0.001	−0.043***	0.017*	0.100***	0.138***	0.130***	0.066***	0.45	158.5	1764
Montgomery County, MD	4.266	−0.070***	0.001	0.045†	−0.104**	0.112***	0.199***	0.023	0.119***	−0.077	0.73	47.9	157
Prince Georges County, MD	4.710	−0.046***	0.012†	−0.015	−0.004	0.017	0.076***	0.113***	0.122***	−0.131†	0.51	28.3	240
Alexandria–Arlington, VA	4.261	−0.034**	0.004	0.066	0.004	0.043	0.083***	0.198***	0.147***	0.043	0.44	15.6	167
Balance in VA, but outside Alexandria–Arlington	4.646	−0.020	−0.003	0.007	−0.053	−0.002	0.091***	0.094***	0.104*	0.078	0.41	13.1	142
Rochester (central city), NY	4.368	0.010	0.007	−0.014	−0.061*	0.073**	0.148***	0.054**	0.135***	−0.006	0.37	21.3	306
Rochester (not central city), NY	4.663	−0.026**	0.004	0.016	0.136†	0.092***	0.050**	0.083***	0.079*	0.074*	0.34	13.2	213
Miami (central city), FL	4.156	−0.002	−0.001	0.027	0.051	0.091***	0.127***	0.109***	0.257***	0.044	0.47	25.8	253
Miami (not central city), FL	4.415	−0.040***	0.012†	0.002	0.012	0.062***	0.137***	0.068***	0.366***	0.059	0.51	37.2	306
Columbus (central city), OH	4.296	−0.016*	0.001	−0.012	−0.054*	0.071***	0.139***	0.054***	0.085***	0.043***	0.31	28.1	539

City												
Columbus (not central city), OH	4.613	−0.050***	0.010	0.021	−0.131*	0.050*	0.104***	0.060**	−0.016	0.012	0.31	8.2	145
Hartford, CT	4.584	−0.006	0.002	0.011	−0.035***	0.071***	0.096***	0.083***	0.073***	0.046**	0.34	35.8	615
New Orleans, LA	3.999	−0.008	−0.002	−0.004	−0.055*	0.073***	0.124***	0.092***	0.246***	0.018	0.45	76.5	815
Milwaukee (central city), WI	4.164	0.004	0.003	0.002	0.028	0.130***	0.145***	0.065***	0.080***	0.037**	0.37	32.0	480
Milwaukee (not central city), WI	4.273	0.013	−0.010	0.035	0.080	0.108***	0.098***	0.124***	0.017	0.109**	0.56	12.7	85
Kansas City (central city), MO	4.033	−0.011	−0.002	−0.019	−0.039	0.215***	0.143***	−0.010	0.141***	0.093**	0.48	26.8	257
Kansas City (not central city), MO	4.568	−0.007	−0.016*	−0.057*	−0.109*	0.126***	0.056***	0.092***	0.091	−0.013	0.34	9.0	146
Kansas City, KS	3.767	0.011	0.002	0.005	−0.051	0.107***	0.177***	0.067**	0.124*	0.114	0.54	12.9	93
Newport News, VA	4.377	0.006	−0.012**	−0.003	−0.006	0.084***	0.102***	0.048***	0.109***	0.044*	0.33	28.0	485
Colorado Springs, CO	4.213	−0.012	0.002	0.017	−0.067**	0.067***	0.112***	0.048***	0.019	0.155***	0.47	47.4	478
Portland (central city), OR	4.441	0.011	−0.011**	0.008	−0.046	0.050***	0.104***	0.059***	0.010	0.109***	0.46	29.1	295
Portland (not central city), OR	4.449	−0.008	−0.008*	0.008	−0.007	0.079***	0.128***	0.053***	−0.007	−0.013	0.33	18.6	325
Atlanta (central city), GA	4.237	−0.023***	−0.001	−0.004	0.002	0.024**	0.142***	0.056***	0.206***	0.054***	0.39	100.2	1400
Chicago (central city in Cook County), IL	4.473	−0.005	0.005†	−0.017**	−0.023***	0.142***	0.089***	0.071***	0.075***	0.003	0.27	65.6	1587
Cook County (not in city of Chicago), IL	4.660	−0.020*	−0.010*	−0.027	0.008	0.087***	0.090***	0.124***	0.016	0.003	0.29	15.4	317
Dupage County, IL	4.749	−0.005	−0.013	−0.078**	−0.016	0.094***	0.159***	−0.090†	0.156*	0.060	0.32	3.8	54
Lake County, IL	4.733	−0.008	−0.017	0.056	−0.079	0.010	0.153***	−0.041	0.144	0.015	0.31	3.1	43
Kane County, IL	4.658	−0.055*	−0.035	0.088	0.270	0.153***	0.150***	−0.340	−0.095	0.030	0.20	2.1	40
Paterson (central city), NJ	4.730	−0.033***	−0.016***	−0.009	0.034	0.111***	0.134***	0.010	0.025	0.036	0.28	11.09	236
Paterson (not central city), NJ	4.605	−0.002	0.003	−0.015	0.031	0.159***	0.116***	0.024	0.053*	0.095***	0.27	12.91	285
San Antonio, TX	3.900	−0.022**	−0.000	0.013	0.042	0.058***	0.136***	0.072***	0.272***	0.136***	0.46	53.10	559
San Diego (central city), CA	4.301	−0.001	0.004	0.001	−0.077**	0.117***	0.120***	0.041**	0.034	0.122***	0.33	21.59	376
San Diego (not central city), CA	4.370	−0.008	−0.003	0.019	−0.066	0.110***	0.147***	0.054***	−0.038	−0.085	0.35	16.74	267
San Bernardino (central city), CA	4.277	0.025	−0.004	−0.003	−0.026	0.072**	0.124***	0.030	0.137***	−0.042	0.19	5.73	182
San Bernardino (not central city), CA	4.128	0.002	−0.010†	0.018	0.035	0.094***	0.133***	0.051***	0.140***	0.106**	0.28	16.11	350

* Significant at 0.01 level, one-tailed test.

** Significant at 0.05 level, one-tailed test.

*** Significant at 0.10 level, one-tailed test.

† Wrong sign and significant at 0.05 level, one-tailed test.

^{a} Top is 1974 variable number and bottom is corresponding 1975 number.

IV

ECONOMIC ANALYSIS OF
ZONING LAWS

INTRODUCTION

As was discussed in Chapter II, a further important area of property law is concerned with zoning ordinances. Modern zoning began in 1916 in New York, but by 1920, 35 cities had zoning ordinances.[1] In 1926 the federal government issued a standard state zoning enabling act, and today most cities have zoning codes.

Zoning is an area that lends itself more than some others to economic analysis, as we will see. In line with Chapter II, zoning involves the division of land into districts or zones having different regulations. These regulations impose legal constraints under which the land market must operate, and rights and entitlements can be exchanged. The constraints are made in accordance with a comprehensive plan, ostensibly designed to promote the health, safety, and general welfare of the population. It must be remembered that zoning in the United States derives its legal basis from the police power of state government. Unlike laws based on the right of eminent domain, zoning regulations do not require payment of compensation to a landowner whose property value is lowered as a result of zoning.

Just as landlord–tenant relations, discussed in the previous chapter, involve important economic issues in the area of applied welfare economics, so does zoning. Efficiency of resource allocation and equity in income distribution are major considerations. The efficiency issue arises because, in the presence of externalities, land use controls in general and zoning in

1. J. Dalafons, *Land Use Controls in the United States* (Cambridge: MIT Press, 1969).

73

particular are designed to improve resource allocation. A major task is to assess the extent to which zoning does or does not accomplish this objective.

The equity issue arises because of direct and indirect influences of zoning. Direct influences relate to zoning's reallocation of rights and entitlements, with the result that some parties gain and others lose. At the same time, there are indirect effects because zoning influences patterns of local government finance, which in turn affect the distribution of income or at least the ability of local governments to redistribute income.

The major purpose of zoning, it is commonly argued, is to prevent offensive land uses (uses that impose negative externalities on neighbors). A second purpose often mentioned is fiscal in nature, reflecting a local government's desire to restrict land uses that result in larger expenditures than receipts. But the accomplishment of these objectives is made difficult because zoning ordinances commonly provide for but a partial assignment of property rights. A complete assignment of property rights would be possible only if government had all the following rights:

1. To exclude, through *controls,* certain economic actors from using specified land resources
2. To enjoy income from the use of a resource by *leasing* it
3. To transfer resources by *selling* them

As Fischel points out, although zoning withholds part of the right to use property as private owners see fit and assigns this control to a local government, the assignment of property rights is far from complete.[2] Only one right can be fully exercised,—the assignment of rights to local political authorities in the form of controls. Courts tend to go along with local zoning ordinances unless the plaintiff can prove that they are unreasonable in their public health, safety, and general welfare implications. However, leasing of property rights is permitted only in limited ways, and their sale is all but prohibited.

One result of this partial assignment of property rights is that land subject to zoning is perceived as having a lower opportunity cost than it would have if all rights were assigned. Inefficiencies can therefore result.

Microeconomic theory can offer some further helpful insights—for example, into the relation between zoning and negative externalities. According to economic theory, the separation of land uses increases the efficiency of property markets to the extent that it causes the price of a parcel of land to equal its true marginal product without causing the prices of equal parcels of land to differ. Thus, for a zoning ordinance to increase the efficiency of the local property market, it should remove any externalities that exist and yet do so without artificially constraining the supply

---

2. W. A. Fischel, "A Property Rights Approach to Municipal Zoning," *Land Economics* 54 (February 1978): 65–81.

of land in any given use. However, as we will see later, increasing efficiency of land use in this manner is not easy. Efforts at reducing, if not removing, externalities can even prove counterproductive. For example, efficiency can decrease if zoning is imposed where in fact different land uses generate few, if any, externalities. Moreover, even in the presence of negative externalities, zoning may be too complex a process to ensure the optimal allocation of land among uses. Matters are so complicated because the zoning process tends to be lengthy and cumbersome and is highly vulnerable to the influence of powerful interest groups.

On the empirical level, economists can make contributions by determining whether unfettered land use generates major externalities, and, if so, how important they are. Furthermore, economists can help estimate some of the major economic effects of zoning ordinances.

In Chapter II I pointed to three major categories of zoning ordinances. I will deal with two of them here: zoning ordinances mainly designed to separate zones that can be put to different residential, commercial, and industrial uses (Category 1), and zoning ordinances mainly concerned with prohibiting certain specified residential land uses in a community (Category 3). I will refer to the former as residential–commercial–industrial (RCI) zoning ordinances and to the latter as exclusionary zoning ordinances. As was discussed in Chapter II, either class of ordinances can involve cumulative or exclusive zoning systems.

2 major categories of zoning ordinances.

1. RESIDENTIAL–COMMERCIAL–INDUSTRIAL ZONING ORDINANCES

Residential–commercial–industrial zoning ordinances do not simply divide land into residential, commercial, and industrial districts or zones. They also provide for separation of, for example, residential districts into various types of residential land uses. Examples are single dwellings, duplexes, and apartment houses of different sizes.

EFFECTS OF RCI ZONING ORDINANCES

Setting aside zones for specified land uses only is designed to cure the market's imperfections. The existence of these imperfections is predicated on the assumption that certain land uses impose major negative externalities on surrounding land uses. A common notion is that, for example, factories, gasoline stations, and commercial laundries impose negative externalities on nearby residences. Zoning is supposed to reduce these externalities. But, if externalities are prevalent and burdensome, does RCI zoning significantly modify the allocation of land to various uses and therefore outcomes in the urban land market? Or do market forces perhaps negate the forces of regulation?

This question cannot readily be answered directly.[3] Instead, the effectiveness of zoning must be approached by seeking evidence on whether zoning has observable side effects. We can argue, for example, that if the amounts of land in the various zoning categories do not match the unregulated market allocations for uses in these categories, then prices of land in the overallocated categories will be depressed relative to prices in the unzoned market, and prices in the underallocated categories will be elevated relative to prices in the unzoned market. If zoning does not induce significant changes in the quantity of land allocated for various uses, we would expect to observe no such elevation or depression, respectively, of land prices attributable to zone category. Thus, one way to measure the effect of zoning is to look for price differentials. Such differentials would show that zoning does modify market outcomes by changing the amount of land allocated to various uses. If there is no price effect, then zoning probably does not affect the allocation of land by type of use, though it may affect specialization and location, and it may reduce or eliminate certain transaction costs.

Since RCI zoning is intended to allocate land differently from the market, the degree to which it succeeds will be reflected in price differentials and can be measured by them. But it is difficult to know a priori whether zoning regulation will modify market outcomes or conform to them. A number of economists have theorized about the effects of zoning regulations. For example, Ohls et al. have argued that it is not in general possible, using a priori theory, to predict the impact of zoning on aggregate land value in a community, regardless of whether the intent of the zoners is to control externalities or to achieve fiscal goals.[4] However, on plausible assumptions, they argue that zoning as practiced in the United States probably lowers aggregate land values in communities with zoning. Additional theoretical research has been carried out by White,[5] Stull,[6] Davis and Whinston,[7] and Davis.[8]

On theoretical grounds a variety of zoning effects can be deduced. For

3. Direct evidence would require the comparison of a map of land use in a zoned city with a similar (hypothetical) map of the same city unzoned. In the presence of such maps it would be possible to identify precisely those changes resulting from zoning in the quantity and geographical specialization of land in various uses.

4. J. C. Ohls et al., "The Effect of Zoning on Land Value," Journal of Urban Economics 1 (October 1974): 428–444.

5. M. J. White, "The Effect of Zoning on the Size of Metropolitan Areas," Journal of Urban Economics 2 (October 1975): 279–290.

6. W. J. Stull, "Land Use and Zoning in an Urban Economy," American Economic Review 64 (June 1974): 337–347.

7. O. Davis and A. Whinston, "Economics of Complex Systems: The Case of Municipal Zoning," Kyklos 17 (1964): 419–446.

8. O. Davis, "The Economic Elements of Municipal Zoning Decisions," Land Economics 39 (November 1963): 375–386.

example, consider the supply of land for single-family use relative to the supply for other dwellings. The emphasis of most zoning ordinances on protecting single-family dwellings probably inspires planners to try to overallocate land for single-family use. Yet competition among jurisdictions for land uses tends to influence planners to allocate land in a manner not different from the market. Likewise, owners of land currently zoned for commercial and industrial use prefer to limit the supply of such land. Owners of residential land may join them for fear of negative externalities. However, owners of land that is zoned for residential use but has industry or commerce as its best use may oppose such restrictions if those owners constitute a special interest that can hope to profit from an increase in the supply of such land. Whenever those who can best afford to pay prevail, zoning will tend to conform to the unregulated market outcome. Since political and economic concerns seldom coincide, it is difficult to theorize whether or not zoning modifies the market outcome. Therefore, an empirical determination is necessary.

There exist a number of such empirical studies; however, they reach conflicting conclusions. Among the studies concluding that zoning does not modify market outcomes are those by Reuter,[9] Crecine et al.,[10] and Maser et al.[11] More or less opposite results were obtained by Sagalyn and Sternlieb,[12] Siegan,[13] Stull,[14] and Avrin,[15] the last concluding that the effects of zoning are not consistent with efficient resource use. The reasons why different empirical studies appear to reach opposing conclusions are many. Perhaps the most important is that each study pertains to a particular geographical area and to a particular point in time. Another reason is the use of different methodologies.

The studies by Maser et al. and Avrin are particularly interesting—the first relating to Rochester, New York, and the second to San Francisco, California; they will be presented in some detail. They were selected be-

9. F. Reuter, "Externalities in Urban Property Markets: An Empirical Test of the Zoning Ordinance of Pittsburgh," *Journal of Law and Economics* 16 (October 1973): 313–350.

10. J. Crecine et al., "Urban Property Markets: Some Empirical Results and Their Implications for Municipal Zoning," *Journal of Law and Economics* 10 (October 1967): 79–99.

11. S. M. Maser et al., "The Effects of Zoning and Externalities on the Price of Land: An Empirical Analysis of Monroe County, New York," *Journal of Law and Economics* 20 (April 1977): 111–132.

12. Lynne B. Sagalyn and George Sternlieb, *Zoning and Housing Costs* (New Brunswick, N.J.: Rutgers University Center for Urban Policy Research, 1973).

13. Bernard Siegan, *Land Use without Zoning* (Lexington, Mass.: Lexington Books, 1972).

14. W. J. Stull, "Community Environment, Zoning, and Market for Single-Family Homes," *Journal of Law and Economics* 18 (October 1975): 535–557.

15. M. E. Avrin, "Some Economic Effects of Residential Zoning in San Francisco," in *Residential Location and Urban Housing Markets*, ed. Gregory K. Ingram (Cambridge, Mass.: Ballinger, 1977), pp. 349–376.

cause of their methodology rather than because of their conclusions about zoning.

The Rochester Zoning Study[16]

In most of the Rochester area, zoning systems are cumulative—single-family houses can be built in any district. However, in the city, industrial districts are exclusive. Data were available for 1950, 1960, and 1970 on sale, physical characteristics, and assessed valuation of property, as well as zoning, variance history, land use of neighboring properties, and average driving time to the central business district (CBD).

Ten samples were analyzed—nine from the city of Rochester and a tenth from the suburban towns. Within each sample, transactions included such residential uses as one-family and two-family uses. Moreover, there was one sample of commercial and industrial uses.

Tests were performed on regressions of the form,

$$P = \alpha_0 + \alpha_B B + \Sigma \alpha_{Z_i} Z_i + \Sigma \alpha_{V_i} V_i + \Sigma \alpha_{A_i} A_i + \Sigma \alpha_{X_i} X_i, \tag{1}$$

where

P = sale price per acre of land plus structure
B = equalized assessed value of structure divided by acreage
Z_i = dummy variables designating zoning category
V_i = dummy variables indicating that other land, visible from the observed parcel, was devoted to some use that might produce an externality for the given land
A_i = dummy variables indicating that land on either side of the observed parcel or directly across the street from it was devoted to some use that might produce an externality (A and V are mutually exclusive)
X_i = variables related to the value of land or the value of the structure, or in some way affecting P

Thus, the regression model of real estate prices contains basically three categories of independent variables: zoning variables Z, externality variables V and A, and a broad range of factors that jointly predict land prices in the absence of either zoning or externalities, that is, value-related variables X. If the predictive power of the regression model in Eq. (1) is significantly decreased when the zoning variables are omitted, the study would support the conclusion that zoning has an impact on real estate prices independent of the other forces operating in the market. On the other hand, if omitting the zoning variables does not reduce the power of the model, one may conclude that zoning does not affect prices. In a similar manner one can test a hypothesis about the impact on land prices of neighborhood uses of land that are thought to produce externalities.

16. Maser *et al.*, "Effects of Zoning and Externalities," pp. 111–132.

To test these hypotheses, Maser *et al.* estimated for each of the 10 samples a regression of the form of Eq. (1). However, instead of treating the effects of zone as simply additive, they consider the effects as varying with distance from the center of the city. Zone and access variables therefore appear in the equations as cross-products. As a result it becomes possible to analyze the impact of zoning within each of the isoaccess bands surrounding the CBD.

Maser *et al.* undertook a number of powerful statistical tests. In all but one sample—the 1971 suburban towns—their tests consisted of dropping the zone variables from the regression and performing an F test to determine whether zoning had a statistically significant effect. The null hypothesis was not rejected in eight cases. In the ninth case—the 1960 two-family sample—the F statistic was significant, and the null hypothesis was rejected.

Accordingly, Maser *et al.* summarized their empirical analysis of the land value side effects of zoning as follows:

> Our principal conclusion is that comparisons we made reveal no price effects attributable to zoning. These comparisons are limited. We compared the several types of residential land and found no evidence of a shortage of multifamily land. We compared industrial and commercial land and found no evidence that either is scarce relative to the other. We did not compare residential land with commercial and industrial land, so we cannot rule out the possibility that zoning does modify the market allocation across that division. So in this case study at least, and within the limits of our tests, it appears that political forces, however much they originally aimed at modifying market outcomes, did not in fact do so.[17]

The San Francisco Zoning Study[18]

M. E. Avrin also sought to determine whether zoning affects land values, with a view of reaching a conclusion as to whether zoning, once imposed, results in inefficiencies in the urban residential property market. Specifically, two different approaches were used to investigate whether zoning leads to nonoptimal pricing by misallocating land among different uses.

The first approach relies on a time-series analysis based on repeat sales prices of given properties in each of four residential zoning categories in San Francisco. A major change in the residential zoning in San Francisco took place in 1960 and provided data to measure the zoning effects by using time-series data. Only three types of zoning existed in the city of San Francisco before 1960—commercial, industrial, and residential, with residential properties divided into two districts. The First Residential District allowed only single-family detached houses, whereas the Second Residential District was unrestricted as to residential use. The new zoning ordinance in

17. *Ibid.*, p. 128.
18. Avrin, "Some Economic Effects of Residental Zoning," pp. 349–376.

1960 divided the Second Residential District into new districts, with their essential differences taking the form of maximum-density restrictions.[19]

Using time-series methods, Avrin sought to estimate the effect of the 1960 ordinance on residential property values. She was specifically concerned with the following issues:

1. How did the 1960 restrictions affect the price of property in the new zoning districts? Did a differential effect occur among districts?
2. Are the prices of properties that are near less-restrictive districts affected differently from those in the interior of a district?

An answer to the first set of questions involves determination of the total price effect of the zoning ordinance, whereas an answer to the second is concerned with the presence of broader effects.

The time-series analysis proceeded in two steps. First, four separate yearly housing price indices for 1950–1973 were constructed. Each index was based on observations of two sales prices of given properties whose zoning changed from Second Residential to one of the post-1960 categories. Use of repeat sales prices was designed to control for the effects of externalities and of neighborhood and housing characteristics on price. Second, each index was tested for a discontinuity at the time of the zoning change to provide evidence of any zoning-related changes in the value of property.

A second approach uses a cross-section analysis. In order to study the economic effects of zoning on sales prices of individual properties, a regression analysis was undertaken. In order to explain the variation in the sales price of individual properties, zoning was introduced as a dummy variable in a regression. Other explanatory variables included structural characteristics of the house, lot, and neighborhood. According to Avrin, "The unique zoning situation in San Francisco makes it possible to determine what the price of residential land would be in an 'unzoned' equilibrium and, therefore, to measure the zoning caused distortion."[20] A reduced-form supply and demand equation for housing was estimated, with the value of a house assumed to be an additive function of its structural characteristics (i.e., lots and neighborhoods).

Both methods produced about the same general conclusions, which should give some confidence in the results. Thus there is strong evidence that residential zoning in San Francisco affected values in the urban residential property market and did so to different degrees depending on the

---

19. The Second Residential District was divided into five new districts: R1, one dwelling per lot, or one dwelling per 3000 square feet; R2, one 2-family dwelling per lot, or one dwelling per 3000 square feet; R3, one dwelling per 400 square feet; R4, one dwelling per 200 square feet; and R5, one dwelling per 125 square feet. Space requirements for R3 were changed in 1963 from 400 to 800 square feet per dwelling.

20. Avrin, "Some Economic Effects of Residential Zoning," p. 364.

zoning classifications. According to both the time-series and cross-section analyses, by providing stable neighborhoods and by limiting the growth of the city in general, zoning appears to have affected the demand for residential property. A direct result was an increase in the value of all properties. However, the effect of zoning on the relative supply of properties among different users caused differential levels of increase in property values in the various zoning districts. The magnitude of the effect increased with allowed density. Thus, the value of the R4 properties, on which high-rise buildings are permitted, was affected most. Based on the time-series analysis, there is some evidence that zoning increased property values in general to a much greater degree than it caused differential rates of increase among uses. Results of the cross-section estimation for each of the zoning districts separately show that zoning interacts with certain property characteristics to create value. A change in value caused by zoning appears to be directly dependent on the characteristics of the properties that are zoned in the various districts.

These results do not indicate optimality in the property market, leading to the conclusion that zoning in San Francisco creates inefficiencies in the urban residential property market, by causing land to be allocated in a nonoptimal way among uses.[21]

TESTING FOR EXTERNALITIES IN LAND MARKETS

Throughout this chapter frequent reference has been made to the presumption that many land uses impose externalities on adjacent properties, particularly residential ones. Both the Maser et al. and the Avrin studies undertook tests to determine the presence or absence of such boundary externalities.

Maser et al. found that the externality effects of different land uses are often insignificant. This finding is consistent with that of Crecine et al. for Pittsburgh.[22] Maser et al. concluded, "We found that—although some external effects from airport noise and nearby bodies of water could be detected—the externalities which zoning is supposed to prevent could not be detected, except in one instance where zoning may have been associated with racial prejudice."[23]

Likewise, the Avrin study could not find evidence that boundary externalities existed in the urban residential property market. Zoning does not appear to cause the values of properties near zones of higher residential or commercial uses either to decrease or to increase less than values of properties interior to a given district. Therefore Avrin concluded, "These findings

21. *Ibid.*, p. 363.
22. Crecine *et al.*, "Urban Property Markets," pp. 79–99.
23. Maser *et al.*, "Effects of Zoning and Externalities," p. 128.

indicate that land use externalities do not exist, but the point is not conclusively proved."[24]

The fact that both studies could not find significant zoning externalities could testify to the success of zoning, a not very convincing conclusion. More to the point is the need to reexamine the presumption of widespread boundary externalities in land markets. Should this presumption prove unwarranted, the call for RCI zoning could be unwarranted.

2. EXCLUSIONARY ZONING

In 1580, Queen Elizabeth I of England proclaimed,

> After the end of this session of Parliament, no person shall within this realm of England make, build, or erect, or cause to be made, builded, or erected, any manner of cottage for habitation or dwelling, nor convert or ordain any building or housing made or hereafter to be made, to be used as a cottage for habitation or dwelling, unless the same person do assign and lay to the same cottage or building four acres of ground at the least . . . being his or her freehold [and] inheritance lying near to the said cottage, so long as the same cottage shall be inhabited.[25]

Clearly, this proclamation is the sixteenth-century precursor of modern exclusionary zoning. It must have been intended to reserve the countryside for the rich, while the poor concentrated in crowded central London. Although large-lot zoning is to this day an important exclusionary instrument, various other instruments exist and deserve examination.

As has been shown in Chapter II, lawyers have been struggling with exclusionary land use problems in terms of the rights and obligations of the parties involved. Examples are *Euclid* v. *Ambler Realty Company,*[26] *Construction Industry Association of Sonoma County* v. *City of Petaluma,*[27] *Village of Bel Terre* v. *Boraas,*[28] *Southern County of Burlington NAACP* v. *Township of Mount Laurel,*[29] *National Land Investment Company* v. *Kohn,*[30] and *Berenson* v. *Town of New Castle.*[31] At the same time economists have been concerned with the nature of efficient communities.

24. Avrin, "Some Economic Effects of Residential Zoning," p. 370.
25. F. Bosselman *et al., The Taking Issue* (Washington, D.C.: U.S. Government Printing Office, 1973).
26. *Euclid* v. *Ambler Realty Co.,* 272 U.S. 365 (1926).
27. *Construction Industry Association of Sonoma County* v. *City of Petaluma,* 375 F. Supp. 574 (N.D. Cal. 1974).
28. *Village of Bel Terre* v. *Boraas,* 94 S. Ct. 1536 (1974).
29. *Southern County of Burlington NAACP* v. *Township of Mount Laurel,* 67 N.J. 151, 363 A.2d 713 (1975).
30. *National Land Investment Co.* v. *Kohn,* 419 Pa. 504, 532, 215 A.2d 597, 612 (1965).
31. *Berenson* v. *Town of New Castle,* No. 430, December 2, 1975.

Economic analysis can be applied to examine the effects on efficiency associated with exclusionary zoning in the presence of local property taxes. Moreover, side effects of different classes of exclusionary zoning instruments can be examined. These two steps will be taken in turn. The analysis will be restricted to those cases in which the goods and services that crowd are augmentable. Schools, roads, libraries, and the like can all be expanded if sufficient revenues are available. These involve resources that are ubiquitous, though not abundant. This is the typical suburban case. The contrasting case is that of unique resources, where the crucial crowding involves an item of unusual historic, scenic, or environmental interest.[32] Here, the usual congestion discussion applies, and the problem is best treated as an externality.

LOCAL PROPERTY TAXES AND THEIR EFFECTS ON LAND USE

The economic side effects of exclusionary zoning should not be examined in a vacuum. They must be considered in a real-world setting, one that takes cognizance of the fact that local governments, which seek to exclude through zoning, raise most of their funds through local property taxes. Thus, local excluding measures are not imposed on a free and unencumbered market. They are, as will be shown here, a correction to some degree of prevailing distortions of a free-market outcome.

An examination of the conditions favoring efficient communities and the effects of both local property taxation and exclusionary zoning is facilitated by the Tiebout model.[33] The original model as well as its follow-up literature sought to identify the conditions under which jurisdictional choice creates an effective market for locally provided public goods and services. However, in contrast to the real world, where local governments raise most funds through property taxation, the model relies on lump-sum taxes and user charges. Such sources force decision makers to consider the true cost of their presence in the community, as well as the difference in the cost of residing in communities that provide different levels of public services. Departing from lump-sum financing generally negates all the normal efficiency results. A further assumption of the model is mobility (i.e., no

---

32. The Santa Barbara Mission and Lake Tahoe are examples of unique resources, one historical, the other scenic. A new entrant increases the crowding experienced by all persons in the jurisdiction, and there is no way to augment the resource to avert crowding. In the ubiquitous resource case, the facilities that become crowded are the schools, the roads, and the parks, all of which can be augmented if sufficient revenues are available. For details, see Werner Z. Hirsch, "The Efficiency of Restrictive Land Use Instruments," *Land Economics* 53 (May 1977): 145–156. For a very important article, see R. C. Ellickson, "Suburban Growth Control: An Economic and Legal Analysis, "*Yale Law Journal* 86 (January 1977): 383–511.

33. C. Tiebout, "A Pure Theory of Local Governments," *Journal of Political Economy* 64 (October 1956): 416–424.

exclusionary zoning or similar intervention). Obstacles to free mobility interfere with the Tiebout results.

It can be shown that local property tax distorts the use of ubiquitous land resources. Since this tax, not the lump-sum charge that makes the Tiebout model work, produces most local funds, the importance of this conclusion is obvious. For convenience's sake it will be assumed that the local property tax is the sole revenue source, although similar results can be obtained under an income tax.

Models of fiscally induced migration are long run, since incentives for migration do not create immediate wholesale relocation. As their circumstances change, households choose communities according to the advantages they provide. These long-run locational effects have produced visible fiscal difficulties for central cities. In such a long-run model, locational decisions are viewed as if a group of prospective residents approached an undeveloped plain with jurisdictional boundaries already established. It is assumed that there is no dominant central business district and, for now, all firms locate in uniformly dispersed commercial jurisdictions. Furthermore, it is assumed that within residential jurisdictions all land is put to residential use, nonconforming uses are dealt with efficiently, and units of different densities are sufficiently separated from one another so that higher-density developments will impose no significant direct externalities on lower-density developments. Finally, absence of racism and snobbery is assumed—the mere presence of members of one race or income class will not, in itself, affect persons of another race or income class. Thus, the analysis is confined to fiscal motives. Although this restriction leaves out important facts, social motives for exclusion tend to reinforce the results.

For any given level of services, the tax rate will be lowest where per capita property values are highest. Individuals will be attracted to communities with low tax rates, causing high growth rates in communities with high property values. However, as will be demonstrated subsequently, the highest-density developers tend to be the highest bidders per unit of land in fiscally favorable locations. Bradford and Kelejian have shown that fiscal advantages are significant in explaining interjurisdictional mobility.[34] Aronson and Schwartz tested their model of fiscally induced movement, to find that 69% of migration in the 1950s and 89% in the 1960s brought fiscal advantages to the mover.[35] The basis for such models is that communities with a relatively high tax base can offer either lower *ad valorem* tax rates to provide a given level of public service, or better public services for a given tax rate, or some combination of the two. A household planning a given amount of housing consumption can reduce tax payments or in-

34. D. Bradford and H. Kelejian, "An Econometric Model of Flight to the Suburbs," *Journal of Political Economy* 81 (May–June 1973): 556–589.

35. J. R. Aronson and E. Schwartz, "Financing Public Goods and the Distribution of Population in a System of Local Governments," *National Tax Journal* 26 (June 1973): 137–160.

crease public-goods consumption, or both, by choosing a community with a very high average value of property. Those choosing small houses impose on others some of the costs of providing them with public goods. Whether low-income householders should have the right to impose such costs on others is an important distributional issue.

SOME EFFICIENCY EFFECTS OF LOCAL PROPERTY TAXES

A first efficiency consequence of the property tax, were no exclusion to apply, is that builders will choose a location not simply on the basis of locational efficiency but also on the basis of fiscal advantages. For example, in the absence of heavy local property taxes builders might find it advantageous to build apartments near places of employment, a location fully consistent with locational efficiency. Yet fiscal advantages emanating from local property tax provisions might overshadow these locational advantages and persuade the builder to construct private homes at these locations instead. Thus, resources are used not where they generate the greatest social value but where the combination of output and tax advantage has the greatest value. The normal tendency of the market to allocate resources to the highest value use is therefore sacrificed by the property tax.

A second inefficiency introduced by the property tax where no zoning constraints apply is the instability of aging communities. Although the property tax is treated by some economists, Henry Aaron for example, as a very general tax on captial, which introduces little distortion, it is more appropriate not to do so.[36] Aside from the obvious capital exemptions, the property tax system as a whole treats capital differently according to its location; clearly, each jurisdiction establishes its own tax rate, except in California in the aftermath of Proposition 13. Certainly there must exist a high degree of substitutability of capital in one location for capital in another, and this is the basis of the instability introduced by the property tax.

As the property tax increases in a given community, the cost of providing housing goes up. In turn, the market value of housing decreases. The consumer's adjustment, when the effective price of housing increases, can take several forms. First, a household will tend to reduce its consumption of housing by reducing maintenance of structures and thus diminishing property values. Second, all new entrants, regardless of income, will tend to build houses of lower value than they would otherwise have built. Third, the initial residents now will be more likely to leave the community, since the conditions for which they initially chose the jurisdiction, and which then represented an equilibrium, no longer exist. Of course, since moving costs are substantial, not all householders will be induced to move immediately.

36. Henry Aaron, "A New View of Property Tax Incidence," *American Economic Review* 64 (May 1974): 212–227.

Adjustments of the quantity of housing services will tend to reinforce the initial disturbance. It is not clear when the process stops, and fiscal catastrophe is not unheard of. The process may be halted, for example, through revenue sharing or a shift of the tax burden to commercial property. In extreme cases, increased tax rates will halt new construction, causing the jurisdiction to decline in population.

A third efficiency effect of local property taxes in the presence of ubiquitous resources relates to reduction in the variety of available communities. Martin McGuire has shown that the segregation of individuals into groups according to their tastes for public goods is efficient.[37] Where all members of a given community pay the same amount toward support of local government, segregation into relatively homogeneous jurisdictions will occur as a voluntary response, with similar incentives for segregation resulting for all groups. McGuire has also shown that forced integration is an inferior redistributing device, since an equivalent wealth transfer by lump-sum taxes and grants will leave both parties better off. After the transfer occurs, each group will be free to choose the combination of public and private consumption that is most preferred by its members, given their tastes and incomes. The property tax does not force integration in any direct sense, but it does compel low-income households to move into higher-income jurisdictions if they are to benefit from the redistributive mechanism.

Where groups are perfectly segregated according to tastes, the choices that the community makes will represent the interests of each member of the community. Where tastes are mixed, individual preferences must be compromised. Aronson and Schwartz have demonstrated that with redistributive tax schemes no equilibrium exists in the allocation of persons to jurisdictions until all communities have the same average incomes and per capita public expenditures.[38] Satisfying this condition will certainly reduce the range of choice of local public services available to consumers, and therefore will reduce their well-being.

Where all individuals are confronted by the full cost that they impose on the local government, "voting with one's feet" can lead to homogeneity within communities, and local decisions can be reached without encountering major conflicts with individual preferences. The local property tax alone, without exclusionary zoning, will create heterogeneity in communities. The potential for redistribution will cause wealthy communities to attract high-density development with smaller individual dwellings, until per capita property values are equalized across communities. Thus, as a redistributive device, the property tax succeeds only where efficiency is sacrificed.

---

37. Martin McGuire, "Group Segregation and Optimal Jurisdictions," *Journal of Political Economy* 82 (January–February 1974): 112–132.

38. Aronson and Schwartz, "Financing Public Goods," pp. 137–160.

The property tax, in the absence of exclusion, probably redistributes from rich to poor. But the redistribution is partial and inaccurate. The poor, unable to move, remain in poor jurisdictions; the rich remain in wealthy, "built-up" jurisdictions, where they avoid redistribution. Property-tax-related fiscal advantages in suburbs have attracted expensive properties; the resulting migration has contributed to the fiscal crisis of cities. Since each generation of affluent Americans tends to locate in new jurisdictions, tomorrow's old suburbs will face similar crises. The result is costly movement of households and unnecessarily rapid depreciation of housing capital. Thus, redistribution is limited by successive rounds of at least in part fiscally induced mobility; what redistribution does occur, occurs only at great cost.

A further consideration is property tax incidence. Normally it is assumed that the tax is entirely shifted to eventual occupants, since the supply of housing is, in the extreme long run, quite competitive. However, a supplier of housing would not "pass on" the benefits of any unusual tax advantages that his unit possessed. Even if "balanced" communities could be ensured, redistribution could not. Rental and sale prices of structures are determined in competitive markets. Therefore tax benefits applying to relatively few properties would not be passed on to consumers as long as their next best alternative is to buy or rent downtown, where tax rates are high and services are poor. Where a community's favorable tax base allows greater per capita expenditures for public services, rent would be bid up by tenants to reflect these advantages. In short, in a competitive market where marginal units remain in areas offering an unfavorable tax–benefit package, the occupant would receive little or no benefit. Consumers get what they pay for and little more; the tax advantages accrue to the initial owners, the builders who manage to acquire the rights to "balance" a community by their action. (Note: Builders are usually the plaintiffs in exclusionary zoning cases.)

THREE MAJOR EXCLUDING DEVICES

Three major classes of excluding devices will be examined as to their economic effects—large-lot zoning, population ceilings and construction quotas, and construction permits.

Large-Lot Zoning

In keeping with the long-run setting, it is assumed that laws are imposed on undeveloped land, or land to be eventually redeveloped. Communities are not differentiated by their present land uses. Thus every community can establish a minimum-lot-size requirement. To attract households that build expensive structures, communities seek to make land (per acre) relatively inexpensive by requiring large lots. Thus, large-lot builders need not compete with higher-density builders who might value land very highly.

Although this strategy may work for a single community acting alone, it must fail when all communities take similar action to attract the rich, since there is a fixed number of rich households. Amenity-rich communities would have the highest prices for fixed-size lots. If these locational amenities are normal goods, the rich will seek them. The poor will get the least desirable locations, since large-lot zoning precludes high-density developments near places of employment. As long as incentives exist to segregate households by income, the emerging patterns will reinforce whatever motives caused the rich to locate in one jurisdiction and the poor in others. Since jurisdictions with expensive structures can support government services at a relatively low *ad valorem* tax rate, every household seeks to locate in the richer communities. But builders of expensive structures derive the greatest tax advantages and will bid highest for lots in communities with high per capita assessed valuation. Households will sort into communities according to housing values. Accordingly, every community seeks the largest legal minimum lot size with expensive structures.

Under large-lot zoning, the property tax approximates a lump-sum tax, with all households paying the same amount for any given level of services. As in a model built by Hamilton, in order to achieve a given number of choice levels for public goods, more communities are required than in the Tiebout case.[39] This first inefficiency is unimportant if the population is large relative to the efficient community size. Residents might also consider themselves better off under a smaller-lot-size constraint, since at the high per-acre land prices, which capitalize tax savings, smaller lots would be chosen. However, this "cost" to the household is an illusion, since the purchase price of a lot reflects the price of the right to construct a residence in the community. If smaller lots were specified, the market clearing price for lots would fall by only the marginal evaluation of space itself, and the price per acre would increase. By adopting large-lot zoning, the community actually accomplishes a transfer of wealth from the previous nonresidential owners to prospective residents. With a large minimum lot size, the owner of undeveloped property must transfer a large amount of land in order to capture the prospective residents' evaluation of the right to locate in a community.

There is a second inefficiency compared to the Tiebout case. Arbitrary lot-size constraints match the marginal evaluation of land with its opportunity cost (recreational uses, agricultural uses, etc.) for only a few residents. For most communities the largest allowable minimum lot size poses an inefficiency that could, however, be eliminated if they were to determine the optimal lot size for the residents that they would ultimately attract. Any jurisdiction acting alone in adopting a minimum lot size below the legal

39. B. W. Hamilton, "Zoning and Property Taxation in a System of Local Government," *Urban Studies* 12 (June 1975): 205–211.

limit would attract smaller dwellings. Thus, where courts do not discriminate but allow all communities to set the same lot requirement, some loss must occur.

A third loss is that efficient community size with respect to public goods consumption is no longer ensured. Given fixed jurisdictional boundaries, population size is determined by the lot size. Incentives for adjusting lot-size requirements may result in a more efficient scale for local governments, but not necessarily for private consumption.

Population Ceilings and Construction Quotas

Population ceilings and periodic construction quotas have the political appeal of appearing not to exclude any particular income group but only to control population size or growth. Still, they affect the composition and size of the jurisdiction. An absolute population ceiling has effects similar to those of the minimum-lot-size requirement. Temporary constraints or moderate population restrictions may merely promote orderly growth. Where a community, acting alone, restricts the rate of growth, distortion toward more expensive structures results. In the long run, minor growth restrictions produce results similar to the no-exclusion case.

Small absolute population limits or new construction quotas allowing merely replacement of obsolete structures have effects similar to those of lot-size requirements—a sorting out of individuals into communities according to the values of their residences. The process is similar to the minimum-lot-size case.

Compared to the Tiebout model, a population ceiling imposes costs by requiring more communities than there are different packages of public output, since purchasers of a given level of service may prefer several different qualities of housing. Again, complementarity in consumption will limit the inefficiency. The population ceiling does not misallocate land between residential and nonresidential uses, since the builder is free to choose an efficient lot size once the right to build has been acquired. There does exist the possibility of inefficient scale, since no automatic forces exist that might produce a community size minimizing average costs. However, public officials could minimize average cost by adjusting the population ceiling.

The property tax without excluding devices will produce a distortion as decision makers reduce consumption to avoid the tax. Under large-lot zoning, the initial entry fees paid in the form of higher lot prices will be larger, the greater the value of structures in the community. Thus there is an excess burden generated by this scheme, since the price for additional units of housing services is equal to the cost of producing this service plus the increased entry fee that would be paid. The population ceiling scheme has similar effects, which governments could alleviate by auctioning off building rights and generating revenue for the community. Revenue could be used to reduce the annual property taxes by an amount equal to the annual earnings on the entry fee, so the fee itself would create no distortion of the housing decision. The sorting out of structures by value is preserved, since anyone building a smaller house than those common in the jurisdiction derives a smaller tax benefit and therefore would not be willing to pay the entry fee. Thus, the population ceiling could provide opportunities for the distribution of building rights in such a way as to eliminate the tax distortion of the housing decision. However, the inefficiency associated with the need for "extra" communities in order to match housing and public-goods preferences remains.

Construction Permits pay a fee for right to build. Thus, excludes these who cannot pay.

Different construction permit fees (payments in cash or kind for the right to build), could be charged for different land uses in the same community. Mieszkowski has pointed out that if local governments can charge permit fees that are equal to the capitalized value of the difference between costs imposed by a land use and revenues generated by it, no incentive exists to zone out any particular land use.[40] Thus, all *ad valorem* taxes can be transformed into a lump-sum tax. A "fair" fee for a given structure is the capitalized value of the difference between actual tax payments and cost imposed on the community servicing an additional household. The latter could be approximated by the average tax payment in the community. Using the community's tax rate, the assessment of the new unit and the average assessment in the jurisdiction, computation of the permit fee would be mechanical.

Construction permit fees pose problems where there is inflation, where costs of existing government services increase, or where local government expands services. When total revenue must be increased, those with low-value properties would pay less than a proportionate share of the increase. New services create a problem if financed by property taxes but not if financed by user fees. Special breaks could accrue to housing with limited service requirements (e.g., housing for bachelors or the elderly).

Why, then, do we not replace the property tax with a lump-sum tax? First, in jurisdictions with fiscal advantages, current residents probably have paid prices that reflect the capitalized value of these advantages; changing to lump-sum taxes can result in decreased capital values and wealth transfers. Construction permit fees have the advantage of countering incentives and justification for exclusion; they promote efficient choices for local government expenditures. Furthermore, if higher levels of government want to provide low-income groups with particular goods—for

---

40. P. Mieszkowski, "Notes on the Economic Effects of Land Use Regulation," in *Issues in Urban Public Finance* (Saarbrücken, West Germany: Institut International De Finances Publiques, 1973).

example, education—they can readily subsidize these fees. In this way, distributional and allocative objectives can be planned specifically rather than determined by accident.

In summary, the efficiency losses of large-lot zoning are (*a*) an increase in the number of communities required to provide a given number of public goods choices, (*b*) inappropriate lot sizes for some communities, and (*c*) inefficient scale of local government operation. Two of these distortions are absent under population ceilings and all are absent under construction permits.

CONCLUSION

In summary, municipal zoning ordinances are products of the twentieth century; most appeared only after 1926. Of the three major zoning categories, two have been singled out for some detailed economic analysis. In relation to the zoning ordinances that assign land to residential, commercial, and industrial uses, theoretical and econometric inquiries raise serious questions about the efficacy of such ordinances. Perhaps somewhat unexpectedly, exclusionary zoning is found to have positive implications for the efficient allocation of resources in the presence of local property taxation, particularly if it takes the form of construction permit fees.

V

CONTRACT LAW

INTRODUCTION

Contract law has developed over the centuries as a means of facilitating economic exchanges. By providing guidelines for transactions other than those involving real property, it helps increase the wealth of the nation.

To facilitate the assessment of contract law, its basic legal premises are first presented. After the nature of a contract is defined and related to the notion of "consideration," a number of formation defenses are explored. Thereafter performance defenses, the notion of anticipatory repudiation, and damages rules are explored.

After setting forth the legal principles of contract law, I examine some of its economic aspects. The economic framework used allows the positions of the buyer and the seller in general, within credit transactions in particular, to be evaluated. The focus is on transaction costs in the formation and performance stages, and on evaluation of different contract clauses. The unconscionability of certain contract clauses and contract terms are also examined within this framework.

THE BASIC LEGAL PREMISES
OF CONTRACT LAW

WHAT IS A CONTRACT?

A contract is a promissory agreement for a future exchange, freely and voluntarily arrived at. The law of contracts is designed to facilitate the process of exchange and to minimize breakdowns, and thus it contributes to transaction efficiencies. Within a system of contract remedies, incentives are provided to make good on promises. If the parties to the bargain agree, the law terms the agreement a contract, and for certain types of agreements society provides legal enforcement remedies should one of the parties decide to breach the contract. Contracts as a societal institution facilitate efficient exchange by providing a social mechanism for enforcing those agreements where aggregate value between the parties can be presumed to have increased. But not all promissory exchanges in society are enforceable as contracts. As we shall see, the law of contracts is structured foremost to enforce efficient exchanges and to deny enforcement to other types of deals.

As was argued in Chapter I, rules provided by contract law protect initial entitlements, so that if others by their activities interfere with the enjoyment of the entitlement, they can be stopped or forced to compensate for damages. Anyone seeking to remove the entitlement to nonreal property must buy it from the entitlement holder in a voluntary transaction guided by contract law. These guidelines can reduce conflicts among transactors and can help resolve conflicts, whether they are settled out of court or in court.

Thus, contract law can help reduce transaction costs by providing transactors with information on normal exchange conditions and on rules that apply, should conflicts arise. When conflicts arise in the face of externalities, the court, in fulfilling its role of externality adjuster in non-real-property transaction cases, is guided by contract law.

One of the primary tenets of contract law is the presumption of voluntary action by both parties. Evidence of duress or compulsion or other nonvoluntary behavior is thus a defense to a contract enforcement action.

The core concept of contracts that are enforceable is *consideration*, a legal term for the judicial inquiry of whether a bargain has been struck. The test of consideration is whether value has been exchanged between parties. The doctrine does not test the fairness of the exchange or the equality of the values exchanged. It seeks merely to ascertain whether an exchange of value has occurred. The maxim is that the law only tests to see if consideration, that is, exchange for value, exists. The parties to the exchange value their respective contributions to the transaction autonomously, and the law only determines whether an exchange has occurred.

On first blush, it might be disconcerting to find that courts inquire only about the existence of a consideration for a contract, and not to its adequacy. However, this is a sound approach. First of all, courts are not in a good position to second-guess those who are actively engaged in specific economic transactions. Second, instead of imposing on experts the court's inadequate view of what a proper consideration should be, the court seeks to establish an environment in which fair and appropriate consideration is offered. Specifically, contract law provides a number of defenses that make it possible for a trading environment to emerge within which fair and appropriate consideration is likely to be offered. Thus, as we will see, contract law provides for such formation defenses as duress and incapacity, and such performance defenses as commercial impracticability and mistake. These defenses should help create an environment in which transactions take place among more or less equal partners. To these defenses antitrust laws and activities by such agencies as the Federal Trade Commission are added to increase the likelihood of a relatively fair balance of bargaining power between trading partners.

The corpus of contract law provides a carefully worked out body of information concerning certain contingencies that may defeat an exchange. This knowledge assists the parties in planning their exchanges. Uncertainty is decreased and efficiency increased; this can reduce the complexity and thus the cost of transactions. Thus the economic rationale for contract law is the creation of incentives for value-maximizing conduct in the future, encouraging a process by which resources are smoothly moved through a series of exchanges into successively more valuable uses. In this spirit, defenses have been stipulated. They are taken up next within the setting of the two major contract phases, formation and performance.

CONTRACT FORMATION AND FORMATION DEFENSES

The first phase of any contract involves the creation of a contractual obligation. During the formation stage various propositions may be advanced, culminating at one point in a meeting of minds when an agreement is reached between the contracting parties. For the contract-formation stage to be completed successfully, an operative offer must be made by one party, and an operative acceptance must be made by a second while the operative offer is still in force. However, after a contract is formed, it may not be binding under certain circumstances.

Within the law of contracts there exist certain *formation defenses* that allow a party to escape judicial enforcement of the contract. One such defense is termed *illusory promise.* Consider the promise: "I'll give you this car *when I feel like it.*" This promise is illusory—it is subject to a condition that makes its value uncertain or possibly nonexistent. An exchange of such promises is not efficient, since the deal is too vague, and a contract involving such vagueness defies enforcement.

Another formation defense relates to promissory exchanges made within *intimate relationships.* They are not legally binding contracts unless there is clear evidence that a legally enforceable contract was contemplated. Thus, if Bill tells Jane he will always need her, and she vows she will love him forever, and then leaves him for Bob, Bill cannot go to court to seek damages for breach of contract. The economic rationale of the doctrine is that imposing legal sanctions in this area would not facilitate efficient exchange. Introducing courts and legal processes into intimate relationships would use up resources, where interference is not called for. This was explicitly recognized in *Balfour* v. *Balfour*. Here the court decided that an agreement, reached in a friendly way, that the wife should be supported by £30 a month while detained in England on doctor's advice was not enforceable because the parties did not intend to have the bargain enforced, and courts do not enforce such an agreement.[1]

A further formation defense is the doctrine of *duress*. The essence of the defense is that the contract was not voluntarily made by one of the parties. If a robber holds a gun to his victim's head and demands, "Your money or your life," the external format of a contract is complete when the victim hands over the money: A promise has been exchanged for a performance—the money was paid for the criminal's forebearance in not pulling the trigger.

A firm principle of Anglo-American law is that the courts will not permit themselves to be used as intruments of inequity and injustice. Courts will not enforce transactions in which the relative positions of the parties were such that one has unconscionably taken advantage of the necessities and distress of the other. Thus, as early as 1761, Lord Chancellor Northington wrote, "And there is great reason and justice in the rule, for necessitous men are not, truly speaking, free men, but, to answer a present exigency, will submit to any terms that the crafty may impose upon them.[2]

In *Atkinson* v. *Denby*, Cockburn, J. C. said that "where the one person can dictate, and the other has no alternative but to submit, it is coercion."[3] In this context, when a mortgagee under the pressure of financial distress conveys his equity of redemption to the mortgagor, the courts will scrutinize the transaction very carefully.[4]

Likewise, when a person heavily in debt, in order to obtain an additional loan with which to meet debts falling due, agreed to buy land at more than twice its value, the court as early as 1826 held that the lender had unjustly taken advantage of the borrower's necessity. It rescinded the contract. "The rule . . . is . . . [that when] a person is encumbered with debts, and that fact is known to a person with whom he contracts, who avails himself of it to exact an unconscionable bargain, equity will relieve upon account of the advantage and hardship."[5]

Enforcing contracts entered into under duress—contracts that involve threat and deny free choice—would encourage extortion. It would undermine confidence in our voluntary exchange system and reduce the general willingness to engage in market transactions.

1. 2 K.B. 571 (1919).
2. *Vernon* v. *Bethell,* 2 Eden 110, 113 (1761).
3. 7 Hurlst. and N. 934, 936 (1862).
4. *Villa* v. *Rodriguez,* 12 Wall. 323, 339 (1870).
5. *Administrators of Hough* v. *Hunt,* 2 Ohio 495, 502.

Another formation defense is *incapacity*. Under this rubric, contracts that would normally be enforceable are denied legal sanction. The defense of incapacity arises when the party who breaches the contract seeks to prove that his assent to the exchange was made under undue influence or strain, or in the presence of mental illness, intoxication, or drug incapacity.

Thus, for example, undue influence was claimed in a 1966 California appeals court case. Plaintiff D. Odorizzi, a teacher, claimed that after he was arrested on criminal charges of homosexual activity representatives of the school board secured his consent to resign.[6] They used the high-pressure technique of assuring him that they were trying to assist him by securing his resignation. Otherwise, they said, the board would dismiss him and publicize the fact, all of which would jeopardize his chances of securing a teaching position elsewhere.

As the court stated in the Odorizzi case,

> Undue influence, in the sense we are concerned with here, is a shorthand legal phrase used to describe persuasion which tends to be coercive in nature, persuasion which overcomes the will without convincing the judgment. . . . The hallmark of such persuasion is high pressure, a pressure which works on mental, moral, or emotional weakness to such an extent that it approaches the boundaries of coercion. In this sense, undue influence has been called over-persuasion. . . . Misrepresentations of law or fact are not essential to the charge, for a person's will may be overborne without misrepresentation. By statutory definition undue influence includes "taking an unfair advantage of another's weakness of mind; or . . . taking a grossly oppressive and unfair advantage of another's necessities or distress [Civ. Code, 1575]."
>
> We paraphrase the summary of undue influence given the jury by Sir James P. Wilde in Hall v. Hall, L. R. 1, P & D 481, 482 (1868): To make a good contract a man must be a free agent. Pressure of whatever sort which overpowers the will without convincing the judgment is a species of restraint under which no valid contract can be made. Importunity or threats, if carried to the degree in which the free play of a man's will is overborne, constitute undue influence, although no force is used or threatened. A party may be led but not driven, and his acts must be the offspring of his own volition and not the record of someone else's.
>
> In essence undue influence involves the use of excessive pressure to persuade one vulnerable to such pressure, pressure applied by a dominant subject to a servient object. In combination, the elements of undue susceptibility in the servient person and excessive pressure by the dominating person make the latter's influence undue, for it results in the apparent will of the servient person being in fact the will of the dominant person.
>
> Undue susceptibility may consist of total weakness of mind which leaves a person entirely without understanding (Civ. Code, § 38); or, a lesser weakness which destroys the capacity of a person to make a contract even though he is not totally incapacitated (Civ. Code, § 39; Peterson v. Ellebrecht, 205 Cal. App. 2d 718, 721–722, 23 Cal. Rptr. 349).[7]

6. *Odorizzi v. Bloomfield School District,* 246 Cal. App. 2d 123 (1966).
7. *Ibid.*

The defense of incapacity has a persuasive economic rationale. The essence of the defense is that true preferences are not revealed in the exchange. Thus, the legal enforcement mechanism should not validate and enforce an exchange where there can be no presumption that value is increased.

CONTRACT PERFORMANCE AND PERFORMANCE DEFENSES

Society has an interest in seeing contracts enforced once they are formed. This attitude is not merely moralistic; it stems from the need to provide parties to a contract with a high degree of confidence in the sanctity of the promise and in its being carried out. If performance were not ensured, few contracts would be entered into and the number of value-creating exchanges would be reduced. Therefore, the law provides incentives to ensure performance.

Once a legally enforceable agreement between the parties exists, the law provides a social mechanism for its enforcement. A party to a contract who later breaches his deal will be held in breach and will be required to provide the nonbreaching party with compensation under specific damages rules. However, there are conditions under which the breaching party may be excused from performing or paying damages. Such conditions, which effectively excuse performance, are often referred to as *performance defenses.* For a performance defense to be invoked, the event claimed to be responsible for the performance inability must not have been preventable by the promisor at a reasonable cost.[8] A performance defense can only be raised where the contract does not explicitly assign the risk in question and the event responsible for claiming the performance defense could not have been avoided by cost-justified precautions. Posner and Rosenfield suggest that, when

> these threshold conditions have been satisfied, economic analysis suggests that the loss should be placed on the party who is the superior (that is, lower-cost) risk bearer. To determine which party is the superior risk bearer three factors are relevant—knowledge of the magnitude of the loss, knowledge of the probability that it will occur, and (other) costs of self- or market-insurance.[9]

A number of performance defenses have been identified in the law. One such defense is *impossibility.* Originally the defense of impossibility did not exist in the common law. If you agreed to manufacture 100 widgets and your factory burned down without any fault of your own, the law held you to your deal and required the payment of damages. Parties to the agree-

This has been changed. Then, you were always liable.

8. R. A. Posner and E. M. Rosenfield, "Impossibility and Related Doctrines in Contract Law: An Economic Analysis," *Journal of Legal Studies* 6 (January 1977): 83–118.

9. *Ibid.,* p. 117.

ment were assumed to have agreed to the allocation of risk between themselves by their specification of performance. The law upheld this agreement, including the resulting allocation of risk between the parties.

Private parties often wished to reallocate the risks of events that cause impossibility-type situations—events such as disaster, death, unforeseeable destruction, or strikes. Specific clauses known as *force majeure* clauses were commonly drafted into commercial agreements. Soon this allocation of impossibility-type defenses became implied as a standard doctrine of the common law, where earlier law had been very hostile to the idea. Moreover, the impossibility defenses have since been included in the Uniform Commercial Code.

Clearly, the risk of losses due to entirely unforeseen events that make delivery on a contract impossible can be assigned in various ways. If the seller assumes the risk, he will want to be compensated for it by including in the price a risk premium. And if the risk is assumed by the buyer, he will want to deduct the risk premium from the price he pays. There is an advantage in having a general risk assignment, as under the impossibility defense, rather than writing special clauses into each and every contract. Such a rule will tend to reduce litigation and transaction costs.

Let us consider some situations where performance may become impossible due to unforeseeable circumstances, and an impossibility defense may be invoked. Clearly for this defense to be applied, the performance must require a more or less unique resource that through unforeseeable circumstances ceases to exist.

One example is the death of a contracting entertainment performer. His estate simply cannot provide performance of the terms of the contract between the decedent and another party. The law implies the risk of nonperformance by death of the purchasing party. That is where the risk is anyway, and the law merely provides legal recognition of this fact, thus discouraging unnecessary suits when parties to the deal have not specifically made provision for the contingency. Here the doctrine promotes efficiency by decreasing the incentives for additional lawsuits and by providing incentives for parties to specify and think out future contingencies to the deal. Thus, efficient exchange is facilitated.

Or consider another unique resource, as in the case of *Taylor* v. *Caldwell*. *Such a clear case of impossibility.* Here a contract was signed for the use of the Surrey Gardens and Music Hall. Just before the concert was to be given under the contract, the hall was destroyed by fire.[10] The court accepted the defense of impossibility, declaring that the hall had ceased to exist, without fault of either party. Therefore, it was impossible for either party to perform its promise.

But in addition to the destruction of more or less unique resources, the defense of impossibility is sometimes invoked more generally. In most

10. *Taylor* v. *Caldwell*, King's Bench, 1863.

commercial-type exchanges the nonperforming party could conceivably substitute conforming performance—by purchasing widgets from other manufacturers even though his own factory was burned down.

When, under these circumstances, will the law excuse performance because of impossibility? The courts seem to look to the intent of the parties at the formation of the contract as to which party was to bear this particular risk. If the terms of the deal, such as the price per widget, evidence an allocation of risk to the seller—liability will be placed there. If otherwise, liability will be excused. Judicial enforcement of the impossibility defense thus seeks to give each party the benefit of the terms of the agreement. Although in certain types of agreements the law implies an impossibility defense, contractual enforcement by the courts is generally flexible enough so that agreements between the parties will be enforced as agreed. By so doing the courts appear to be promoting efficient exchange.

Clearly, much depends on how financially ruinous and unforeseen the result of the erroneous underlying assumptions turn out to be. For example, a contract between two parties for the construction of a concrete bridge across the Arroyo Seco in South Pasadena, California, stipulated that all gravel and earth necessary for the project would come from the plaintiff's land, and a certain price would be paid for it by the defendants. When only about half of the gravel was taken from the plaintiff's land, he filed suit for breach of contract. However, the court found that "no greater quantity could have been taken by ordinary means except by the use, at great expense, of a steam dredger, and the earth and gravel so taken could not have been used without first having been dried at great expense and delay."[11] The defendants had apparently not anticipated that taking more than half of the gravel from the plaintiff's land would require work below the water level and involve very high costs. Therefore, they bought the rest of the gravel from a cheaper source.

Consequently, the court concluded,

> . . . And, in determining whether the earth and gravel were "available," we must view the conditions in a practical and reasonable way. Although there was gravel on the land, it was so situated that the defendants could not take it by ordinary means, nor except at a prohibitive cost. To all fair intents then, it was impossible for defendants to take it.
>
> "A thing is impossible in legal contemplation when it is not practicable; and a thing is impracticable when it can only be done at an excessive and unreasonable cost." 1 Beach on Contr. § 216. We do not mean to intimate that the defendants could excuse themselves by showing the existence of conditions which would make the performance of their obligation more expensive than they had anticipated, or which would entail a loss upon them. But, where the difference in cost is so great as here, and has the effect, as found, of making

11. *Mineral Park Land Co.* v. *Howard,* 172 Cal. 289, 156 p. 458 (1916).

More difficult to rule than previous case.

performance impracticable, the situation is not different from that of a total absence of earth and gravel.

Judgment for defendants.[12]

Thus, if crucial assumptions underlie the deal as a foundation to the performance agreed upon, then failure of the assumption is a defense to actual performance. This rule clearly has an economic rationale, since enforcement of the performances agreed upon, once the underlying assumptions to the deal have been destroyed, would cause inefficient exchange. When the deal was struck neither party contemplated performance unless the underlying assumptions remained in force. That was the deal. Once assumptions are destroyed, this excuses performance, a rule that encourages efficient exchange.

The Uniform Commercial Code deals extensively with the doctrine of *commercial impracticability*. Section 2-615 indicates that a party seeking to be discharged from his contractual obligations must show all of the following and that the party seeking excuse has the burden of the proof:

1. A failure of an underlying condition of the contract must occur. Part of Section 2-615 reads,

(*a*) Delay in delivery or non-delivery . . . is not a breach of his duty under a contract for sale if performance as agreed has been made impracticable by the occurrence of a contingency the non-occurrence of which was a basic assumption on which the contract was made or by compliance in good faith with any applicable foreign or domestic governmental regulation or order whether or not it later proves to be invalid.

2. The failure must have been unforeseen at the time the contract was signed. Official Comment 1 reads,

This section excuses a seller from timely delivery of goods contracted for, where his performance has become commercially impractical because of unforeseen supervening circumstances not within the contemplation of the parties at the time of contracting.

3. The risk of failure must not have been assumed either directly or indirectly by the parties seeking excuse.

4. Performance must be impracticable. In this connection Official Comment 4 states that

Increased cost alone does not excuse performance unless the rise in cost is due to some unforeseen contingency which alters the essential nature of the per-

12. *Ibid.*

formance. Neither is a rise nor a collapse in the market in itself a justification, for that is exactly the type of business risk which business contracts made at fixed prices are intended to cover. But a severe shortage of raw materials or of supplies due to a contingency such as war, embargo, local crop failure, unforeseen shutdown of major sources of supply or the like, which either causes a marked increase in cost or altogether prevents the seller from securing supplies necessary to his performance, is within the contemplation of this section.

5. The seller must have made all reasonable attempts to assure himself that the source of supply will not fail. Official Comment 5 states that

there is no excuse under this section, however, unless the seller has employed all due measures to assure himself that his source will not fail.

6. Finally, both in terms of court-made law and the implication of Official Comment 5, the seller's own conduct must not have created the situation leading to the impracticability of performance.

An interesting examination of the claim by Westinghouse Electric Corporation in 1975 that it was not legally bound to honor fixed price contracts to deliver about 70 million pounds of uranium by appealing to section 2-615 of the Uniform Commercial Code can be found in an article by Joskow.[13] The paper was written before the case had been disposed of by the courts. (In October 1978, a U.S. district court ruled that Westinghouse's claim of commercial impracticability was invalid, holding that it illegally had reneged on its uranium supply contracts.) Joskow correctly concluded that "Westinghouse appears to fail on all counts to justify a discharge of its contractual obligations under U.C.C. paragraph 2-615."[14]

The defense of *mistake* is a further performance defense. A party claiming under the defense of mistake asserts that though the explicit terms of the contract may give rise to the interpretation of the agreement the plaintiff suggests and thus the resulting breach that the plaintiff asserts, they also give rise to an alternative reasonable interpretation that the defendant reasonably believed was the agreement. The essence of this defense to a contract enforcement action is thus that parties have not reached an agreement, though in form it might appear that they had.

Such a difference in interpretation faced the court in the *Frigaliment* case, in which Judge Friendly raised the question as to what, for contract purposes, a chicken is.[15] Two contracts were entered into involving hundreds of thousands of pounds of chicken, yet without an explicit definition of the commodity traded—the chicken's age. The court agreed that the word

13. P. L. Joskow, "Commercial Impossibility, the Uranium Market and the Westinghouse Case," *Journal of Legal Studies* 6 (January 1977): 119–176.

14. *Ibid.,* p. 175.

15. *Frigaliment Importing Co.* v. *B.N.S. International Sales Corp.,* D.C.N.Y. 190 F. Supp. 116.

chicken was ambiguous. The defendant produced a witness who testified that a chicken is everything, except a goose, a duck or a turkey.

The court concluded,

> When all the evidence is reviewed, it is clear that defendant believed it could comply with the contracts by delivering stewing chicken in the 2 ½–3 lbs. size. Defendant's subjective intent would not be significant if this did not coincide with an objective meaning of "chicken." Here it did coincide with one of the dictionary meanings, with the definition in the Department of Agriculture Regulations to which the contract made at least oblique reference, with at least some usage in the trade, with the realities of the market, and with what plaintiff's spokesman had said. Plaintiff asserts it to be equally plain that plaintiff's own subjective intent was to obtain broilers and fryers; the only evidence against this is the material as to market prices and this may not have been sufficiently brought home.[16]

What are the efficiency implications of a defense of mistake? The judicial enforcement of the external form of the contract where the defendant's evidence is strong enough to show that the parties never really agreed would not be efficient. Efficient exchange requires agreement between the parties both to their explicit terms and to their underlying assumptions. Otherwise, no true bargain has been struck in the sense that each party sought to equate its true marginal costs and revenues.

In summary, formation as well as performance defenses invalidate a contract when it can be shown that actual agreement has not occurred. Under such a circumstance, the economic rationale of a contract is not met, and therefore efficient resource use is unlikely to result.

Anticipatory Repudiation

Anticipatory repudiation results when a party to a contract gives formal advance notice of his intention not to perform. It is a break by anticipatory repudiation in contrast to a breach by failure to perform when due. Suppose two parties exchange promises to perform in the future. Specifically, one agrees to buy and another agrees to sell 100 widgets at $1 apiece 1 year from the date the contract is signed. Now that a contract exists, both parties have an enforceable obligation to perform or pay damages when the time of performance comes. During the intervening year before the seller's duty to deliver is due, he begins to have reservations about the deal and expresses them to the buyer. "I'm not sure I can perform." Yet, when the deal was made, both parties believed in the reliability of the promises exchanged. The agreement, by solidifying the deal between the parties, had concluded in an exchange of reliable promises between the parties. Was there not an exchange of a promise for a promise, a key ingredient of a contract? And were not both promises of future performance deemed

16. *Ibid.*

reliable by the parties to the contract and did they not therefore contribute a basis for reliance in future dealings? The buyer knew that he had a deal that would give him 100 widgets a year from the date the contract was signed, and he therefore was able to act in reliance upon this deal. Moreover, the reliability of the deal had perhaps become the basis for reliance by other parties. The fact that a contract between the parties existed gave both parties a basis for contracts with others.

The legal step of anticipatory repudiation is an expression of intent not to perform in the future, but to breach the contract. When the expression of intention not to perform in the future destroys the nonbreaching party's confidence in the reliability of the promise exchanged, a material breach of contract has occurred and the nonbreaching party has legal rights of action.

In connection with such anticipatory repudiation, the court stated in *Hawkinson v. Johnston,*

> The real sanctity of any contract rests only in the mutual willingness of the parties to perform. Where this willingness ceases to exist, any attempt to prolong or preserve the status between them will usually be unsatisfactory and mechanical. Generally speaking, it is far better in such a situation, for the individuals and for society, that the rights and obligations between them should be promptly and definitely settled, if the injured party so desires, unless there is some provision in the contract that, as a matter of mutual intention, can be said to prevent this from being done. The commercial world has long since learned the desirability of fixing its liabilities and losses as quickly as possible, and the law similarly needs to remind itself that, to be useful, it too must seek to be practical.[17]

According to the Uniform Commercial Code, the aggrieved party in the light of anticipatory repudiation may

1. Await performance for a commercially reasonable time
2. Resort to any remedy for breach
3. Suspend his own performance or proceed in accordance with the provisions of the seller's right to identify goods to the contract notwithstanding breach or to salvage unfinished goods[18]

The economic rationale of the doctrine is clear. Efficiency in exchange is enhanced by certainty between the parties to the deal. Therefore, if one party is convinced that unforeseen circumstances make the deal unprofitable, being permitted to cancel the deal while leaving the other party no worse off than he otherwise would have been is efficient. As Vold has stated,

---

17. *Hawkinson* v. *Johnston,* 122 F.2d 724, 729–730 (8th Cir. 1941).
18. Uniform Commercial Code, section 2-610.

The substantial practical reason for permitting the aggrieved promisee to sue at once for anticipatory repudiation is that allowing an action at once tends to conserve available resources and prevent waste. If no legal recognition is extended to the promisee's valuable contractual relation pending performance, if no cause of action is recognized until there is a failure to perform at the time for performance, large losses may be incurred which suing promptly might avoid. . . . Unless the aggrieved promisee can at once come to court in an action for anticipatory repudiation he must either struggle on with hostile or possibly insolvent parties, incurring expense and loss of time in preparations which may be of no use to anybody, or he must cease such further preparations for performance at the peril of being found in default after all in later litigation at the time for performance. . . . Very often by such settlement through litigation, the controversy can be adjusted and the productive work of the business in hand continued without serious interruption.[19]

DAMAGES RULES

The law of contracts does not require parties to a contract actually to perform. Contracting parties are given the option of performance or breach. But if a contracting party breaches his deal, he is required to pay damages. As Oliver Wendell Holmes, Jr., has stated, "The only universal consequence of a legally binding promise is, that the law makes the promisor pay damages if the promised event does not come to pass."[20] Thus, a breach of contract is not a tort, and the party in breach is not held liable for consequences of nonperformance. Instead, the basic measure of damages for breach of contract is the *rule of financial equivalent performance.* Under this rule, a breaching party must pay the financial equivalent of his breach of the contract to the nonbreacher. The objective is to put the innocent party in the position he would have been in if the contract had not been breached. Suppose a party contracts to sell a buyer one sack of sand at $6. He then notifies the buyer that he will not deliver. The current market price of equivalent sacks of sand on the open market is $7. The financial equivalent performance of the deal from the buyer's perspective is the difference between the market price and the contract price for the sand, or $1.

The underlying economic rationale for this rule is that if one party determines that breach is in its self-interest, actual breach is efficient, as long as the other party is not harmed. The rule of financial equivalent performance ensures such an outcome by giving the nonbreacher the value of his deal; it releases the breaching party from an actual performance that he believes would be more expensive for him than payment of damages. Thus, the party best able to evaluate the cost of actual performance versus

19. L. Vold, "Repudiation of Contracts," *Nebraska Law Bulletin* 5 (February 1927): 269, 279–285.

20. Oliver Wendell Holmes, Jr., *The Common Law,* ed. Mark D. Howe (Boston: Little, Brown, 1963), pp. 234–237.

the payment of financial equivalent damages is given the power to decide. The nonbreacher is given his full financial equivalent for performance of the deal and may purchase conforming performance on the market. Resources are saved and the lowest-cost performance is revealed to the contracting parties.

Next, let us turn to a further damages rule, the *avoidable-consequences rule*, and demonstrate it. Suppose, as in *Rockingham County v. Luten Bridge Co.*, a construction company ~~and~~ a ~~municipality~~ contract to build a bridge.[21] As the company proceeds with bridge construction, the municipality reaches a decision to breach the contract. The bridge order is thereby canceled. Once notice of breach is given to the construction company, the law of contracts imposes the avoidable-consequences rule on the nonbreaching party. Specifically, the construction company is legally required to mitigate damages and minimize the loss from the breach. In this case, the construction company would be required to stop building the bridge. Its damages for materials expended and incidental costs in bringing the operation to a halt would be determined as of the time of breach. Any additional damages piled on after notification of the breach would be denied judicial enforcement.

As Judge Parker explained in the *Luten Bridge Company* case,

> There is a line of cases running back to 1845 which holds that, after an absolute repudiation or refusal to perform by one party to a contract, the other party cannot continue to perform and recover damages based on full performance. This rule is only a particular application of the general rule of damages that a plaintiff cannot hold a defendant liable for damages which need not have been incurred; or, as it is often stated, the plaintiff must, so far as he can without loss to himself, mitigate the damages caused by the defendant's wrongful act. The application of this rule to the matter in question is obvious. If a man engages to have work done, and afterwards repudiates his contract before the work has been begun or when it has been only partially done, it is inflicting damage on the defendant without benefit to the plaintiff to allow the latter to insist on proceeding with the contract. The work may be useless to the defendant, and yet he would be forced to pay the full contract price.[22]

The avoidable-consequences rule puts the burden on the nonbreacher to minimize damages and preserve resources for redirection toward other uses. This rule creates incentives for efficient use of resources once a deal has gone sour. To allow the innocent party to a breached contract to increase its award of damages via the courts by artificially increasing damages occurring from a contractual breach would be wasteful and inefficient in the use of resources.

Finally, there is the *rule of consequential damages*, which entitles the non-

---

21. *Rockingham County* v. *Luten Bridge Co.*, 35 F.2d 302.
22. *Ibid.*

breaching party only to those damages that are neither too speculative nor too remote. Instead it entitles him merely to those damages that flow naturally from the breach of contract. This is a very limiting rule, with the breaching party, according to *Hadley* v. *Baxendale*, liable merely for the foreseeable consequences of the breach.[23] In this famous case of the mid-nineteenth century, a mill was stopped by the breakage of a crankshaft. The shaft was taken to a well-known carrier for shipment to Greenwich for repair. The carrier was told that the breakage had stopped the mill, and that the shaft should be shipped immediately. When the carrier delayed delivery by some neglect, the plaintiff claimed damages for the resulting loss in profits. Applying the rule of consequential damages, the court ruled,

> It follows, therefore, that the loss of profits here cannot reasonably be considered such a consequence of the breach of contract as could have been fairly and reasonably contemplated by both the parties when they made this contract. For such loss would neither have flowed naturally from the breach of this contract in the great multitude of such cases occurring under ordinary circumstances, nor were the special circumstances, which, perhaps, would have made it a reasonable and natural consequence of such breach of contract, communicated to or known by the defendants. The Judge ought, therefore, to have told the jury, that, upon the facts then before them, they ought not to take the loss of profits into consideration at all in estimating the damages. There must therefore be a new trial in this case.[24]

Thus, the law of contracts generally denies recovery for consequential damages, unless the risk of consequential damages was specifically bargained for between the parties. If the buyer, for example, told the seller of the consequential damages that would result when nondelivery occurred and the seller and buyer made the deal with those damages in mind, such that the seller bargained to take the risk for a price, the law of contracts would hold the seller liable for the ensuing consequential damages. If either party agreed to take the risk of consequential damages, any resulting consequential damages would be placed there. Normally, in the absence of an agreement to transfer risk from buyer to seller, the law presumes that the buyer takes the risks of consequential damages. He is the party best able to avoid any resulting damages. This rule thus has an economic rationale and the resulting signals should lead to an efficient use of resources.

The Damage Rule of Quantum Meruit

A plaintiff claiming damages under a breach of contract can often avail himself of an alternative to the rule of financial equivalent performance. According to Mueller and Rosett,

23. *Hadley* v. *Baxendale*, 9 Exch. 341, 156 Eng. Rep. 145 (1854).
24. *Ibid.*

. . . a party to an agreement may have paid in advance, or expended money, materials and time in performing his part of the contract. In the event of a breach, such a party may just want his money back or compensation for what he has expended on a performance, the benefit of which the breaching party is enjoying. The law permits him to elect this form of relief if he wants it, and sue under the rule of quantum meruit. Under quantum meruit, the plaintiff is entitled to the fair market value of his performance until the time of breach, i.e., the judicial valuation of the performance given.[25]

Quantum meruit is well illustrated by the following instruction to the jury in *Mooney* v. *York Iron Co.:*

It is the law that if an employer terminate a contract without any fault on the part of the employe or contractor, that then the employe or contractor may sue upon the contract to recover damages, or he may sue in *assumpsit* upon the common counts, as they are called—the *quantum meruit*—to recover what his services were worth. That does not mean what they were worth to the employer. It is the fair values; that is, the value of work and labor. Of course, the main question is first as to whether the contract was performed up to that time by the plaintiffs. If it was not, then the defendant had the right to stop the work, and discharge them, and they could not recover.[26]

Let us consider a hypothetical example. Suppose a painter made a contract to paint a house. During the negotiations he made a mistake and priced his services too low—he made a bad deal. His price is lower than the market price for similar work. Partway through the painting job the house owner breaches his deal. The nonbreaching party's options now include suit on the contract price (which is below the market valuation of similar performance) or suit under a *quantum meruit* theory for a fair market valuation of the performance given. He naturally takes the highest valued option—the *quantum meruit* theory. This option scheme of contract damages places a great incentive on the party making a good deal to perform his bargain fully and not breach.

Suppose, however, that the painter breaches his deal. In this situation the nonbreaching party is entitled to financial equivalent performance, which would be the difference between the market price of the same performance and the contract price. He thus cannot escape the consequences of his deal by breach.

The *quantum meruit* option for breach of contract has an economic rationale. It gives the party who makes a sweet deal an incentive to perform in order to obtain the full value of the bargain. As long as he fully performs his side of the bargain, incentives are created to ensure actual performance of the contract. The other side cannot escape the consequences of a bad

25. A. Mueller and A. I. Rosett, *Contract Law and Its Applications* (Mineola: Foundation Press, 1971), p. 164.

26. *Mooney* v. *York Iron Co.,* 82 Mich. 263, 46 N.W. 376.

deal by breach, which would result in the payment of financial equivalent damages at the market price.

Thus, suit in *quantum meruit* can be a valuable remedy when a nonbreaching party has a losing contract; it allows that party to get out of the deal without the loss he would have suffered if he had been required to complete the contract. When *quantum meruit* is used to allow a breaching party to recover for the reasonable value of what he delivered before he breached, the value is measured by the vague yardstick of value to the recipient of the performance, as opposed to a value to the deliverer of the performance. This difference in valuation loads the dice in favor of a nonbreacher. A further difference in the valuation is that where a breacher is claiming, his recovery is limited by the contract price. Otherwise, if prices had sharply risen, the breacher would recover more by breaching than by performing.[27]

reimbursment costs + profit !!

plaintiff, entitled to fair market value of costs before breach. Not just made equal whole again (as you are in financial equivalent performance)

ECONOMIC CONSIDERATIONS OF CONTRACT LAW

EXCHANGES AND TRANSACTION COSTS

In order to explore certain economic implications of contract law, I propose a framework that focuses on the activities and costs associated with contract formation and contract performance. The intent is to clarify the transaction costs incurred by the seller and the buyer in these successive contract activities.

As a simplified case, assume that seller–creditor A has V goods, all of which he seeks to sell to buyer–borrower B. The transaction goes through three stages—in t_0, A has V goods and B has no goods, but usually money or earning capacity; t_1 is the contract-formation stage, when both A and B incur certain transaction costs (FC); at its conclusion A no longer has V, having incurred FC_A; B has V and has incurred FC_B. In t_2—the contract-performance stage—both A and B incur certain transaction costs in connection with performance C, for example, debt payment (collection). After performance is completed at the end of t_2, A will have V returned to him together with an interest payment (I). However, he will have incurred transaction costs in both t_1 and t_2, that is, $FC_A + C_A$. At the same point in time, B will no longer have V, but will have incurred the interest costs plus transaction costs, that is, $FC_B + C_B$.

The length of t_2, that is, the duration of the loan, which can extend from a day or two to a number of years, is important for various reasons. One reason relates to the risk of price-level changes (PC). By and large, the longer the period, the greater the price-level risk. The risk PC goes hand-

27. Mueller and Rosett, *Contract Law*, p. 166.

in-hand with another risk in credit transactions, that is, the risk of default D. Both can be looked upon as involving transaction costs in a credit transaction. Thus, the transaction costs facing the seller, for example, in the performance stage (C_A) can be written as follows:

$$C_A = C_{PC_A} + C_{D_A}.$$

Costs related to risk—for example, risk of default—can be evaluated by recognizing that the seller could contract with a third party for insurance against such a risk.[28] The insurance premium the seller would have to pay reflects the risk level he transfers to the insurance company.

The relation between uncertainty (or risk) and costs was well stated by Arrow and Lind: "In private capital markets, investors . . . choose investments to maximize . . . the present value of returns properly adjusted for risk."[29]

The effects of changes in the value of a risk or uncertainty-reduction factor T can be illustrated by approximating the insurance premium one would have to pay a third party to whom one could shift the risk. For simplicity's sake purely competitive conditions and a constant net uncertainty-reduction factor will be assumed, that is, one that is value-adjusted for costs and invariant with output, and a partial equilibrium analysis will be applied. If an uncertainty-reducing contract is signed, the value of the uncertainty-reduction factor can be subtracted from the industry supply function S. The result is a parallel, downward shift of the supply function. (The magnitude of the uncertainty-reduction factor could also have been added to the industry demand function D, which would have resulted in a parallel, upward shift to the right.) As can be seen in Figure 5-1, *ceteris paribus,* the equilibrium output will have increased, and the larger the uncertainty-reduction factor, the more the output will increase from Q_0 to Q_1. The increased output will be accompanied by a lower price—P_1 instead of P_0.

Transaction Costs during Contract Formation

The transaction costs of both the seller–creditor and the buyer–borrower during contract formation, FC, have two main components:

1. Costs of negotiating the contract (a_1)
2. Costs of preparing and signing the contract form (a_2)

---

28. Frank H. Knight's distinction between risk and uncertainty is helpful. Risk refers to insurable liabilities and uncertainty to uninsurable liabilities and outcomes. See Frank H. Knight, *Risk, Uncertainty and Profit* (London: London School Reprints of Scarce Works, No. 16, 1933).

29. K. J. Arrow and C. Lind, "Uncertainty and the Evaluation of Public Investment Decisions," *American Economic Review* 60 (June 1970): 364.

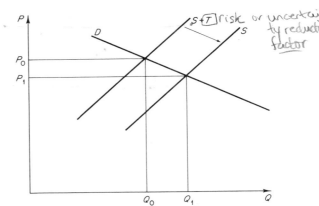

FIGURE 5-1 Effects of uncertainty-reduction T on quantity of output Q and price P; D is the industry demand function and S is the industry supply function.

Thus,

$$FC = a_1 + a_2.$$

Since the seller in consumer transactions has more knowledge, experience, and ability to spread cost over more transactions, FC_A usually is smaller than FC_B. Although in consumer transactions the seller usually benefits more from economies of scale than does the buyer, both tend to do so in nonconsumer transactions.

Transaction Costs during Contract Performance

In most instances the seller–creditor and the buyer–borrower perform as agreed upon in the contract. In such a routine case, both A and B incur bookkeeping costs and check-writing (collection) costs b_1. But in the absence of complete performance by both parties, additional costs can occur to A in each of three successive contract cases:

1. Default is threatened and A takes self-help measures and incurs costs b_2.
2. Default occurs and A takes self-help measures and incurs costs b_3.
3. Default occurs and A initiates judicial coercive collection under due process and incurs costs b_4[30]

---

30. Coercive collection takes place under due process, with costs according to Leff substantial for four reasons: (a) due process requires a court that at the outset is altogether ignorant, and it is costly to educate it; (b) since each case is theoretically different, the process of education cannot be generalized but must be handcrafted; (c) this crafting, save in a court of small claims, is done by specialists (i.e., lawyers); and (d) in allocating docket space, the court disregards the size of the creditor's claim at stake. Thus those having very large claims at stake will queue behind plaintiffs with relatively small claims. See A. A. Leff, "Injury, Ignorance and Spite—The Dynamics of Coercive Collection," *Yale Law Journal* 80 (November 1970): 1–46.

Thus, the default-related transaction costs facing a seller during contract performance CD_A can be stated as

$$CD_A = b_{A_1} + b_{A_2} + b_{A_3} + b_{A_4}.$$

Likewise, the default-related transaction costs for the buyer CD_B are

$$CD_B = b_{B_1} + b_{B_2} + b_{B_3} + b_{B_4}.$$

Clearly, each cost item can be very different for buyer and seller, with b_{B_2} virtually nil in most instances. There are also price-level-related transaction costs (C_{PC}), which, as was mentioned earlier, change with the length of the loan period.

Particularly in case of default, A and B are concerned about reducing their transaction costs. They would tend to take steps to write a contract that, should default become a possibility and occur, would minimize the ensuing transaction costs. Seller–creditors will seek contract terms that tend to persuade the buyer–borrower not to default. Such terms have been of concern to the courts as possibly unconscionable, and I will say more about the matter subsequently.

Likewise, rational buyer–borrowers will seek terms that reduce their risk and transaction costs in case they themselves default or the seller defaults.

In connection with Case 1, self-help can take the form of the seller–creditor threatening to repossess the commodity or to initiate legal action. The ensuing costs b_2 can range from efforts at persuasion to lawyers' fees.

Once the buyer has defaulted, Case 2, the seller can rely on self-help. For example, in certain states, after due notice is given, the seller can repossess a car. If he does so, he will incur certain transaction costs associated with the repossession, such as hiring and manning a tow truck. Moreover, he may recover a value that is smaller than the outstanding debt plus transaction costs. Note that the value of the repossessed car depends on the down payment and the rate of depreciation.

Commonly the costs of b_2, b_3, and b_4 are different for the seller–creditor than for the buyer–borrower. For example, in connection with b_2, the cost of repossession deprives the buyer of use and resale of the item bought on credit; the traveling salesman who has his car repossessed may be unable to make a living.

In Case 3, which involves judicial coercive collection, both A and B can incur court fees, attorney fees, time costs, and psychic costs. The seller–creditor faces an outside chance of losing the case, perhaps because of some technicality. In that case he will have incurred substantial costs not only in connection with the court case, but also in connection with his deprivation of debt repayment. The court may however call for such execution techniques as repossession, which has been discussed, or garnishment.

From a creditor's point of view, garnishment is a powerful technique for the noncooperative collection of debts. Like any lien, garnishment will interfere with the use of a liened property, be it a worker's wages or a businessman's bank account. Garnishment of wages imposes transaction costs on the employer, who is forced to organize and administer the withholding of wages at the risk of occasional error. As a result employers tend to be outraged at their worker's apparent improvidence and seek steps to disassociate themselves from the complicated affair. Employers therefore tend to fire workers whose wages have been garnished. Thus garnishment of wages imposes relatively low costs on the creditor, some costs on the debtor's employer, and very high costs on the debtor himself.

Normally, costs associated with judicial coercive collection are higher for the buyer–borrower than for the seller–creditor, particularly in consumer transactions. The borrower may have his reputation damaged and may incur very high costs of repossession and/or garnishment.

BARGAINING POWER IN EXCHANGE RELATIONS

The relative strengths of a buyer and a seller are seldom equal. This is particularly so in consumer transactions and even more so when low-income buyers are involved.

Retailers commonly have an advantage over consumers because a seller engages in many more repetitive transactions than does a buyer, particularly one who is poor. The retailer can spread his transaction costs in both the formation and the performance stages of the contract over many similar transactions, which greatly reduces his costs compared to those of the buyer, who has engaged in very few such transactions during his lifetime. The buyer's disadvantages are particularly great if he is poor, in which case his investment in signing a contract and knowing the law is large relative to his income. Thus, legal costs take a smaller percentage of the income and wealth of the rich than of the poor, and the poor tend to be less well educated and have greater difficulty in interpreting laws than do the rich. Finally, the seller might be more accommodating to a wealthy person from whom he expects repeat purchases than to a poor person whose purchases are likely to be few. Thus, the seller's inclination to take full advantage of his legal rights might depend on the buyer's wealth.

Compared to the retail level, bargaining power tends to be more equal on the wholesale level, and even more so on the manufacturing level. In relation to the comparative cost advantages and bargaining power of parties to a contract, Leff distinguishes three types of relationships between the buyer–debtor and the seller–creditor.[31] First, the buyer may be a consumer who also assumes the role of creditor, for instance, in a defective-products case. Second, the seller may be a professional creditor who sells to a consumer. Third, the buyer and the seller may be professionals, as might be the case on the manufacturing or wholesale levels. These

31. *Ibid.*, pp. 19–26.

three cases are of interest, since they have different effects on the transaction costs of the buyer and the seller.

Let us start with the case where the consumer acts as creditor. In the purchase by consumers of large-ticket-item durable goods it is not uncommon for the buyer to have fully or substantially performed on his contract although the seller has not.[32] For example, Leff discusses the case where a consumer

> has just bought a color television set from a retailer for $500 in cash. The consumer takes the set home, tries it, and finds that it is defective to the tune of $50; that is, that it would cost $50 to bring the television up to warranty. In these circumstances the consumer is a creditor; the retailer has possession of $50 of parts and services that belong to him. The consumer approaches the retailer and asks him to repair the set. The retailer refuses. This leaves the consumer with only coercive collection if he is to recover the $50.[33]

The consumer as creditor can recover through judicial coercion no more than the amount by which the seller is in default. As I have argued, the consumer–creditor is at a distinct disadvantage, because during his lifetime he engages in one or at best a very few such transactions, but the seller does so continuously. The seller has more knowledge and experience, and because he engages in a larger number of similar transactions he can spread parts of the legal costs. Moreover, repossession and garnishment affect professional debtors very little.

The same point is made in a somewhat different way by Mueller, when he states,

> Two factors combine to bring about the modern consumer's lack of effective legal power when he buys a product which is faulty but does not cause physical injury. Both of them stem from the fact that he is a little man in the scheme of things. First, there is an all-pervasive difficulty: our machinery of justice is simply not designed for easy use by the average citizen with a minor claim of any kind. If anything, it is designed to discourage him. He is not apt to know a lawyer and he does not particularly want to know one. And if he does muster up his courage and finds a lawyer, he will almost surely discover that his small claim is of no interest to that lawyer unless he is prepared to guarantee what to him will seem a preposterous sum. Even in those localities where small claims courts are supposed to be readily available, the use of the law remains a mysterious and a frightening prospect for the average citizen. It is especially frightening for the below-average citizen, for "the poor man looks upon the law as an enemy, not as a friend. For him the law is always taking something away."[34]

---

32. The consumer's position is likely to be the same whether he has paid cash or has "only" given a negotiable note. Because of the holder-in-due-course doctrine he will probably have to pay cash to the eventual holder of the note, no matter what is wrong with the deal or the product.

33. Leff, "Injury, Ignorance and Spite," p. 21.

34. Address by Attorney General Robert F. Kennedy on Law Day, University of Chicago,

The unavailability of simple process handicaps the little man regardless of the nature of his small claim, and it is handicap enough. But when he claims as a consumer against a seller, he encounters a second difficulty. Unless his claim is based on accidental injury to person or property caused by a defective product and is thus eligible for relief in tort, he claims in contract and must use a deck of doctrine that is stacked against him.

Most of his losing cards are colored "freedom of contract." Contract (says the jurisprudence) is a voluntary association, and the parties are therefore free within broad limits to adopt such terms as they see fit. The reasonably equal bargaining power that is manifestly required to support this basic principle is presumed.[35]

The second case is much more common. Here the seller, who is a large merchant, also serves as creditor and faces the probability that a consumer defaults. In the writing of a contract as well as the execution, the professional creditor has a distinct advantage over the buyer. He benefits from scale economies, mainly in the form of standardization and repetition. A lawsuit ordinarily requires an attorney; but at the summons and complaint stages the creditor needs only a little extra time or effort to file 10 suits, rather than one. Likewise, specialization and standardization reduce costs in procuring a judgment by default or pursuing a regular lawsuit. By obtaining legal aid at relatively low unit costs, moreover, the creditor can readily shift some portion of the cost to others, including employers of delinquent workers who must in case of garnishment organize an installment plan.

In the third case, professionals are at both ends of the transaction. The buyer and the seller can have very similar knowledge and bargaining power, and if default is threatened there are strong incentives to work out a compromise while holding transaction costs to a minimum.

STRATEGIES TO REDUCE TRANSACTION COSTS

Within the microeconomic framework developed, we can identify a number of strategies that can be pursued during the contract-formation stage in order to reduce a party's transaction costs. Although transaction costs in this stage are relatively small, they can be reduced by using standard forms, often referred to as *boilerplate forms.* They make it unnecessary to draft a new contract form each time. As will be shown later, in consumer transactions reliance on standard forms usually gives the seller–lender an advantage over the buyer–borrower.

More interesting are the strategies that can be used, particularly by the seller–creditor, to improve his position during the performance stage should default be threatened or occur. Within our microeconomic

May 1, 1964. See Patricia M. Wald, *Law and Poverty* (Washington, D.C.: U.S. Government Printing Office, 1965), ch. 3.

35. A. Mueller, "Contracts of Frustration," *Yale Law Journal* 78 (March 1969): 578–581.

framework the seller–creditor can, if the buyer–borrower defaults, take steps that will increase the latter's costs, thus reducing the likelihood of default. Interesting provisions that have been incorporated into contracts in this connection are,

1. Add-on clauses
2. Waiver-of-defense clauses
3. Due-on-sale clauses
4. Termination-at-will clauses[36]

Most of these clauses have been challenged under the rule of unconscionability, which is examined after these clauses are explored.

Add-On Clauses.   Certain clauses provide that all previous goods purchased by the buyer from the seller will secure the debts incurred with the current purchase. Moreover, each payment made with respect to any of the items purchased is applied against all outstanding balances, allowing the seller in effect to retain his security interest in all the goods sold until all debts are discharged. Default on a single payment permits the seller to repossess all the goods subjected to the comprehensive security arrangement. Such clauses greatly reduce the risk of the seller of personal property, since the goods sold can lose value through use or abuse more rapidly than the purchase price minus the time payments. In turn, the buyer can end up having a negative equity in the goods. Thus, the seller who takes back a security interest only in the goods sold risks that by repossessing the single item sold he will be left with a loss on the transaction as a whole in the light of interest and transaction costs.

An alternative that could be used to reduce the seller's risk would be to insist on larger cash down-payments, which are often unacceptable to buyers with limited means. Thus, the add-on clause permits the buyer and the seller to benefit from a reduction in costs associated with the setting up of the security arrangements. The seller can collect on his unpaid debt without having to initiate costly procedures established for unsecured creditors. Moreover, the seller is assured that the value he has furnished buyer will, should the occasion arise, first be used to satisfy his own claims and not those of third parties. Yet the disadvantage to the buyer is that he will not be able to use any of the goods bought from the buyer, should he default on paying for any one item.

Waiver-of-Defense Clauses.   In order to insulate itself from disputes between a buyer and a seller of goods, a finance company, having bought the right to collect the payments as they come due, favors original contracts of sale that include a waiver-of-defense clause. Such terms require the buyer

36. R. A. Epstein, "Unconscionability: A Critical Reappraisal," *Journal of Law and Economics* 18 (October 1975): 293–316.

to continue paying his installments to the finance company, even if the seller has not made good on his warranty obligation.[37] *inequality of bargaining power*

✱ *Due-on-Sale Clauses.*   Some contracts allow a lender to call in the out- *reduces* standing balance on the loan whenever the mortgagor either sells his *period* interest in the property or further encumbers it with a second mortgage. *during* Such a due-on-sale clause protects the lender against increased "moral risk" *which* that might be associated with the new buyer and against undesirable price- *mortgage is out-* level changes. The clause has been challenged as an unreasonable restraint *standing* on alienation.[38]

The due-on-sale clause allows the lender to use the natural turnover in *Wallenkamp* real estate to become a relatively short-term lender, which is in his favor, *State court* should interest rates increase. Thus the lender's risk associated with price- *Glendale:* level changes is reduced; he should therefore be able to offer the borrower *Fed court* better credit terms. Moreover, the clause may reduce the risk of default faced by the lender, who at the time of sale would otherwise have to deal with an unknown party.   *McDonalds sells a franchise —*

Termination-at-Will Clauses.   In commercial transactions, a common provision to many franchise agreements allows the franchisor to terminate the franchise at will without having to give any justification for his action. The clause has been attacked because it allows the franchisor to act as a tyrant who can cut off his franchisee any time he chooses, in extreme cases even before the franchisee has recouped his start-up costs in the venture.[39] Although such a clause gives the franchisor a distinct advantage, he is likely to exercise his right only when it is to his advantage. To the extent that in the formation stage a franchisee fully understands the implications of the clause, and its potential inconvenience and losses are properly reflected in the terms of the contract, the clause can be efficient. It removes all uncertainty as to who has the exclusive right to terminate an agreement.

In summary, this framework considers credit costs to be composed of the pure interest rate that is related to a person's time preference, the risk of default, and the risk of price-level changes. The seller–creditor can reduce the risk of default he faces by including in the contract an add-on, a waiver-of-defense, and/or a termination-at-will clause. In order to reduce his risk of price-level changes, he can include a due-on-sale as well as a termination-at-will clause.

THE RULE OF UNCONSCIONABILITY   *Posner. pg 84*
Trebelcock- imp.

The Uniform Commercial Code and the courts have taken a strong interest in the possibility that an otherwise legal contract may involve

37. *Ibid.*, pp. 308–309.
38. For example, according to California Civil Code §711 conditions restraining alienation when repugnant to the interest created are void.
39. Epstein, "Unconscionability: A Critical Reappraisal," p. 314.

unconscionable terms. Standards have been advanced to facilitate detection of unconscionability. Contracts containing oppressive clauses or exorbitant prices are considered unconscionable when more equal terms or lower prices would have been achieved had the bargaining process been adequate.[40] Unconscionability is thus related to imperfect markets that could produce oppressive terms or exorbitant prices compared to a perfect market. (Such terms or prices are not considered unconscionable if they result from fraud, duress, or misrepresentation.)

Using a perfect market, a market that has never existed, as a standard raises serious philosophical questions with regard to the economic determination of unconscionability. This issue will be taken up later. Here I will only say that two extreme policies are possible. One assumes that perfect market conditions are possible and use of the law is therefore desirable to bring them about. A second policy realistically concludes that perfect markets cannot be attained and seeks to penalize seller–creditors who have written into a contract oppressive clauses or exorbitant prices. Remember that what may appear to be oppressive or exorbitant may not be so if careful consideration is given to transaction costs, particularly the risk of default and the risk of price-level changes. I will consider this issue in some detail.

Section 2-302 of the Uniform Commercial Code authorizes the court to find, as a matter of law, that a contract or a clause of a contract was "unconscionable at the time it was made," and upon so finding the court may refuse to enforce the contract, excise the objectionable clause, or limit the application of the clause to avoid an unconscionable result.

The court's interest in unconscionable terms is perhaps best reflected in *Williams* v. *Walker-Thomas Furniture Co.*,[41] involving an appellant with limited education separated from her husband, maintaining herself and her seven children by means of public assistance. During the period 1957–1962 she had a continuous string of dealings with appellee from which she purchased many household articles on the installment plan. These included sheets, curtains, rugs, chairs, a chest of drawers, beds, mattresses, a washing machine, and a stereo set. In 1963 appellee filed a complaint in replevin for possession of all the items purchased by appellant, alleging that her payments were in default and that it retained title to the goods according to the sales contracts. By the writ of replevin appellee obtained a bed, chest of drawers, washing machine, and the stereo set.

Appellant signed fourteen contracts in all. They were approximately six inches in length and each contained a long paragraph in extremely fine print. One of the sentences in this paragraph provided that payments, after the first purchase, were to be prorated on all purchases then outstanding. Mathematically, this had the effect of keeping a balance due on all items

40. L. A. Kornhauser, "Unconscionability in Standard Forms," *California Law Review* 64 (September 1976): 1151–1183.
41. *Williams* v. *Walker-Thomas Furniture Co.*, 121 U.S. App. D.C. 315, 350 F.2d 445.

until the balance was completely eliminated. It meant that title to the first purchase remained in appellee until the fourteenth purchase, made some five years later, was fully paid.

The Appeals Court held,

> The record reveals that prior to the last purchase appellant had reduced the balance in her account to $164. The last purchase, a stereo set, raised the balance due to $678. Significantly, at the time of this and the preceding purchases, appellee was aware of appellant's financial position. The reverse side of the stereo contract listed the name of appellant's social worker and her $218 monthly stipend from the government. Nevertheless, with full knowledge that appellant had to feed, clothe and support both herself and seven children on this amount, appellee sold her a $514 stereo set. . . .

> Accordingly, we hold that where the element of unconscionability is present at the time a contract is made, the contract should not be enforced.

> Unconscionability has generally been recognized to include an absence of meaningful choice on the part of one of the parties together with contract terms which are unreasonably favorable to the other party. Whether a meaningful choice is present in a particular case can only be determined by consideration of all the circumstances surrounding the transaction. In many cases the meaningfulness of the choice is negated by a gross inequality of bargaining power. The manner in which the contract was entered is also relevant to this consideration. Did each party to the contract, considering his obvious education or lack of it, have a reasonable opportunity to understand the terms of the contract, or were the important terms hidden in a maze of fine print and minimized by deceptive sales practices? Ordinarily, one who signs an agreement without full knowledge of its terms might be held to assume the risk that he has entered a one-sided bargain. But when a party of little bargaining power, and hence little real choice, signs a commercially unreasonable contract with little or no knowledge of its terms, it is hardly likely that his consent, or even an objective manifestation of his consent, was ever given to all the terms. In such a case the usual rule that the terms of the agreement are not to be questioned should be abandoned and the court should consider whether the terms of the contract are so unfair that enforcement should be withheld.

> In determining reasonableness or fairness, the primary concern must be with the terms of the contract considered in light of the circumstances existing when the contract was made. The test is not simple, nor can it be mechanically applied.[42]

In short, although the court in *Williams* v. *Walker-Thomas* spoke in terms of unfairness, gross inequity of bargaining power, and no reasonable opportunity to understand the contract terms, it did not undertake an empirical evaluation of terms and prices. Basically it refused to condone an add-on clause, without examining whether such a clause produced substantially better terms for the borrower than she could have gotten had she made every purchase an independent contract.

An explicit attempt at establishing whether finance charges might be exorbitantly high was made in *Jones* v. *Star Credit Corporation:*

42. U.S. App. D.C. 315, 350 F.2d 445 (1965).

↑ good ex. for unconscionability

On August 31, 1965 the plaintiffs, who are welfare recipients, agreed to purchase a home freezer unit for $900 as the result of a visit from a salesman representing Your Shop At Home Service, Inc. With the addition of the time credit charges, credit life insurance, credit property insurance, and sales tax, the purchase price totaled $1,234.80. Thus far the plaintiffs have paid $619.88 toward their purchase. The defendant claims that with various added credit charges paid for an extension of time there is a balance of $819.81 still due from the plaintiffs. The uncontroverted proof at the trial established that the freezer unit, when purchased, had a maximum retail value of approximately $300. . . .

The question which presents itself is whether or not, under the circumstances of this case, the sale of a freezer unit having a retail value of $300 for $900 ($1,439.69 including credit charges and $18 sales tax) is unconscionable as a matter of law. The court believes that it is. . . .

No doubt, the mathematical disparity between $300, which presumably includes a reasonable profit margin, and $900, which is exorbitant on its face, carries the greatest weight. Credit charges alone exceed by more than $100 the retail value of the freezer. These alone, may be sufficient to sustain the decision. Yet, a caveat is warranted lest we reduce the import of section 2-302 solely to a mathematical ratio formula. It may at times, be that; yet it may also be much more. The very limited financial resources of the purchaser, known to the sellers at the time of the sale, is entitled to weight in the balance. Indeed, the value disparity itself leads inevitably to the felt conclusion that knowing advantage was taken of the plaintiffs. In addition, the meaningfulness of choice essential to the making of a contract can be negated by a gross inequality of bargaining power. (*Williams* v. *Walker-Thomas Furniture Co.*, 350 F.2d 445.)

There is no question about the necessity and even the desirability of installment sales and the extension of credit. Indeed, there are many, including welfare recipients, who would be deprived of even the most basic conveniences without the use of these devices. Similarly, the retail merchant selling on installment or extending credit is expected to establish a pricing factor which will afford a degree of protection commensurate with the risk of selling to those who might be default prone. However, neither of these accepted premises can clothe the sale of this freezer with respectability.[43]

The court in the *Star Credit* case explicitly took cognizance of the social desirability of installment sales. As a matter of fact, it recognized that except for credit, poor people could hardly hope to acquire certain durable goods.

Therefore, it is important to determine carefully whether the interest rate charged is or is not commensurate with the risk assumed by the merchant. Should merchants fear that they cannot be properly compensated for the risk they assume, credit sales will dry up, to the detriment of all those with low incomes.

FORM CONTRACTS AND CONTRACTS OF ADHESION

There are strategies that, although perhaps designed to reduce transaction costs in the formation stage, have their main impact on transaction costs in the performance stage. I have in mind form contracts. Mueller and

---

43. *Jones* v. *Star Credit Corp.*, 59 Misc. 2d 189, 298 N.Y.S. 2d 264 (1969).

Rosett have identified the form contract as posing the "most urgent unre-solved set of problems in modern contract law. . . . Form contracts have many practical commercial virtues. . . . The difficulty with form contracts is that they offer a too-tempting way of loading a contract with a variety of very favorable terms and conditions that will probably be unnoticed."[44] In consumer transactions, the concern about form contracts relates to bargain-ing power, with is frequently unequal. The consumer who buys a defective appliance or car often finds himself in the position of a creditor. He discovers that the seller has taken full advantage of the presumption that parties to a written agreement know, or ought to know, the terms of their agreement. In some cases he will find that the printed contract with his dealer contained one or more conditions designed to give the dealer, and everyone above him in the distribution chain, maximum protection against consumer claims. He has, in short, entered into what has come to be called a *contract of adhesion.*

As Mueller has stated,

> Some of this printed boilerplate is apt to come in an envelope containing assorted other literature that is sealed in the carton or is taped to the chassis of the purchased equipment. In consequence it is seldom seen by the buyer until after delivery. Clearly, then, the buyer might persuasively claim that he cannot be bound by it because he never accepted it as part of his bargain. But it would make little practical difference if he not only saw it but read it and even understood it before his purchase. The result of an attempt on his part to reject it would be no purchase; it would be a rare and imaginative dealer indeed (to say nothing of a rare and imaginative customer) who would act in so non-institutional a fashion as to agree to a special warranty arrangement. Even if a dealer were willing to do so, his action would almost surely be held not to have involved the deeper pockets of his supplier or the manufacturer of the product. And though theoretically the buyer could go elsewhere and buy from a merchant who did not so limit his obligations, he would almost certainly find that all competing goods were similarly limited. So to turn the matter on the buyer's lack of knowledge would simply put dealers to the useless task of saying, "look at this," before they say, "Sign here." A requirement that full disclosure be made concerning terms that can in face be accepted or rejected is a meaningful and important element of contract law. But standard disclaimers and limitation of remedy clauses such as make up the bulk of the printed boilerplate in contracts for the sale of consumer goods are not such choice-offering terms. The problem with such clauses is not lack of notice but lack of consumer power to bargain about them. The problem is that they are parts of contracts of adhesion.[45]

The implications of boilerplate contract forms in the presence of a buyer's limited bargaining power are extensively discussed in *Henningsen v. Bloomfield Motors, Inc.*;

44. Mueller and Rosett, *Contract Law,* p. 354.
45. Mueller, "Contracts of Frustration," pp. 578–579.

Plaintiff Clause H. Henningsen purchased a Plymouth automobile, manufactured by defendant Chrysler Corporation, from defendant Bloomfield Motors, Inc. His wife, plaintiff Helen Henningsen, was injured while driving it and instituted suit against both defendants to recover damages on account of her injuries. Her husband joined in the action seeking compensation for his consequential losses. The complaint was predicated upon breach of express and implied warranties and upon negligence. At the trial the negligence counts were dismissed by the court and the cause was submitted to the jury for determination solely on the issues of implied warranty of merchantability. Verdicts were returned against both defendants and in favor of the plaintiffs. . . .

The type used in the printed parts of the form became smaller in size, different in style, and less readable toward the bottom where the line for the purchaser's signature was placed. The smallest type on the page appears in the two paragraphs, one of two and one-quarter lines and the second of one and one-half lines, on which great stress is laid by the defense in the case. These two paragraphs are the least legible and the most difficult to read in the instrument, but they are most important in the evaluation of the rights of the contesting parties. They do not attract attention and there is nothing about the format which would draw the reader's eye to them. In fact, a studied and concentrated effort would have to be made to read them. De-emphasis seems the motive rather than emphasis. More particularly, most of the printing in the body of the order appears to be 12 point block type, and easy to read. In the short paragraphs under discussion, however, the type appears to be six point script and the print is solid, that is, the lines are very close together.

The two paragraphs are:

The front and back of this Order comprise the entire agreement affecting this purchase and no other agreement or understanding of any nature concerning same has been made or entered into, or will be recognized. I hereby certify that no credit has been extended to me for the purchase of this motor vehicle except as appears in writing on the face of this agreement.

I have read the matter printed on the back hereof and agree to it as a part of this order the same as if it were printed above my signature. I certify that I am 21 years of age, or older, and hereby acknowledge receipt of a copy of this order.

The reverse side of the contract contains 8½ inches of fine print. It is not as small, however, as the two critical paragraphs described above. The page is headed "Conditions" and contains ten separate paragraphs consisting of 65 lines in all. The paragraphs do not have head-notes or margin notes denoting their particular subject, as in the case of the "Owner Service Certificate" to be referred to later. In the seventh paragraph, about two-thirds of the way down the page, the warranty, which is the focal point of the case, is set forth. It is as follows:

7. It is expressly agreed that there are no warranties, expressed or implied, *made* by either the dealer or the manufacturer on the motor vehicle, chassis, or parts furnished hereunder except as follows.

A large number of further limiting provisions follow in small print on the reverse side.[46]

46. *Henningsen v. Bloomfield Motors, Inc.*, 32 N.J. 358, 161 A.2d 69 (1960).

The court concluded,

> The conflicting interests of the buyer and seller must be evaluated realisti-
> cally and justly, giving due weight to the social policy evinced by the Uniform
> Sales Act, the progressive decisions of the courts engaged in administering it
> . . . , and the bargaining position occupied by the ordinary consumer. . . .
>   The warranty before us is a standardized form designed for mass use. It is
> imposed upon the automobile consumer. No bargaining is engaged in with
> respect to it. . . . The form warranty is not only standard with Chrysler but
> . . . it is the uniform warranty of General Motors, Inc., Ford, . . . the "Big
> Three" . . . represent 93.5% of the passenger-car production for 1958. . . .
>   The gross inequality of bargaining position occupied by the consumer in the
> automobile industry is thus apparent. There is no competition among the car
> makers in the area of express warranty.[47]

THE ECONOMICS OF DAMAGES FOR BREACH OF CONTRACT

As was implied earlier, a major goal of common-law courts is expectation
protection—that is, providing protection for agreed-upon expectations to
be fulfilled.[48] The goal is to be attained through the rule of financial
equivalent performance that is designed to restore the plaintiff to a position as good as if the promise had been honored. Another goal of contract
law is the maintenance of incentives; parties should be motivated to honor
their promises. However, courts do not explicitly recognize this goal.[49]
Since, in line with Justice Holmes, the obligation imposed by a contract is
not to comply, but either to comply or to pay damages, the goal of expectation protection is all too clear. The offended party is to be given a sum of
money in damages to place him in as good a position as he would have
enjoyed had the contract been honored.

Specifically, if a contract exists according to which one party sells 100
widgets at price p on a specific day, and on that date the market price s is
higher than p, a breach may result. The buyer will want to enforce the
contract, whereas the seller will want to avoid its enforcement. Should the
seller breach, the buyer is forced to purchase the widgets on the open
market at price s. The difference between the two prices, d, would be the
damages that would compensate the buyer for not obtaining the widget at
price p. Thus, for each widget the damage measure d is equal to or larger
than $s - p$. It can be larger than $s - p$ because of transaction costs.

Implementing the rule of financial equivalent performance requires an
active market for the contracted commodity. In its absence, the plaintiff
cannot find a replacement to make up for the breach, and the price for a
reimbursement cannot be properly determined. Thus, for example, when

47. *Ibid.*
48. J. H. Barton, "The Economic Basis of Damages for Breach of Contract," *Journal of Legal Studies* 1 (June 1972): 277–304.
49. *Ibid.*, p. 278.

a contract is entered into for the purchase and sale of a product manufactured to order, Barton talks about a nonmarket transaction.[50] Under such circumstances there is no market by which a measure of damages can be defined or by which the injured party can protect himself. Costs and benefits to the different parties may not provide an unequivocal basis for estimation of damages mainly because the cost incurred by the injured party tends to be different from the benefit accrued to the breaching party. Under such conditions completion of a transaction under all'circumstances may not be efficient.

In nonmarket transactions there is a strong incentive for parties to create rules to deal with this breach, and in the absence of such rules courts are called upon to promulgate them. Clearly such rules will affect resource allocation by influencing the probability that parties will continue a performance that is not economically justifiable, and by changing the manner in which parties allocate the cost of covering various risks. Under a number of simplifying assumptions—all markets are competitive except for the goods manufactured to order and sold under contract, parties have similar risk aversion, and parties have complete knowledge of each other's utilities—Barton produces a number of interesting propositions. He shows that if parties have substantial and approximately similar knowledge of the risks involved in the transaction as a whole, any bargained-for allocation of risks incorporated in the contract should be enforced. Such clauses are also referred to as _liquidated-damages clauses_ and are often rejected by the courts, perhaps because courts look upon them as intruding upon their own prerogatives. However, Barton maintains that liquidated-damages clauses should only be rejected on the ground that the negotiation was unfair.[51] Altogether, when parties with equal bargaining power negotiate about risks that both understand equally, the court does best from an economic viewpoint to enforce their understanding much as it enforces a contract where damages are automatically ascertained in an organized market.

Barton also shows with the aid of economic theory that the court in _Hadley_ v. _Baxendale_ was correct in singling out the importance of notice and information.[52] Thus, if the seller knows the risk at the time of entering the contract, damages in the event of casualty loss should be measured by the buyer's full expectation, but disclosure of the magnitude of this expectation must be made to the seller at the time of negotiation.

CONCLUSION

In summary, contract law provides guidelines by which voluntary exchanges of intitial entitlements are expeditiously carried out and disputes

50. _Ibid.,_ p. 280.
51. _Ibid.,_ pp. 286–287.
52. _Hadley_ v. _Baxendale,_ 9 Exch. 341, 156 Eng. Rep. 145 (1854).

in case of breach are settled. The process of contracting goes through a contract-formation stage followed by contract performance, and during each phase specified conditions serve as legal defenses. Financial equivalent performance and *quantum meruit* are the dominating damages rules. Economic analysis of contract law concentrates on the efficiency with which exchanges take place and on whether they are in fact voluntary. In connection with the former, strategies to reduce transaction costs, and in connection with the latter, unconscionable behavior of merchants and their use of form contracts and contracts of adhesion are of interest.

Stipulated damages in agreement

VI

TORT LAW'S BASIC
LEGAL PREMISES

INTRODUCTION

Though tort law has a long and distinguished history, it is today a most dynamic branch of the law, dealing with situations where an initial entitlement has been unintentionally destroyed. In this chapter some major legal concepts and premises are explored, starting with the nature of a tort. The concepts of negligence, duty, and proximate cause are examined, and tort defenses are reviewed. Thereafter, major liability rules are presented and compared, before an examination of damages is undertaken. Trends in tort law are reviewed last.

WHAT IS A TORT?

Broadly speaking, a tort is a civil (seldom a criminal) wrong. Such a wrong occurs when one party, usually unintentionally, destroys another party's initial entitlement by imposing a negative externality on him. The courts can then provide a remedy in the form of damages. When externalities result in the forcible taking of initial entitlements—for example, when a slaughterhouse pollutes the air of the surrounding neighborhood—liability rules can be invoked. Concomitantly government assumes responsibility for the imposition of objectively determined compensation and its prompt payment to the party harmed. *This are of great diffr btwn contract + tort law.*

This issue can be related to transaction cost. Although property rules assume that voluntary transactions can be carried out at relatively low transaction costs, in many circumstances they cannot. When market evaluation of entitlements involves high transaction costs (i.e., market evaluation is either unavailable or very costly compared to collective valuation), and therefore is inefficient, a property rule can be replaced by a liability rule. Thus, for example, accidental damages are a special case of externalities with very high transaction costs, and such damages are covered by liability rules under tort law. As Calabresi and Melamed have stated, whenever "there is no reason to believe that a market, a decentralized system of valuing, will cause people to express their true valuations and hence yield results which all would *in fact* agree are desirable," an argument can be made for moving from a property rule to a liability rule.[1]

In relation to accidents, these authors argue,

> If we were to give victims a property entitlement not to be accidentally injured we would have to require all who engage in activities that may injure individuals to negotiate with them before an accident, and to buy the right to knock off an arm or a leg. Such pre-accident negotiations would be extremely expensive, often prohibitively so. . . . And, after an accident, the loser of the arm or leg can always very plausibly deny that he would have sold it at the price the buyer would have offered.[2]

The law treats a thief differently from an injurer in auto accidents or a polluter in a nuisance case. One reason is found in transaction costs. (A second reason is society's collective decision not to tolerate criminal conduct, even though some individuals are willing to pay to engage in it.) Since before an accident the injured person is unknown, transaction costs in negotiations with a potential victim for the transfer of entitlements are very high. Not so for the thief who often knows what he is going to do and to whom. He could have negotiated for a good that is allowed to be sold. Likewise, relatively low transaction costs are incurred by a stationary-source polluter. It has control over externality-causing events. The polluter knows what it will do, how often, and whom it is likely to hurt. However, it faces a holdout problem; one or more potential victims may be unwilling to sell it their entitlement to clear air or water. Moreover, there may be a freeloader problem—a very high exclusion cost. For example, once one polluter has bought all the entitlements, another may proceed to pollute without paying.

Tort law has a price-system rationale. Individual tortfeasors may meet their tort duties for a price, for an appropriate compensation. Thus, if enterprises unintentionally injure individuals they are not prohibited from operating; they need only pay compensation for the breach of their tort

1. G. Calabresi and D. A. Melamed, "Property Rules, Liability Rules, and Inalienability: One View of the Cathedral," *Harvard Law Review* 85 (April 1972): 1107; see also G. Calabresi, "Torts—The Law of the Mixed Society," in *American Law: The Third Century,* ed. B. Schwartz (South Hackensack, N.J.: Rothman 1976).

2. Calabresi and Melamed, "Property Rules," pp. 1108–1109. Copyright © 1972 by the Harvard Law Review Association.

duty. (These principles, by the way, are substantially different from those of the criminal law system, which is little concerned with compensation of the injured individual against whom the crime is committed.) The civil action for a tort is commenced and maintained by the injured person himself, and its purpose is to compensate him for the damage he has suffered, at the expense of the wrongdoer. The tort system thus reallocates the costs of harm that is unintentionally imposed by a tortfeasor. It is the legal format created to protect the distribution of income from the interferences brought about by certain injurious interactions. If an individual breaches his tort duty to others—if he destroys an initial entitlement—he is required to pay for the imposition. The compensation is essentially an income transfer from one party to the other and creates a deterrent to wrongdoing. Specifically, incentives are created not to destroy entitlements unless the expected gains from the destruction offset at a minimum the anticipated required compensation.

Let us look at the main elements in an important tort, negligence, with an injured individual seeking compensation from his injurer (tortfeasor) for damages. To be awarded compensation in a negligence suit, the plaintiff must prove that the following technical requirements are met:

1. That the defendant's actions were negligent, that is, that the defendant's actions fell below the standard of those of a "reasonable" man and thereby caused injury. An injury without proof of negligence and of defendant's deficient conduct is not compensable.

2. That the defendant owed the plaintiff a "duty," that is, an obligation to pay for any injuries the defendant caused with respect to this particular class of plaintiffs. Duties, as will be seen later, are defined by the statutes and cases of each particular jurisdiction and essentially define the class of persons to which the defendant owes an obligation not to injure without compensation.

3. That the particular defendant in fact caused the particular injury complained of. A further requirement, known as proximate cause, is the legal determination that a particular defendant was so intimately involved in causing the injury complained of that the legal system will hold him liable for the damage.

NEGLIGENCE   *unintentional tort*

The tort of negligence is probably the most commonly known tort. It involves a failure to exercise the care of an ordinary prudent and careful man. Accident cases, mainly negligence cases, constitute the single largest item of business on the civil side of the nation's trial courts.[3]

3. Richard A. Posner, "A Theory of Negligence," *Journal of Legal Studies* 1 (January 1972): 29.

[handwritten margin note at top: Shifted burden of creating an export industry put on backs of workers. (by Shaw) for 60-65 yrs, growth of industry on back of poor. Finally, worker's compensation came about]

Negligence as a legal concept has substantively changed over time. Until the nineteenth century, a person was liable for harm caused by his actions whether or not he was at fault. In the landmark case of *Brown* v. *Kendall*, Chief Justice Lemuel Shaw of the Massachusetts Supreme Court set aside the old application of a writ of trespass.[4] In turn, he formulated the beginnings of a doctrine of liability. This 1850 case dealt with a defendant seeking to separate two fighting dogs by beating them with a stick. Of course, the dogs moved about a good deal and when the defendant raised his stick over his shoulder to strike them, he happened to hit the plaintiff in the eye. *[handwritten margin note: from writ of trespass, he would have been liable]* The report did not indicate whether the defendant or the plaintiff was in any way negligent. Shaw developed the principle that when harm occurs as the consequence of an unintended contact, it is actionable only on the basis of negligence. He thereby established that unintentional contact on one's interests, achieved through the conduct of another, was not a trespass at all in the sense that it was a tort, even if damage ensued.

As C. O. Gregory concluded, "under this new principle the tort of trespass could occur *only* when there was an intentional invasion of one's interest . . . no longer was there any theory of absolute liability without fault in our common law to govern the disposition of cases where one sustained harm unintentionally inflicted as a result of another's conduct."[5]

It appears that a major reason for Shaw's ruling was his interest in reducing the liability of the young industrial firms that were springing up by the hundreds in the mid-nineteenth century; in this way he hoped to expedite the industrialization of Massachusetts in particular and of the United States in general. In a sense, Shaw's ruling amounted to subsidies for young industrial enterprises by removing the costs of compensating injured workers or employing expensive safety devices.

However, it did not take long for juries to become uncooperative and usually rule in favor of the plaintiff. In rural areas, in particular, juries tended to side with the local plaintiff, harboring strong feelings against remote corporate giants. To counteract "biased" juries, the courts began, particularly in New York State where most of the railway-crossing injury cases were initiated, to apply the doctrine of *contributory negligence*. Under this doctrine, as will be discussed later, any even minor negligence of the plaintiff that could be causally linked to the injury implied that the defendent was not liable. The plaintiff therefore was bound to show that he did not, by his negligence, bring the misfortune upon himself. The argument of contributory negligence was used by the court to justify a nonsuit. It was an ingenious device that gave the court almost complete freedom to accept or reject jury participation at its pleasure.

---

4. *Brown* v. *Kendall*, 60 Mass. (6 Cush.) 292 (1850).
5. C. O. Gregory, "Trespass to Negligence to Absolute Liability," *Virginia Law Review* 37 (April 1951): 367.

Tort (Shaw
Law (Cardozo 1920
(Trainer

At the end of the nineteenth century, the tort system was found wanting when tested against social needs. Particularly, tort law was found unacceptable to an industrialized society when applied to workers who were injured *around* by a job-related cause. Workers' compensation laws were passed in the *WWII* United Kingdom and the United States, thus removing job-related accidents from the tort system. *→ does NOT put burden on employer*

In addition to human considerations, the extraordinarily high transaction costs of the existing system played an important role in the enactment of workers' compensation laws. They have also led to consideration of no-fault accident insurance.[6] Since motor vehicle injuries tend to involve very costly litigation, Robert E. Keeton and Jeffry O'Connell proposed a no-fault insurance system,[7] to be taken up in detail in the next chapter.

So far we have discussed the evolution of negligence in tort law in the face of prevailing social and economic conditions; it is time now to turn to more operational issues. A fundamental determination that must be made in the vast majority of tort claims revolves around the issue of the defendant's negligence. The question of actual negligence is almost always factual, requiring a jury determination. A key issue in determining liability relates to the defendant's conduct: Has it been such that under the same or similar circumstances a reasonable man would not have caused the resulting injury? Thus, would the conduct of a reasonable man have avoided the ensuing harm?

In *Osborne v. Montgomery*, Chief Justice Rosenberry carefully considered the dimensions of negligence:

> Every person is negligent when, without intending to do any wrong, he does an act or omits to take such precaution that under the circumstances he, as an ordinarily prudent person, ought reasonably to foresee that he will thereby expose the interest of another to an unreasonable risk of harm. In determining whether his conduct will subject the interests of another to an unreasonable risk of harm, a person is required to take into account such of the surrounding circumstances as would be taken into account by a reasonably prudent person and possess such knowledge as is possessed by an ordinarily reasonable person and to use such judgment and discretion as is exercised by persons of reasonable intelligence under the same or similar circumstances.[8]

Judge Learned Hand provided a more formal definition of the legal standard of negligence (i.e., the standard of care required by the law). In

6. John G. Turnbull *et al.*, *Economic and Social Security,* 3rd ed. (New York: Ronald Press, 1968).

7. For a very early statement see, Robert E. Keeton and Jeffry O'Connell, *Basic Protection for the Traffic Victim: A Blueprint for Reforming Automobile Insurance* (Boston: Little, Brown, 1965). A particularly thoughtful analysis of no-fault automobile compensation plans can be found in G. Calabresi, *The Costs of Accidents: A Legal and Economic Analysis* (New Haven, Conn.: Yale University Press, 1970).

8. *Osborne* v. *Montgomery*, 203 Wis. 233, 234 N. W. 372 (1931).

United States v. Carroll Towing Company, he offered the following algebraic formula: "If the probability be called P; the injury L; and the burden B; liability depends upon whether B is less than L multiplied by P; i.e., whether B is smaller than PL."[9] In short, in line with the Hand formula, the defendant is guilty of negligence if the loss caused by the accident multiplied by the probability of the accident occurring exceeds the burden of the precautions that the defendant might have taken to avert the mishap. Although the burden of precautions is the cost of avoiding the accident, the loss multiplied by the probability of the accident is the expected harm that the precautions would have averted. If a larger cost could have been avoided by incurring a smaller cost, Judge Hand would have preferred the smaller cost to be incurred.

The philosophy underlying the Learned Hand formula can be summarized as follows: A reasonable man, before taking any action, weighs the costs and benefits of that action not only from his own personal perspective but also from the broader perspective of all the individuals within the possible scope of any resulting harm. From the economist's point of view, the Learned Hand formula seeks a tort system that maximizes social welfare over the action of all individuals involved in a given tortious act. When an individual's actions fall below the reasonable-man standard, he is assessed liability for any resulting harm. Knowledge of this compensatory requirement creates incentives for individuals to weigh their actions from a social welfare point of view.

The Hand formula, that negligent behavior is the failure to invest resources up to a level that equals the expected saving in damages, is in harmony with common sense, as is well demonstrated by an example given by Schwartz and Komesar:

> A customer walking down the aisle of a supermarket knocks a jar of baby food to the floor, where it shatters. A few seconds later, another customer turns in to the aisle, fails to see the puddle on the floor, slips, and breaks a leg. It would not have been "reasonable" to expect that the owner of the market would station personnel in each aisle to offer continuous warnings about wet spots and to provide for instant cleanup. In this case, the cost of preventing the injury would far exceed the expected loss ($P \times L$). Common sense would almost certainly lead a jury to conclude that negligence had not occurred. But if the wet spot had been left for thirty to forty minutes, the verdict would be likely to go the other way, because the cost of policing the aisles at such an interval is relatively low, and the likelihood of injury occurring during the longer interval is considerably greater. As the cost of preventing a mishap

9. *United States v. Carroll Towing Co.,* 159 F.2d 169 (2d Cir. 1947). Hand's formula's "utilitarian" origin can be seen clearly in H. Terry, "Negligence," *Harvard Law Review* 29 (November 1915): 40–54. In it Terry defined fault as conduct involving unreasonably great risk, and isolated magnitude, principal object, collateral object, utility, and necessity of risk as determining whether a particular risk was so great as to be "unreasonable."

rises and the likelihood becomes more remote, failing to avoid it becomes increasingly reasonable.[10]

Despite its presumed algebraic precision and common sense, the Learned Hand formula poses a number of serious problems. It makes stringent assumptions about the attitude of different people toward risk. Although transactors can be risk-averse, risk-preferring, or neutral, the Learned Hand formula implicitly assumes risk neutrality. Yet in the real world it is not uncommon to find some parties to a tortious act who are risk-preferring and others who are risk-averse. Further shortcomings will be taken up in detail in the next chapter.

DUTY

One essential element of negligence is the demonstration of a duty. It relates to a person's responsibility not to destroy another person's initial entitlement. The defendant who owes no duty to the plaintiff cannot be negligent. Thus, the definition of the duties owed by defendants to plaintiffs in part determines the scope and range of the negligence tort. The scope and range of duties have been evolving and expanding over time. This expansion has been directed toward making individuals more concerned about the results of their actions on others. It has encouraged greater internalization of the costs and benefits associated with various actions. In general, the concept of duty has become much more inclusive.

One example of the expansion of a duty can be seen in the changes in case law over time as it relates to the duty of landowners and land occupiers toward trespassers. Initially, landowners were not bound by a duty of due care to regulate their conduct in contemplation of the presence of trespassers intruding on private structures. They only owed a "duty" of due care to *invitees*. But as the 1921 case of *Hynes v. New York Central Railroad Company*[11] reveals, the courts had trouble with the conceptual distinction between a trespasser, an invitee, or a traveler upon the adjacent public way. In *Hynes* the landowner's obligation with respect to the particular plaintiff was dependent on this classification. Even though, by definition, a negligent act that would cause an injury to an invitee is no different than one causing an injury to a trespasser, the landowner was not required to compensate the trespasser. He owed the trespasser only the duty of no willfull or wanton harm. Thus, the wealth relationship between landowner and trespasser was such that the landowner's negligent acts gave rise to no

10. W. B. Schwartz and N. K. Komesar, *Doctors, Damages and Deterrence: An Economic View of Medical Malpractice,* R-2340-NIH/RC (Santa Monica: Rand Corporation, June 1978), p. 3.
11. *Hynes* v. *New York Central Railroad Co.,* 231 N.Y. 229 (1921).

liability for compensation. Perhaps the reason for this rule was the implicit discouragement of would-be trespassers.

However, the concept of duty of landowners and hosts toward trespassers and others changed as time passed. In *O'Keefe* v. *South End Rowing Club*,[12] the California Supreme Court in 1966 distinguished between varying duties toward invitees, trespassers, implied licensees, and trespassing children. Although the distinctions are much finer in this case, the trend of the law is toward expanding the scope and range of the duty concept, giving rise to a greater scope of liability for a variety of acts. As the scope of duties expands, actors must internalize more and more costs and benefits and balance them in their choice calculus.

✱ In the case of *Rowland* v. *Christian*,[13] the landowner and host's duty was further expanded. The plaintiff, while a social guest in the defendant's apartment, severed some tendons and nerves when the porcelain handle on a bathroom faucet cracked in his hand. Although the defendant had told the plaintiff about the handle some weeks earlier, she did not mention it before the plaintiff went to the bathroom. The California Supreme Court ruled that

> The proper test to be applied to the liability of the possessor of land . . . is whether in the management of his property he has acted as a reasonable man in view of the probability of injury to others, and although the plaintiff's status as a trespasser, licensee or invitee may in the light of effects giving rise to such status have some bearing on the question of liability, the status is not determinative.[14]

The court went on to hold that

> where the occupier of land is aware of a concealed condition involving in the absence of precaution an unreasonable risk of harm to those coming in contact with it and is aware that a person on the premises is about to come in contact with it, the trier of fact can reasonably conclude that a failure to warn or repair the condition constitutes negligence.[15]

Thus, landowners (and hosts) have thrust upon themselves an increased responsibility to care for those who use their property. Consequently, the range and scope of their responsibility are expanded to cover further classes of prospective plaintiffs.

Courts not only have expanded existing duty concepts but also have imposed new duties where none existed previously. For example, in *Ellis* v. *Trowen Frozen Products, Inc.*[16] a California court of appeals ruled in 1968

---

12. *O'Keefe* v. *South End Rowing Club,* 64 Cal. 2d 729 (1966).
13. *Rowland* v. *Christian,* 69 Cal. 2d 108 (1968).
14. *Ibid.*, p. 319.
15. *Ibid.*
16. *Ellis* v. *Trowen Frozen Products, Inc.,* 264 Cal. App. 2d 499 (1968).

that a frozen food company is under a duty to watch out for small children using its services. It must use reasonable care to guard for their safety as regards the premises of the ice cream truck or face the prospect of civil liability for resulting injuries. The activity of providing ice cream bars to children must now bear the added expense of watching out for the children's safety by using lookouts or other devices to prevent accidents. Creation of this duty of ice cream sellers has distributional effects. The burden of protecting small children buying ice cream from trucks has been shifted from the child and his family to the vendors. How much of this cost is shifted forward to the customer depends on the relative demand and supply elasticities of truck-catered ice cream.

Since an injury to a small child is a loss of great magnitude, a wide range of cost-preventive activities can be considered using the Hand formula. They must be considered if the ice cream supplier is to escape liability for harm resulting from his failure to use these devices. Although children and their families may assume part of the burden for these additional safety devices by paying part of the cost incurred by the ice cream vendor, this cost could become so great as to make truck catering of ice cream unprofitable.

Moreover, an additional major tort duty has been added, for negligently inflicted emotional distress and its consequent physical harm. Past law held that there could be no recovery for injuries, physical or mental, incurred by fright negligently induced. In *Battalla* v. *State of New York*, the court considered the negligence of an employee of the state of New York who, placing an infant in a chair lift at a mountain ski center, failed to secure and properly lock the belt intended to protect the occupant. As a result the infant became frightened and hysterical on the descent and "suffered severe emotional and neurological disturbances with residual physical manifestation."[17] Although earlier courts, such as the *Mitchell* court,[18] had found that individuals negligently exposed to fright or fear were not eligible for compensation, the court here ruled that the inflictor of the fright must bear the cost.

Individuals exposed to fright or scare are in a poor position to avoid injury. To attempt to escape such an injury would require them to engage in very extensive cost-avoidance procedures. Placing the duty of liability for negligently caused emotional distress upon the party who inflicts it—for example, the chair lift acitivity operator—assigns liability to the most cost-effective place. The activity operator is usually in the best position to evaluate the most cost-effective steps to prevent emotional distress and resulting physical harm. He knows the activity, its production function, and the range and scope of variations that can be made to reduce the risk of emotional distress.

17. *Battalla* v. *State of New York*, 10 N.Y. 2d 237 (1961).
18. *Mitchell* v. *Rochester Ry. Co.*, 151 N.Y. 107 (1896).

PROXIMATE CAUSE

Proximate cause "is that cause which, in natural and continuous sequence, unbroken by an efficient intervening cause, produced the injury (or damage complained of) and without which such result would not have occurred."[19] In an injurious event, the rules and doctrines of proximate cause seek to determine which actor is to be held legally responsible for the resulting harm. Often the combined negligence of many actors causes a given injury. The doctrine of proximate cause determines which of the actors must bear the cost of the resulting harm. As an example, suppose two negligent drivers collide and injure a pedestrian. Under the rules of proximate cause, both drivers would be held liable for the full extent of the injury, although in some states they would share the liability. They are both held liable because the resulting harm caused by their negligence was foreseeable; consequently the expectation of it should have entered their choice calculus and affected their behavior. In terms of the Hand formula, when harm resulting from an actor's negligence is foreseeable the burden that the defendant carries in order to avoid a judgment of liability due to his negligence is higher than if it were not foreseeable. (Since the resulting harm is foreseeable the probability of occurrence to be placed in the Hand formula is higher than it would be otherwise.) Thus, whenever a resulting harm is foreseeable, the rules of proximate cause will impose liability on the actor, forcing him to be concerned about the foreseeable effects of his actions upon others.

However, suppose the resulting harm of an actor's negligence is unforeseeable, as in *Overseas Tankship Ltd.* v. *Morts Dock and Engineering Company Ltd.*[20] As this case illustrates, foreseeability of the resulting harm from an actor's negligence makes a substantial difference in determining the extent and scope of the negligent actor's liability. The court declared that "it is the foresights of the reasonable man which alone can determine responsibility."[21] The rationale for this legal doctrine is that an actor can only internalize a foreseeable result of his negligence into his choice calculus. Any other result, by definition unforeseeable, cannot be effectively brought into the actor's choice calculus and cannot affect his behavior. Consequently, the proximate-cause rule that liability only extends to foreseeable issues has a clear economic rationale.

Another aspect of this general rule limiting liability to foreseeable harms concerns the rule that a negligent tortfeasor is not liable to the unforeseen plaintiff. This is essentially the rule of the famous 1928 New York Court of

---

19. *Kettman* v. *Levine,* 115 Cal. App. 2d 844, 253 P.2d 102 (1953).

20. *Overseas Tankship Ltd.* v. *Morts Dock and Engineering Co., Ltd.,* Privy Council, A. C. 338 (1961).

21. *Ibid.* This case has not generally been accepted in the United States.

Appeals case of *Palsgraf* v. *Long Island Railroad Co.*[22] Writing for the majority Justice Cardozo stated, "Life will have to be made over, and human nature transformed, before provision so extravagant can be accepted as the norm of conduct, the customary standard to which behavior must conform."[23] Clearly, liability based on unforeseeable consequences is so unpredictable that a person cannot bring within his choice calculus such a system of legal responsibility. Thus the probability of a freak accident is by definition very low and the expected accident cost will usually be low. In a truly freak accident, such as that in *Palsgraf*, the expected accident cost may come close to zero.

DEFENSES

A number of defenses may be invoked to avoid a tort liability. These will be discussed under the headings Assumption of Risk, Immunities, and Contributory Negligence. But first a few words about custom as a defense are in order.

In medical malpractice cases, as will be discussed later in more detail, a special point is made of the defense of custom. The duty of care of a physician toward his patient is to comply with the *customary* standards of the medical profession in the *area* in which the physician is practicing. Thus, the physician implicitly promises to treat patients with the care customary among physicians in the area, and if he fails to do so he is guilty of malpractice. However, customary compliance is more "some evidence" of nonnegligence than a complete defense.

I. ASSUMPTION OF RISK

People vary greatly as to their willingness to take risks. Some are risk-neutral, others are risk-averse, and still others are risk-preferring. A risk-preferring person may evaluate the dangers and decide that he can increase his welfare by taking the risk; he is thus held accountable for any resulting injury to himself.

For example, in *Murphy* v. *Steeplechase Amusement Co.*,[24] the plaintiff was injured in an amusement park. He stepped into a "Flopper," which is a moving belt running upward on an inclined plane. Jerking motions tend to throw visitors to a padded floor. The plaintiff, a vigorous young man, entered the "Flopper" with a young woman, later his wife, who said, when asked whether she thought that a fall might be expected, "I took a chance." The plaintiff took the chance with her, but was less lucky than his companion and suffered a fracture of the kneecap. Justice Cardozo, writing for the

22. *Palsgraf* v. *Long Island Railroad Co.*, 248 N.Y. 339 (1928).
23. *Ibid.*, p. 343.
24. *Murphy* v. *Steeplechase Amusement Co.*, 250 N.Y. 479 (1929).

court, held that "one who takes part in such a sport accepts the dangers that inhere in it so far as they are obvious and necessary, just as a fencer accepts the risk of a thrust by his antagonist or a spectator at a ball game the chance of contact with the ball."[25]

The rationale of this case is that a person who foresees the risks of his prospective activity and enters them into his choice calculus accepts the responsibility for the resulting outcome. He takes the risk only after being able to evaluate the relevant costs and benefits. The plaintiff's implicit or explicit evaluation of those risks apparently was such that he decided he could increase his welfare by his action and thus could be held to have assumed the risk and to have been accountable for any resulting injury to himself.

2. IMMUNITIES

In general, government officials and agencies have been granted sovereign immunity. It precludes them from being sued for tortious acts. However, a distinction prevails concerning the nature of the decision made by government. Sovereign immunity is granted for harm that governmental decisions cause if these decisions are discretionary policy decisions. However, to the extent that the decisions are ministerial in nature, no immunization is granted. In the following chapter more will be said about sovereign immunity and its economic aspects.

3. CONTRIBUTORY NEGLIGENCE

If a defendant has been found to be negligent with respect to a particular plaintiff, he may still escape liability upon proof that the plaintiff was contributorily negligent. To be contributorily negligent, the plaintiff must have failed to exercise due care and this breach must have contributed to the tortious result. A victim who is found contributorily negligent may then be barred from recovery, even though the defendant was negligent.

A number of different defenses based on contributory negligence can be made. In the orthodox form, the defense completely bars the plaintiff's recovery as long as he failed to exercise due care. Thus, one modified form could be that the plaintiff's contributory negligence bars his recovery if, and only if, the plaintiff's prevention costs were lower than the defendant's.

Although these two forms of contributory negligence involve an all-or-nothing (binary) approach to liability, comparative negligence also considers the contributory aspect. However, instead of being binary, comparative negligence reduces rather than bars recovery. Basically the reduction is by the percentage by which the victim's negligence contributed to the result of the tortious act. Since contributory negligence and comparative negligence are major liability rules, they will be taken up in detail.

25. *Ibid.*, p. 250.

LIABILITY RULES—INTRODUCTORY CLASSIFICATION

By what rule or standard should we determine whether a defendant, having destroyed an initial entitlement, is liable and therefore should pay for the tortious act? J. P. Brown has identified eight different liability rules.[26]

No liability (the victim is liable under all circumstances) and *strict liability* (the injurer is liable under all circumstances) are symmetrical.

Under the *negligence rule,* the victim is liable unless the injurer is found negligent. Under a *strict liability with contributory negligence rule,* the injurer is liable unless the victim is found negligent. Thus, these two rules, too, are symmetrical.

Under the *negligence rule with contributory negligence*, the injurer is liable only if he is negligent and the victim is not, with the victim liable otherwise. Under *strict liability with dual contributory negligence,* the victim is liable if he is negligent and the injurer is not, with the injurer liable otherwise. Again these two rules are symmetrical.

A further rule is *relative negligence*. The injurer is liable under this rule if the increment to accident avoidance per dollar of avoidance by him is greater than that per dollar of avoidance by the victim—in short, if the money that could be spent by the injurer on avoidance is more cost-effective than that which could be spent by the victim.

Finally, there is the *comparative-negligence* rule. Under this rule liability is apportioned according to the relative liability of the two parties. Under the comparative-negligence rule, negligence can be defined as a marginal or an average concept. In the former case, negligence is the incremental reduction in accident probability per dollar spent, and the liability of the injurer is his negligence divided by the negligence of both parties.

The different liability rules, except that of comparative negligence, are presented graphically in Figure 6-1. The graphs are taken from Brown, "Toward an Economic Theory of Liability."[27] Here, X represents the effort of the injurer to prevent harm, and Y represents the effort of the victim to avoid harm; X^* represents the legal standard of negligence for the injurer, and Y^* that for the victim. Finally, Ω is the optimal amount of protection from an overall point of view, where the marginal cost of protection is equal to the marginal expected benefit from the protection. The injurer is liable in the shaded area. Thus in part *a* (no liability), there is no shaded area since the injurer is never liable, but in part *b* (strict liability), the entire area is shaded with the injurer liable under all circustances.

---

26. J. P. Brown, "Toward an Economic Theory of Liability," *Journal of Legal Studies* 2 (June 1973): 323–349.

27. *Ibid.,* pp. 330–331.

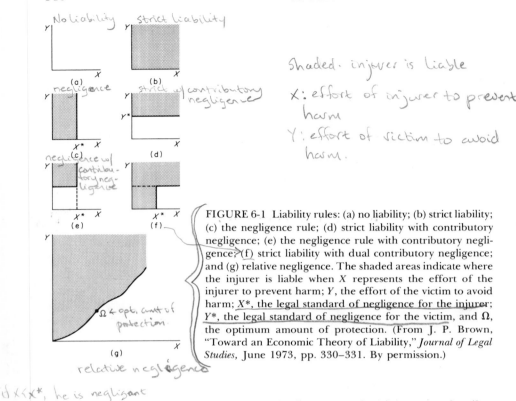

Handwritten annotations:

Shaded: injurer is liable

X: effort of injurer to prevent harm

Y: effort of victim to avoid harm.

(a) No liability
(b) strict liability
(c) negligence
(d) strict w/ contributory negligence
(e) negligence w/ contributory negligence
(f) strict w/ dual contributory negligence
(g) relative negligence

Ω ← opt. amt of protection

if x < x*, he is negligent

FIGURE 6-1 Liability rules: (a) no liability; (b) strict liability; (c) the negligence rule; (d) strict liability with contributory negligence; (e) the negligence rule with contributory negligence; (f) strict liability with dual contributory negligence; and (g) relative negligence. The shaded areas indicate where the injurer is liable when X represents the effort of the injurer to prevent harm; Y, the effort of the victim to avoid harm; X^*, the legal standard of negligence for the injurer; Y^*, the legal standard of negligence for the victim, and Ω, the optimum amount of protection. (From J. P. Brown, "Toward an Economic Theory of Liability," *Journal of Legal Studies*, June 1973, pp. 330–331. By permission.)

I will next discuss three major negligence rules in some detail—contributory negligence, comparative negligence, and strict liability.

THE RULE OF CONTRIBUTORY NEGLIGENCE

Handwritten: all or nothing (binary) approach to liability; good expla.- pg. 143

In terms of Figure 6-1, under the contributory-negligence rule the shaded area (indicating that the injurer is liable) covers the case where the victim has met his legal standard of negligence but the injurer has not done so.

As mentioned earlier, both orthodox and modified contributory negligence are affirmative defenses that are traditionally afforded by tort law. The defense of contributory negligence has a long history. It entered English law in the beginning of the nineteenth century;[28] *Brown* v. *Kendall* introduced contributory negligence as an integral part of American negligence doctrine in 1850.[29]

28. *Butterfield* v. *Forrester,* 103 Eng. Rep. 926 (K. B. 1809).
29. *Brown* v. *Kendall,* 60 Mass. (6 Cush.) 292, 296 (1850).

[handwritten note at top: This led industry (railroad) to not put brakes on locomotives led to build up of railroad industry.]

Let us examine the contributory-negligence rule and some of its compli-cations. Assume a $100 risk that the defendant could prevent for $80, but that the plaintiff himself could prevent for $10. Although the defendant may be negligent, the plaintiff is more efficient in preventing the accident. The economic justification of the rule is to give the plaintiff an incentive to spend his $10, since he is the most efficient accident preventer.

Complications arise when we reverse the numbers. Now the plaintiff can prevent the risk for $80 and the defendant for only $10. Although the plaintiff is contributorily negligent, the defendant should be held liable since the defendant is in a better position to eliminate the risk. The modified contributory-negligence rule takes care of this matter, since the plaintiff's contributory negligence should bar his recovery only if his pre-vention costs are lower than the defendant's.

Thus, contributory negligence focuses on the fact that the plaintiff may *[handwritten: Posner]* be an efficient risk preventer. Although negligence law without any contributory-negligence defense is unlikely to be socially efficient, various scholars have argued that the contributory-negligence rule as a complete defense fails to produce efficient results.[30]

Although economists can build models that include risk neutrality and zero information costs under which contributory negligence is an efficient standard, in real-life situations efficient results are unlikely to prevail. Some reasons follow.

For the Learned Hand formula to be applied effectively, all parties must be risk-neutral and know that this neutrality is a fact. If one party is indeed risk-neutral but the other is risk-averse or risk-preferring, no efficient accident prevention is likely.

Turning to the zero-information-cost assumption, it is in fact very costly for the potential victim to be able to predict that his injury will occur and that another party will assume tort liability. Moreover, it is costly for the potential victim to know and understand the contributory-negligence rule and its applications. And if such understanding is too costly, the rule will not reliably deter.

A further reason why contributory negligence is unlikely to generate efficient safety incentives relates to the probability that compensating dam-ages will not cover the full cost of the accident. Reasons include the prevalence of contingency-fee arrangements in personal-injury litigations (if successful, the plaintiff receives only part of the award); the fact that the victim who files a tort claim subjects himself to the misery of litigation with its time costs and very real emotional costs; and the low probability that tort damages will fully compensate the victim.

In the literature two additional claims have been made against the ef-

30. G. Schwartz, "Contributory and Comparative Negligence: A Reappraisal," *Yale Law Journal* 87 (March 1978): 710.

ficiency of contributory-negligence rules. G. Schwartz points to psychological complexities and specifically to the victim whose action was mindless rather than rational. As examples, he gives motorists who absentmindedly take their eyes off the road or who drive across well-marked railroad crossings without slowing down, and pedestrians who jaywalk into the path of cars.[31] Although I do not deny such events, I wonder whether they cannot be placed within an economic benefit–cost framework. Thus, depending on the harm that jaywalkers must fear to befall them and the likelihood of such harm, it is more or less likely that they will absentmindedly jaywalk. Finally, it has been argued that "the plaintiff's unreasonable conduct may effectively be prevented by the defendant."[32] G. Schwartz offers a number of examples in which the defendant appears better able than the plaintiff to prevent conduct likely to result in accidents. Thus, the employee who is uncomfortable wearing protective goggles might wear them if comfortable ones were provided by the employer. Or the manufacturer can more easily design products that offer little opportunity for injuries due to carelessness.

Schwartz concludes, in relation to efficiency, that "in sum, there is inadequate reason to believe that any contributory negligence rule is a good idea in safety terms; the traditional rule, moreover, appears to be a distinctly bad idea."[33]

Though economists have been particularly interested in the safety rationale, and therefore the accident-prevention aspects, of negligence rules for the sake of resource-allocation efficiency, there are also fairness considerations. Fairness commands that if the defendant is found to have engaged in tortious acts, faulty, unreasonable, or wrongful behavior by the plaintiff himself should be reflected by either denying the plaintiff a defense or by reducing the plaintiff's damages. As long as an accident would not have occurred except for the plaintiff's faulty, unreasonable, or wrongful behavior, it is not fair to ignore the plaintiff's contribution to the outcome. Contributory negligence as a liability-denying rule raises serious questions as to its fairness, compared to a liability-dividing rule, such as comparative negligence. This will be taken up next.

→ ② THE RULE OF COMPARATIVE NEGLIGENCE

As mentioned earlier, comparative negligence can be looked upon as a special case of the broadly interpreted rule of contributory negligence. The all-or-nothing (binary) approach to liability adopted by the rule of con-

---

31. *Ibid.*, pp. 713–719.
32. *Ibid.*, p. 720.
33. *Ibid.*, p. 721.

tributory negligence has been widely criticized, with some justification. Harper and James state,

> There is no justification—in either policy or doctrine—for the rule of contributory negligence, except for the feeling that if one man is to be held liable, because of his fault, then the fault of him who seeks to enforce that liability should also be considered. But this notion does not require the all-or-nothing rule, which would exonerate a very negligent defendant for even the slight fault of his victim. The logical corollary of the fault principle would be a rule of comparative or proportional negligence, not the present rule.[34]

In consequence, a significant number of jurisdictions have adopted general comparative-negligence schemes, among them 32 states,[35] Great Britain, all Canadian provinces, New Zealand, and some Australian states. These statutes or decisional laws provide that contributory negligence reduces, rather than bars, recovery. The reduction is by the percentage by which the victim's negligence contributed to the accident. Thus in California, for example, the rule is that in an action for negligence resulting in injury to a person or property, the contributory negligence of the person injured in person or property does not bar recovery, but the damages awarded shall be diminished in proportion to the amount of fault attributable to that person. Still, though "liability in proportion to fault"[36] is the slogan of comparative-negligence rules, several variations are possible. Thus, although in many United States jurisdictions, comparative-negligence standards generally call for a comparison of the extent to which the plaintiff and the defendant have departed from the standard of due care, in the United Kingdom the emphasis is on the parties' relative responsibility for the accident. Responsibility here is a concept that seems receptive to a number of considerations, including, for example, the relative extent to which the parties' conduct has caused the accident.

Some jurisdictions in the United States rely on a pure form of comparative negligence, whereas others use modified forms. Under the pure form the recovery of the plaintiff is reduced by the proportion of his negligence to the sum of his and the defendant's negligence. Under the modified forms, the plaintiff's recovery is reduced in this very manner, but he receives no recovery whatsoever either if he was more negligent than the defendant or, depending on the variant of the modified form, if he and the defendant were equally negligent.

Matters are complicated by the fact that there are different ways in which the negligence of the plaintiff and defendant can be compared.[37] On the

34. Fowler Harper and Fleming James, Jr., *The Law of Torts* (Boston: Little, Brown, 1956), sect. 22.3, p. 1207.
35. H. L. Sherman, "An Analysis of Pennsylvania's Comparative Negligence Statute," *University of Pittsburgh Law Review* 38 (Fall 1976): 55.
36. *Li* v. *Yelllow Cab Co.*, 13 Cal. 3d 804, 810, 532 P.2d 1226, 19 Cal. Rptr. 858, 862 (1975).
37. Schwartz, "Contributory and Comparative Negligence," pp. 705–706.

one hand, the *a.* comparison can be in terms of prevention cost. For example, if A could have prevented the accident for $20 and B for $60, A would bear a liability three times as great as B. Each party's share of total liability could be determined as follows:

Party's share of liability

$$= \frac{(\text{total prevention costs}) - (\text{party's prevention costs})}{\text{total prevention costs}}$$

On the other hand, the *b* comparison could be in terms of net losses incurred by the parties' failure to take preventive measures—the differences between A's and B's prevention costs and expected value of the risk that A and B allowed to materialize. For example, if the expected value of the risk is $100 and again the respective prevention costs are $20 and $60, the differences are $80 and $40, respectively. Thus, A would bear a liability twice as large as B. The liability of A and B could be determined as follows:

Party's share of liability

$$= \frac{(\text{expected value of risk}) - (\text{party's prevention costs})}{2 \times (\text{expected value of risk}) - (\text{total prevention costs})}$$

The two methods of comparison can give very different results, especially when the difference between the prevention costs of A and B is either very large or very small. Thus, if the expected value of the risk is again $100 and the prevention costs are $1 and $4, the first method would divide liability 80% to 20%, whereas the second method would divide liability 51% to 49%. However, should prevention costs be $96 and $98, the ratios would be 51% to 49% and 67% to 33%, respectively.

As to its accident-prevention and therefore efficiency aspects, comparative negligence in real-life situations differs little from orthodox or modified contributory negligence. The efficiency argument in connection with comparative negligence is similar to that made in the discussion of contributory negligence. Among the major reasons why comparative-negligence schemes are unlikely to be more efficient than contributory ones is high information cost. Thus, each party would have to invest heavily in order to learn about the prevention possibilities and costs of the other party. Only in the presence of information on the prevention possibilities of both parties can efficient decisions be made.

However, in terms of fairness, comparative negligence is much superior to contributory negligence. For this reason Schwartz concludes that "the fairness criterion establishes a preference for a liability-dividing rule . . . and, among liability-dividing rules for comparative negligence. . . . Comparative negligence is thus the proper rule."[38]

38. *Ibid.*, p. 727.

③ THE RULE OF STRICT LIABILITY

In terms of Figure 6-1, under the strict liability rule the shaded area (indicating that the injurer is liable) is all-inclusive. Thus the defendant is liable under all circumstances.[39]

Strict liability was first applied to cases involving trespassing animals and ultrahazardous activities—often referred to as *traditional strict liability*. I will take this up before turning to product liability.

a) TRADITIONAL STRICT LIABILITY

Traditional strict liability in tort holds that the defendant, even though he did not intentionally cause an injury, must pay damages if he did not live up to an objective, reasonable-care standard. For example, in regard to trespassing wild animals and domestic animals with known dangerous propensities the owner is strictly liable for all injuries resulting from this dangerous propensity. Domestic animals that are not dangerous are usually entitled to one "free bite." The rationale, similar to the negligence theory, is that the utility of keeping a potentially dangerous animal is outweighed by the likelihood and possible extent of the harm.

Traditional strict liability for an ultrahazardous activity relates to an activity that involves a serious risk of harm to persons, land, or chattels of others that cannot be eliminated by exercising utmost care and is not a matter of common usage. Thus blasting, explosive storage, crop dusting, water collection, tunnel construction, drilling of oil wells, and fumigation are considered to engender strict liability. The plaintiff must show that the defendant committed the act or omitted to act and thereby breached his absolute duty, such breach being the cause of the damage sustained. The duty is limited to foreseeable harm to plaintiffs who are damaged from the normally dangerous propensity of the condition or act involved. Therefore, strict liability for blasting extends to the damage caused by flying debris, but not to completely unforeseen events.[40]

If the dangerous act is reasonable and permissible in cost–benefit terms, the actor is still held strictly accountable for the act's miscarriage. For example, in *Luthringer* v. *Moore,* fumigation was allowed, but the sprayer was

---

39. G. Calabresi and J. T. Hirschoff, "Toward a Test for Strict Liability in Torts," *Yale Law Joournal* 81 (May 1972): 1055–1085.

40. An example of the limitation of foreseeable damage is *Madsen* v. *East Jordan Irrigation Co.,* 101 Utah 552, 125 P.2d 794 (1942). The defendant was repairing a canal with the use of explosives, which disturbed the plaintiff's mother mink and caused the mink to kill 230 of their offspring. It is normal for mother minks to kill their offspring when they become excited, and a blaster is held strictly liable for damage caused by flying debris or vibrations. But the defendant was not held liable in this case. The court held that the act of the mother mink was so peculiar that it broke the chain of causation and the plaintiff had to prove negligence on the part of the blaster.

held absolutely accountable, despite all possible precautions, when his dangerous hydrocyanic spray poisoned people in the neighborhood, though he had left a notice warning of the danger.[41]

An economic rationale for strict liability is to deter uneconomical accidents. For example, in *Whitman Hotel Corporation* v. *Elliott and Watrous Engineering Co.* the blaster who used dynamite was found to be able to limit the costs of such an activity better than the neighbor whose house was damaged by the vibrations.[42] Strict liability for ultrahazardous activities forces the actor to consider the social benefits and costs. Therefore, if the necessary activity can be performed by a similar but safer device at the same cost, there is incentive for the actor to adopt the safer method.

The only defense in ultrahazardous liability cases, other than causation, is that the plaintiff voluntarily participated in the ultrahazardous activity and that he negligently caused the miscarriage. This defense provides an incentive for the individual to avoid a possible accident.

b) PRODUCT LIABILITY

The use of products, from soft-drink bottles to automobiles, often results in accidents and damages, sometimes to the purchaser and sometimes to the bystander. Accidental harm in general and accidental harm from a defective product in particular comprise a special case of externalities. In the extreme, and usually at prohibitively high transaction costs, potential victims of harm caused by a defective product could be given an entitlement not to be injured accidentally. They would then negotiate with producers and/or distributors of products who would buy from them the right to impose on them accidental damages. In this manner, externalities would be internalized, but at very high transaction costs. But there are alternatives, and I will review how product liability began as a negligence theory, was expanded under a contract-warranty approach, and now is considered a special case of strict liability.

Historical View of Product Liability

In the nineteenth century product liability was predicated on a contract theory, and the seller was liable only to an individual with whom he was in privity of contract, that is, the immediate buyer. Therefore a manufacturer would be liable to a wholesaler, a wholesaler to a retailer and a retailer to a consumer. The seminal case was *Winterbottom* v. *Wright*, which involved damage caused by a carriage that overturned because of a defective wheel.[43] It was held that an injured coach passenger could not sue the manufacturer because he had no contract with the maker of the carriage.

---

41. *Luthringer* v. *Moore*, 31 Cal. 2d 489, 190 P.2d 1 (1948).

42. *Whitman Hotel Corp.* v. *Elliott and Watrous Engineering Co.*, 137 Conn. 562, 79 A.2d 591 (1951).

43. *Winterbottom* v. *Wright*, 10 M. & W. 109, 11 L.J. Ex. 415, 152 Eng. Rep. 402 (1842).

In the presence of competitive conditions, even under this privity limitation, the manufacturer had an incentive to reach an efficient safety level, since he feared to be sued along the contractual chain eventually. Therefore he would seek to invest in the safety of his product to a point where marginal cost equaled marginal revenue. However, the courts later rejected the privity limitation. The first major basis of liability for negligence in the production of a product that could normally be expected to inflict substantial damage if it was defective occurred in *MacPherson* v. *Buick Motor Co.*[44] In that case a car maker was held liable for negligence when a wheel was defectively manufactured, causing the car to collapse and to injure the plaintiff. The case was unique because the product was not inherently dangerous; nevertheless the defendant manufacturer was declared liable to a plaintiff who was not the immediate purchaser.

Under this negligence theory, the manufacturer is required to exercise the care of a reasonable man under the circumstances. This involves the familiar negligence test of balancing the likelihood and severity of the damage against the benefit of the product and the cost of safety devices. The negligent manufacturer is therefore forced to internalize the costs and benefits from the broad perspective of all the individuals involved. However, courts were slow to extend liability from the producer to the ultimate consumer and to those injured by the defective product.

Today negligence liability for defective products is primarily used to determine whether a manufacturer is negligent in designing a product. Such liability extends even to bystanders foreseeably within the scope of use of the defective product. The manufacturer is forced, therefore, to consider all possible repercussions of his negligence. However, repetitive and costly multiple suits along the chain of privity are eliminated. Still, when a dealer or middleman has no reason to know of the negligent defect, he is not held liable; to do so would not increase efficiency but merely effect a transfer from the dealer to the injured party.

Defenses include the injured parties' contributory negligence or assumption of the risk. Both defenses create economic incentives for the injured party as well as the negligent manufacturer to avoid negligent behavior.

Because of the difficulty in proving negligence on the part of someone along the production chain and a desire to reduce litigation along the chain, courts next developed liability based on breach of warranty. *Breach of warranty* is a contract action based either on a warranty made expressly by the seller or on one implied in law, that the product will do no harm in normal use. However, as a contract action the injured party often had to show that he was in privity of contract with the alleged liable party.

Originally, the manufacturer's implied warranties covered only those to whom he sold his good. Therefore, the producer often could not be sued

---

44. *MacPherson* v. *Buick Motor Co.*, 217 N.Y. 382, 111 N.E. 1050 (1916).

by the purchaser or consumer of the product because there was no contract between the two parties. Illustrative of this early court interpretation is *Chysky* v. *Drake Brothers Co. Inc.*, which involved a waitress working in a lunchroom who was badly injured when she bit into a nail hidden in the defendant's cake.[45] The court held the baker not liable because the plaintiff's employer had bought the cake from the defendant and the implied warranty ran only to those parties in privity of contract. Interestingly, the court speculated that the baker would have been liable to the plaintiff under a negligence theory, but since warranty was a contract action, the plaintiff's action failed for want of privity.

Finally, privity of contract in warranty cases was overriden, leading to the overruling of *Chysky* in *Randy Knitwear* v. *American Cyanamid Co.*[46] In this case a plaintiff consumer sued the wholesaler and manufacturer of a fabric that shrunk, contrary to an express representation within the garment itself. The court ruled that the ultimate consumer could sue the manufacturer despite the lack of privity.

Similarly, the scope of warranty liability was expanding. Originally a warranty of fitness was implied in law only to delicate objects such as food as in *Chysky*. However, in *Henningsen* v. *Bloomfield Motors, Inc.*,[47] the implied warranty of fitness was extended to the manufacturer of automobiles despite the lack of a contractual arrangement between the manufacturer and the plaintiffs. The case signaled the end of the doctrine of privity of contract, and thereafter an implied warranty of safety was held to apply to a wide assortment of products.

There are several possible reasons for the extension of warranty liability. One view is that the consumer is helpless to protect himself against dangerous products, and that the manufacturer is best able to defend against such hazards. Since only the manufacturer, barring a patent defect, is able to provide the optimal level of safety, he should be given the incentive to adopt cost-effective measures to reduce damage. If the two parties were free to bargain and had equal bargaining power, the duty to search for the hazard would often be placed on the manufacturer, since he frequently has a comparative advantage. If so, the law is merely trying to reinforce the likely market solution. Another view is that the manufacturer solicited the product's use and should not be able to disclaim liability by stating that he had no contract with the ultimate consumer. Theoretically, liability would force the manufacturer to stand behind his goods and advertisements. Finally, a direct action for warranty eliminates costly suits against intermediate suppliers that waste valuable court resources.

45. *Chysky* v. *Drake Brothers Co., Inc.*, 233 N.Y. 468, 139 N.E. 576 (1923).
46. *Randy Knitwear* v. *American Cyanamid Co.*, 11 N.Y. 2d 5, 226 N.Y.S. 2d 363, 181 N.E.2d 399 (1962).
47. *Henningsen* v. *Bloomfield Motors, Inc.*, 32 N.J. 358, 161 A.2d 69 (1960).

The defenses to warranty action were limited in many instances, and, since warranty was a contract action, the buyer had to give notice to the seller within a reasonable time after he knew or should have known of the breach.[48] However, the seller often included in the contract a disclaimer of liability that defeated the warranty.[49] Furthermore, courts have been reluctant to extend the rights of a two-party contract involving a good to all foreseeable users of that good. Therefore, a new basis of liability without these restrictions was needed.

Strict Liability for Products

The answer to these considerations has been the formulation of tort liability, which holds manufacturers and suppliers of defective products strictly liable in tort to consumers and users for injuries caused by the defect. Specifically, according to the *Restatement of Torts,*

> (1) One who sells any product in a defective condition unreasonably dangerous to the user or consumer or to his property is subject to liability for physical harm thereby caused to the ultimate user or consumer, ... (2) (a) although the seller has exercised all possible care in the preparation and sale of his product.[50]

The first case to apply this theory to defective products was *Greenman* v. *Yuba Power Products, Inc.,* in which a power tool proved to be defective and caused injury and the plaintiff was foreclosed from suing on a warranty theory because he had failed to give timely notice of breach to the seller. A new rule of strict liability was formulated: "A manufacturer is strictly liable in tort when an article he places on the market, knowing that it is to be used without inspections for defects, proves to have a defect that causes injury to a human being."[51] Therefore, the defendant was held strictly accountable for the defect that made the product unsafe for its intended use. Within a short time the doctrine of *Yuba* largely displaced the warranty theory.

There are three major types of defect—*design, concealed dangers,* and *manufacturing.* Design liability is primarily a negligence theory of liability with a determination of whether or not the design was reasonable. Usually a producer is liable for a concealed danger because he failed to give an adequate warning. Most strict liability cases center around actual defects in the manufacturing process. Manufacturers are liable if it can be shown that the defect is attributable to them and if the defect caused the injury. Often the proof is difficult. For example, in *Friedman* v. *General Motors Cor-*

---

48. U.C.C. §2-316.
49. U.C.C. §2-607.
50. *Restatement (Second) of Torts,* §420A.
51. *Greenman* v. *Yuba Power Products, Inc.,* 59 Cal. 2d 57, 27 Cal. Rptr. 687, 377 P.2d 897 (1963).

poration[52] the issue was whether a defective gearshift that caused a car to start in the drive position could be attributed to the manufacturer of the 2-year-old car. Holding that reasonable minds could differ on the evidence, the court reversed a directed verdict for the defendant. It stated that it was possible for Friedman to prove that the car was defective, that the defect existed when the car left the factory, and that the defect was the proximate and direct cause of the injuries.

Ultimate users and consumers, and even a bystander, can invoke strict liability. The rationale is that industry should be responsible for all the foreseeable harm done by its defective products. Therefore, when a defective car strikes a pedestrian, the car manufacturer will be held liable to the victim because the resultant injury caused by the accident was within the scope of the risk. This approach is sound to the extent that the bystander had no chance to inspect the goods for defects and is in need, therefore, of greater protection than the consumer. Also, the likelihood that a third party may have insurance to protect against the risk of another's defective product may be minimal, making it more efficient to hold the producer liable.

The major defense in strict liability cases is that the victim was engaged in unreasonable use of the product. The plaintiff has no duty to discover the danger and guard against it, but if he knows of the risk and continues to use the product unreasonably, then he has assumed the risk of the defect. He has also assumed the risk if he was adequately warned of the danger of continued misuse. The defense of mishandling has a solid rationale; the victim is not allowed to recover when he could have prevented the accident at lower cost than the producer. This is assumed to have happened when the victim knows of the danger yet continues to use the product in an unreasonable manner.

Efficiency of Product-Liability Standards for Different Prevention Scenarios

In this section I examine some of the efficiency characteristics of major liability rules and standards under a variety of scenarios under which harm that products cause can be prevented. Although I focus on defective products and therefore product liability, it should be easy to infer to other tortious acts. Strict liability in terms of all harms occasioned by a given product, negligence with contributory negligence as a defense, and comparative negligence are selected for analysis. The five scenarios explored involve different relations between industry as a potential injurer and the consumer as a potential victim. They mainly differ as to who has a comparative advantage (and incentive) to prevent accidents caused by defective products.

52. _Friedman_ v. _General Motors Corp.,_ 43 Ohio St. 2d 909, 331 N.E.2d 702 (1975).

If transactions are free, all forms of liability, including no liability, are equally optimal. This is to be expected since all externalities can be negotiated away if people agree to accept the results of voluntary exchanges. Once transaction costs are introduced, however, the results change depending on how these costs are distributed.

1. *Only industry can prevent the accident.*

If only the potential injurer can take preventive action, strict liability and negligence are equally efficient standards of liability. There is no negligence by the plaintiff, and the defendant has the incentive to adopt efficient safety precautions until the judgment cost is lower than the cost of the precaution. This is true whether the industry is held strictly liable or liable only for negligent or unreasonable acts.

Other factors may favor a strict liability standard, however. Holding the industry strictly liable for the injury, where it alone could have prevented it, may lead to more long-term investment in safety research and development than would be undertaken by consumers if there were no liability or liability solely for negligent acts. Also, there may be an incentive for manufacturers to provide more safety information to consumers.

Government may mandate insurance to be taken out by the industry. The bundling of a compulsory insurance policy with the good would increase costs and reduce freedom of choice. The resulting increase in the cost of the hazardous goods would lead to a shift to safer products. Demand for the hazardous good would be increased because the producer would be liable for defects; but the supply would be reduced because the costs of production would have increased. The cost of the insured good may be higher than the cost of good and insurance purchased separately.

2. *Neither industry nor the consumer can prevent the accident.*

In the case of an entirely unforeseen accident that neither party could have prevented, both strict liability and negligence liability are equally efficient. Even if the industry is strictly liable it would not adopt safety measures, since it would be cheaper to pay the occasional judgment than to adopt costly precautions. By hypothesis neither party would be negligent. The form of liability would only affect the distribution of wealth. Court costs involved in such a transfer, as well as the other concerns outlined in Case 1, would have to be considered.

3. *Both parties can take precautions but the individual consumer can more effectively adopt the safety measure.*

In cases in which the potential victim can more readily prevent the accident than can the injurer, a negligence standard with contributory negligence is generally preferred over strict liability or negligence without a contributory-negligence defense. The defendant may be negligent in causing the accident, but it would be inefficient to allow the plaintiff to recover it he could have prevented the accident at less cost than the defendant. The contributory-negligence standard provides the potential accident victim with an incentive to take measures for an efficient level of safety. It is equally valid whether the defendant is held strictly liable or adjudged negligent.

The contributory-negligence standard is not always more efficient. Given the assumption that one party is acting in an optimal manner and that this fact is known to the other party, the negligence rule with contributory negligence as well as strict liability provide the optimal result as demonstrated by Brown.[53] However, if the other party has not in fact operated in the optimal manner, no social optimum can be obtained using comparative negligence, strict liability, or negligence standards, with or without contributory negligence as a defense. Instead, the optimum is reached only when the injurer could have bought more avoidance with the same expenditure than the victim could have.

4. *Both parties have incentives to take precautions but the injurer can prevent the accident at less cost.*

Either party could have avoided the accident at less than the expected cost of the accident, but under the doctrine of contributory negligence the injurer would not be liable at all. This outcome is inefficient and penalizes the injured party. Comparative negligence is a response to this problem and is more efficient in this case, because it apportions at least some liability to both negligent parties. However, since both parties now have an incentive to invest in safety to avoid being partly negligent, both may invest even though only one party could efficiently take the precaution. The result can be overinvestment in safety (i.e., inefficiency).

A better rule may be to hold the injurer negligently liable without any defense of contributory or comparative negligence. Under such a rule there is still an incentive for the injured party to avoid being negligent because he normally does not know that the injurer will also be negligent. Given that he has this incentive, it would be preferable on efficiency grounds to hold the injurer liable because he can provide the most cost-effective method of preventing or limiting damage.

5. *Only the consumer can prevent the accident.*

The reasoning in Case 1 is applicable with the roles of consumer and manufacturer reversed. In real life this is a rare case since in fact the producer usually knows most about his product. To hold the industry strictly liable is clearly inefficient, because only the consumer can take precautions to reduce injuries.

---

53. Brown, "Economic Theory of Liability," pp. 337–343.

DAMAGES

To compensate for the destruction of initial entitlements through the imposition of negative externalities, two classes of damages can be awarded by the court: *compensation* and *punitive damages.*

① COMPENSATION

If accidental damages occur (i.e., negative externalities are imposed on a victim), the tortfeasor who is found guilty must compensate the victim. The role of the court is to provide the victim with appropriate compensation from the tortfeasor or his insurer. (As will be seen later, in a few cases punitive damages may be levied to deter occurrence of tortious acts.) Some awards have involved large amounts of money. For example, a California appeals court affirmed in 1978 an award of $4,239,996 to a worker hurt by a pipe that fell on him in an industrial accident and $500,000 to his wife for loss of consortium.[54]

The primary rule of compensation for nonintentional tort is that the defendant is required to compensate the plaintiff for the dollar value of the damages inflicted, so as to maintain the earlier income distribution between the various parties. Calculating compensatory damages that provide just enough compensation to return the injured party to his prior condition revolves around the fundamental issue of evaluating the various component parts of a tortious injury. Some components are relatively easy to assess, such as medical costs and lost wages in injury cases. Other aspects of a tortious injury pose difficulties. For instance, in *Seffert* v. *Los Angeles Transit Lines* [55] the plaintiff was dragged some distance by a bus. How does one place a value upon the pain and suffering incurred by such an accident?

Another problem of valuation occurs when attempts are made to compensate the deceased's relatives for the loss of a life. As the case of *Zanovich* v. *American Airlines, Inc.* illustrates, the law seeks only to compensate the deceased's relatives for pecuniary loss of the lost life.[56] No compensation is generally included for the emotional elements of such a tragic event. The legal theory behind this explicit limitation of damages in wrongful-death cases is that life, to the person now dead, had such great value that no value at all can be placed on its loss.

As I have stressed, the law of torts is concerned only with civil, and not ✳ with criminal, liability. Therefore damages for tortiously caused death do not relate to criminal liability or moral culpability. To the dead plaintiff the loss is so high, and by definition unshiftable, that the law does not attempt

---

54. *Rodriguez* v. *McDonnell Douglas Corp.,* App. 3d, 151 Cal. Rptr. 399 (1978).
55. *Seffert* v. *Los Angeles Transit Lines,* 56 Cal. 2d 498 (1961).
56. *Zanovich* v. *American Airlines, Inc.,* 26 App. Dov. 2d 155 (1966).

to place the entire amount on the tortfeasor. However, the dead person's relatives may sue for the pecuniary loss of the injured party, and to that extent the law places a value on human life. But this valuation does not compensate for the loss of a life. In so doing, it might be argued that this rule fails to create an appropriate incentive to prevent negligently caused death.

Pain and suffering presents problems of valuation as to both past and future. For example, *Seffert* involved not only the plaintiff's pain and embarrassment about limping and the permanent disfigurement of her thigh, but also her dread of needing an amputation. It is difficult to put price tags on such consequences, but if the law seeks to restore the plaintiff to her prior condition or its equivalent, these intangibles must be assessed.

Or consider the case of *Sandifer Oil Co.* v. *Dew*, in which a 14-year-old girl was burned in an explosion caused by the defendant's negligence:

> Approximately ninety percent of her body was burned and the greater portion of this consisted of second and third degree burns. Over a large area, the skin was destroyed and the flesh cooked. In this condition, she lived ninety-nine and one-half hours, . . . conscious until about eighteen to twenty-four hours before death. According to the doctors and nurses who attended her, she endured the most intense and excruciating pain.[57]

What value should be set for the pain and suffering endured by the victim in this case?

(2) PUNITIVE DAMAGES

On occasion the legal system awards punitive as well as compensatory damages. Punitive damages are generally awarded in cases involving concealable or intentional acts or in situations where the plaintiff's damages, though real, are not normally compensable under traditional legal standards. The economic rationale for punitive damages is thus multifaceted.

Some torts such as reckless driving are intentionally concealed by the actor. Here the probability of catching the appropriate defendant can be very small. If caught, the legal system imposes punitive damages as a bonus factor for both deterrent and compensatory reasons. By forcing the defendant to pay punitive damages, the law is in effect extracting compensation for the defendant's undetected torts. Substantial punitive damages can also effectively create a deterrent to future tortious conduct both in respect to this particular defendant and as a precedent with regard to possible future actors.

Another rationale for punitive damages is as an implicit compensation mechanism for damages and expenses not normally compensable under our legal system. Particularly in situations where mental anguish, personal

---

57. *Sandifer Oil Co.* v. *Dew*, 220 Miss. 609 (1954).

discomfort, and damage to reputation are not normally provable or compensable under the usual compensatory damages standard, punitive damages can provide the plaintiff with some measure of relief. For instance, since under American law plaintiffs must pay their own attorney's costs, punitive damages are used to compensate for these expenses implicitly.

Perhaps the most fundamental rationale for punitive damages is their role of protecting the sanctity of the market system's structure of consensual exchange and production. Punitive damages are imposed to prevent the substitution of *post ad hoc* adjudications of legal rights for market transactions. Individuals in our society own property rights, and nonconsensual violations of those rights are punished by punitive damages to create a framework of consensual market exchange.

The imposition of punitive damages also reinforces the private property system. The fact that punitive sanctions are imposed for nonconsensual violation of property rights creates security in those entitlements and discourages encroachments. By maintaining the market system of consensual exchange, costs and benefits are internalized into each actor's choice calculus and through this mechanism a more efficient economic allocation of goods and services is achieved.

Cases arising from the 1975 crash of a DC-10 near Paris and from Ford Pinto fires, respectively, illustrate some of the inherent tensions in our legal system, where one alternative to litigation is settlement and where punitive damages are allowable in personal injury cases but not in wrongful-death cases.[58] For example, in February 1978 a Santa Ana, California, superior court jury awarded $125 million in punitive damages to a passenger in a Ford Pinto automobile, an award that was however reduced substantially by the court. The victim was burned over 90% of his body but survived. The plaintiff successfully argued that the Ford Motor Company had deliberately fitted Pinto cars with poorly designed gas tanks that ruptured on light impact. However, the driver of the car was killed and no punitive damages were awarded to his family because that portion of the case was limited to a wrongful-death claim.[59]

---

58. In January 1977, U. S. District Judge Manuel L. Real ruled that neither the California state legislature nor the California courts had made any rational distinction as to why punitive damages were allowable in personal injury cases but not in wrongful-death cases. Consequently the prior limitation of punitive damages in wrongful-death cases was held unconstitutional. In its immediate context, this ruling was highly favorable to the plaintiffs' attempts for remunerative out-of-court settlements since it increased the defendants' potential liability. Over the long run the decision could correct the economically anomalous structure of the law in this area.

As we have seen, wrongful-death actions do not adequately compensate the victim or his family for the loss of life. Incorrect incentives for the defendant are thus arguably created. The prior limitation of punitive damages in wrongful-death cases perhaps only exacerbated this problem (*Los Angeles Times*, January 9, 1977).

59. *Los Angeles Times*, February 7, 1978.

TRENDS IN TORT LAW

Tort law has been one of the most dynamic areas of the law. A number of forces have converged to result in this development. First and perhaps foremost has been the rapid increase in industrialization and urbanization, which has greatly increased the interdependence of each and every one of us. Thus there has been a great increase in externalities, and many have become more severe.

Another factor is the growth of social consciousness, dedicated to satisfying the economic goals of the "common man," which spread the desire to protect the common man from the destruction of his initial entitlement.

Finally, since judges cannot seek out issues that will result in changes in the law but must wait for cases to come to them, tort law had to wait for a new breed of lawyers. This happened when tort practitioners became more innovative and began engaging in creative advocacy. Moreover, a comprehensive system of civil discovery was adopted to remove the "game element" from litigation.[60] The process was initially designed to inform each party of its opponent's case so as to avoid surprise at trial, ease preparation, and enhance the possibilities of settlement.

As a result some major developments have taken place, particularly since 1960. For example, in California explosive developments in tort law occurred between 1961 and 1976. They can be divided into two classes—extension toward stricter liability, and reduced immunity. Here are several California examples that indicate the extent to which a move toward stricter liability has taken place:[61]

1. Introduction of employer negligence into workers' compensation disputes by denial of the employer's right to reimbursement from third persons if the employer is negligent[62]
2. Extension of land-occupier liability by elimination of the concept of degrees of duty to persons on the land for different purposes[63]
3. Imposition of liability on lending institutions for negligent acts of their borrowers[64]
4. Extension of recoverable damage to include emotional distress caused by observation of negligently inflicted injury to a close relative[65]
5. Extension of rule of strict product liability[66]

60. *Greyhound Corp.* v. *Superior Court,* 55 Cal. 2d 555 (1961).
61. Robert S. Thompson, "One Judge's View of the Future of Tort Liability," *UCLA Law and Economics Workshop,* November 9, 1977.
62. *Witt* v. *Jackson,* 57 Cal. 2d 57 (1961).
63. *Rowland* v. *Christian,* 69 Cal. 2d 108 (1968).
64. *Connor* v. *Great Western Savings & Loan Association,* 69 Cal. 2d 850 (1968).
65. *Dillon* v. *Legg,* 68 Cal. 2d 728 (1968).
66. *Elmore* v. *American Motors Corp.,* 70 Cal. 2d 578 (1969).

6. Liability imposed on bartender for injury caused by his drunken customer[67]
7. Refusal to apply the *Restatement (Second) of Torts* limitation defining a defective product as one that is unreasonably dangerous[68]
8. Application of strict liability for defective products to those that are patently defective[69]
9. Imposition of a stricter test of "informed consent" to medical procedures[70]
10. Rejection of "guest statute" on the theory that it denies equal protection of the law[71]
11. Rejection of the former rule barring proof of subsequent improvement of a product to show it was defective before improved[72]
12. Imposition of a standard of care on lawyers requiring them to research obscure authority to evaluate the possibility that the court-made law may change[73]
13. Imposition of liability on a landowner for negligence of his tenant[74]
14. Imposition of a duty on a psychiatrist to warn third persons of danger to them disclosed by a patient in professional consultation[75]

The following are examples of reduced immunity:

1. Abrogation of the doctrine of sovereign immunity insulating public entities from tort liability except in unusual circumstances[76]
2. Abolition of interspousal immunity[77]

However, in 1975 the California Supreme Court may have given a signal indicating a change in direction away from strict liability.[78] It rejected a statutory rule of contributory negligence in favor of a rule of comparative negligence. By 1976, 29 states had legislatively established comparative negligence, and another 3 states had done so by court-made law.[79]

---

67. *Vesely* v. *Sager*, 5 Cal. 3d 153 (1971).
68. *Cronin* v. *J. B. E. Olson Corp.*, 8 Cal. 3d 121 (1972).
69. *Luque* v. *McLean*, 8 Cal. 3d 136 (1972). Mans arm disentangled by a lawnmower when he fell in front of their it's
70. *Cobbs* v. *Grant*, 8 Cal. 3d 229 (1972).
71. *Brown* v. *Merlo*, 8 Cal. 3d 855 (1973).
72. *Ault* v. *International Harvester*, 13 Cal. 3d 113 (1974).
73. *Smith* v. *Lewis*, 13 Cal. 3d 349 (1975).
74. *Ucciello* v. *Landenslayer*, 44 Cal. App. 3d 504 (1975).
75. *Tarasoff* v. *Regents of the University of California*, 13 Cal. 3d 177 (1974).
76. *Muskopf* v. *Corning Hospital District*, 55 Cal. 2d 211 (1961).
77. *Klein* v. *Klein*, 58 Cal. 2d 692 (1962).
78. *Li* v. *Yellow Cab Co.*, 13 Cal. 3d 804 (1975).
79. Sherman, "Analysis," p. 55.

CONCLUSION

In summary, tort law has found more and more applications, since the world has become one of increasing interdependence, replete with externalities, many of which have forcibly though unintentionally destroyed initial entitlements. Some tort law concepts and standards lend themselves especially well to economic analysis, which will be undertaken in the following chapter in relation to malpractice, industrial accidents, product liability, accident law, and sovereign immunity.

VII

ECONOMIC ANALYSIS OF
TORT LAW

INTRODUCTION

A number of concepts common to tort law were presented in the preceding chapter. An effort will now be made to infuse some further economic content into these concepts, in the hope of sharpening them and offering additional insight. Medical malpractice is examined first. A brief review of the legal history and major characteristics of malpractice is followed by economic considerations, including the application of the Learned Hand formula and an examination of the signals emanating from the malpractice system. Then effects of liability standards on industrial accidents are considered. The strict liability standard applied to product liability is then examined in terms of some of its economic effects. Thereafter, an economic analysis of accident law is undertaken, and the Learned Hand formula is further examined, here within a social-welfare-maximizing benefit–cost framework. Sovereign immunity is then examined in an economic framework, and, finally, the effects of the American and Continental rules of assigning liability for litigation cost are compared.

ECONOMIC ANALYSIS OF MEDICAL
MALPRACTICE

LEGAL BACKGROUND

The first medical malpractice case reported in the United States was *Cross* v. *Guthrey* in 1794.[1] Malpractice was soon related to the standard of care

---

1. *Cross* v. *Guthrey*, 2 Root 90 (1794).

applied by physicians, which was defined in the New York Supreme Court case of 1898, *Pike* v. *Honsinger*:

> The physician and surgeon, by taking charge of a case, impliedly represents that he possesses, and the law places upon him the duty of possession, that reasonable degree of learning and skill that is ordinarily possessed by physicians and surgeons in the locality in which he practices, and which is ordinarily regarded by those conversant with the employment as is necessary to qualify him to engage in the business of practicing medicine and surgery . . . it becomes his duty to use reasonable care and diligence in the exercise of his skill and the application of his learning to accomplish the purpose for which he was employed. He is . . . to use his best judgment in exercising his skill and applying his knowledge. The law holds him liable for an injury to his patient resulting from want of the requisite skill and knowledge or the omission to exercise reasonable care or the failure to use his best judgment.[2]

The locality rule of *Pike* not only established a standard for comparison, but also required that a medical expert testifying for the plaintiff in a malpractice action must have practiced in the defendant's community. Since, particularly in small communities, there are few physicians and, moreover, physicians are often reluctant to testify against colleagues, the locality rule greatly favors the defendant. Therefore, the Massachusetts Supreme Court in *Brune* v. *Belinkoff* in 1968 flatly announced that it was abandoning the locality rule.[3] Other states have followed suit.

Plaintiffs in the past have also been handicapped by the inadmissibility of medical treatises as evidence because what is written in the treatises was not given under oath. Pertinent here is the belief that the validity of testimony can be evaluated by jurors only if the witness is on the witness stand and can be subjected to cross-examination. Such states as Massachusetts, Kansas, Nevada, and Rhode Island have enacted statutes specifically to admit learned books and articles to establish the standard of care. The value of using medical treatises can be particularly great when used in conjunction with the examination of the defendant physician. Most states today have "adverse witness statutes," although they were long opposed. These statutes expressly permit a litigant to call the opposing party for cross-examination.

The doctrine of *res ipsa loquitur* ("the thing speaks for itself") is of particular interest in malpractice action. It can be viewed as simply a characterization of those conditions in which circumstantial evidence, by itself, is sufficiently strong to warrant the conclusion that the defendant was probably negligent and that the negligence was the proximate cause of the alleged damages. *Res ipsa* simply creates the presumption of negligence, which can however be overturned by evidence to the contrary by the

2. *Pike* v. *Honsinger,* 155 N.Y. 201 (1898).
3. *Brune* v. *Belinkoff,* 354 Mass. 102 (1968).

defendant. (For example, American courts almost always apply *res ipsa* to cases where sponges, and sometimes other foreign bodies, were not removed from the patient before the operation was concluded.) In many medical situations, particularly where the plaintiff has been given anesthesia, he is in no position to know whether the physician employed due care. Where there is little evidence of negligence, but the defendant knew about the likely harm and could have done more to avoid its occurrence than the plaintiff could, *res ipsa* is applied in ways that approach a strict liability standard.

Medical malpractice, which gained great notoriety in the middle 1970s, is however only one of a number of battlegrounds. Lawyers, architects, real estate agents, corporate officers and directors, and travel agents have increasingly been subjected to malpractice suits and have seen their insurance premiums soar.

THE HAND FORMULA AND *HELLING v. CAREY*

ex. of incremental standard of reasoned Hand form.

Next, I will analyze a medical malpractice case, *Helling* v. *Carey*, which illustrates many facets and tensions within the field of medical malpractice in court, but in addition lends itself in part to an empirical implementation of the Hand formula.[4] The plaintiff Helling, who first consulted the defendant ophthalmologists in 1959 for myopia (nearsightedness), was fitted for contact lenses and became blind from glaucoma because no tonometry to detect glaucoma was performed. She experienced a minimal amount of irritation during the next 8 years, but in September of 1967 she consulted the defendants again, complaining of eye irritation. They diagnosed conjunctivitis (inflammation of the mucous membranes) and gave her a prescription. During several more visits in the course of the following month the defendants decided Helling had corneal abrasions due to the contact lenses. In May 1968, the plaintiff returned, again complaining about irritation. On October 1, 1968, the defendants tested for glaucoma and found it.

Glaucoma can result in blindness; but it can be treated and ameliorated if detected early enough. There are few symptoms until the harm is irreversible. It can be detected by a simple tonometry test, the major cost of which is the ophthalmologist's time. The plaintiff contended that the defendants should have tested for glaucoma in 1967 when she was 32 years of age, and that they ignored both their training and advances in the profession in not doing so.

The defendants presented evidence that, although there were some ophthalmologists who favored giving the glaucoma test to patients under 40 years of age, the accepted national practice did not require giving glaucoma tests to patients under 40 unless symptoms and complaints would indicate the presence of glaucoma. There was inconsistent evidence as to

4. *Helling* v. *Carey*, 83 Wash. 2d 514, 519 P.2d 981 (1974).

whether the defendants should have suspected glaucoma, and it was also unclear whether testing in 1967 would have made any difference.

The Washington Supreme Court held that the defendants were negligent *as a matter of law* for not administering the glaucoma test. The court stated,

> Under the facts of this case reasonable prudence required the timely giving of the pressure test to this plaintiff. The precaution of giving this test to detect the incidence of glaucoma to patients under 40 years of age is so imperative that irrespective of its disregard by the standards of the ophthalmology profession, it is the duty of the courts to say what is required to protect patients under 40 from damaging results of glaucoma.
>
> . . . as a matter of law . . . the reasonable standard that should have been followed . . . was the timely giving of this simple, harmless pressure test. . . . In failing to do so, the defendants were negligent, which proximately resulted in the blindness sustained by the plaintiff.[5]

To support its decision, the court cited two nonmedical cases, including the *T. J. Hooper* decision, in which Justice Learned Hand stated,

> . . . In most cases reasonable prudence is in fact common prudence; but strictly it is never its measure; a whole calling may have unduly lagged in the adoption of new and available devices. It never may set its own tests, however persuasive be its usages. Courts must in the end say what is required: there are precautions so imperative that even their universal disregard will not excuse their omission.[6]

In justifying its holding, the court emphasized that the glaucoma test is "simple, harmless, and inexpensive."

Empirical evidence of the incidence of glaucoma was recognized by the court: For those under 40, the expected incidence is 1 per 25,000 persons; among all those over 40, it is around 1 to 2 per 100 persons. The test is not totally without risk, since any time an instrument is placed on the eye there is a risk of scratching the cornea.

Standards for the test were evaluated by R. P. Crick, an expert in the field, who concluded, "The prevalence of glaucoma is too low and the methods of detection such as to make population screening an uneconomic use of medical resources at present."[7]

Since *Helling* v. *Carey* has the distinction of citing generally agreed-upon quantitative estimates on the probability of harm occurring, it is useful to place these estimates into the Hand formula. Judge Learned Hand, it will

---

5. *Ibid.,* p. 519.

6. *T. J. Hooper,* 60 F.2d 737 (1932).

7. R. P. Crick, "Chronic Glaucoma: A Preventable Cause of Blindness," *Lancet,* February 9, 1974, p. 207.

be recalled, defined the legal standard of liability applicable to most unintended acts of negligence as follows: The defendant is guilty of negligence if the loss caused by the event, for example, an accident, L, multiplied by the probability of the event occurring, P, exceeds the costs of the precautions that the defendant might have taken to avert it, C.

In relation to glaucoma in general and *Helling* v. *Carey* in particular, the following numbers might be illustrative: The medical profession indicates that P for persons below 40 is 1/25,000, and for persons above 40, 2/100. The cost of preventing the occurrence of glaucoma, C, is about 10 minutes of a doctor's time, let us say $30; the loss associated with the occurrence of glaucoma, namely blindness, L, is the most difficult parameter. Ideally, one would need to estimate the losses incurred by a person who goes blind, and do so year by year with each year reflecting the particular age. Since these losses constitute a flow over time, discounting would be necessary.

We can use a bounding technique and estimate for the two age groups at what L value the Hand formula would find the defendant liable for the ill effects of glaucoma, should he have omitted an examination. For persons under 40 years of age the defendant would be liable if the loss due to glaucoma was more than $30/(0.00004) or $750,000. For persons 40 years or older, the defendant would be liable if the loss due to glaucoma was more than $30/(0.02) or $1500.

Thus, the critical loss figure for young people is about 500 times as large as for older people. Younger people can look forward to a longer productive life than older persons, but the income difference is unlikely to be more than 3–10 times on average.[8] Although admittedly, there are other than income losses to be considered, such as mental anguish, or any harm from unintended scratching of the eye by the testing procedure, these harms are unlikely to entirely offset the 500-fold greater loss.

Another way of applying the Hand formula makes use of the average jury verdict for total or legal blindness in 1973–1977: $678,000.[9] Accordingly,

$$\$30 > \$678,000 \ (0.00004) = \$27.$$

It would therefore be interesting to contemplate whether the Washington Supreme Court would have ruled in favor of plaintiff Helling, had it explicitly placed its figures into the Hand formula. But perhaps it would have priced a tonometry test below $30.

8. For example, if the average person starts to be gainfully employed at age 22 and retires at 65, and the average of persons 1 to 39 years old is 20, then those 1–39 years old could have been gainfully employed 17 + 26 or 43 years in the absence of glaucoma. With similar assumptions, the equivalent number of years is 15 for persons 40 years and older.

9. Injury Valuation Reports, Tables of Verdict Expectancy Values for Eye Injuries, in *Personal Injury Valuation Handbooks* (Cleveland: Jury Verdict Research, in press).

THE MALPRACTICE SYSTEM'S SIGNALS TO PHYSICIANS

Aided by the Hand formula, the malpractice system provides a means, through litigation, to redress the loss and suffering caused by carelessness; but in addition it signals potentially negligent individuals that to be careless will cost them more than to invest in an appropriate level of prevention.[10] Damages awarded to a victim induce potentially negligent individuals to compare the cost of avoiding an injury with the cost of paying for it. Prospective compensation provides a victim with an incentive to sue, and thus to him, too, a signal is given.

The signal to the physician—once it is received and considered together with the potential time loss, anxiety, and loss of reputation—guides his decision of how much to invest in avoiding mishaps. As was stated in the previous chapter, the correct response is for him to invest his resources up to the level that equals the expected saving in damages.

Here then are some of the efficiency effects of the signals. To the extent that the usual fee for a service accurately reflects the training and the investment of time needed to meet customary standards of care, nonnegligent physicians are appropriately remunerated. By contrast, the negligent physician, who fails to provide the full service but accepts the full price, is shortchanging his patient. With an effective malpractice signal, the potentially negligent physician would be stimulated to invest more time for no increase in pay because he probably could not set his fees higher than those of his more competent colleagues. What would this mean in practice? The negligent physician who tends to rush through physical-examination procedures may take the time needed for more careful work. But to the extent that the physician's shortcoming is less shortage of time than of training, the damages award would signal that he should invest in further training. Alternatively, the signal may persuade him to abandon procedures he is not competent to perform, even though they are highly remunerative.

This leads us to the ideal negligence signal, which is achieved only when every significant incident of malpractice leads to a claim and every valid claim leads to a full award. If the physician's sole objective is to maximize his income, he would invest in mishap reduction up to the point where the last resource unit spent toward this goal would equal the expected saving in damages. Further investment would increase the net costs to society. But what if not all mishaps result in suits? Then the physician is likely to invest less than the optimum and the overall outcome would be less efficient. I should hasten to point out that I am fully aware that physicians neither seek to maximize their income in this manner nor engage in the sort of quantita-

---

10. For a detailed development of this issue, one on which this section relies heavily, see W. B. Schwartz and N. K. Komesar, *Doctors, Damages and Deterrence: An Economic View of Medical Malpractice,* R-2340-NIH/RC (Santa Monica: June 1978).

tive analysis implied in this discussion. However, I think that intuitively they may act more or less in line with the model.

What is the meaning of the existence of a "malpractice crisis"? In the economist's view the malpractice system would be regarded as not working properly when awards exceed losses suffered by claimants, and when there are successful claims that are not warranted. Merely looking at the size of awards or number of claims filed tells us little about the effectiveness of the malpractice system. High awards have been found to contain a large compensation element for pain and suffering, as in catastrophic injury, and they are not necessarily excessive. Moreover, awards below $50,000 were found to cover only one-third to two-thirds of medical expenses and lost earnings.[11]

Although between 1972 and 1977 the number of malpractice claims increased by nearly 50%, at most only one out of every six or seven incidents resulted in a claim.[12] Therefore, the number of suits, though burgeoning, falls far short of the level required to signal the complete expected loss $(P \times L)$ resulting from negligence.

This statement, however, is not entirely correct. It leaves out important transaction costs—resources in the form of lawyers, physicians, witnesses, judges, juries, and insurance companies—spent on administering the malpractice system. These resource costs must be deducted from the savings attained under the malpractice system. Some mishaps are therefore not worth preventing through the malpractice system, since some suits are not worth bringing.

To the extent that courts make mistakes, the malpractice system falls short of the optimum. When a court fails to detect real negligence, expected losses to defendants are smaller than they should be. Physicians are therefore given signals to invest in mishap avoidance below the optimal level. Concomitantly, transaction costs are incurred though they do not yield benefits.

When a court penalizes nonnegligent behavior, physicians are given signals that can lead them to provide medically unjustifiable services in order to avoid malpractice suits, that is, to practice defensive medicine. They overinvest, particularly if third-party payments enable use of diagnostic tests and hospitalization that directly burden neither physician nor patient. Immunity is bought, then, by physicians at social costs in excess of expected benefits.

Malpractice insurance can be shown to interfere with the appropriate response of physicians and to lead to suboptimal results. Since the malprac-

11. *Ibid.*, p. 11.
12. California Medical Association and California Hospital Association, *Report on the Medical Insurance Feasibility Study* (San Francisco: Sutter Publications, 1977), and *Malpractice Digest* (St. Paul, Minn.: St. Paul Fire and Marine Insurance Co., April/May 1977).

tice premium of a given physician is inadequately related to his record of claims, settlements, and verdicts—he pays a group rate—the signals he receives are muted. He has only a minor pecuniary incentive to reduce the expected losses resulting from his own behavior, which is further reduced as much of the insurance cost is passed on to patients in the form of health insurance premiums.

Despite these negative effects, malpractice insurance, by spreading the physician's risk, protects him from a ruinous verdict, though it may even be an erroneous one. This advantage could be retained and efficient signals provided if the medical profession would agree on individual experience ratings for determining malpractice premiums. With the premium reflecting the risk a particular physician poses to the insurer, the physican could act in line with this signal. Moreover, physicians with poor ratings and high premiums are unlikely to pass these costs on in higher fees, since they would be out of line with prevailing fees.

SOME PROPOSALS FOR THE MALPRACTICE SYSTEM

Economic analysis can be further applied to examine the merits of two proposals—replacing contingency fees in malpractice cases by fee-for-service payments, and introducing no-fault malpractice insurance.

Contingency fee arrangements under which attorneys are paid a fixed percentage of damage awards are often accused of encouraging lawyers to initiate suits. These arrangements, it is argued, lead to the filing of too many suits, many of which are frivolous, rather than to the careful selecting of meritorious cases.

Yet a rational lawyer who is paid only if the court rules in his favor or if a settlement is reached out of court would compare his costs in time and money with the likely fee to be obtained. Cases with little prospect for success will not be attractive to most lawyers. The result is less litigation and harassment of physicians compared to fee-for-service arrangements. At the same time, meritorious cases are likely to be filed even on behalf of poor clients, as long as a contingency fee can be expected. Altogether there will be more screening out of frivolous cases and more reliable signaling under a contingency fee than under a fee-for-service system. The former appears to offer greater net social benefits than the latter.

My discussion of no-fault insurance in relation to malpractice will be brief, since this subject will be discussed in greater detail later, in relation to accident law. Most proposals would exclude from litigation certain events in which bad outcomes result usually, though not exclusively, from negligence. Malpractice procedures, and with them transaction costs, including the physician's anxiety, would be avoided. Although some disputes and ensuing litigation would continue, transaction costs would no doubt decline, but at a cost and perhaps a not-insignificant one. Specifically, since the individual physician no longer pays the damages—he does not pay a premium that closely relates to the cost of compensable damages caused by him—he recieves no reliable signals. Without such signals he is unable to select efficient steps toward optimal care.

For the sake of efficient deterrence, as I showed earlier, premiums should be based on individual experience ratings; but under no-fault insurance this could have undesirable effects. These include the practicing of defensive medicine as well as a disinclination of physicians to employ high-risk procedures even where they are medically necessary to help high-risk patients. Thus, altogether, no-fault malpractice insurance is unlikely to produce net social benefits over the existing fault system.

THE REDER MODEL

M. W. Reder has built a model within which some other economic aspects of medical malpractice can be examined.[13] In this model, differences in outcomes of treatment (i.e., the quality of care), depend on differences in physicians' efforts, and not on differences in their abilities. Reder argues that in the long run differences in ability or competence are largely the result of differences in amount and kind of training. Moreover, the model assumes that medical care is produced by economically efficient physicians and that differences in costs and returns, including specialized training undergone, affect the techniques used. Under these assumptions, the fee for a unit of medical service has two components: the fee proper and a "liability-sharing" component. The larger the percentage of the liability the patient is willing to share, the lower the fee the physician will supposedly charge him.

Reder argues that if courts would cease to refuse honoring malpractice liability waivers and instead would permit doctors and patients to negotiate individual exchanges of malpractice waivers for abatement of fees, the malpractice crisis would be resolved. Patients and doctors could agree on how much malpractice liability the doctor would bear and how much the patient would pay. Such an environment, Reder argues, would permit doctors concerned about malpractice insurance premiums and patients concerned about high fees to do something about their separate, though related, concerns through individual negotiations. Unfortunately, when patients come to see physicians they are usually in a poor bargaining position. Thus the precondition for negotiating a fair contract is missing.

However, the Reder model can be used to show that a regime in which the terms of malpractice liability are set by negotiation between individual doctors and patients would establish or reinforce a positive association of the quality of medical care with the patient's wealth. Thus, although such a

13. M. W. Reder, "An Economic Analysis of Medical Malpractice, *Journal of Legal Studies* 5 (June 1976): 267–292. The shortcoming of such a market approach to malpractice is criticized in G. Calabresi, "The Problem of Malpractice: Trying to Round Out the Circle," *University of Toronto Law Journal* 27 (1977): 132.

regime might be efficient, it would have undesirable redistributive implications.

EFFECT ESTIMATION OF LIABILITY
STANDARDS ON INDUSTRIAL ACCIDENTS

Although I hypothesized earlier that the various tort standards will affect behavior differently and therefore will result in different levels of accident risk, I have waited until now to present an empirical test of this hypothesis. Specifically, I will now consider how a universal shift from a negligence rule with contributory negligence to a stricter negligence or strict liability standard (in the form of workmen's compensation) has affected levels of accident risk in the United States.

It must be remembered that at the beginning of the twentieth century negligence was the basis by which all states determined industrial accident costs. Under this system, the employer had an easy time invoking such defenses as the negligence of fellow servants, the assumption of risk by employees, and contributory negligence by injured workers. For example, under the fellow-servant rule, an employer was not liable for the negligent acts of co-workers to each other unless a co-worker was acting as the employer's representative.

Early in the twentieth century, states began to pass employer's liability laws, which greatly modified or altogether abolished the three employer's defenses just mentioned. As employer's liability laws were enacted, a further set of accident laws was considered in various states. Thus, in 1911 the first state introduced a system of strict liability—workmen's compensation—and by 1949 all states had switched to this standard. Under the new system, an employer must pay employees or their heirs a predetermined compensation, regardless of what caused the accident, as long as it was work related. Although under the earlier standard 6–30% of all industrial accidents were compensated, under workmen's compensation *all* accidents are compensated, though substantially below the employee's full accident cost.[14] Litigation is sharply reduced. Only whether injury is work related and how serious it is can be contested. Moreover, employees covered by workmen's compensation cannot sue an employer for negligence.

The question now arises whether employers modified work conditions when the switch to stricter tort standards increased their risk. Specifically, I would like to estimate the effect of this switch of tort standards on the level of accident risk. In a study by Chelius the level of accident risk is approximated by the ratio of the machinery death rate for a state to the machinery

---

14. W. L. Prosser, *Handbook of the Law of Torts,* 4th ed. (St. Paul, Minn.: West, 1971), pp. 416–417.

death rate for the United States in a given year.[15] (*Machinery death rate* is defined as the number of deaths caused by non-motor-vehicle machinery accidents per number of employees.)

In order to account for changes in factors such as per capita exposure to machinery, the business cycle, and the status of medical care, risk was measured as a ratio of the experience of a particular state for a particular year to the average experience in that year for the United States.

Since safety regulations other than tort standards can also affect the risk level in work places, a dummy variable testifying to the presence or absence of such state regulatory efforts was introduced.

Chelius' model is as follows:

$$D_{ij}/D_{USj} = \alpha_0 + \alpha_1(EL) + \alpha_2(WC) + \alpha_3(\text{Controls}) + \mu, \qquad (1)$$

where

D_{ij}/D_{USj} = the ratio of the machinery death rate in state i in year j to the machinery death rate for the United States in year j

EL = a dummy variable representing the presence of an employer's liability law lagged 1 year

WC = a dummy variable representing the presence of a workmen's compensation law lagged 1 year

Controls = a dummy variable representing the presence of a regulatory system using safety standards lagged 1 year;

μ = error term.

The right-hand variables were lagged 1 year because laws went into effect during different times of the year and changes were not likely to be instantaneous. In using dummy variables for employer's liability and workmen's compensation, the coefficients α_1 and α_2 are interpreted as the impact of these laws on the death rate compared to the impact of the common law. Similarly, the coefficient α_3 measures the impact of safety standard regulation compared to the absence of such regulation.

An ordinary least squares analysis produced the results that are reproduced in Table 7-1. Specifically, it was found that although during 1900–1940 both employer's liability and workmen's compensation laws were associated with significantly lower death rates, safety-control regulation was not. The larger value of the *WC* coefficient (1.4) in comparison with the *EL* coefficient (0.6) indicates that the strict liability system (workmen's compensation) had a greater impact on the relative death rate than did the employer's liability system.

There was the possibility that during 1900–1940 the 26 sample states had coincidentally developed a safer technology than was used by the average

15. J. R. Chelius, "Liability for Industrial Accidents: A Comparison of Negligence and Strict Liability Systems," *Journal of Legal Studies* 5 (June 1976): 293–302.

TABLE 7-1

Impact of Liability Changes on Death Rates (D_{ij}/D_{USj}): As Measured by
Coefficients on Employer's Liability (EL) and Workmen's Compensation (WC)

	Coefficients and t values associated with the independent variables		
	EL	*WC*	Controls
I	−0.6*	−1.4*	+0.6
	(−4.0)	(−14.0)	(1.7)
	$R^2 = 0.29$, $F = 12.9*$, $n = 907$		
	Estimated using available data 1900–1940		
II	−0.8*	−1.4*	+0.6
	(−3.8)	(−10.8)	(1.3)
	$R^2 = 0.53$, $F = 8.3*$,- $n = 621$		
	Estimated using available data 1900–1930		
III	−0.8*	−1.4*	+0.7
	(−3.5)	(−8.8)	(1.3)
	$R^2 = 0.51$, $F = 5.9*$, $n = 491$		
	Estimated using available data 1900–1925		
IV	−1.0*	−1.5*	+0.7
	(−3.0)	(−6.4)	(1.0)
	$R^2 = 0.50$, $F = 9.0*$, $n = 361$		
	Estimated using available data 1900–1920		

Source: J. R. Chelius, "Liability for Industrial Accidents: A Comparison of Negligence and Strict Liability Systems," *Journal of Legal Studies* 5 (June 1976): 305.

* Significant at the 1% level. All equations were estimated using dummy variables for each state except Connecticut as dictated by the covariance analysis. The coefficients for these dummy variables and the constant term are not presented.

state. Should this be the case, the safety benefits of these changes would be inappropriately assigned to changes in liability systems. This possibility was investigated by alternatively restricting the sample to 1900–1930, 1900–1925, and 1900–1920 (Table 7-1, Eq. II, III, and IV). Restricting the sample in this manner allows less time for technological change than the full period of 1900–1940. The results using each of the restricted samples confirm the results of the full sample—employer's liability and workmen's compensation were associated with lower death rates and safety-standard regulation had no impact.

An analysis focusing more sharply on the changeover from a negligence to a strict liability system was undertaken. For this purpose, the average machinery death rate for the 5-year period before and the 5-year period after the change to workmen's compensation was analyzed using a dummy variable to represent the difference in liability arrangements. The same was done for a 3-year period. In both cases, death rates were found to be significantly lower under a strict liability standard.

❋ SOME ECONOMIC CONSIDERATIONS OF
PRODUCT LIABILITY   *Increasing incredibly*

The discussion of the legal aspects of product liability developed in the previous chapter will now be supplemented by an inquiry into certain economic aspects. Specifically, I will examine some of the aggregate effects of strict liability for products on efficiency, inflationary pressures, competition, and innovation.

In the early 1970s litigation regarding product liability (as well as malpractice) took a sudden turn upward. The awards made in such cases have been numerous and many have been extremely large. By the mid-1970s, premiums for product-liability insurance had become a major cost item. At $1.5 billion a year, premiums for product-liability insurance ran twice the total of those for medical malpractice coverage. According to *Business Week*, for some small companies, those with annual sales of less than $75 million, premiums have jumped from less than 1% of sales to 15% or more.[16] Not only has their profit been placed in jeopardy, but their competitiveness with larger enterprises has been reduced. Depending on demand and supply elasticities, the costs of insuring against product liability (and malpractice) are passed on to the consumer, thereby substantially increasing the costs of goods (and services). Product-liability insurance has been especially costly for manufacturers of industrial machinery, industrial chemicals, and such high-risk consumer goods as pharmaceuticals, automotive parts, and medical devices.

The escalation in premium payments has been attributed to an increasingly broad application of strict liability standards. There may indeed be justification for this development, as suggested by *Morisett* v. *United States*, where the Supreme Court stated,

> The industrial revolution multiplies the number of workmen exposed to injury from increasingly powerful and complex mechanisms, driven by freshly discovered sources of energy, requiring higher precautions by employers. Traffic of velocities, volumes and varieties unheard of, came to subject the wayfarer to intolerable casualty risks if owners and drivers were not to observe new cares and uniformities of conduct. Congestion of cities and crowding of quarters called for health and welfare regulations undreamed of in simpler times. Wide distributions of goods became an instrument of wide distribution of harm when those who dispersed food, drink, drugs, and even securities, did not comply with reasonable standards of quality, integrity, disclosure and care.[17]

Another problem relates to courts holding manufacturers liable for the full life of their products and for "foreseeable" design defects that might not show up for years. Thus, for example, a tool manufactured 30 years

16. *Business Week,* January 17, 1977, p. 63.
17. 342 U.S. 246 (1952).

ago and originally equipped with the required safety guard may presently injure a worker, with the manufacturer possibly held liable. Furthermore, some courts have dismissed all consideration of contributory negligence, although there are cases when a worker's negligence has greatly contributed to the injury.

Although a strict liability standard is designed to protect potential victims in general and consumers in particular, we must worry about the standard's side effects. In the presence of a strict product-liability rule, at least four major aggregate effects can result: distorted resource allocation, enhanced inflationary pressures, reduced competition, and slowed innovation.

Should manufacturers become exceedingly fearful of being held responsible for all product defects and liable for all ensuing harm, they will be inclined to design and manufacture products with such high reliability that failure is virtually ruled out. They could do so, however, only at very high resource costs, and major misallocation of resources is likely to result. The nation's electronics and aerospace firms who have participated in the exploration of outer space, for example, have learned to manufacture to very fine specifications and have built redundancy into many space-exploration devices. As a result, the probability of failure has been greatly reduced, but at a high cost. If we were to adopt similarly high standards for fear of being found liable for the failure of such items as lawnmowers, washing machines, and automobiles, too many resources would go into these safety devices. Some resources and skills would be bid up in price and further distortions would result.

Enhanced safety can only be provided at a cost, and someone will have to bear the increased cost. Though the shifting of these costs will depend on the demand and supply elasticities of the safe product, under virtually all circumstances consumers will end up bearing part of the cost in terms of higher prices. Some of the price increases can be readily justified, since a very safe product is a better product than an unsafe one. However, strict liability that results in exceedingly safe products not only will distort resource use by preventing customers from choosing the safety level they prefer—admittedly above a floor that meets minimum requirements—but will result in a general rise in the price level. Thus, inflationary forces are generated, a condition feared today by most countries.

Exceedingly high safety levels also have an effect on the state of competition in the particular industry. As was mentioned earlier, only very large firms enjoying the benefits of producing a wide variety of goods and services—with only a few of them subject to strict liability—can hope to pay the high cost of insurance or of carrying out research, development, and production of products meeting the very high safety standards. Smaller firms will go under, and the industry is likely to become increasingly monopolized.

But perhaps most damaging is the chilling effect strict liability rules are likely to have on new discoveries and innovation. Particularly feared are chilling effects on investment by industries that are otherwise well situated to seek new drugs and medical equipment. The risk and cost of developing such new drugs and devices may be so high that most firms will prefer to stay with their old products. Should this happen, great societal losses will result.

In the light of these potential aggregate effects, certain steps can be taken to provide reasonably safe products without placing unduly high burdens on society. Perhaps the single most important, yet perhaps the most difficult, step is to make sure that courts are reasonable in setting safety levels. Beyond this, courts may allow a consideration of contributory negligence by workers who have been grossly negligent in taking minimum precautions against industrial accidents. Shifting some such liability to a negligent employer makes sense in the light of statistics showing that nearly seven out of eight industrial accidents result from either worker or employer neglect.[18] Also, a "state-of-the-art" defense can be suggested. It would permit manufacturers to plead that a modern safety feature was not technologically available when the product was originally manufactured. This defense could be accompanied by a statute of limitations beyond which the manufacturer is no longer liable, possibly 10–15 years. Resource allocation could be improved if federal legislation and regulation would standardize product liability rather than leave it up to the states to deal with these problems. Competition could be enhanced if federal guidelines and assistance were given toward the formation of a national product-liability pooling mechanism to help smaller manufacturers of "high-risk" products, and toward federal chartering of "captive" or in-house insurance subsidiaries.

Pg 141 posner

ECONOMIC ANALYSIS OF ACCIDENT LAW

The laws and institutional arrangements concerning automobile accidents, in short accidents, are closely related to those dealing with malpractice and product liability, which similarly aim to protect against the destruction of initial entitlements. But there are some unique features, and therefore the subject of accident law deserves to be treated separately. This analysis examines the goals of accident laws and evaluates various methods used toward their attainment. Because of the great interest in no-fault accident compensation plans, special attention is given to them.

The major goals of accident laws are, by general agreement, justice and

18. *Business Week,* January 17, 1977, p. 63.

accident-cost reduction. Justice through fair compensation of injured parties is an often-mentioned but elusive goal.[19] Posner finds compensation to
be both costly and incomplete.[20] Regardless of these difficulties, the law
cannot close its eyes to seeking justice for those injured in automobile
accidents. Providing fair protection against the destruction of initial entitlements remains a large order.

Economists can contribute to estimating compensation, but they are also
interested in shaping accident law so as to reduce accident costs to efficient
levels, and in accomplishing this objective efficiently. In this connection it is
useful to define accident costs broadly, in terms of social costs of accidents.
Such a broad view does not deny the importance of reducing the number
and severity of accidents, a cost item that is a subset of the broader social
costs of accidents. Furthermore, note that the application of tort law to
accidents in such a way as to protect against the destruction of initial
entitlements can involve high administration costs. It is in this connection
that we seek to reduce accident costs with the aid of cost-effective administrative procedures.

Frequency and severity of accidents can be affected by the methods
selected for risk distribution. Calabresi has identified three major risk-
distribution methods—*risk-spreading, deep-pocket,* and *deterrence* methods.[21]

Risk spreading in its most extreme form seeks the broadest possible
spreading of losses both over people and over time. Through social insurance schemes the most universal spreading of risk is possible. The question
remains, however, of how funds should be raised to cover all accidents.
Social insurance could be paid out of general taxes. An alternative that
involves high transaction costs is to tax people on the basis of their tendency
to cause accidents costs, a scheme that would offer some incentive to avoid
accidents; the first scheme would not do so. More commonly, risks are
distributed through private or voluntary insurance. Most such insurance is
a combination of intertemporal and interpersonal spreading, with some
adjustment made in the rates for accident-proneness.

A further risk-spreading device is referred to by Calabresi as *enterprise
liability.*[22] By placing losses on buyers of products or factors employed in
their production, a fairly wide distribution of accident losses occurs. However, it is very difficult to determine the degree to which enterprises
succeed in shifting losses forward to consumers and backward to production factors—mainly workers. The analysis of these shifts is similar to that

19. G. Calabresi, *The Costs of Accidents: A Legal and Economic Analysis* (New Haven, Conn.:
Yale University Press, 1970), p. 24.

20. Richard A. Posner, *Economic Analysis of Law,* 2nd ed. (Boston: Little, Brown, 1977),
p. 154.

21. Calabresi, *Costs of Accidents,* pp. 21–23.

22. *Ibid.,* pp. 50–54.

of tax shifting and heavily depends on the relative elasticity of the relevant demand and supply functions.

Although it is difficult to determine precisely how much of the losses are shifted forward and backward, it is quite clear that payers under enterprise liabilities are different from those under social insurance. Under enterprise liability those on whom the burden comes to rest are those who are engaged in the activity that produced the loss. A system of enterprise liability can therefore provide deterrence.

A number of objections to risk spreading through private insurance have been voiced: People do not know what is best for them; most people are unable to value properly the risk they face; certain individuals will not bear the costs of failing to insure; and the cost of loss spreading differs depending on who chooses whether to insure.

The deep-pocket method places losses on those who can afford to pay— the well-to-do. It is therefore an income-redistribution scheme. The method assumes that a dollar taken from a wealthy person causes less pain than one taken from a poor person.

Finally, the deterrence method places losses on activities that engender accidents. This method attempts to decide what the accident costs of activities are likely to be and then lets the market determine the degree to which and the manner in which activities are desired at such costs. People are given the freedom to choose whether they will engage in the activity and pay the cost of doing so—including accident costs—or whether in the light of the expected accident costs they would prefer safer activities even though these might otherwise be less desirable. Moreover, the incentives might result in investments that produce a general reduction in the likelihood of accidents.

The deterrence method relies on the market to help make rational decisions. Accident costs are treated as one of the many costs faced by the automobile driver, who would trade off the costs and benefits associated with his driving activities and seek the most advantageous balance. The driver thus faces a conventional problem in welfare economics. Its solution assumes that he knows what is good for him, which, if correct, leads under ideal conditions to an optimal resource allocation. But the presence of monopoly, unemployment, and unequal income distribution, among other factors, will tend to prevent the attainment of Pareto optimum.[23]

The fault system succeeds best in deterring accidents when victims belong to the class of actors who can best decide whether accident avoidance is worthwhile and can most efficiently accomplish such avoidance.[24] More-

---

23. For a detailed discussion see Calabresi, *Costs of Accidents,* pp. 78–85.
24. G. Calabresi, "Optimal Deterrence and Accidents," *Yale Law Journal* 84 (March 1975): 657–671.

over, transaction costs, including administration costs, should be low. In fact, however, all risk-distribution methods under the fault system entail high administrative costs related mainly to litigation. In an effort to reduce these transaction costs, and on the assumption that fear of self-inflicted bodily injury and of criminal prosecution can deter careless conduct, no-fault automobile compensation plans have been advanced. The progenitor of all such plans is the proposal of Keeton and O'Connell.[25] These plans, regardless of their nuances, would remove fault liability from automobile accident law and substitute in its place a system of first-party insurance. Every motorist would be required to carry basic protection insurance, which would entitle him in case of accident to recover his medical expenses plus lost earnings regardless of the injurer's negligence. In most plans, pain and suffering would not be compensated and collateral benefits would be deducted. Under most plans, victims may waive basic protection and sue in court, but only if they sustain more than a reasonable amount of damages—for example, $10,000 other than pain and suffering.[26] Basic protection would be first-party (accident) rather than third-party (liability) insurance. The automobile driver would pay premiums to and collect damages from his own insurer. The injurer and his insurance company are liable only if the victim waives basic protection and sues in court.

As of January 1, 1976, the states of Arkansas, Delaware, Kentucky, Maryland, Oregon, North Dakota, South Dakota, Texas, and Virginia had no-fault laws with first-party benefits, but no tort restrictions. In another 16 states there existed no-fault laws with first-party benefits as well as tort restrictions. However, in all cases these restrictions involved a very low threshold, with $200 in New Jersey the lowest, and $2000 in Minnesota the highest.[27]

The positive side effects are lower administration costs. But what are some of the negative side effects? One drawback is a possible lessening of deterrence. Another is an unwarranted differential incentive to various groups to reduce the likelihood of accidents. For example, an insurance company might favor relatively low premiums to drivers of large, heavy automobiles, since they tend to sustain less serious losses than drivers of

25. Robert E. Keeton and Jeffry O'Connell, *Basic Protection for the Traffic Victim: A Blueprint for Reforming Automobile Insurance* (Boston: Little, Brown, 1965).

26. A $10,000 economic loss as ceiling for unconditional reparation appears reasonable for the late 1960s in view of accident statistics. Thus in the late 1960s, 99% of all persons injured in automobile accidents incurred losses below $10,000. The remaining 1% incurring $10,000 or more in economic losses accounted for 69% of the aggregate economic losses resulting from automobile accidents. The reason is that the gravest economic losses occur in a few, though very serious, accidents. See W. Blum and H. Kalven, "Ceilings, Costs and Compulsion in Auto Compensation Legislation," in *Perspectives on Tort Law,* ed. R. L. Rabin (Boston: Little, Brown, 1976), p. 269.

27. C. O. Gregory, H. Kalven, and R. A. Epstein, *Cases and Materials on Torts,* 3rd ed. (Boston: Little, Brown, 1977), p. 870.

small, vulnerable cars.[28] These comparatively low premiums would reduce the incentive of drivers of heavy cars to avoid accidents while unduly increasing the incentive for drivers of small cars to do so. Avoidance measures taken in light of the incentives given to the two groups are likely to lead to distortion and inefficiency. Nevertheless, if transaction costs can be reduced greatly and fear of self-inflicted injury and of criminal prosecution is a major deterrent to unsafe driving, no-fault compensation plans can provide efficient means of protecting against the destruction of initial entitlements.

REEXAMINATION OF THE LEARNED HAND FORMULA WITHIN A WELFARE FRAMEWORK

The Learned Hand formula, though an algebraic expression, is much less clear-cut than is commonly recognized. Carefully considered, it is seen to be ambiguous in a number of respects. J. P. Brown has shown that at least three closely related standards of negligence can be inferred from the Learned Hand formula.[29]

The first standard is called by Brown the *Literal Learned Hand Standard.* It constitutes the most common interpretation and compares the *total* costs of harm prevention with the expected costs of the accident. Brown argues that this Literal Standard can only answer the question of whether it is better to provide complete protection against potential harm or to provide none at all. This question is neither of interest nor common in tort proceedings.

Brown therefore derives what he calls the *Incremental Standard* of the Learned Hand formula. It assumes complete information about the underlying technology of accident prevention. Under these circumstances the "negligence for one party is determined on the *assumption that the other party is already acting in an optimal manner.*"[30]

It can be shown that conditions associated with the Incremental Standard coincide with the condition for social-cost minimization independently for both the injurer and the victim. Thus, the determination of the Incremental Standard also determines the social-cost-minimizing solution. Courts applying the Incremental Standard for the determination of a social optimum define avoidance below the optimum as negligent.

Although the Incremental Standard has very desirable attributes, it suffers from excessively stringent information demands. These are relaxed in a third standard identified by Brown and referred to by him as the *Limited Information Incremental Standard.* It assumes rather realistic conditions, in

28. Posner, *Economic Analysis of Law,* p. 156.
29. J. P. Brown, "Toward an Economic Theory of Liability," *Journal of Legal Studies* 2 (June, 1973): 331–335.
30. *Ibid.,* p. 333.

terms of both the knowledge usually available to potential tortfeasors and the argument frequently advanced in tort cases. It does not assume that courts have information on all accident-prevention alternatives and their cost–benefit implications. Rather, the court is assumed to be able merely to investigate effects of small changes away from the preventive steps actually chosen by the two parties on the probability of harm. Under the Limited Information Incremental Standard the court declares an avoidance level as negligent if it is below the optimal level in the light of the steps taken by the other party.[31]

The appropriateness of the last two standards is well summarized by Brown:

> The Incremental Standards are a good approximation, I think, of the way that courts actually proceed. The attorney for the plaintiff will try to find some act which, if the defendant had taken it, would have significantly reduced the probability of the accident at low cost. But that is precisely the statement that the increment in the expected loss was greater than the cost of avoidance, which is the definition of the Incremental Standards of negligence. The defendant will try to respond that the expected benefits of the proposed act were, in fact, less than the costs of undertaking it. When the court is asked to decide between the two points of view it is being asked to compare the incremental expected benefits with the incremental costs. Thus it is not peculiar that the outcome of large, important cases often seems to turn on the value of small changes in the behavior of one party or the other.[32]

In summary, negligence law does not require the defendant to be altruistic in the sense of being self-abnegating. But he is required to place the welfare of others and his own on an equal footing. Conduct that embodies a failure to do so leads to a judgment of negligence under the Incremental Standards of the Learned Hand formula.

SOVEREIGN IMMUNITY

LEGAL BACKGROUND

From the beginning of judicial history in the United States, there has been great confusion about sovereign immunity. It was a rule that began in England, as the personal prerogative of the king. The basic position was that "the king can do no wrong," but even local governments were held not liable for tort. _Russell_ v. _Men of Devon_ involved an action in tort against an unincorporated county.[33] The court ruled that since the groups were unin-

└→ + had no money

31. In more precise terms, the injuring party is held negligent whenever he or she takes preventive steps below those required to minimize social costs, treating the preventive steps of the injured party as fixed.

32. Brown, "Economic Theory of Liability," pp. 334–335.

33. _Russell_ v. _Men of Devon_, 100 Eng. Rep. 359 (1788).

corporated there was no fund out of which the judgment could be paid, and, moreover, it was more appropriate for an individual to sustain an injury than for the public to suffer an inconvenience. This ruling of an English court was first applied in the United States in _Mower v. Leicester._[34] Although the county was incorporated, could sue, and had corporate funds out of which a judgment could be satisfied, the Massachusetts court used _Russell_ as a leading case, and it became the basis for the treatment of governmental tort liability in the United States. _Russell_ has been attacked on all three levels of government; on the federal level, the Federal Tort Claims Act of 1946 waived the government's general tort immunity.[35]

On the state level, too, there has been much action. In 1963 the California legislature enacted the first general law dealing with governmental liability.[36] This legislative action followed two important California Supreme Court decisions. In _Muskopf_ v. _Corning Hospital District,_ the court held that the doctrine of sovereign immunity would no longer protect public entities from civil liability for their torts.[37] In _Lipman_ v. _Brisbane Elementary School District,_ the court stated that the doctrine of discretionary immunity might not protect public entities from liability in all situations.[38] Other states that enacted sovereign tort immunity acts in the early 1960s include Illinois,[39] Minnesota,[40] and Oregon.[41]

Sovereign immunity has been based in the past on two classes of distinctions: governmental versus proprietary activities and discretionary versus ministerial functions. Wherever legislatures have acted, the govern-

---

34. _Mower_ v. _Leicester,_ 9 Mass. 247, 249 (1812).

35. Under the Federal Tort Claims Act the federal government is made generally liable for money damages, for injury or loss of property, or for personal injury or death caused by the negligent or wrongful act or omission of any employee of the government while acting within the scope of his office or employment, under circumstances where the United States, if a private person, would be liable to the claimant.

There are three principal exceptions to this general rule of suability. First, the government is absolutely immune from suit for torts occurring while it is engaged in a set of specific tasks, including collecting taxes and fighting wars. Second, the government is granted immunity from a set of causes of action, including any claim arising out of assault, battery, false imprisonment, false arrest, malicious prosecution, abuse of process, libel, slander, misrepresentation, deceit, or interference with contract rights. Third, the United States may escape liability if it can show that the acts or omissions complained of were based on the exercise or performance of or the failure to exercise or perform a discretionary function or duty on the part of a federal agency or an employee of the government, whether or not the discretion involved be abused. Federal Tort Claims Act, 28 U.S.C. 1291, 1346, 1402, 1504, 2110, 2401–2404, 2411–2414, 2671–2680 (1970), as amended by Act of March 16, 1974, Pub. L. 93–253, 2, 88, Stat. 50, 28 U.S.C. 2680 (h) (Supp. IV 1974).

36. California Tort Claims Act (1963).

37. _Muskopf_ v. _Corning Hospital District,_ 359 P.2d 457 (1961).

38. _Lipman_ v. _Brisbane Elementary School District,_ 359 P.2d 465 (1961).

39. Illinois Tort Immunity Act (1965).

40. Minnesota Tort Claims Act (1963).

41. Oregon Tort Claims Act (1967).

mental–proprietary distinction has been discarded, most likely for good reason. There never was a logical reason why, for the same tortious act, for example, a private hospital could be sued but a government hospital could not.

Much of today's argument in favor of sovereign immunity is based on the distinction between discretionary and ministerial functions of government. Discretionary acts have been defined as "those wherein there is no hard and fast rule as to the course of conduct that one must or must not take."[42] Thus, discretionary activities relate to basic policy decisions as well as planning operations, as opposed to operational-level day-to-day decision making, which involves ministerial functions.

The distinction between discretionary and ministerial functions has been elucidated in *Ramos* v. *County of Madera.*[43] In September 1967 the Madera County schools were closed so that pupils could assist in the grape harvest. The county welfare department, although lacking the authority to so act, announced that Aid for Dependent Children (AFDC) recipients aged 10 years and older must work in the fields or face aid termination. When 19 families refused to send their children to the harvest, their assistance payments were halted immediately. Consequently the California Supreme Court reversed the finding. The court ruled that "a public entity may be liable in tort . . . where it knows or should know that its failure to exercise its duty to reasonably supervise employees will result in coercing others to violate state laws, and where such violation proximately results in an injury of the kind the law was designed to prevent."[44]

Moreover, the court held that governmental immunity did not protect defendants since immunity is only for decisions of a policy-planning nature, not for the operational level of day-to-day decision making. Since welfare-eligibility standards are determined at state and federal levels, the court decided that the defendants' actions were not discretionary in the statutory sense even though welfare employees often exercise judgment in determining whether individual recipients fulfill aid eligibility requirements. The court, realizing that almost all actions involve some element of discretion, rejected any rule of law based on such a semantic distinction, and opted for a rule considering whether policy reasons justified immunity. Local welfare departments, for example, are not protected by governmental immunity when they merely enforce and administer mandatory eligibility standards established at state and federal levels. They do not perform the policymaking function necessary for governmental immunity and their actions leave no room for discretion.

---

42. *Elder* v. *Anderson*, 205 Cal. App. 2d 326, 331.
43. *Ramos* v. *County of Madera*, 4 Cal. 3d 685; 94 Cal. Rptr. 421, 484 P.2d 93.
44. *Ibid.*, pp. 695–696.

A FRAMEWORK OF ANALYSIS

Tort law reallocates the costs of unintentional harm, and we need a framework within which we can weigh the circumstances under which government should be held responsible for a tortious act, or should be held immune. Moreover, we would like to inquire into the circumstances under which, if ever, public employees or officials, rather than public entities, should be suable.

Before attempting to answer, I would probe into some side effects. There can be no doubt that whenever decision makers can be sued, both for action or inaction, they are given an incentive that can lead to more efficient decisions. Clearly there is a difference as to whether a public official or only a public agency can be sued, although even if an official is immune personally, heavy burdens can be placed on him when his agency is sued. Public agencies, unless they are immune, must fear the possibility of fines, large amounts of time being required in the discovery and trial stages of suits, adverse publicity, and the like. In the face of such a threat, public agencies are likely to be induced to consider seriously whether their action or inaction is likely to result in litigation. Though considering these issues will require resources, these costs under certain circumstances are likely to be small compared to the benefits that result from more careful decision making.

As long as there are circumstances in which government can be sued, we must decide whether the public agency or the public official should be suable. Under the doctrine of *respondeat superior*, the government agency *and* the employee are responsible. As a practical matter, however, government, with its deeper pocket will be sued. This arrangement takes advantage of government's unique ability to spread the cost of harm. However, the concept of strict liability inherent in *respondeat superior* can result in inefficient solutions to conflicting resource use problems. In the narrow sense, the doctrine gives the public official relatively little incentive to take steps to prevent harm. In order to counteract this tendency, government would have to devote resources to monitor the activities of employees so as to eliminate careless individuals and carelessness. Moreover, it might have to impose sanctions for carelessness. Monitoring and policing public employees are severely circumscribed by civil service provisions and increasingly strong unionization. Both reduce government's power to fire employees or in other ways enforce compliance with appropriate standards of performance. In short, the doctrine of *respondeat superior*, which shifts tort liability to the agency, weakens the incentive of public officials to make every effort toward the best possible solution and its implementation.

Yet refusing personal immunity to public officials under most circumstances would be a mistake. Most people, particularly the ablest ones, would tend to refuse public employment, should they be suable. For this reason, no doubt, many states give public officials a nearly ironclad guaranty of indemnification from the employing public entity. Still, the recruitment of top government officials is handicapped, since as public officials they forfeit the legal protection relative to privacy and defamation accorded high-ranking corporate officials. This issue is exacerbated by the Freedom of Information Act and the fact that compensation in the private sector is more commensurate with the personal risks associated with the position. Thus, even if the agency and not the official is sued, great inconvenience, mental stress, and losses of time and privacy can result, both during the discovery period and when the case reaches the courts.

For these reasons, the total absence of sovereign immunity would tend to reduce the caliber of persons who fill top government positions. The chilling effect would be even more significant in relation to the filling of positions on boards where remuneration is insignificant or plays a minor role.

Thus, in order to determine whether a government agency should or should not be immune, it is necessary to balance two considerations at the margin. The costs to government, in the absence of sovereign immunity, of being served by generally less qualified public servants and the costs of legal action must be balanced against the benefits that can be expected from conditions that give decision makers incentives and signals conducive to the best possible decisions.[45] Whether the gains exceed the costs is not easily answered. The aspect of fairness must also be considered.

There exists some literature on this matter. Spitzer has argued that since tort law "is a system of reallocating the costs of accidents, when one of the parties in an accident is the government, sovereign immunity in tort may preclude any reallocation. Hence, the government and private citizens face different structures of incentives to be careful (or to take risks)."[46] He concludes by advancing "the preferred rule . . . that the government should be suable to tort for monetary damages."[47]

Based on a large number of assumptions, including one that government behaves in accord with one of nine specific models, Spitzer's analysis is quite thorough, and perhaps even excessively mathematical. However, by having picked the example of the locomotive sparks that can burn up a farmer's wheat field, first used by Coase, he misses many of the public-goods aspects of government immunity. He fails, for example, to place sufficient em-

45. In a more general way this issue had already been stated in 1969 by the California Appeals Court, when it stated that immunity be given "flexible definition which balances the harm that may be caused by inhibition of the governmental function against the desirability of providing redress for wrong that may have been done." See *Jones* v. *Oxnard School District*, 270 Cal. App. 2d 587.

46. M. L. Spitzer, "An Economic Analysis of Sovereign Immunity in Tort," *Southern California Law Review* 50 (March 1977): 515.

47. *Ibid.*, p. 548.

phasis on the social costs that are incurred in the absence of immunity in the case of essential public services for which there are only very costly alternatives. Yet, for many public goods there exist very few substitutes. The social costs can be very great, as I stated earlier, when key government jobs cannot be filled by the very best people because of fear that their agency might be sued and their own reputations tarnished by adverse publicity.

In addition, the administrative cost of providing a record for evidence that alternatives have been weighed and discretion exercised, and the expense of defending the agency in court, can become very high. Spitzer finally modifies his Simple Welfare Maximizing model into one of Welfare/Tort Balancing, in which the "bureaucrat wants to do the best that he can for the citizens, . . . [but he] dislikes tort judgments against his bureau."[48] In this model, which is perhaps his most realistic one, Spitzer finds that "immunity is the preferable rule."[49] Yet, in arriving at his general conclusion quoted earlier, Spitzer appears to neglect this more realistic model.

SOVEREIGN IMMUNITY AND PAROLE DECISIONS

The foregoing framework will next be applied to decisions about the parole of prisoners. When a felonious act is committed the shock and outrage expressed is particularly strong if the crime was perpetrated by a parolee. One of the first questions often asked under such circumstances pertains to preventability. If there were no sovereign immunity, would parole boards and parole agencies not make more careful parole decisions and would they not implement them more efficiently?[50] Then, would not fewer crimes be committed by parolees?

Most states provide explicit immunity to all those who deal with parolees.[51] However, some court decisions appear to limit sovereign immunity.[52] Thus, for example, according to California case law, although

48. *Ibid.*, p. 538.

49. *Ibid.*

50. A parole agency is the government unit that supervises and otherwise deals with convicts who are on parole. In some cases it may be part of the prison system; in others it may be independent and it may also deal with persons on probation.

51. The California Tort Claims Act, for example, is quite specific about tort liability of both a public entity and its employees. Section 845.8(a) of the act states, "Neither a public entity nor a public employee is liable for . . . any injury resulting from determining whether to parole or release a prisoner or from determining the terms and conditions of his parole or release or from determining whether to revoke his parole or release [California Tort Claims Act, Section 845.8(a)]."

52. In *Johnson* v. *State of California*, the California Supreme Court in 1969 carefully distinguished between two separate activities of state juvenile parole officers: (a) the decision to place a youth with foster parents and (b) the decision of a parole officer as to the warnings he should give to foster parents. The court held that "once the proper authorities have made the basic policy decision—to place a youth with foster parents, for example—the role of

parole boards are basically immune, many activities of agencies may not be immune. But, before we attempt to place the parole function into the balancing framework developed earlier, it must be remembered that parole decisions can be incorrect, whether they are positive or negative. Still, on balance it would appear easier to prove that a decision had been erroneous if a prisoner was prematurely released than if he was kept too long.

As long as decisions by parole boards involve discretion and are therefore immunized and most other parole decisions are not, the efficiency of parole decisions is increased if all parole and prison functions are vertically integrated. Then boards would look upon themselves, the prison agency, and the parole agency as parts of a single integrated system through which criminals move after conviction by the courts. The board would stand in the middle of this vertically integrated system whose overall costs and benefits it would seek to balance. The more supervisory functions of the parole agency (though not of the board) are classified as ministerial and known to be so, the more efficient the parole decisions that will result. This statement, however, should be tempered by the possibility that as parole agencies enjoy fewer immunities, recruiting of able probation officials will become more difficult. How serious the recruiting problem will become is an empirical question that remains to be researched.

The board should take into consideration the various cost and benefit elements associated with paroling a convict on the one hand and with keeping him incarcerated on the other. Costs of paroling include losses to victims of crimes committed by parolees, to parole boards and parole agen-

---

section 845.8 immunity ends; subsequent negligent actions, such as the failure to give reasonable warnings to the foster parent actually selected, are subject to legal redress (69C.2d 785)."

Johnson mandates the balancing of the following three policy considerations: importance of function involved, extent to which immunity would impair the exercise of this function, and the availability of other remedies. Moreover, *Johnson* emphasizes that for immunity to hold, the official who is accused of action must show that he exercised discretion and either consciously considered the risks involved or determined that such risks were justified by other policies.

In *Elton* v. *County of Orange,* the California Appeals Court held that "while the . . . Probation Department performs functions . . . which could be classified as involving basic policy decisions (such as recommending a child be, or not be, declared a dependent child), and hence warrants immunity, it does not follow [that] its subsequent ministerial acts in implementing such decisions rise to the same level [53 Cal. App. 3rd 1058, 54 Cal. Rptr. 30 (1970)]."

Applied to parole board decisions, these two cases can mean that the board is immune when it makes a parole decision; but the probation department is not immune in implementing the decision, if it does not take all appropriate action to prevent a parolee from committing a crime. However, in *Santa Barbara County* v. *Superior Court for Santa Barbara County,* the California Supreme Court ruled that the conduct of county employees who, it was alleged, negligently released a prisoner on bail after the prisoner demonstrated extreme violent behavior while incarcerated, was inherently a part of the process of determining whether to release him. Thus, the county was held immune from liability for the wrongful death of a person stabbed by the arrestee while on bail [93 Cal. Rptr. 406, 15 C.A. 3d 751 (1971)].

cies resulting from a dissatisfied public, to parole officials as their reputations are beclouded, and to parole agencies in defending themselves in court and possibly being forced to pay damages.

Benefits of paroling include those to parolees whose sentences are shortened, who are able to leave early the often-damaging prison environment, and who may thus be more successfully rehabilitated; and to prison authorities who will have fewer prisoners to look after and who can effectively use parole as a means to elicit good behavior from prisoners.

The last two issues deserve some elaboration. First, although the capacity of the prison system is more or less fixed, and all too often inadequate, the number of prisoners that require incarceration varies over time. Strong evidence exists that parole decisions today are heavily influenced by prison vacancy rates. Thus, one cost of not paroling prisoners is overburdened prisons in the short run and adding prison space in the long run. Second, costs are incurred when the paroling of prisoners is altogether abandoned. Then a potent inducement to good behavior is lost. No doubt, the administration of prisons has been made easier by prisoners' knowledge that their term might be shortened for good behavior, and prison authorities are likely to be reluctant to give up this valuable enticement.[53] Yet perhaps too much emphasis has been placed on good behavior. Norval Morris, former dean of the University of Chicago Law School, points to "the hypocrisy of parole decisions, in which it is pretended against the evidence that behavior in the cage is a reliable guide to behavior in the community."[54]

Thus, should it be generally known that if crimes are committed by parolees (and thus might have been prevented by ministerial decisions) parole agencies will be held strictly accountable, these agencies would seek to exert increasing pressure on legislatures for funds to ensure that their responsibilities can be met. (In this connection a careful spelling out of relevant ministerial functions would be helpful.) Legislators would then perhaps respond more fully to responsible claims. Likewise, a prison system that can no longer rely on parole boards to stabilize its occupancy rates will seek to exert more pressure and possibly receive a fair hearing for proper funding. A parole board located in the middle of the prison–parole system is likely to take into consideration all the system's activities, and their costs and benefits.

Two extreme, and less efficient, solutions would virtually disappear from

53. For example, in relation to the California Youth Authority, good behavior or satisfactory performance means attendance at some kind of school, or work at some kind of chore for 6 hours a day; not being cited more than once a month for attempted escape, fighting, drug use, or drug smuggling; and not being cited more than twice a month for talking back to a counsellor, not making a bed, and pushing ahead in the food line. See *Los Angeles Times*, December 18, 1977.

54. Norval Morris, "Prison Sentencing: A Way out of Anarchy," *Los Angeles Times*, January 5, 1978.

the scene. The first is the common case discussed earlier of parole boards being influenced by prison occupancy rates, which can lead to premature paroling of prisoners. The second is an issue of particular concern to courts who argue in favor of the immunity of discretionary functions—that boards would become increasingly reluctant to grant parole for fear of being sued. Since within the proposed framework boards would seek to consider the difference between benefits and costs of incarcerating versus paroling prisoners, they would not necessarily vote against parole.

In summary, there is obvious merit in more carefully classifying parole decisions into discretionary and ministerial ones. Most decisions by parole agencies to implement those made by parole boards should fall into the second category. Removing immunity from many parole agency activities, though leaving individual officials and parole boards immune, is likely to lead to more carefully considered parole decisions. Moreover, improved decisions would result if parole boards were fully integrated with the parole and prison system, and if they were required to show that in their decisions they have carefully traded off expected costs and benefits. These steps, however, should be taken in a manner that will keep to a minimum the possibly chilling effects of reduced immunity on the recruitment of probation officials. In this new environment, gains from providing efficient incentives, as immunity of parole agencies is reduced, can exceed the costs incurred.

RULES FOR ASSIGNING LIABILITY FOR LITIGATION COSTS

Once courts have determined that a negative externality has been imposed on a plaintiff and initial entitlements have been destroyed, they can assess compensatory and punitive damages. But should the assessment of damages also include the payment of the plaintiff's litigation costs? And if so, what are the effects of rules that assign liability for litigation costs to the unsuccessful party in tort (and contract) cases?

As one surveys the legal scene, one finds two major rules for allocating litigation costs—mostly attorney fees—in civil cases. The American rule, prominent in all states but the state of Alaska and applicable to most types of litigation at the federal level, directs each party to pay its own fees regardless of which litigant prevails.[55] Admittedly there are some exceptions. For example, U.S. equity courts reserve the right to assign litigation costs as a punitive measure where a party has willfully disobeyed a court

---

55. "Court Awarded Attorneys' Fees and Equal Access to the Courts," *Pennsylvania Law Review* 122 (January 1974): 637–713.

order or has engaged in an oppressive activity. Moreover, litigation fees have been awarded to successful plaintiffs for bringing litigation that promotes the effective implementation of public policy.

The second rule—the Continental rule—is specified in 29 federal statutes and is in force in the state of Alaska and in the United Kingdom, Canada, and other Western countries. It awards to the prevailing litigant some or all of his litigation costs, according to some predetermined schedule.[56]

What are some of the effects of these two rules? The American rule, it has been argued, leads to an excessive initiation of suits, an inordinate amount of litigation relative to settlement, and prolongation of litigation.[57] Since it is also said to encourage nuisance suits and to discourage plaintiffs with strong but small suits without legal aid, the American rule may be inefficient and inequitable.

Yet the American rule has been supported by the courts because it "allegedly" places the parties "on a footing of equality" and because it avoids the problem of adopting a "fixed standard" against which reasonable fees would be measured.[58] Chief Justice Warren has defended the American rule on grounds that "since litigation is at best uncertain one should not be penalized for merely defending or prosecuting a lawsuit."[59]

As an example of how economic theory can be applied to derive rigorous statements about the likely effects of the different rules, some work by D. L. Martin will be discussed. It should be emphasized that this work is presented merely as an example, one that explicitly assumes that the parties to a dispute are risk-neutral, court costs are not prohibitive, and the subjective probability of a verdict favoring the plaintiff is larger in the eyes of the plaintiff than of the defendant.[60]

According to Martin, parties who are risk-neutral and pursue as their sole behavioral objective wealth maximization will go to court only if the plaintiff's minimum acceptable compensation is larger than the defendant's maximum offer. These discounted values of trial activity differ, *ceteris paribus*, according to how litigation costs are allocated among litigants. In terms of Martin's model, therefore, the Continental rule will result in

---

56. Although the Continental rule usually applies to the prevailing party in the suit, several U.S. federal statutes allow only plaintiffs to recover attorney fees if they prevail.

57. C. McCormick, "Council Fees and Other Expenses of Litigation as an Element of Damages," *Minnesota Law Review* 15 (May 1931): 619–643, and John Tunney, "Financing the Cost of Enforcing Legal Rights," *Pennsylvania Law Review* 122 (January 1974): 122, 632–635.

58. *Oelricks* v. *Spain*, 82 U.S. (15 Wall.) 211, 231 (1972).

59. *Fleischmann Distilling Corp.* v. *Maier Brewing Co.*, 383 U.S. 714 (1967).

60. D. L. Martin, *Assigning Liability for Attorney Fees: An Economic Analysis* (UCLA Law–Economic Workshop, February 1, 1978).

relatively more litigation than the American rule if the parties are risk-neutral, court costs are not prohibitive, and the plaintiff is more optimistic about the outcome than the defendant is.[61] However, when the defendant is more optimistic about the likely outcome than the plaintiff is, Martin's model indicates that both the American and Continental rules imply settlement, and no statement can be made that a particular rule will be more likely to achieve that result.

These conclusions clearly neglect a number of important considerations. For example, the American rule may often be circumvented by juries who include in their awards to plaintiffs some equivalent of litigation costs. Moreover, court costs are often deductible for federal and state income tax purposes and many defendants fall into distinctly different income categories than do plaintiffs.

61. Let ϕ_p and ϕ_d be the plaintiff's and defendant's subjective probabilities of a verdict favoring the former. Under the American rule, the plaintiff's expected value of going to trial then is $\phi_p(A_d) - k_p$ and the defendant's is $\phi_d(A_d) + k_d$, where A_p and A_d are the parties' respective estimates of the award that would result from trial, and k_p and k_d are their respective litigation costs. (Litigation costs, for the sake of simplicity, are assumed to be zero. This assumption, however, does not affect the analysis, because of the assumption that court costs exceed settlement costs). Thus, trials or settlements will occur depending on whether the left-hand expression in (1) is larger or smaller than the right-hand expression.

$$\phi_p(A_p) - k_p \gtrless \phi_d(A_d) + k_d. \tag{1}$$

If we assume $A_p = A_d$, expression (1) may be rewritten as

$$A(\phi_p - \phi_d) \gtrless k_p + k_d, \tag{2}$$

which shows that, under the American rule, if $\phi_p > \phi_d$ the court costs are not prohibitive, and adversaries will choose trials over settlements.

Martin defines prohibitive litigation costs as those that make settlements more economical than trials, even though adversaries have differing estimates of the probability that the plaintiff will prevail. For each set of probabilities held by adversaries there is one set of court costs that are just nonprohibitive. Where these costs obtain, differences in subjective probabilities that make the plaintiff relatively optimistic are both necessary and sufficient for a trial to take place. See J. P. Gould, "The Economics of Legal Conflicts," *Journal of Legal Studies* 2 (June 1973): 285, 299.

Now compare these conditions with those obtained under the Continental rule. The expected values of a trial, as viewed by the plaintiff and the defendant, are the expressions on the left- and right-hand sides, respectively, of the inequality in (3):

$$\phi_p(A + k_p) - k_p - (1 - \phi_p)k_d \gtrless \phi_d(A + k_p) + k_d - (1 - \phi_d)k_d. \tag{3}$$

These expressions show the minimum acceptable settlement offer for the plaintiff and the maximum settlement offer for the defendant, respectively. Obviously, if the latter's offer is smaller (larger) than the minimal amount acceptable to the former, a trial (a settlement) will ensue. If the costs of litigation are the same for both parties, then $k_d = k_p$, and expression (3) may be restated as

$$A(\phi_p - \phi_d) \gtrless 2[(\phi_d + 1 - \phi_p)k]. \tag{4}$$

The difference between (2) and (4) is the expression $\phi_d + 1 - \phi_p$ on the right side of (4). If this is smaller than 1, if $\phi_p > \phi_d$, the right side of (4) is smaller than the right side of (2).

CONCLUSION

Rather than concentrating on how damages under tort law can be estimated, I have attempted to show how economic theory and, in one case, econometric techniques can enrich the application of tort law. Although the examples presented here are beginnings and, no doubt, more work will be forthcoming in this dynamic field of the law, it is hoped that they indicate the promise of such efforts.

VIII

CRIMINAL LAW

INTRODUCTION

In the past, the discussion of criminal justice was often the domain of philosophers, civil libertarians, and politicians; law enforcement officers and lawyers, obviously, also played a major role. But economists have also developed an interest in the field, and they have begun to produce analytic work.[1] This work casts new light on important policy issues and may even call into question some of the basic assumptions of criminal law and some current criminal justice practices. At the same time, economic analysis is providing a useful underpinning for basic concepts found in criminal law.

The scope of the field is well described by Greenwood:

> The problems of crime and justice are important public policy issues because they touch so many lives and because they involve such fundamental values— personal safety, property rights, privacy, due process and punishment. In 1975 there were more than 11 million serious crimes reported to police agencies and 9 million arrests for non-traffic offenses. Public expenditures for criminal justice functions exceeded 15 billion dollars, 60 percent of which was spent at the local government level. At any one time in this country there are more than 400,000 persons confined in jails or other correctional facilities.[2]

A country's criminal law reflects and also determines governmental roles or objectives in curbing crime. Key issues are whether penalties for those

---

1. Some of the more important work will be presented here.
2. P. W. Greenwood, *Criminal Justice Research at RAND*, P-5886 (Santa Monica: RAND, 1977), p. 1.

who are caught should be severe, in the hope of deterring others, and how the conflicting aims of punishment and rehabilitation should be resolved. This chapter intentionally omits consideration of victimless and white-collar crimes, because of their complexity. I shall attempt to deal with them, therefore, in a detailed, separate effort.

To facilitate the understanding of criminal law, this chapter begins with a discussion of the premises and tenets on which it is based: what makes an act a crime, defenses that may be employed by those accused of crime, and the imposition of penalties and sanctions. The discussion also touches on the economic rationale of these premises. Next a comprehensive theoretical framework is presented, within which crime, its motivation and deterrence, can be given economic content, and the role and effect of criminal law can be evaluated.

THE BASIC LEGAL PREMISES OF CRIMINAL LAW

THE LEGAL DEFINITION OF A CRIME

American criminal law is founded upon certain basic premises concerning what constitutes a crime. Thus, a crime consists of an act, a mental state, concurrence of the act and the mental state, and causation of harm. Crimes are socially responded to by prosecution and punishment. Underlying the criminal law in both its individual and social aspects is an economic rationale, which I shall examine next.

As argued in Chapter I, the destruction of initial entitlements by acts that meet the requirements for a crime is protected by criminal laws. Society, since it places a high premium on human life and on respect for the prevailing property rules, is unwilling to tolerate the negative externalities imposed by persons who commit a crime. Opposing the unleashing of such externalities, society refuses to convert property rules into liability rules and merely to seek compensation for the victim. Instead, for the sake of deterring future externalities of this sort, criminal sanctions are imposed.

Let us next look at the legal requirements necessary for an act to be considered a crime.

Volitional Act

The criminal law imposes liability only when there has been an act of commission or when there has been an act of omission at a time that there is a legal duty to act. An act is defined as a volitional bodily movement. Reflex actions, for example, are not criminal acts regardless of the harm they cause. This definitional requirement of a crime may be said to have an economic rationale. The criminal must have had a choice between action and inaction. Since the criminal law seeks to guide human behavior by the imposition of costs on certain types of activities, it would be inefficient to impose penalties on activities that either do not occur or are not subject to a person's choice calculus. Enforcement bodies have limited resources, which must be efficiently used.

J. G. Murphy has stated that

> an act or omission [is] involuntary (and thus excusing liability) . . . . if and only if the behavior or the failure in question is explainable by factors which causally prevent the exercise of normal capacities of control or eliminate such capacities entirely. By "causally prevent" here I mean simply the following: that the factors and the incapacity can be related by submission under a scientific law. Thus: Prince Miskin (who, in an epileptic seizure, flails his arms and breaks a valuable vase) acted involuntarily (or really did not act at all, if you prefer) in breaking the vase, because epilepsy is a factor we know to be related (in a lawlike way) to capacities of control. The switchman who fails to pull the lever omitted to do so involuntarily if, for example, he was having a seizure at the time he was supposed to be pulling the lever. The merely negligent man, however, has the normal capacities. He simply did not exercise them.[3]

Some crimes are defined in terms of a duty to act or an omission to act. For example, a father has a legal duty to save his child from drowning in a small stream if he is physically able. Such crimes are always defined in terms of circumstances when the omission sought to be punished must clearly have entered the actor's choice calculus. Any objective observer of an omission to act would perceive that the criminal actor involved must consciously have taken account of the costs and benefits of the omission to act. Thus, the nonaction was volitional and would be responsive to the imposition of criminal penalties.[4]

2. Criminal State of Mind

To be a crime, an act must not only be volitional but also have a criminal mental element. Most crimes require some sort of subjective fault. Others require only an objective fault and still others are defined in terms of strict liability crimes. For instance, the crime of receiving stolen property may be defined in terms of "knowing that such property is stolen." Thus, the prosecutor must prove that the criminal actor knew in his own mind that the particular property was stolen. If the crime is defined as "having reason to know" the property was stolen, the proof required is an objective deter-

---

3. J. G. Murphy, "Involuntary Acts and Criminal Liability," *Ethics* 51 (1971): 332.

4. For instance, in *Jones* v. *United States*, 308 F.2d307, the defendant was found guilty of involuntary manslaughter through failure to provide for the 10-month-old illegitimate baby of Shirley Green, who had been placed with the defendant, a family friend. According to medical evidence the baby had been shockingly neglected and died of malnutrition, although the defendant had ample means to provide food and medical care. The court concluded that the defendant's nonaction was clearly the result of a volitional choice not to act, and therefore liability was upheld.

mination of whether a reasonable person would have known the property was stolen. If the crime is defined as "received stolen property," no mental element other than the volitional action of receiving property is necessary.

Within the criminal law such gradations of fault for crimes are correlated closely with the severity of the crime and, as we will see, with the types of punishments imposed. In crimes requiring a subjective fault, the prosecutor has to prove that the criminal consciously weighed the costs and benefits of his act in his mental calculus.

Objective-fault crimes are defined as acts that would have entered the choice calculus of an "objective person." For example, a reasonable person would have known that the property received was stolen. The law is less certain that the act entered the actor's choice calculus. However, the act would have entered an average or objective person's choice calculus.

Strict liability crimes do not require a determination of fault. They are crimes that usually carry light penalties and often involve high transaction costs. With such crimes it is not efficient, given the types of lesser penalties that are imposed, to make a judicial inquiry into whether the act entered the criminal's conscious choice calculus. It is assumed to have so entered and the penalty is imposed if the act occurred.[5]

Motive is not relevant on the substantive side of criminal law. If, for instance, a person steals food to feed his impoverished family, the law will not take motive into account in the determination of the crime. Motive is related to a person's set of preferences, which respond to the costs and benefits imposed by the criminal law. The commission of a crime testifies that, given the costs and benefits of the criminal act as valued by the criminal, he chose the crime. Since the criminal law seeks to impose penalties in order to direct objective behavior, the person's preferences are not relevant to the determination that a crime occurred. However, motive is

---

5. For example, in *State v. Arizona Mines Supply Co.*, 107 Ariz. 199, the county attorney's office charged the Arizona Mines Supply Co. with two counts of "air pollution," a misdemeanor. The information charged that the defendant–respondent did cause, suffer, allow, or permit the discharge into the atmosphere, from a single source of emission, air contaminants for a period or periods aggregating more than 3 min in 1 hour as dark or darker in shade than that designated at No. 2 on the Ringelmann Chart in violation of Section IV, Regulation 1, Maricopa County Air Pollution Control Regulations, February 9, 1970, and ARS § 36-779 and § 36-789.01, May 18, 1970.

At trial, the state sought to exclude (*a*) any evidence as to the amount of money expended by Arizona Mines Supply Co. for air pollution equipment and (*b*) any testimony the defendant might have sought to introduce with regard to its lack of criminal intent to violate the statute and regulations. The state contended that it did not need to prove intent or knowledge since this offense was more in the nature of *malum prohibitum* or strict liability.

The doing of the inhibited act constitutes the crime, and the moral turpitude or purity of the motive by which it was prompted and knowledge or ignorance of its criminal character are immaterial circumstances on the question of guilt. The only fact to be determined in these cases is whether the defendant did the act.

often considered relevant in the determination of guilt when the evidence of guilt is merely circumstantial.

3. Concurrence of Act and State of Mind

A further requirement of a criminal act is that the act and the mental part concur; the state of mind must actuate the commission or omission. Likewise, if the crime requires certain attendant circumstances, these circumstances must exist at the time of the conduct; thus no criminal act occurs when the bad state follows the physical conduct, for here it is obvious that the subsequent mental state is in no sense legally related to the prior act of commission or omission of the defendant. Thus, it is not criminal battery for A accidentally to strike and injure his enemy B, though A, on realizing what has happened, may rejoice at B's discomfiture.

Clearly, the criminal law seeks to impose penalties only in situations where the actor's choice calculus will be affected—when the actor has made a conscious decision to commit the act. The requirement that the act and the mental part concur ensures that the act in question is the result of the actor's conscious choice calculus. This has an economic rationale since penalties on criminal acts will tend to result in an efficient redirection of human behavior.

4. Causation of Harm

Most crimes require not merely conduct but also a resulting harm—the defendant's conduct must be the proximate cause of the result that turns out to be harmful. Proximate cause, as was discussed in Chapter VI, denotes a legal determination that the specified actor is responsible for the cause that produced the harm complained of, without which the result would not have occurred. Then the imposition of a criminal penalty would serve some social purpose. The criminal requirement of causation thus has a rationale in that the imposition of a penalty on a particular actor serves no purpose if that actor did not cause the harm. (Exceptions are certain cases of criminal "attempt.") Causation has a further rationale in the sense that conduct that does not cause harm does not merit punishment, given the limited resources available for the control of criminal behavior. Thus, A is not liable for murder if he shoots at B intending to kill but misses. The question of causation is whether there is a sufficient causal connection between the defendant's conduct and the result of his conduct so that the imposition of a penalty will affect the actor's choice calculus and thereby tend to redirect his behavior.

The goal of the criminal justice system and its system of penalties is thus the creation of a pattern of costs that will create incentives against criminal acts. Therefore penalties are in order only when an actor's prior conduct has caused the crime in question.

DEFENSES TO CRIMES

Not all criminal acts warrant criminal prosecution. Instead, there exist a number of defenses and they are taken up next.

Insanity

When charged with a criminal act, the actor can escape the imposition of liability if, at the time he committed the act, he was laboring under such a defect of reason—from a disease of the mind—as not to know what he was doing; or if he did know it, as not to know that what he was doing was wrong. Generally stated, insanity is a defense when the defendant had a mental disease that kept him from controlling his conduct.[6] The rationale behind the insanity defense is that imposition of costs so as to direct human behavior will only be effective where those costs can enter the actor's choice calculus. If a person is insane, by definition his actions are not responsive to a cost and benefit calculus. He will not respond to criminal penalties and it would therefore be inefficient to attempt to redirect his behavior by that method.

The insanity defense is different from other defenses in that the result, if successfully interposed, is commitment of the defendant in a mental institution. Here, therapeutic methods are employed to seek redistribution of his behavior into socially acceptable norms.

Automatism

One who engages in otherwise criminal conduct is not guilty of a crime if he does so in a state of unconsciousness or semiconsciousness. This is the defense of *automatism*. Its rationale is apparent—the actor is not engaged in a voluntary act and thus will not be responsive to the imposition of normal incentives or penalties. The costs and benefits of criminal action clearly do

---

6. One exception to this statement is when a criminal actor voluntarily takes steps to become insane. In *State* v. *Hall*, 214 N.W.2d 205, the defendant shot and killed a person from whom he had hitched a ride in Oregon. Defendant's version was that shortly before the shooting he took a pill (apparently LSD) given to him by an acquaintance in California who told him it was a "little sunshine" and would make him feel "groovy." The pill induced hallucinations and the deceased, who was sleeping in the car, seemed to turn into a rabid dog like one the defendant's father had shot before his eyes when the defendant was a child. In panic he seized the deceased's gun and shot him.

Here the court ruled that the temporary mental condition caused by voluntary intoxication from alcohol does not constitute a complete defense. The rule is the same when the mental condition results from voluntary ingestion of other drugs as long as the defendant did not take the pill by mistake.

Thus the rule that imposes liability for voluntarily induced insanity fits in with our theory concerning the rationale of the criminal law. One who consciously chooses the risk of the resulting harm is liable for criminal penalties because those criminal sanctions will affect his behavior. One who is insane or in a criminal state not voluntarily induced cannot have his behavior affected by criminal sanctions and thus they are not imposed.

not weigh upon the conscious choice calculus of a person in a state of unconsciousness or semiconsciousness.

Involuntary Intoxication

Involuntary intoxication is a defense to a crime. However, if a lack of awareness of a risk is due to voluntary intoxication there is no defense. These legal rules have the following justifications: If by voluntary intoxication an actor can escape criminal liability, the rationale of the criminal law would be defeated. Consequently, when intoxication is volitional, the foreseeable consequences of intoxication can enter the actor's choice calculus and consequently the imposition of penalties will create behavior-modifying incentives.

Duress

In some instances a criminal confronts a person with a tragic choice. A person's unlawful threat, which causes a defendant reasonably to believe that the only way to avoid imminent death or serious bodily injury is to engage in conduct that violates the literal terms of the criminal law, and which causes the defendant to engage in that conduct, allows the defense of duress. An exception is the case where the violation of the criminal law consists of the equally great cost of intentionally killing an innocent third person. Thus, the duress rule—with this one exception—allows a person caught in the predicament of a threat of imminent death or serious bodily harm to choose the lesser evil in order to avoid the greater evil threatened by the other person. This rule, it can be argued, is socially beneficial in that it reduces the costs incurred by the threat of intentional death or serious bodily injury, both of which involve extremely high costs. However, forbidding such a defense for any lesser violation of the criminal law, one that avoids such high costs, increases social benefits. Note, however, that the defense is inapplicable when the actor has only the alternative of intentionally killing an innocent third person. In a formal way, in such a situation the intentional killing of an innocent third person would merely amount to a wealth transfer, a transaction between the defendant and the third person, without any likely net social benefit.

Necessity

The tragic choice may have an impersonal origin. Thus, pressure of natural physical forces sometimes confronts a person in an emergency with a choice of two evils: Either he may violate the literal terms of the criminal law and thus produce a harmful result, or he may comply with these terms and thus produce great harm. For reasons of social policy, if the harm that will result from compliance with the law is greater than that which will result from violation of the law, he is justified in violating it.

United States v. *Kroncke* well summarizes this defense:

The common thread running through most of these cases in which the defense of necessity was asserted is that there was a reasonable belief on the part of the defendant that it was necessary for him to act to protect his life or health, or the life or health of others, from a direct and immediate peril. None of the cases even suggests that the defense of necessity would be permitted where the actor's purpose is to effect a change in governmental policies which, according to the actor, may in turn result in a future saving of lives.[7]

The rule of necessity has an economic rationale in that it allows the actor to weigh the costs and benefits of a particular action even though it violates the criminal law. He should act in a manner that maximizes social welfare.

Defense of Another Person

This defense is well stated in *People v. Williams,* where the court held,

> A person is justified in the use of force against another when and to the extent that he reasonably believes that such conduct is necessary to defend himself or another against such other imminent use of unlawful force. However, he is justified in the use of force which is intended or likely to cause death or great bodily harm only if he reasonably believes that such force is necessary to prevent imminent death or great bodily harm to himself or another, or the commission of a forcible felony.[8]

By encouraging value-enhancing behavior over the aggregate of individuals, total social welfare is increased.

Self-Defense

One who is not the aggressor in an encounter is justified in using a reasonable amount of force against his adversary when he reasonably believes (*a*) that he is in immediate danger of unlawful bodily harm from his adversary and (*b*) that the use of such force is necessary to avoid this danger. Notice that the key emphasis is on the term *reasonable.*

In general, courts hold that it is not reasonable to use deadly force against a nondeadly attack. Thus, the courts' dealings with the term *reasonable* implicitly value the costs and benefits of each response to the threatening attack and give judicial sanction only to those responses that over the aggregate of the parties decrease the net social costs of the resulting harm.

Defense of Property

A person is justified in using reasonable force to protect his property from trespass or theft when he reasonably believes that the property is in immediate danger of such an unlawful interference and that the use of such force is necessary to avoid that danger.

---

7. *United States* v. *Kroncke,* 451 F.2d 697.
8. *People* v. *Williams,* 56 Ill. App. 2d 159 (1965).

It is generally held that no force is reasonable if a request to desist will be successful. Under another view, deadly force is never reasonable except where the unlawful interference with property is accompanied by a threat of deadly force (in which case it is proper to use deadly force in self-defense), or where the unlawful interference involves an invasion of an occupied dwelling under circumstances causing the defender reasonably to believe that the invader intends to commit a felony therein or to do serious bodily harm to its occupants.

This legal rule creates incentives and sanctions costs that tend to minimize the resulting harm from criminal conduct and encourage the defender of property to use the minimum force necessary to defend his property. It thus minimizes the aggregate of costs over all the parties. Thus it is not efficient to use deadly force to protect mere property since the value of human life is greater than that of property. Furthermore, it is most efficient for the defender to use the minimum force necessary to achieve his desired result, and the rule encourages the defendant actor to use a minimum force consistent with the judicial determination of whether such force would be reasonable. The determination of reasonableness relates to the costs and benefits of an action.

PENALTIES AND SANCTIONS

Criminal law employs sanctions against those who are found guilty of a criminal act. These sanctions and penalties are designed to affect a potential criminal's choice calculus so as to deter the occurrence of criminal acts. Some states have embarked on experiments to compensate, with public funds, victims of certain crimes. Moreover, the federal government is considering similar legislation that can be looked upon as forcing defendants to pay, in addition to the criminal penalties, an objectively determined amount to the victim for having destroyed his initial entitlement.

I mentioned earlier that the law distinguishes among crimes with subjective, objective, and strict liability faults. A crime that requires a subjective-fault determination is usually a serious crime and, if proven to have been committed, is therefore associated with heavy penalties to deter recurrence. Since it is only efficient to impose heavy penalties where the court is satisfied that the defendant consciously considered the costs and benefits he was likely to derive from the criminal act, proof of subjective fault is required.

An objective-fault crime—for example, one where the court merely asks whether a reasonable person would have known that the property received was stolen—is less serious than a subjective-fault crime. It is less likely to have entered the defendant's choice calculus, and moderate penalties may suffice to deter such lesser crimes.

Finally, when transaction costs are high and crimes are of relatively minor consequence, strict liability rules are applied—we have a strict liability fault. Such crimes without fault determination lead to automatic sentencing, but usually to lesser penalties.

Motive, though not relevant to the substantive determination of a crime, can enter into sentencing. Thus, motive is often considered in individual determinations of criminal penalties and a good motive may result in leniency. This makes sense, since once this person's preferences are revealed, a penalty can be chosen that most accurately affects behavior.

ECONOMIC ANALYSIS OF CRIMINAL LAW

The model presented in this section provides a rational explanation for criminal activities. It also provides a framework for the examination of some early econometric attempts at estimating crime-deterrent effects, and for the exploration of police production functions and deterrence.

ECONOMIC MODEL OF A CRIME

In order to understand under what conditions criminal law imposes a liability, what defenses are available, and how the court seeks to determine appropriate penalties we must look at the economic choice calculus that underlies criminal activity. Economists have developed a framework that seeks to explain how rational men trade off expected returns from legal and illegal activities. Perhaps best known is the work of Gary Becker.[9]

Becker's economic choice framework views crime, with the exception of crimes of passion, as an economic activity with rational participants. A person commits a criminal offense if his expected utility exceeds the level of utility he could derive from alternative (legal) activities. He may choose to be a criminal, therefore, not because his basic motivation differs from that of other persons, but because his options and the evaluation of their benefits and costs differ. The criminal law seeks to influence human behavior by imposing costs on criminal activities, thereby providing the individual with an economic incentive to choose *not* to commit a criminal offense; that is, a deterrent incentive.

Within Becker's framework, the number of crimes committed by an individual depends on his probability of conviction, the expected severity of his punishment, and variables reflecting his legal-income-earning potential, environment, and tastes. This can be represented as

$$O_j = O_j(p_j, f_j, u_j), \tag{1}$$

where O_j denotes the number of offenses committed by the jth individual in a given period, p_j is the probability of conviction per offense, f_j is his

9. Gary Becker, "Crime and Punishment: An Economic Approach," *Journal of Political Economy* 78 (March/April 1968): 169–217.

expected punishment per offense, and u_j is a composite variable representing all other influences. An increase in either p_j or f_j would reduce the expected utility associated with a criminal offense, so that

$$\frac{dO_j}{dp_j} < 0, \quad \frac{dO_j}{df_j} < 0. \tag{2}$$

That is, increasing the probability of conviction or the severity of punishment increases the incentive not to commit crimes and so influences the jth individual to commit fewer criminal offenses.

This rational-choice framework is based on the assumption that the person deciding whether or not to commit a crime behaves as if he is responding to the relevant economic incentives. The fact that those who commit certain crimes may differ systematically in certain respects from those who do not commit them does not contradict this basic assumption that both the latter and the former respond to economic incentives. However, this assumption would clearly be inappropriate if a person is insane, since the actions of an insane person are by definition not responsive to normal costs and benefits in a socially acceptable manner. This is indeed the rationale for the use of insanity as a defense to a crime.

The total number of offenses in a community is simply the sum of the offenses committed by all individuals, the sum of all the O_j's. Although the variables p_j, f_j, and u_j are different for each individual j because of differences in such factors as intelligence, education, wealth, and family upbringing, Becker hypothesizes that the total number of offenses, O, can be expressed as the function

$$O = O(p, f, u), \tag{3}$$

where p, f, u represent the average value of these variables for all individuals in the community. It is assumed that, as for each individual, the number of offenses, O, committed in a community is negatively related to p and f.

Becker's innovative model of rational choice can readily be extended to include other variables that affect the costs and benefits of criminal activities relative to alternative legal activities. One law enforcement variable that should perhaps be included in an extension of his rational-choice framework is the probability that a person will be arrested given that he has committed an offense. That is, irrespective of whether he is later convicted, the embarrassment, anxiety, fear, and temporary restriction of activity associated with arrest in itself provide the individual with an incentive not to commit a crime. Furthermore, a person's perception of the costs associated with a criminal offense may well be influenced by the very "visibility" of police patrols. Thus, police activities may act as a direct deterrent on crime over and above the effect they exercise via increasing probabilities of arrest, conviction, and imprisonment.

The rational-choice framework can also be extended to include policy variables that aim at increasing the benefits associated with legal activities rather than at imposing increased costs on illegal alternatives. For example, the government may be able to reduce the level of criminal activity by increasing the education level of the community, thereby increasing the individual's income-earning possibilities associated with legal employment activities. Alternatively, reducing the level of unemployment could increase a person's chance of success in searching for legal employment, and so increase his expected returns from legal employment searching activity relative to his illegal alternatives.

ECONOMETRIC ESTIMATES OF CRIME DETERRENCE

The rational-choice framework that we have examined so far provides specific predictions about the crime-deterrent influences of certain law enforcement (and other) variables, and I shall now consider empirical studies to see if these predictions are observed in reality. Several empirical studies by Ehrlich,[10] Carr-Hill and Stern,[11] Sjoquist,[12] and Phillips and Votey[13] provide evidence that various law enforcement variables do indeed exert an observable deterrent effect on crime.

Ehrlich used simultaneous equations estimation techniques applied to cross-sectional data for the United States to examine the effect of Becker's law enforcement variables p, the probability of conviction, and f, the expected severity of punishment, on the number of criminal offenses. The variable p was measured by the ratio of convictions to reported offenses and f was measured by the average time served by offenders in state prisons. In addition, Ehrlich extended Becker's model to include variables such as unemployment rate, education level, and income distribution so that both rewards from legal activities and costs imposed on illegal activities are taken into account. He found that a 1% increase in the probability of conviction on the average was associated with a reduction in the number of crimes of 0.99%, but a 1% increase in the average prison sentence was associated with a reduction of crimes of 1·12%. Both of these estimated deterrent effects are statistically significant at the 99% confidence level.[14]

Despite the comprehensive nature of his statistical analysis, Ehrlich did

---

10. I. Ehrlich, "Participation in Illegitimate Activities: A Theoretical and Empirical Investigation," *Journal of Political Economy* 81 (1973): 521–565.

11. R. A. Carr-Hill and N. H. Stern, "An Econometric Model of the Supply and Control of Recorded Offenses in England and Wales," *Journal of Public Economics* 81 (1973): 289–318.

12. D. L. Sjoquist, "Property, Crime and Economic Behavior," *American Economic Review* 63 (1973): 439–446.

13. L. Phillips and H. L. Votey, "Crime Control in California," *Journal of Legal Studies* 4 (June 1975): 327–350.

14. Ehrlich, "Participation in Illegitimate Activities," table 5, p. 551. The elasticities quoted here refer to the all-offenses equation using two-stage least squares estimation for 1960 data.

not take into account the effect of any law enforcement variables other than Becker's p and f. For example, he ignored the possible deterrent effects of both the probability of arrest (as opposed to conviction) and the visibility aspect of police patrol activities.

Carr-Hill and Stern also used simultaneous equations estimation techniques, applied to United Kingdom data for urban police districts for 2 years, 1961 and 1966, to investigate the deterrent effect of two law enforcement variables on crime. The two enforcement variables they examined were the clear-up rate (an offense is cleared up if the police clearly know the identity of the offender) and the proportion of those convicted given custodial treatment. For the year 1961, they found that a 1% increase in the clear-up rate on the average was associated with a reduction in the number of crimes of 0.66% and that a 1% increase in the proportion of convicted offenders given custodial treatment was associated with a reduction of 0.28%. Both of these enforcement variable coefficients were found to be statistically significant at a 99% level of confidence, using 1961 data. However, for the year 1966, Carr-Hill and Stern were unable to find evidence at a 99% confidence level that either of these two law enforcement variables exerted any deterrent effect on crime.[15] Thus their findings appear to be somewhat inconclusive when viewed over both time periods.

A possible, though unlikely, explanation of these findings is that potential criminals were indeed responsive to these particular law enforcement variables in 1961 but had ceased to be responsive to them by 1966. However, there is a much more likely explanation. Perhaps the significant deterrent effect detected in 1961 was not observed in their model using 1966 data because of a correlation between their enforcement variables and other variables that are not included in their model, a correlation that existed in 1966 but not in 1961. This would be the case if, for example, courts in some of the police districts surveyed decided some time between 1961 and 1966 to reduce the proportion of convicted offenders sentenced to imprisonment but to maintain the expected severity of punishment by simultaneously imposing heavier prison sentences on those who were imprisoned. In this case, Carr-Hill and Stern's findings for both years would be consistent with the hypothesis that the expected severity of punishments exerts a deterrent effect; but their model would be misspecified in that the proportion of convicted offenders sentenced to custodial treatment fails to reflect variations in the expected severity of punishment in 1966.

Phillips and Votey applied simultaneous equations regression techniques to 1966 data for 50 California counties. They investigated the deterrent effect on the number of crimes committed of the following two enforce-

15. R. A. Carr-Hill and N. H. Stern, "An Econometric Model," pp. 302–303. The proportion of offenders given custodial treatment was found to exert a statistically significant deterrent effect using a 95% confidence level and a one-tailed test.

ment variables—proportion of convicted offenders receiving felony sentences and likelihood of conviction (convictions per arrest). They found that a 1% increase in the probability of conviction on the average was associated with a 0.70% reduction in the number of offenses committed, and a 1% increase in the fraction of convicted offenders receiving felony sentences was associated with a 0.38% reduction.[16] Both coefficients are significant at a 95% level of confidence.

Sjoquist applied single equation estimation techniques to 1960 cross-section data of municipalities in the United States. He examined the deterrent effect of three variables, each reflecting a component of the risk of being punished for an offense. In three separate equations, one for each law enforcement variable, he estimated the impact of arrests per offense, convictions per offense, and convictions per arrest on the number of offenses, respectively. He demonstrated the existence of a deterrent effect at a 99% level of confidence using either arrests per offense or convictions per offense as the appropriate measure of the risk of punishment. In particular, he found that a 1% increase in either the ratio of arrests or the ratio of convictions to offenses on the average was associated with a reduction in the number of offenses of approximately 0.35%.[17] However, the deterrent effect of the ratio of convictions to arrests was not found to be statistically significant even at a 95% level of confidence.[18]

Combining the empirical evidence contained in the four studies reviewed here indicates that law enforcement variables relating both to the risk of being punished (either being arrested or being convicted) and to the severity of punishment appear to exert a deterrent effect. Nevertheless, variables that have been used to measure the extent of law enforcement have not been found to have a statistically significant deterrent effect. Estimates of the magnitude of the deterrent effect vary, but it appears that an increase in law enforcement activity that increases either the probability of punishment or the expected severity of punishment by 1% is on the average associated with a reduction in the number of offenses somewhere between 0.3 and 1.1%. Further empirical investigation is necessary in order to gain a more accurate estimate of the magnitude of this deterrent effect coefficient, though the true value of the coefficient is probably closer to 1 than to 0.3.[19]

16. Phillips and Votey, "Crime Control," table 1, p. 336. These figures refer to the authors' four-equation model using two-state least squares estimation.

17. Sjoquist, "Property, Crime and Economic Behavior," equations 1 and 2 of table 1, p. 444.

18. *Ibid.*, equation 3 of table 1, p. 444. This deterrent effect was found to be significant at a 90% confidence level using a one-tailed test.

19. Carr-Hill and Stern reported the smallest statistically significant coefficient, 0.28, but this coefficient refers to their severity-of-punishment variable (for 1961), which performed badly using a different data set (1966). Sjoquist, whose statistical techniques are the least sophisticated of all the papers reviewed here, reported the next lowest coefficient, 0.35.

ECONOMETRIC ESTIMATES OF CAPITAL PUNISHMENT AS CRIME DETERRENT

An explosive issue that has been at the center of much public controversy concerns the death penalty as a deterrent for the crime of murder. Leaving aside the moral and ethical aspects of this issue, beyond the question of whether or not the death penalty exerts a deterrent effect over and above that exerted by life imprisonment comes the question of the relative magnitudes of the deterrent effects. It is a question that can be elucidated by empirical research.

Before reviewing two attempts to measure the deterrent effect of the death penalty, it should be emphasized that the *current* debate merely relates to the use of this penalty for the crime of murder. Remember, before a person can be convicted of murder—the most serious form of homicide—the jury must be convinced that the criminal was sane at the time of the act, was not under duress, and was generally in the position of knowing what he was doing and of being able to weigh the costs and benefits of his action. If these conditions are not present the criminal may still be convicted of a lesser homicidal offense (e.g., manslaughter), but the death penalty is not at issue. Thus the economist's rational-choice framework and the deterrence hypothesis are especially relevant in the case of murder.[20] And since murder is one subcategory of homicide, the deterrence of one murder constitutes the deterrence of one homicide.

Empirical studies investigating the deterrent effect of the death penalty on homicides have yielded conflicting results. Most prominent among these studies are those by the criminologist Sellin,[21] the economist Ehrlich,[22] and the economist Wolpin.[23] Sellin selected clusters of neighboring states "closely similar" to each other in certain respects. Within each cluster, he then compared homicide rates in those states that had abolished death penalty statutes as opposed to those that had retained such statutes, irrespective of whether the retentionist states actually executed any homicide offenders. He also examined homicide rates before and after abolition of the death penalty in those states where it had been abolished. He found

Furthermore, Ehrlich reported the largest coefficients, and his is the most sophisticated and comprehensive work to date. For all these reasons, we can have more confidence in the papers reporting the higher estimated coefficients.

20. Conversely, it is acknowledged that this rational-choice framework is of much less relevance in the case of lesser homicidal offenses, especially crimes of passion involving a person who is emotionally related to his victim.

21. T. Sellin, *The Death Penalty* (Philadelphia: American Law Institute, 1959); T. Sellin, ed., "Capital Punishment," 25 *Federal Probation* 3 (1961); T. Sellin, "Homicides in Retentionist and Abolitionist States," in *Capital Punishment,* ed. T. Sellin (New York: Harper, 1967).

22. I. Ehrlich, "The Deterrent Effect of Capital Punishment: A Question of Life or Death," *American Economic Review* 65 (June 1975): 397–417.

23. K. L. Wolpin, "Capital Punishment and Homicide in England," *American Economic Review* 68 (May 1978): 422–427.

that homicide rates in abolitionist states were not significantly or system-atically different from the rates in retentionist states, and so concluded that the death penalty has no measurable deterrent effect beyond that of life imprisonment.

The validity of Sellin's technique of clustering similar states depends heavily on just how "closely" the states within each cluster are "similar" to each other with regard to those variables that are likely to influence homicide rates. To the extent that he failed to identify specific variables that are likely to have the greatest impact on homicide rates, so that he was unable to show that his clustered states were closely similar with respect to these specific variables, his clustering technique is a very weak attempt to hold other influences constant while examining differences in homicide rates.

Ehrlich used more sophisticated regression techniques, within the con-text of a simultaneous equations model of the supply of homicides and society's defense against homicides. He sought to measure the effect of three law enforcement variables on the number of homicides. The three enforcement variables he investigated were the probability of arrest per homicide, the probability of conviction per arrest, and the probability of being executed per conviction. Of particular interest to the capital punish-ment debate is his finding that a 1% increase in the number of executions per homicide conviction on the average reduced the number of homicides by 0.06%. Ehrlich pointed out that this implied that "on the average the trade-off between the execution of an offender and the lives of potential victims it might have saved was of the order of magnitude of 1 for 8 for the period 1933–67 in the United States."[24]

Despite subsequent criticism of Ehrlich's model, structural form, and data, his work represents a most comprehensive and sophisticated theoreti-cal and empirical study of the deterrent effect of the death penalty.[25] Although criticism of Ehrlich's data and structural form may have some validity, the problems of weak data and inappropriate structural form should make it more rather than less difficult to detect significant evidence of a deterrent effect. The fact that Ehrlich was able to discover significant evidence of his hypothesized deterrent effect despite these problems is evidence that the deterrent effect of the death penalty in reality may well be greater than Ehrlich's reported estimates.

A note of caution is required regarding the interpretation of Ehrlich's statement about trading off one execution for eight homicides. This state-

24. Ehrlich, "Deterrent Effect," p. 398.

25. For criticisms of Ehrlich, and his reply to these criticisms, see the following three articles in *Yale Law Journal* 85 (1975): D.C. Baldus and J. W. L. Cole, "A Comparison of the Work of Thorsten Sellin and Isaac Ehrlich on the Deterrent Effect of Capital Punishment"; W. J. Bowers and G. L. Pierce, "The Illusion of Deterrence in Isaac Ehrlich's Research on Capital Punishment"; and I. Ehrlich, "Deterrence: Evidence and Inference."

ment assumes that the probability of an offender's being executed (given that he is convicted) is independent of the probability that the jury will convict him for murder. In a world where some jurors and judges disagree with the imposition of the death penalty they may well be reluctant to find an offender guilty of murder if they feel he is likely to be executed. Thus the deterrent effect of additional executions could be offset by a tendency to convict fewer offenders. The measurement of this offsetting effect, though possibly amenable to empirical research, so far has not been undertaken.

Ehrlich himself stresses that his findings do not necessarily constitute an endorsement of capital punishment. Any decision regarding the desirability of the death penalty must be made within the content of the ethical and moral standards of the society and must take into account the risks of executing an innocent person who has been erroneously convicted of murder. Ehrlich's finding can only constitute one input of information into the decision-making process within this wider context.

Wolpin undertook an econometric analysis of the deterrent effect of capital punishment, conceptually similar to Ehrlich's work but using 1929–1968 data for England and Wales. He employed ordinary least squares regression techniques in both linear and logarithmic functional form and found his result quite robust (i.e., unchanged regardless of functional form and time period). Wolpin's conclusions parallel those of Ehrlich in principle, but not in detail. Thus he finds capital punishment to have had a statistically significant deterrent effect in England and Wales during 1929–1968, but the effect is only half as large as that found by Ehrlich in the United States during 1933–1967. Specifically, he estimates that four fewer murders are committed, and therefore four lives saved, for each additional execution of a convicted murderer.[26] This effect is relative to the alternative punishment of a prison sentence, generally not exceeding 10–15 years.

Although Wolpin himself points out several qualifications to his empirical findings, the list is actually longer. First, there are some serious data problems. In 1957, the Homicide Act reduced the frequency of a trial verdict of "guilty but insane," and eliminated the earlier rule that subjected all convicted murderers to execution. Moreover, in the 5 years subsequent to the act, 10% of convicted murderers were executed, whereas in the 5 years preceding it 52% were executed, perhaps in anticipation of the legal change. Then, in 1965, the Murder Act abolished the death sentence.

Perhaps even more damaging is the absence of a variable that reflects the average time served by convicted murderers sentenced to prison. For example, if the average time served declined along with the probability of execution, the deterrent effect of execution produces an upward bias.

---

26. Wolpin, "Capital Punishment and Homicide," p. 426.

Since starting in 1956 crimes increased greatly and jails most likely became overcrowded, the time served for all crimes may very well have decreased.

Finally, a word about the absence of a variable testifying to the immigration of racial groups into an otherwise homogeneous society. Average net immigration dropped by about 50% between 1956–1961 and 1962–1966, and the homicide rate increased rapidly. For example, if racial friction increases with the absolute or relative number of minority group members, and this fact in turn results in homicides, the rapid increase in murders after 1961 would be explained.

Altogether, we have so far only tentative information about the deterrent effect of capital punishment. The Ehrlich and Wolpin studies appear to be consistent with the deterrence hypothesis. A 1978 report by the National Academy of Sciences Panel on Research on Deterrent and Incapacitative Effects concludes, "We cannot tell from the studies done so far just how much effect . . . capital punishment [has] on the number of . . . crimes committed."[27]

POLICE PRODUCTION FUNCTIONS AND DETERRENCE

The finding that law enforcement variables may exert a deterrent effect on crime would confirm one of the major tenets upon which our criminal law system has always been based. Should empirical research succeed so that it can contribute to our knowledge of the magnitude of this effect, this knowledge can assist in the allocation of law enforcement resources so as to maximize society's welfare. Increasing the probability of arresting offenders requires that society incur additional costs. By devoting more resources to police activities aimed at arresting offenders society must forgo the use of those resources in alternative uses, such as, education, health services, or personal consumption. Similarly, increasing the average length of prison sentences imposes on society additional costs associated with building and operating penal institutions. In order to compare these costs of increased law enforcement with the benefits resulting from reduced crime rates, we need to know two things: (a) the extent to which increases in specific law enforcement variables will reduce crime rates—that is, the magnitude of the deterrent effect—and (b) the extent to which devoting additional resources to police and court activities will increase the probability of arrest and conviction—that is, the magnitude of the effect that extra police and court inputs have on the probability that criminals will be apprehended and punished.[28]

27. National Academy of Sciences Panel on Research on Deterrent and Incapacitative Effects, "Deterrence and Incapacitation: Estimating the Effects of Criminal Sanctions on Crime Rates," *Newsletter Assembly of Behavioral and Social Sciences* 6 (March 1978): 3.

28. Knowledge of a third variable is also required; namely, we need to know the cost to society (measured in dollars) of an additional crime. However, this empirical issue will not be pursued here.

Having knowledge of these two variables we can maximize the net benefits to society of allocating resources to various law enforcement activities up to the point where the last $1 of resources devoted to each enforcement activity yields a benefit to society (in the form of reduced losses from crime) of $1.

I turn now to review some of the empirical research related to measuring this second magnitude, the impact of extra police resources on the probability of arrest or conviction. This research involves the estimation of police production functions, where the probability of arrest or conviction is regarded as a measure of the output of police activities.

A production function measures the specific service outputs that result from different sets of physical inputs at different scales of operation, under different service conditions, and in the long run with different states of technology. In more formal terms,

$$O = j(I, S, T),\qquad\qquad(4)$$

where O represents output, I represents input factors, S represents service conditions (i.e., the more or less intangible environment within which services are to be rendered), and T represents the state of technology. In the short run T changes very little, whereas S is largely beyond the control of the relevant police department. Hence we are primarily interested in measuring the relationship between outputs O and inputs I, holding service conditions S and technology T constant.

But how can police "output" be measured? Several alternative measures of police output have been proposed in the literature. Walzer has proposed the use of an index composed of the number of police services rendered, such as the number of complaints investigated.[29] Because this discussion is concerned with measuring the relationship between police inputs and the probability of apprehension or punishment of criminals, I will review only those empirical studies of police production functions that use the probability of arrest or conviction as the measure of output.

I must emphasize, however, that the probability of arrest suffers from a serious defect as a measure of police output. It ignores the crime-prevention effect of police activities other than those directed specifically toward the arrest and conviction of criminals. For example, it ignores the crime-deterrent effects of warning potential wrongdoers, guarding people and property, and the general visibility aspect of police patrols. Despite this defect, the probability of arrest or conviction is still the most useful single measure of police output because it best conforms to the rational-choice theoretic framework discussed earlier.

Police production functions of the form we are interested in here have

29. N. Walzer, "Economies of Scale and Municipal Police Services: The Illinois Experience," *Review of Economics and Statistics* 54 (1973): 431–438.

been estimated as one part of a simultaneous system of equations by Ehrlich,[30] Carr-Hill and Stern,[31] and Vandaele.[32] Unfortunately, the empirical results reported in these three papers are inconclusive and contradictory.

Ehrlich estimated a production function in which the probability of apprehension and imprisonment is used as a measure of output. Thus, the crime-prevention effects of all police activities devoted to the apprehension and conviction of criminals who are not subsequently imprisoned (i.e., they may be convicted and fined) are ignored. Ehrlich's production function is also weak in that he uses per capita police expenditures as the only measure of the extent of input usage. It neglects the differential efficiency with which resources are combined. Furthermore, expenditures only reflect the extent of input usage if there are no variations in factor prices, such as policemen's wages, which is most unlikely to be the case. Ehrlich estimated that a 1% increase in per capita police expenditure would increase the probability of imprisonment per crime by 0.3%, but this estimated coefficient is not statistically significant even at relatively low confidence levels (less than 80% confidence).[33] His failure to find a statistically significant coefficient could indeed result from the weaknesses in his measures of inputs and outputs, as noted.

Vandaele estimated a police production function for the crime of auto theft, using the probability of arrests and conviction as his measure of police output and the number of policemen per capita as his measure of input. This input measure suffers from the defect that it ignores any differences in the amount of capital inputs (e.g., vehicles, equipment) per policeman used by different police departments. Vandaele estimated that a

---

30. Ehrlich, "Participation in Illegitimate Activities," p. 557.

31. Carr-Hill and Stern, "Econometric Model," table 2 (i), pp. 302–303.

32. W. Vandaele, "The Economics of Crime: An Econometric Investigation of Auto Theft in the United States" (Ph.D. diss., University of Chicago, 1975). The Vandaele police production function estimates are part of a larger study in which he constructs an economic model of crime that is in many respects analogous to an economic industry supply and demand model. He views crime as an industry producing illegal goods that are supplied to a crime product market, such as markets for drugs and stolen goods. In order to produce this supply of illegal goods, the crime industry purchases inputs of illegal labor time. Law enforcement activities exert an important influence on demand and supply in both the product market for illegal goods and the factor market for illegal labor services.

Vandaele applied his crime industry model to data referring to automobile thefts in the United States. He used simultaneous equations regression techniques to investigate the impact of law enforcement variables on demand and supply in the product market for stolen autos. He found that on the average a 1% increase in the probability of arrest was associated with a 1.29% reduction in product demand for stolen autos and a 0.44% reduction in product supply, whereas a 1% increase in the probability of conviction given arrest was associated with a 0.33% reduction in product demand. All of the reported coefficients were found to be statistically significant at a 99% level of confidence.

33. Ehrlich, "Participation in Illegitimate Activities," p. 577.

1% increase in the numerical strength of police departments would increase the probability of conviction per auto theft by 0.4%. Like Ehrlich, however, he found that this estimated coefficient is not statistically significant even at relatively low levels of confidence (less than 80%).[34] Once again, this failure to find a statistically significant relationship between police inputs and outputs could possibly result from problems with the specific measures used to represent them.

Carr-Hill and Stern used the number of police to measure police inputs and the clear-up rate to measure output.[35] However, their results are even more confusing than those reported in the two other papers, since they found evidence of a statistically significant *negative* relationship between inputs and outputs; that is, an increase in the number of police is associated on the average with a reduction in the clear-up rate for criminal offenses. This result is hard to believe, and Carr-Hill and Stern are unable to provide a satisfactory explanation of their perverse result.

The overall conclusion of the findings in these three papers is that researchers have been unable to find statistically significant evidence to confirm the belief that devoting extra resources to police activities will increase their arrest and conviction rates.

HANDGUN CONTROL AND HOMICIDES

For many years there has been a lively debate about handgun control. This debate can be joined within the general framework of a police production function, Eq. (4), presented earlier. Statutory gun control would change the service conditions S within which the police produce their output.

The arguments in favor of gun control proceed from the premise "that one of the major sources of homicide is assault and that the use of firearms increases both the feasibility of attack and the fatality rate."[36] Phillips *et al.* have developed a model that gives expression to the implied objective of minimizing both the losses due to crime and the costs of control. Constraints are the budgets of law enforcement agencies and the behavioral relations specifying crime generation and crime control. Two-stage least squares methods are used to estimate the crime-control and crime-generation equations for homicides.

Phillips *et al.* found that, based on multiple regression analysis, a 10% reduction in handgun density is associated with a 27.4% reduction in the homicide offense rate.[37] They concluded that, for the sake of social-cost minimization, about 19.5% of California's law enforcement personnel

34. Vandaele, "Economics of Crime," table 22, p. 156.
35. Carr-Hill and Stern, "Econometric Model," table 2 (i), pp. 302–303.
36. L. Phillips *et al.*, "Handguns and Homicide: Minimizing Losses and the Costs of Control," *Journal of Legal Studies* 5 (June 1976): 463–472.
37. *Ibid.*, pp. 474–475.

should be assigned to homicide-related activities, although they find the present percentage to be much smaller.

CONCLUSION

In summary, criminal law is predicated on the premise that initial entitlements must and indeed can be protected from criminal encroachment by a specially fashioned class of laws, criminal laws. In order to deter such encroachment and the ensuing negative externalities, society imposes criminal sanctions. Models have been developed by economists to relate deterrence measures to the commission of a crime, and some econometric models have attempted to provide estimates of the deterrent effects. Though some studies have found statistically significant relations, it may be too early to be sure of their existence and nature. Police production functions can help provide improved understanding of the effects of various police inputs on police output and thereby deterrence. Moreover, these functions can also shed light on the extent to which the conditions under which the police must function, such as easy access to guns by the general public, affect the performance of the police.

IX

ENVIRONMENTAL LAW

INTRODUCTION

Environmental law has moved to front stage. The intense attention given to it on the legal scene has resulted from the spread of industrialization and urbanization in many areas of the world. Externalities abound; environmental problems have been emerging at an increasing pace, and society has become concerned, even alarmed, about the degradation of the environment. In light of these developments, courts and legislatures have generously responded. Many areas of the substantive law, we find, overlap to form the legal framework that now seeks to define environmental property rights and entitlements, identify their allocation or misallocation, reduce impediments to exchange, and, if necessary, intervene. To cope with these complex problems, property law, tort law, and contract law have been drawn upon in evolving environmental law.

ENVIRONMENTAL EXTERNALITIES, PROPERTY RIGHTS, AND ENTITLEMENTS: SOME THEORETICAL CONSIDERATIONS

In an affluent, technologically advanced world where the parties engaging in transactions are highly specialized and mobile and live close to one another, everyone's acts affect everyone else. As persons, firms, or governments exercise their property rights or entitlements, they commonly affect the utility or production functions of others. As was stated in Chapter I, when such exchanges take place outside the market and therefore no appropriate compensation is exchanged, we speak about externalities.

Under conditions of close environmental interdependence, a direct relationship exists between the assignment of property rights or entitlements and the concomitant nature and extent of the externalities. Assignment of private resource rights or entitlements does not necessarily produce the internalization of all externalities. Often the incentive for internalization of an externality under government intervention may be called for. In this spirit, conditions for forced optimal intervention will next be explored.

GOVT. OPTIMAL INTERVENTION INTO THE ENVIRONMENT

In order to determine an optimal intervention we must carefully define the economic and legal relationships between property rights and entitlements on the one hand, and externalities on the other hand. In line with the *Restatement of Property,* which defines *right* as "a legally enforceable claim of one person against another," a person who has a property right or entitlement is legally able to compel another to commit or not to commit a given act.[1] In the abstract, when one person's activity causes damage to another person's property rights (i.e., imposes negative externalities), the owner of the rights can force the person causing the damage to cease the activity or pay for any damage incurred. Such externalities, which can impose costs on (or avoid benefits to) persons who hold property rights or entitlements, can take many forms relative to such environmental conditions as air, water, solid waste, noise, or view. What, then are the conditions of optimal intervention?

If the assumptions that underlie the economist's model of perfectly competitive markets were satisfied in real life, all impacts on the natural environment, no matter who was responsible for them, would be appropriately incorporated into the decisions of each party in those markets. However, these assumptions are not met, in part because of the very existence of externalities. The externalities of concern here do not result from the performance of malicious acts by decision makers but are for the most part produced incidentally in the pursuit of a legitimate activity. The presence of externalities prevents the market mechanism from reaching an economically efficient allocation of resources. Thus when parties to a transaction generate externalities but fail to consider their implications in making the decision, the resource allocation is unlikely to be Pareto optimal. Hence, it will be theoretically possible to reallocate resources and increase the welfare of at least one member of society without decreasing that of any other member. For example, if a manufacturer pollutes the air, adversely affecting the health and welfare of people living in the neighborhood, and fails to incorporate these external costs into his production decisions, in-

1. *Restatement of Property,* § 1.

cluding those dealing with smoke-generation decisions, then the manufacturer's equilibrium level of pollution will tend to exceed the economically efficient level. Under such conditions, efficiency increases if the manufacturer reduces his pollution to a level at which the cost of additional pollution abatement exceeds the gain accruing to neighbors therefrom, and if the abatement is financed exclusively from the gains obtained by the manufacturer's neighbors as a result of this smoke reduction.

In theory such a solution can be negotiated under contract law, if only a very small number of parties are involved. The principle of this solution is stated by Coase:

> The traditional approach has tended to obscure the nature of the choice that has to be made. The question is commonly thought of as one in which A inflicts harm on B and what has to be decided is: how should we restrain A? But this is wrong. We are dealing with a problem of a reciprocal nature. To avoid the harm to B would inflict harm on A. The real question that has to be decided is: should A be allowed to harm B or should B be allowed to harm A? The problem is to avoid the more serious harm.[2]

This principle can be applied to our example: Unrestricted generation of smoke by a manufacturer gains him additional profits while imposing external costs on his neighbors; pollution-control activities provide gains to the firm's neighbors while imposing smoke-abatement costs on the manufacturer. Thus, the external effect is caused by both the resource owner who generates the effect and the resource owner who receives it. Optimal resource allocation demands that both of these resource owners take into account all external effects related to their resource decisions. This situation obtains if those who seek to modify the behavior of a second party engage in a trade with that party, moving both to preferred positions where all additional mutually agreeable trades are available and thus a Pareto optimum prevails.

However, trade requires a careful assignment of resource rights in externality situations. Such determination will indicate either that the manufacturer possesses the right to generate any quantity of smoke that he deems desirable or that his neighbors possess the right to an environment that contains at most a specified level of smoke, possibly zero. Once these rights are assigned, and if these rights are transferable and rigidly enforced and no costs are associated with the negotiations and enforcement, then any particular assignment of resource rights will produce an economically efficient resource allocation.[3] Under such conditions, the stipulated

2. Ronald Coase, "The Problem of Social Cost," *Journal of Law and Economics* 3 (October 1960): 1–2.

3. Property rights with respect to liability damages are transferable if the government enforces liability rules only upon appeal by one of the parties involved in the externalities situation. Such an enforcement policy introduces the possibility of exchange between these parties.

property-right assignment provides incentives to one of the parties in the externalities situation to seek changes in the externality-producing activity by offering inducements to modify its behavior.

Since the marginal cost associated with any particular increase in the production of an external effect is unaffected by resource-right assignment, the very same economically efficient resource allocation can be obtained as long as the differences in wealth distribution that are associated with the various systems do not affect demand patterns. In short, if the income elasticity of demand is zero in all markets, including the market for the external effect, and if the cost of negotiating and enforcing transactions is zero, the market resolution of any externality problem will be both economically efficient and allocatively neutral with respect to the assignment of liability. However, several studies have demonstrated that the asserted allocative neutrality of alternative assignments of resource rights will not prevail when some of the resource owners who are involved in the externalities situation are merely consumers, when the income elasticity of demand for at least some goods in the economy is not zero, or when the costs of negotiating and enforcing transactions are positive.[4] Since one or more of these conditions tend to prevail in real life, negotiated resolutions of externality situations are unlikely to be allocatively neutral with respect to alternative assignments of property rights.

Different assignments of property rights usually generate different economically efficient allocations of resources. Specifically, more of the externality will be produced if the resource owner responsible is declared to have no liability for the damages attributable to this external effect than if he is liable for damages. Moreover, since positive transaction costs inhibit exchange, the disparity between resource allocations at equilibrium and under different assignments of rights in any externality situation increases as transaction costs increase. As the externality situation becomes more complex and the number of resource owners involved in the situation increases, transaction costs increase and so do deviations from allocative neutrality. In the extreme, transaction costs may be so high that movements away from the initial allocation of resources that is specified by the prevailing system of property rights may be impossible.

LIABILITY RULES FOR ENVIRONMENTAL EXTERNALITIES

In the literature there is much debate concerning the proper liability rule in the presence of externalities. E. J. Mishan favors a liability rule that incorporates a strong bias against the production of externalities when

---

4. F. T. Dolbear, "On the Theory of Optimum Externality," *American Economic Review* 56 (March 1967): 95–97; W. J. Samuels, "The Coase Theorem and the Study of Law and Economics," *Natural Resources Journal* 14 (January 1974): 6–12; and A. Randall, "Coasian Externality Theory in a Policy Context," *Natural Resources Journal* 14 (January 1974): 43–44.

substantial uncertainties exist.[5] H. Demsetz takes an opposite view: "The greater the uncertainty of effect, the less inclined we should be to require that prior compensation should be paid to those harmed or prior fees be charged of those benefited. The cost of sorting out and measuring legitimate claims in cases of great uncertainty would be so high as to undermine efficient resource use."[6]

These diametrically opposed positions may result from the fact that Mishan regards uncertainty effects as major and irreversible, whereas Demsetz considers them relatively insignificant and reversible. G. Calabresi acknowledges that either of these conditions might prevail in different externality situations, hence he argues that, in any particular uncertain situation, society should adopt that liability rule for which the market is most likely to correct an error in the initial assignment of property rights.[7] A generalization of this principle is provided by S. N. S. Cheung, who suggests that in uncertain situations the socially most desirable liability rule can be determined by comparing the risk associated with the adoption of each alternative liability rule with all of the other costs and benefits attributable to the adoption of that rule.[8] According to Cheung's principle, since all externality situations do not involve the same degree of uncertainty, different internalization mechanisms will be socially most desirable in different externality situations. Moreover, since communities may exhibit different degrees of risk aversion, they rationally may adopt different internalization mechanisms for essentially identical externality situations.

Because of these considerations, there exists no single most desirable mechanism for the internalization of externalities in different externality situations. The appropriate internalization mechanism for any particular externality situation can be determined only after the relative strengths and weaknesses of each available alternative internalization mechanism have been carefully evaluated.

Toward Forced Internalization

To the extent that the observed purchasing behavior of a person in a market situation is generally acknowledged to be the most reliable available indication of his economic preferences, it is desirable to adopt those assignments of property rights that will maximize opportunities to engage in market exchanges promoting the internalization of an externality. In the

5. E. J. Mishan, "The Economics of Disamenity," *Natural Resources Journal* 14 (January 1974): 81–82.

6. H. Demsetz, "Some Aspects of Property Rights," *Journal of Law and Economics* 9 (October 1966): 64.

7. G. Calabresi, "Transaction Costs, Resource Allocation and Liability Rules: A Comment," *Journal of Law and Economics* 11 (April 1968): 69–73.

8. S. N. S. Cheung, "Transaction Costs, Risk Aversion, and the Chioce of Contractual Arrangements," *Journal of Law and Economics* 12 (April 1969): 24–29.

absence of overriding social considerations, therefore, there is <u>virtue in</u> <u>relying on the negotiated resolution of externality problems wherever</u> <u>voluntary negotiation of the permissible level of the externality is feasible.</u> Feasibility, however, depends on the number of parties involved in the externality situation. The smaller the number, the lower the transaction costs. In turn, when many parties are affected by a particular externality situation and internalization of the externality assumes the nature of a public good for all these parties, the economic and social desirability of governmental intervention is virtually ensured. Thus, all too frequently, externality problems cannot be resolved by negotiated solutions, and other means must be applied, often involving the courts.

COURT-MADE ENVIRONMENTAL LAW

As has been pointed out, the market provides an effective mechanism by which rights or entitlements to the possession and use of goods and services are exchanged. When this exchange of rights or entitlements is complicated by an abundance of externalities that affect many persons and prevent the market mechanism from achieving an economically efficient allocation of resources, government intervention is often called for. Government then takes steps to guide, and if necessary to adjudicate, conflicting property rights and entitlements. High on the list of laws relevant to these circumstances is nuisance law, and this will be explored next.

NUISANCE LAW

The law of nuisance[9] has been applied to determine whether someone's property right or entitlement has been violated.[10] The courts have recognized the need to resolve a deep-seated conflict between two opposing legal principles:

The law of nuisance plys between two antithetical extremes: The principle that every person is entitled to use his property for any purpose that he sees fit, and the opposing principles that everyone is bound to use his property in such a manner as not to injure the property or rights of his neighbor. For generations, courts, in their tasks of judging, have ruled on these extremes according to the wisdom of the day, and many have recognized that the contemporary view of public policy shifts from generation to generation.[11]

9. This section has benefited from F. H. Reuter and P. Kushner, *Economic Incentives for Land Use Control*, EPA-600/S-77-001 (Washington, D.C.: U.S. Environmental Protection Agency, 1977), sect. 2.34–2.53.

10. A private nuisance has been defined as "an interference with the use and enjoyment of land." W. L. Prosser, *Handbook of the Law of Torts*, 4th ed. (St. Paul, Minn.: West, 1971) p. 591.

11. *Antonik* v. *Chamberlain*, 81 Ohio App. 465, 475, 78 N.E.2d 752, 759 (Ct. App. Summit County 1947).

The use of nuisance law as a deterrent to pollution and as a means to internalize the costs of land use has a long history, beginning in English case law.[12] A private nuisance action has been used to abate nearly every common form of pollution: air,[13] water,[14] solid waste,[15] noise,[16] and sight pollution.[17]

The Supreme Court in *Euclid* v. *Ambler*[18] indicated, as early as 1926, that "a nuisance may be merely the right thing in the wrong place, like a pig in the parlor instead of the barnyard."[19] In general, "a nuisance may undoubtedly arise from a land use incompatible with the surrounding neighborhood."[20] Thus, the first element of a nuisance is the unreasonable use of one's land as determined by the character of the neighborhood. Certain activities that may be perfectly reasonable in industrial areas or in the country are not suitable in residential communities. Courts have found that a powder mill,[21] a factory,[22] or a stable,[23] if located in residential areas, are nuisances, but these same activities are surely permissible in the proper setting.

Once it has been determined that the *activity is unreasonable for the area,* it must also be proven that the *interference is substantial.* For instance, a slight amount of noise or smoke is permissible,[24] but the activity will be considered a nuisance if it is sufficient to "interfere with the ordinary comfort of human existence."[25] The Supreme Court of New Hampshire considered substantial harm to be that "in excess of the customary interferences a land user suffers in an organized society. It denotes an appreciable and tangible interference with a property interest."[26] Both of these required elements introduce the possibility that a landowner will be able to externalize the costs of his land use.

Nuisance law permits two general forms of remedy: damages and injunctive relief. Normally, only if the damages cannot be determined or if the nuisance would require continued litigation will the court permit injunctive

---

12. William Aldred's Case, 77 Eng. Rep. 816 (K.B. 1611).
13. *Campbell* v. *Seaman,* 63 N.Y. 568 (1876).
14. *Johnson* v. *City of Fairmont,* 188 Minn. 451, 247 N.W. 577 (1933).
15. *Lind* v. *City of San Luis Obispo,* 109 Cal. 340, 42 P. 437 (1895).
16. *Hennessey* v. *Carmony,* 50 N.J. Eq. 616, 25 A. 374 (1892).
17. See "Torts—Aesthetic Nuisance: An Emerging Cause of Action," *New York University Law Review* 45 (November 1970): 1075–1097.
18. *Euclid* v. *Ambler Realty Co.,* 272 U.S. 365 (1926).
19. *Ibid.,* p. 388.
20. *Township of Bedminster* v. *Vargo Dragway, Inc.,* 434 Pa. 100, 253 A.2d 659 (1969).
21. *Cumberland Torpedo Co.* v. *Gaines,* 201 Ky. 88, 255 S.W. 1046 (1923).
22. *Riblet* v. *Spokane Portland Cement Co.,* 41 Wash. 2d 249, 248 P.2d 380 (1952).
23. *Johnson* v. *Drysdale,* 66 S.D. 436, 285, M.W. 301 (1939).
24. Prosser, *Handbook,* p. 79.
25. *Holman* v. *Athens Empire Laundry Co.,* 149 Ga. 345, 351, 100 S.E. 207, 210 (1919).
26. *Roble* v. *Lillis,* 112 N.H. 492, 299 A.2d 155, 158 (1972).

relief. In two cases, _Boomer_ v. _Atlantic Cement Co._[27] and _Baldwin_ v. _McClendon_,[28] the courts permitted the payment of damages that would compensate the injured party, not only for the past and present, but for future injury as well.

In _Boomer,_ the defendant operated a large cement plant near Albany, New York, and neighboring landowners sought an injunction and damages to compensate for costs imposed on their properties from dirt, smoke, and vibration emanating from the plant. The court found the defendant guilty of a nuisance in that the company was making an "unreasonable" use of its land. This use created such externalities upon neighboring landowners that in order to maintain the relative economic position of all the parties before the court, the defendant had to pay for damages inflicted.

But the plaintiffs in _Boomer_ also asked the court to enjoin the defendant from continuing the nuisance; on the facts of the case and the state of technology in cement production this would have required the factory to shut down. The court denied the plaintiffs' motion for an injunction, noting that the defendant's investment in the plant was in excess of $45 million and that it employed 300 people. The court decided, therefore, that on balance closing the plant was too costly. It allowed continuation of the nuisance upon the payment of damages, thereby allowing the company to continue its activity if it was able to pay the costs involved.

There are two doctrines that a court may apply to deny an injunction and possible damages even after a nuisance is found: the _balancing-the-equities doctrine_ and the _coming-to-the-nuisance doctrine._

The doctrine of balancing the equities sometimes requires a court to deny a remedy to the plaintiff even if a nuisance is otherwise proven. The courts have examined the harm alleged by the plaintiff and compared it to the harm that the defendant and society would suffer if the defendant had to cease operations. Thus, in _Clifton Iron Company_ v. _Dye_,[29] the development of mining interests was judged to be more important than the pollution the defendant caused by his operations. Some earlier cases have similar holdings. For example, in _Pennsylvania Coal Co._ v. _Sanderson_ the court found,

> The plaintiff's grievance is for a mere personal inconvenience; and we are of the opinion that mere private personal inconveniences . . . must yield to the necessities of a great public industry, which, although in the hands of a private corporation, subserves a great public interest. To encourage the development of the great natural resources of a country trifling inconveniences to particular persons must sometimes give way to the necessity of a great community.[30]

Similarly, the defendant's own financial interests must be examined:

> If the resulting damage . . . because of the nuisance cannot be avoided, or only at such expense as would be practically prohibitive to a person in the

27. _Boomer_ v. _Atlantic Cement Co._, 26 N.Y. 2d 219, 257 N.E.2d 870, 309 N.Y.S. 2d 312 (1970).
28. _Baldwin_ v. _McClendon_, 292 Al. 43, 288 S.2d 761 (1974).
29. _Clifton Iron Co._ v. _Dye_, 87 Ala. 468, 6 So. 192 (1888).
30. _Pennsylvania Coal Co._ v. _Sanderson_, 113 Pa.126, 6 A. 459 (1886).

enjoyment of his own land, he (the defendant) may not be required to abate the nuisance.[31]

In this Pennsylvania case, the commonwealth was attempting to stop the pollution of a stream, but lost because of its inability to formulate a practical plan of abatement.

The coming-to-the-nuisance doctrine prevents the plaintiff from recovering because "one who voluntarily places himself in a situation whereby he suffers an injury will not be heard to say that his damage is due to the nuisance maintained by another."[32] Thus, a person who moves next to a golf course cannot complain that golf balls are falling on his property.[33] But in order to discourage inefficient "first come" use of land, a party coming to the nuisance should and can recover.

Taking (with Just Compensation) versus Applying the Police Power

In framing laws that are designed to deal with a nuisance, it is necessary to make a decision as to whether or not the police power should be applied. The police power has been described by the Supreme Court as

> one of the most essential powers of government, one that is least limitable. It may, indeed, seem harsh in its exercise, usually is on some individual, but the imperative necessity for its existence precludes any limitation upon it when not exerted arbitrarily.[34]

Yet this power can be in conflict with another fundamental tenet of American law, the Fifth Amendment of the Constitution of the United States, which prohibits the taking of property without just compensation. This provision is a "seemingly absolute protection" against the possibility of confiscation by the government of a private party's property without compensation.

In *Pennsylvania Coal Co.* v. *Mahon*, the Supreme Court held that the police power qualifies the protection granted under the Fifth Amendment. Justice Holmes, speaking for the Court, concluded,

> The natural tendency of human nature is to extend the qualification more and more until at last private property disappears. . . . We are in danger of forgetting that a strong public desire to improve the public condition is not enough to warrant achieving the desire by a shorter cut than the constitutional way of paying for the change.[35]

Since the decision in *Pennsylvania Coal Co.* v. *Mahon*, the state courts have struggled to strike the proper balance between the police power qualifica-

31. *Commonwealth* v. *Wyeth Laboratories*, 12 Pa. Commw. Ct. 327, 315 A.2d 648, 653 (1974).
32. *Oetjen* v. *Goff Kirby Co.*, 38 Ohio L. Abs. 117, 124, 49 N.E.2d 95, 99 (Ct. App. Cuyahoga County, 1942).
33. *Patton* v. *Westwood Country Club*, 18 Ohio App. 2d 137, 247 N.E.2d 761 (1969).
34. *Hadachek* v. *Sebastian*, 239 U.S. 394, 410 (1915).
35. *Pennsylvania Coal Co.* v. *Mahon*, 260 U.S. 393, 413 (1922).

tion and the seemingly absolute prohibition against taking property without paying just compensation. As in the area of nuisance law, since the state courts are independent, there is a lack of uniformity among the state decisions.

But under what circumstances does diminution of property value warrant compensation?[36] The Supreme Court, in *Pennsylvania Coal Co.* v. *Mahon,* stated the diminution-of-value test as follows:

> Government hardly could go on if, to some extent, values incident to property could not be diminished without paying for every such change in the general law. . . . One fact for consideration . . . is the extent of the diminution. When it reaches a certain magnitude, in most cases if not all cases there must be an exercise of eminent domain and compensation to sustain the act.[37]

Since the *Pennsylvania Coal* decision, courts have sought to determine what magnitude of diminution is the "certain magnitude" mentioned by Justice Holmes. Courts have concluded that neither financial hardship nor substantial diminution is sufficient for a taking. They have instead required that "a property owner be unable, permanently, to use his property . . . and is therefore deprived of all beneficial use thereof."[38] Despite what appears to be an insurmountable burden for a plaintiff, many property owners in environmental cases have succeeded in satisfying the test.

In *Morris County Land Improvement Co.* v. *Township of Parsippany–Troy Hills,* zoning regulations had created meadowlands to promote flood control.[39] The uses permitted the plaintiff were very limited and severely reduced the property's value. The New Jersey Supreme Court concluded that the regulations "are clearly far too restrictive and as such are constitutionally unreasonable and confiscatory."[40] The court, in determining the property's value, examined not only its existing value as a swamp, but its potential value if filled. For that reason there was a great diminution of value, which resulted in a taking without compensation.

In *State* v. *Johnson,* the Maine State Wetlands Control Board attempted to prohibit the filling of coastal wetlands.[41] The landowner argued that such a regulation made his property "commercially valueless land."[42] The Supreme Court of Maine agreed, holding that the prohibition amounted to a taking of property without just compensation, and an unreasonable exercise of the police power. As in the *Morris* case, the value of the property included its potential after landfill.

---

36. See, Bruce A. Ackerman, *Private Property and the Constitution* (New Haven: Yale University Press, 1977).

37. *Pennsylvania Coal Co.* v. *Mahon,* 260 U.S. 413.

38. *Bureau of Mines of Maryland* v. *George's Creek Coal and Land Co.,* Md., 321 A.2d 748, 762 (1974).

39. *Morris County Land Improvement Co.* v. *Township of Parsippany–Troy Hills,* 40 N.J. 539, 193 A.2d 232 (1963).

40. *Ibid.,* p. 242.

41. *State* v. *Johnson,* 265 A.2d 711 (Me. 1970).

42. *Ibid.,* p. 716.

In *Dooley* v. *Town Plan and Zoning Commission of Town of Fairfield,*[43] the plaintiff's property was zoned as a floodplain with a limited number of uses, and in fact, the court found that "use of the plaintiff's land has been, for all practical purposes, rendered impossible."[44] The diminution in value was estimated to be approximately 75%, which the Supreme Court of Connecticut found to be a taking without just compensation.

On the other hand, an early case permitting extreme diminution of value within the police power is *Hadachek* v. *Sebastian.*[45] Despite the plaintiff's loss of nearly 90% of the value of his property, the Supreme Court in 1915 found no taking, commenting that the exercise of the police power is sometimes "harsh."

Recently, courts have again begun to permit substantial diminution, verging on total deprivation, without compensation. In *Turnpike Realty Co.* v. *Town of Dedham,*[46] the zoning board had established a floodplain district. The case was very similar to the cases just mentioned, but the result was vastly different. The diminution of the plaintiff's land was approximately 90%, but the Massachusetts Supreme Court concluded,

> We realize that it is often extremely difficult to determine the precise line where regulation ends and confiscation begins. The result depends on the "peculiar circumstances of the particular instance." . . . In the case at bar we are unable to conclude, even though the judge found a substantial diminution in the value of petitioner's land, that the decrease was such to render it an unconstitutional deprivation of property.[47]

Just v. *Marinette County* approaches the diminution problem from a different perspective.[48] When the plaintiff attempted to fill some property along a shoreline, he was prohibited by the zoning ordinance. The zoning board fined the Justs and the conviction was appealed. The court basically redefined the valuation criteria.

> The Justs argue their property has been severely depreciated in value. But this depreciation of value is not based on the use of the land in its natural state but on what the land would be worth if it could be filled and used for the location of a dwelling. While loss of value is to be considered in determining whether a restriction is a constructive taking, value based on changing the character of the land at the expense of harm to public rights is not an essential factor or controlling.[49]

A COST–BENEFIT FRAMEWORK

The preceding section has shown how the courts have been struggling to determine whether a nuisance is present—whether a given land use is

---

43. *Dooley* v. *Town Plan and Zoning Commission of Town of Fairfield,* 151 Conn. 304, 197 A.2d 770 (1964).

44. *Ibid.,* p. 772.

45. *Hadachek* v. *Sebastian,* 239 U.S. 394, 410 (1915).

46. *Turnpike Realty Co.* v. *Town of Dedham,* 284 N.E.2d 891 (Mass. 1972).

47. *Ibid.,* p. 894.

48. *Just* v. *Marinette County,* 56 Wis. 2d 7, 201 N.W.2d 761 (1972).

49. 56 Wis. 2d 23, 201 N.W.2d 771.

unreasonable for an area—and, if so, whether the resulting interference is substantial. Similarly, the courts have found it difficult to decide what would constitute a fair remedy under such circumstances. The resolution of these issues can be facilitated by applying a powerful framework developed by economists—cost–benefit analysis. Moreover, there are indications that courts have implicitly applied such an analysis.

Cost–benefit analysis works in the following manner: The more relevant environmental alternatives are identified and for each alternative all benefits and costs are listed, evaluated to obtain dollar figures, and adjusted by a discount rate to determine their present value. The present values of the social costs and benefits of each alternative are compared and the one with the highest overall excess of social benefits over social costs in terms of present values is chosen. It is the socially optimal alternative.

In most instances these steps are not easy to carry out. Difficulties exist because of serious evaluation problems, absence of clear-cut guidelines for the selection of discount rates, and a host of theoretical issues.[50]

THE COURT'S TREATMENT OF ENVIRONMENTAL
PROBLEMS, RECONSIDERED

A judge deciding an environmental law case may be considered to act as the owner of all the property rights and entitlements affected by the environmental question under consideration. His role is to seek a solution that optimizes the aggregate value of the environment's use insofar as all individuals are affected, thereby maximizing total social welfare. Thus, in *Boomer* v. *Atlantic Cement Co.*, the court may be interpreted as viewing the plant as an unreasonable land use for the area, resulting in substantial interference. The defendant, forced to pay damages to surrounding neighbors, was in effect paying the price for the nuisance he was causing to adjacent owners. The court thus forced the defendant to purchase the value of the nuisance his usage was creating on the others' land.

There is also a pricing system rationale to the damage award. If the damage award on top of other costs is higher than the price at which the cement factory can operate satisfactorily, it will close down. If the plant can operate profitably while paying all the costs, then aggregate social value will tend to be maximized. At the margin, then, the total social benefits generated from the cement activity are greater than the total social costs, and under such conditions production should continue.

The plaintiffs in *Boomer* also asked the court to enjoin the defendant from continuing the nuisance. Such injunctive relief, which here would have meant shutting down the factory, often has a great disadvantage. In the presence of an injunction, all opportunity is lost for distinguishing between economic activities that are able to pay their total social cost and

50. For a summary of some of the problems common to most of welfare economics, see John V. Krutilla and Anthony C. Fisher, *The Economics of Natural Environments* (Baltimore: Johns Hopkins, 1975), pp. 28–35.

those that are unable to do so. Generally, injunctions are therefore inefficient solutions to externality situations. Consistent with this view, the court denied the plaintiffs' motion for an injunction, as courts have generally shown great reluctance to enter permanent injunctions prohibiting the operation of useful enterprises.

THE FEE–TAX ALTERNATIVE

An additional way to guide the use of the environment is to impose financial burdens. Theoretical and empirical difficulties prevent the design of an optimal tax for protecting the environment in general and for controlling and abating pollution in particular. There are two classes of tax alternatives. One involves periodic taxes that are paid immediately before, after, or at the time firms or people impact on the environment. These *ex post* taxes can be distinguished from a second class of taxes, that is, *ex ante,* lump-sum taxes. In both instances, a tax should be levied equal to the marginal net damage, that is, the difference between marginal social and private costs.[51]

In the case where a factory's pollution damages a laundry, the *ex post* tax levied on the factory should equal the damage its smoke caused the laundry during the preceding period. The tax restrains factory smoke emission and the costs of operating the factory, including pollution control, are internalized to the factory owner, a step consistent with optimal resource allocation.

An *ex ante,* lump-sum tax is set at a level equal to the discounted present value of the damage expected to be caused by a given activity in the future. As will be seen below, determining the proper *ex ante* tax is even more difficult than determining an *ex post* tax.

EX POST ALTERNATIVES   *periodic*

Five alternative *ex post* taxes will be examined. An ideal tax would directly reflect the damage imposed on victims by a given source. Such a step often is difficult since damage assessment as well as the relations between cause and effect are complex and information costs increase with the number of polluters and victims.[52]

1. *Ex Post Tax on Single Large (Mainly Stationary) Polluters.* Ideally, the government would like to know the level of factory output and its concommitant smoke damage in each period. This requires knowledge of the technical relation between output and smoke emission, the relation between smoke emission and damage to victims and the level of factory output in a period. Only when all three of these conditions are met will the tax be the socially efficient one.

---

51. A. C. Pigou, *The Economics of Welfare*, Macmillan, 1932.
52. Japan imposes a noise pollution fee on airliners depending on tonnage and noise level at time of takeoff. (*Wall Street Journal*, May 30, 1979).

Thus, even in the presence of a single, large polluter, whether of air, water, or the auditory environment, it will be extremely difficult to directly assess the actual damage caused. Obtaining the required information is exceedingly costly. For this reason, indirect damage assessment must usually be relied upon. In such an effort, we seek to estimate the amount of environmental externalities produced by a specific activity. In the case of water and air pollution, we seek to measure the ambient concentration, and in the case of noise pollution the number of decibels found in specific locations. Such measurements can be taken by placing appropriate metering devices at locations where different damage levels are expected; however, such steps are very costly.

In order to more fully reflect the damage done, rather than the externality produced, steps can be taken to adjust the readings of ambient concentration or decibels for natural conditions which make marginal emissions more damaging and costly, such as time of day, atmospheric conditions, etc. Even such indirect damage estimates involve very high transactions costs. Measurements and taxes of this kind are, therefore, often replaced by the establishment of surrogate fees, based on past experience and therefore harm to be expected.

2 *Ex Post Tax Levied on Large Numbers of (Mainly Stationary) Polluters.* While it is almost impossible to assess the actual damage caused by a single large polluter, the problem becomes virtually insurmountable in the presence of numerous polluters. Instead of direct annual fees based on actual damage assessment, often only an indirect or indirect surrogate approach is feasible.[53]

Thus, plants emitting either air or water pollution could be forced to add to their emissions a unique, identifiable chemical. Then with the aid of monitoring stations placed in different locations it would become possible to estimate how much each polluter has added to the general pollution level at a particular point in space and time. Indirect fees could be based on these estimates, possibly adjusted for specific natural conditions exacerbating the harm in specific locations.

A substantially less costly, and yet also less reliable, tax system would use indirect surrogates. Thus, for example, an annual ad valorem, that is, property, tax could be levied and related to a given land use's pollution output. The tax could be based on estimates of last year's damage caused by the particular land use.

3 *Ex Post Tax on Numerous Nonstationary Polluters (Mainly Automobiles).* When there are many moving polluters, the main options are indirect and indirect surrogate taxes. In relation to air and noise pollution caused by automobiles, it would be possible to attach to each engine a unique, electric beam emitting identification. Signals from the automobile could then be picked up and monitored by a centrally located device connected to an electronic computer that meters and records time of day, date, and length

---

53. G. H. Hagevik, *Decision Making in Air Pollution Control,* New York, 1970.

and location of trip. This information could be used to charge drivers an appropriate indirect air and/or noise pollution fee depending on the automobile's emission characteristics. Such an arrangement is not only costly in money terms but imposes enormous social costs in terms of privacy infringement.

For all practical purposes, therefore, an indirect surrogate method might have to be used. It can take the form of a gasoline tax, a registration fee, an inspection fee, a parking fee, or a fee for a zone sticker permitting entry and/or parking in a given zone, all related to the automobile's emission characteristics. Thus, for example, to the extent that fuel efficiency is inversely correlated with engine displacement and emissions, a gasoline tax is a step in the right direction. Another method is the scaling of automobile registration fees to the characteristics of the vehicle. Automobiles that are older, heavier, and have larger engines will tend to emit more pollutants per mile than their newer, smaller, smog-control-fitted counterparts. The gas guzzlers should be taxed more heavily in proportion to their greater emissions. Of course, neither of these taxes has the virtue of distinguishing between the volume of emissions and the extent of damage.

Ex Post Taxes on Sewage Disposal and Solid Waste Disposal. Sewage and solid waste disposal services tend to relate to more limited externalities than do air, water and noise pollution controls.[54] Still, because of the large number of externality generators as well as victims, direct damage assessment is excessively costly. An attractive alternative in the case of sewage disposal is to charge an indirect annual or monthly fee reflecting the expected effluence emission. Reliance on an indirect surrogate, such as a user fee on nonagricultural water purchase, can reduce transaction costs. A further indirect surrogate can take the form of an annual ad valorem tax related to a given land use's effluence.

In connection with solid waste disposal, it is possible to levy an indirect monthly or annual fee per can of garbage collected, particularly once the size of permissible garbage cans has been legally and enforceably standardized. Also, an indirect surrogate is available in the form of a user fee levied on the purchase of plastic garbage bags, when the law permits pick-up of garbage only in such bags.

Moreover, it is possible to design a combination of a flat user fee for picking up a fixed, contracted for number of garbage cans, and a collection fee that could be added to the purchase price of plastic garbage bags should the household ask for collection of additional garbage at particular times.

EX ANTE TAX ALTERNATIVES

Under some circumstances, *ex ante* taxes or fees are alternatives that deserve examination. However, it is well to realize that while the setting of appropriate *ex post* environmental taxes or fees pose serious theoretical and empirical difficulties, the problems raised by *ex ante* taxes are even more

54. F. H. Rueter and P. Kushner, *op. cit.*, 5.16–5.25.

severe. Thus, setting an appropriate *ex ante* tax or fee requires estimates of the full cost of given activities during their lifetime. The ideal fee must be set on the assumption that each activity is carried out at an optimum level in each period. It must be of a magnitude that prevents the pollutants' levels during the lifetime of the activity to inflict more marginal damages on victims than what would be the marginal prevention costs incurred by the emitter. Thus, unless we assume a world of perfect foresight, *ex ante* taxes will always be inferior to *ex post* taxes.

A major shortcoming of an *ex ante*, lump-sum tax or fee, in addition to its great information costs, is that once paid, all incentive is lost to perform the activity in a manner that preserves the environment. Once the *ex ante* fee has been paid, the firm's marginal cost of polluting is zero. A second major shortcoming relates to the fact that government is likely to incorrectly estimate the extent of damage. For example, if subsequent technological advances in the art of producing the product of a factory changes, then the resulting allocation of resources as between the factory and victims will diverge from optimum.

A positive aspect of *ex ante*, lump-sum taxes is that they tend to deny, for example, construction permits to prospective factory owners who are relatively inefficient in reducing smoke emissions. High emissions are likely to lead to high taxes. Their net discounted receipts (exclusive of the lump sum tax) are unlikely to exceed the tax and they therefore will not seek a permit.

Two classes of *ex ante*, lump-sum taxes on land uses will be considered as well as taxes levied at the time an automobile is sold or a sewage connection is installed.

Ex Ante Lump-Sum Payment Preceding Zoning Change—Rezoning Fee. A rezoning fee in the form of a lump-sum payment should approximate the costs that are likely to be imposed on society by a given land use during its life time and levied when rezoning takes place. As was discussed earlier, zoning can be cumulative or exclusive. The former is hierarchical in that any particular land use is prohibited in districts reserved for higher uses only. Exclusive zoning specifies a particular use to which a parcel can be put. Clearly, uncertainties about the specific future use of land are greater under cumulative than exclusive zoning.

Ex Ante Permit Construction Fee. A construction permit fee is a lump sum tax charged the petitioner of a construction permit. It is designed to cover all the costs a polluter is expected to impose on society during the lifetime of the contemplated investment. Clearly the uncertainties about the use to which a particular parcel will be put are somewhat reduced once a developer has specific plans and seeks permission to initiate construction. While the uncertainties are smaller than those faced at the time of a zoning change request, they still are very high. By and large, the general formulation of what constitutes an efficient construction permit fee differs only by degree from that levied prior to rezoning.

Ex Ante Automobile and Sewage Connection Tax. At the time an automobile is sold a lump-sum tax may be levied that directly relates to emissions per mile. Alternatively, there could be an income tax deduction for the purchase of certain types of automobiles that have been identified as relatively clean burning. This would be similar to the current deduction for energy-installation of conserving devices in the home.

Similarly, before a new sewage connection is made, a fee could be levied relating the size and type of building and its location relative to the overall sewage system.

THE SUBSIDY ALTERNATIVE

A further approach is subsidies, basically the obverse of the polluter's fee approach. Selective cash grants can be made to polluters in return for their restricting emissions to an optimal degree. These cash grants could in principle be equivalent to the off-site costs imposed by increments of waste discharge and could vary with conditions as well as quantity and quality of pollutants. This sort of payment resembles the polluter's fee scheme in theory, though its approach is the opposite, and therefore criticisms discussed in relation to the latter would also apply here. The strongest criticism has been advanced by E. S. Mills, who declares,

> They are simply payments for the wrong thing. The investment credit proposal will illustrate the deficiency that is common to others. An investment credit on air pollution abatement equipment reduces the cost of such equipment. But most such equipment is inherently unprofitable in that it adds nothing to revenues and does not reduce costs. To reduce the cost of such an item cannot possibly induce a firm to install it. The most it can do is to reduce the resistance to public pressure for installation. Common sense and scattered bits of evidence suggest that these payments policies are costly and inefficient ways to achieve abatement.[55]

Some theoretical work has shown that subsidization will be less effective than taxation in inducing the internalization of external diseconomies, but it will be more effective than taxation in inducing the internalization of external economies.[56] Moreover, subsidization is likely to be inefficient in that it will frequently stimulate the purchase of special equipment when other methods might be superior. Furthermore, it would be difficult to determine who should be subsidized and by how much. Also, taxpayers' feelings of equity might be violated, since the industrial firm, in not having to consider pollution abatement a cost of production in the same sense that

55. E. S. Mills, "Federal Incentives in Air Pollution Control," *Proceedings,* National Conference on Air Pollution, December 12–14, 1966, p. 576.

56. F. T. Dolbear, "On the Theory of Optimum Externality," *American Economic Review,* March 1967, 56: 90–103; G. A. Mumey, "The 'Coase Theorem': A Re-examination," *Quarterly Review of Economics and Statistics* 85 (November 1971): 718–723; and R. A. Tybout, "Pricing Pollution and Other Externalities," *Bell Journal of Economics and Management Science* 13 (Spring 1972): 252–266.

labor and capital are, would rely on payments raised at least partially by higher taxes on other taxpayers. Apparently, the only advantage that subsidies have to recommend them is political. It is easier to subsidize than to tax, although ultimately subsidies have to be raised in terms of taxes or fees.

THE REGULATORY ALTERNATIVE

An additional way to guide the use of the environment and to raise the necessary public funds to do so is to impose regulations on individual usage and enforce these prohibitions directly. For example, government can and does speciy maximum pollution levels. When regulations are not heeded, fines are imposed.

A key question is the determination of the pollution limit deemed desirable by society. Cost–benefit analysis can be applied to help determine the optimal use of society's scarce resources, by trading off environmental amenities against other goods and services. Specifically, it involves weighing the social costs of environmental amenities against their social benefits. Such a determination would vary according to the current state of society's preferences, the particular characteristics of the environmental region in question, for example, a watershed, and the alternatives that must necessarily be forgone in order to achieve the desired quality level.

Theoretically, once society has chosen an overall maximum permissible level of a particular pollutant (e.g., carbon monoxide), then the most efficient method to achieve the desired level is to have each polluter reduce his level of pollution output until the marginal costs of an incremental decrease in pollution are the same for all polluters.

One example of environmental regulation is the Clean Air Act passed by Congress to regulate the use of air resources. This law uses a uniform national air pollution standard as a regulatory framework. Each state is required to implement a plan designed to achieve a stringent national standard, whether pollution is a problem in that state at the time or not. Such a system is inefficient by the economic standards previously outlined. To begin with, the social cost of a given level of pollution varies from region to region depending on the natural characteristics of each area. A high level of pollution output in one area may entail a low social cost because of such natural dispersement features as high winds or proximity to the ocean. However, the same pollution output may generate high social costs in a geographically hemmed-in area like the Los Angeles Basin. To be efficient, pollution levels and standards should vary from area to area depending on the range and level of costs imposed. The Clean Air Act, by imposing a uniform national pollution limit across every air space region in the nation, would appear to be inefficient. Yet, by providing all regions with about equal air quality, it is equitable in a certain sense.

The regulatory alternative can also mandate action to control pollution. For example, the California legislature mandated, but later counter-manded, the installation of crankcase pollution devices in every new and used car sold in California. The cost of the device and its installation was estimated to average about $35 per car and the requirement was absolute. The results would have been inefficient, since cars with long and short life expectancies had to have the same expensive device installed. Further-more, the pollution decrease from putting the device on an old car would initially be much greater than that from putting the device on a new car. However, a new car would have a decreased pollution output over a much longer life span and the device would have a much lower average cost for the new car than for the old. Clearly the economically efficient standard previously outlined for the control of pollution is violated by this regulatory mechanism. As we can see, the marginal cost for each decrement of pollu-tion for all polluters is not the same, and a more efficient reallocation of pollution-control resources should be possible.

In general, the purely regulatory approach leads to inefficiencies when it imposes a uniform aggregate standard; a more efficient attainment of the same level of environmental cleanliness could be achieved by marginal adjustments over the various regions and individual polluters involved.

A number of different approaches have been applied to determine fines. One method calculates the "opportunity for profit" a firm is likely to have derived from using equity capital that otherwise would have been invested in pollution control and from the accompanying savings in operating and maintenance costs. An example will illustrate this opportunity-for-profit concept: Assuming that the pollution-control equipment would have cost $100,000, had a 10-year tax life, and required $10,000 a year to operate, and that the company had a 10% after-tax return on equity and a marginal tax rate of 48%, the economic advantage after 2 years would be $27,464.[57]

A second method calculates the amount a company is likely to save by avoiding capital and operating costs over the useful life of the pollution-control equipment. On the basis of the numbers just given, the economic advantage after 2 years comes to $23,358, with both examples assuming a 10% investment tax credit and an inflation rate of 6%.[58]

GOVERNMENT-FACILITATED
INTERNALIZATION REQUIRING NO REVENUE

Government can take a number of steps that, though involving different degrees of direct intervention, can bring about internalization of some of

57. *Business Week*, December 19, 1977, p. 27.
58. *Ibid.*, p. 27.

the externalities without requiring government funds.[59] They range from government-induced publicly negotiated settlements among all affected parties to government-sanctioned formation of landowner development corporations.

PUBLICLY NEGOTIATED SETTLEMENT

Government can arrange for the holding of public hearings involving all the individuals affected by an externality, and by so doing it can facilitate the initiation of negotiations among these parties. In order to establish a basis for such negotiations, a rigidly enforced assignment of transferable property rights relative to the externality must be specified. This assignment of property rights will affect the motivations for emitters and recipients of the externality to engage in negotiations.

Since externality situations are reciprocal in nature, there exists some rationale, and sometimes even an incentive, for negotiations to get under way. The generation of an external diseconomy, for example, provides benefits to the emitters but imposes costs on the recipients. Thus, for any positive quantity of external diseconomy rationally generated, a reduction thereof provides benefits to the recipients of the externality, a reduction in external costs. At the same time it imposes costs on the emitters by reducing their profits or satisfaction. Yet there may exist strong political, social, and moral pressures to reduce the negative externality. Therefore, both emitters and recipients of the externality may be motivated to explore the possibility of a negotiated, mutually beneficial modification of the generated externality. For example, in the absence of legal restrictions on the generation of an external diseconomy, the recipients may be motivated to offer to the emitter some portion of the reduction in external costs that the recipients will obtain as a result of a decrease in the externality. This may induce emitters to accept the reduction in their profits or satisfaction accompanying a decrease in externality generation. The emitters may be motivated to accept payments and decrease externality generation if these payments exceed the costs they will incur in efforts to decrease externality generation. The opposite will hold if there are binding legal restrictions on the generation of the external diseconomy.

Public hearings of this type are likely to succeed in producing socially desirable negotiated settlements only in externality situations involving a very small number of individuals. However, usually pollution of the air, streams, and lakes generates externalities affecting very many firms and individuals. Under such circumstances, a freely negotiated settlement is unlikely unless unanimous consent of all affected parties is not required for the adoption of the settlement. But unless unanimous consent is required the resulting resource use is likely to be less efficient than that which would result from alternative mechanisms.

59. Reuter and Kushner, *Economic Incentives,* sect. 5.40–5.90.

Arrangements can be made whereby government negotiates on behalf of neighbors with the polluting firm. In a limited sense this occurs in England and Wales where the Alkali and Clean Air Inspectorate negotiates with industry on the best practicable means to ensure that potentially dangerous emissions are not discharged except in a harmless and inoffensive form.[60] The negotiations, no doubt, are helped along by industry's knowledge that the Inspectorate can, in case of unsuccessful discussions, lay down limits it considers appropriate.

FORMATION OF LANDOWNER DEVELOPMENT CORPORATIONS

Government can either take initiating steps or sanction the formation of a landowner development corporation with the purpose of merging the control of externalities. By unifying within a single decision-making unit the authority to control all activities relative to a given parcel of land, many of the externalities are likely to be internalized.

Yet a landowner development corporation is likely to be socially undesirable since, in order to control externalities effectively, the corporation will require substantial monopoly power over the development and use of land in the area. To formulate public policy that regulates the corporation's exploitation of this monopoly power requires about the same large quantity of information needed for a policy to control generation of externalities among private land users. Thus, there is very little merit in such a policy and it is unlikely to have political appeal.

GOVERNMENT-FACILITATED INTERNALIZATION FINANCED THROUGH GENERAL TAXES

A final mechanism has government taking affirmative steps to internalize major externalities and financing the activity out of general taxes. The specific steps involve public purchase of environmental easements.

PUBLIC PURCHASE OF ENVIRONMENTAL EASEMENTS

Government can force property owners to surrender the right to use their property in certain specified ways (e.g., to cause pollution of the air and/or rivers), in exchange for a monetary payment. One such method is to purchase environmental easements. For the public purchase of an environmental easement to promote the attainment of efficiency, certain

---

60. The Alkali Act explicitly specifies emission limits for only four processes. For all other processes the limits are negotiated. Department of the Environment, *Pollution Control in Great Britain: How it Works* (London: 1976), p. 7.

conditions must be met. Specifically, the easement-related costs that are incurred by the property owner from whom the easement is purchased should not exceed the net benefits expected to be obtained therefrom by all other members of society. These costs incurred by property owners and the net benefits obtained by society constitute the lower and upper bounds, respectively, of the compensation range for the easements that promote efficiency. Clearly, estimating such values is extremely difficult. Moreover, because easements are essentially negative control mechanisms, attainment of efficient resource use is difficult.

Since establishing environmental easements requires someone to exercise the power of eminent domain, two legal conditions must be fulfilled. First, "just compensation" must be paid for the damages inflicted on the property owner as a result of the easement. Second, the constraints imposed on the use of the property to which the easement is applied must serve a public purpose.

The purchase of environmental easements has the great advantage of flexibility at any point in time as well as of adaptability over time. However, it also has serious shortcomings, including large information requirements. Moreover, property owners may fool the government by displaying a convincing interest in initiating activities on the property that will impose substantial externalities. Yet they may have no actual intention of initiating these activities. Thus a property owner may succeed in inducing government to purchase an easement on his property to avoid pursuit of an activity that the property owner never seriously considered undertaking.

CONCLUSION

We have seen that environmental law has grown out of society's concern with defining, enforcing, and allocating environmental property rights and entitlements. Defining and enforcing specific rights to the use of the environment is a complex task because of the interrelated and therefore nonexclusive nature of environmental resources. By their inherent nature, the use of environmental resources generates complex externalities, thereby making specific enforceable rights to their usage difficult to define. Because environmental entitlements are hard to define they are also difficult to exchange and reallocate to their highest-valued alternative use. The courts and the legislatures have been called on to interfere. They have done so in various ways, applying a host of techniques with varying success. The application of nuisance law and the attempts at reconciling the conflict between the police power of the state and the citizen's right to just compensation have not been easy for the courts in their efforts to internalize widespread externalities. No single technique for such internalization exists for all externality situations. Although a single public policy that is socially most desirable is lacking, there exists a uniformly applicable analytical framework appropriate for the comparisons of strengths and weaknesses of alternative mechanisms and policies: cost–benefit analysis. Courts and legislatures have been slow in making use of empirical cost–benefit analyses but appear to have in many cases implicitly applied this general outlook.

Legislatures have sought to deal with threats to the environment by levying a variety of taxes and fees. In some cases they have done the obverse; they have provided subsidies to induce environmentally safer practices. Moreover, governments can take steps to facilitate the internalization by firms and households of externalities, steps that in some cases require revenues and in others do not.

X

ANTIMONOPOLY LAW

INTRODUCTION

Contract law, as was discussed earlier, is based on the premise that all parties to a transaction are reasonably equal in bargaining power. This equality of bargaining power is a prerequisite—a necessary though not sufficient condition—for a competitive market, where important characteristics of a competitive market are,

1. A large number of firms
2. Homogeneous products
3. Free entry into and exit from the market
4. Independence of decisions among firms
5. Perfect knowledge

Economists differentiate between perfect and pure competition. *Perfect competition* requires all five characteristics; for *pure competition,* some economists consider the first four characteristics essential; others, merely the first two. In the absence of pure or perfect competition, markets are monopolistic or oligopolistic to varying degrees, depending on whether the industry has one or a small number of members.

However, as E. S. Mason has effectively argued, lawyers and economists use the word *monopoly* (and therefore the word *competition*) in distinctly different ways.[1] For lawyers, the term *monopoly* is used as "a standard of

1. E. S. Mason, "Monopoly in Law and Economics," *Yale Law Journal* 47 (November 1937): 34–49.

evaluation," designating a situation not in the public interest. *Competition,* in comparison, designates situations in the public interest. For the lawyer, monopoly means a restriction of the freedom of business to engage in legitimate economic activities.

Economists use monopoly and competition as tools of analysis rather than as market situations that are or are not in the public interest. They define monopoly to involve the power of a business unit to influence the terms under which transactions take place, and in the extreme case a single seller of a product devoid of close substitutes.

The legal definition of monopoly clearly has the great advantage of simplicity, defining a situation whose elimination is salubrious. Thus restrictive practices are to be eliminated for the public good. The economic view is more complicated. It is widely agreed that transactors exert themselves to the limit and put forth their very best efforts when threatened by effective rivals. But, although economic theory demonstrates with great rigor that competitive markets produce greater allocative efficiency than any other market, they may result in fewer new or improved products and processes. More important, pure competition does not exist in real life. Moreover, the mere existence of control or power does not always lead to undesirable results.

Matters are further complicated by the precedent-setting nature of rulings by the courts, which may lead, for example, to the denial of a specific merger even though it would not have lessened competition, because of the fear that most similar mergers would indeed have adverse effects.

Why should government interfere with the sanctity of a contract? The reason is quite simple. When there exists great inequality in bargaining power, a contract, even if freely arrived at, can have major ill effects on others who are not parties to it. Government intervention, it can be argued, is then needed to champion resource-allocation, and even social, efficiency.

From a theoretical point of view it is easy to see, therefore, why Congress passed antimonopoly laws; it is not so clear, however, why in the presence of such laws great concentrations of economic activity continue to exist. Furthermore, it is not clear whether such concentration is in fact socially undesirable, and if so under what circumstances it is undesirable. Economists who seek to evaluate antimonopoly laws can raise some major questions: Have these laws produced consistent, socially desirable results? Or was an initially valid concern to use antimonopoly laws to enhance consumer welfare diverted from the original objective, contaminated, and abused? Specifically, have antimonopoly efforts lost their direction so that some of them seek social and political equality rather than efficiency? Moreover, is this misguided objective being sought by protecting inefficient firms while penalizing aggressively efficient ones?

Some authors have expressed strong opinions on these issues. For example, R. H. Bork argues,

The present misshapen look of antitrust doctrine is due in large measure to the Supreme Court's habit of regarding business efficiency as either irrelevant or harmful. Insufficient regard for efficient methods of production and distribution meant that hardly any business practice challenged could survive.[2]

Clearly, as will be seen, this is not the only view of antimonopoly laws.

Much of the difficulty perhaps stems from the fact that the benchmark to which economists tend to compare real-life markets is a highly theoretical construct—the purely or perfectly competitive market. It has never been shown to exist and is a most improbable phenomenon. Therefore we cannot be sure that rigorous economic theory of pure or perfect competition can, as is often claimed, provide powerful policy guidelines. (The fact that competitive markets produce efficient resource allocation is based on a number of restrictive assumptions, discussed in Chapter I.)

This issue is recognized by H. Demsetz when he states, "The proper issue for antitrust, then, is not the degree to which a market descriptively diverges from perfect competition, but the degree to which it diverges in either direction from that intensity of competition which takes account of the real social costs of competing."[3]

There is at least one more issue that must be considered in framing antimonopoly laws. Even if competitive markets lead to efficient resource allocation, they perpetuate existing income-distribution patterns. Though a competitive market gives expression to people's willingness to pay, it does not necessarily do much about people's ability to pay. Since it does very little to change the existing income distribution, the welfare results of effective competition are desirable only if the existing income distribution is looked upon as optimal. In a world of a widely unequal income distribution, high transaction costs, and pervasive externalities, an antimonopoly policy designed to approximate the results of a perfectly competitive market has serious limitations.

THE ECONOMIC INCENTIVE TO MONOPOLIZE MARKETS

In the most simplistic textbook version, profit-maximizing solutions of the single-firm monopolist and of competitive firms in the same industry are compared. Numerous simplifying assumptions are made, including the presence of identical firm demand functions as well as cost functions, and the absence of any transaction cost. The two solutions are presented in

2. R. H. Bork, "Vertical Constraints: Schwinn Overruled," 1977 *Supreme Court Review*, ed. P. Kurland and G. Caper (Chicago: University of Chicago Press, 1977), p. 172.

3. H. Demsetz, "Economics as a Guide to Antitrust Regulation," *Journal of Law and Economics* 19 (August 1976): 374.

Figure 10-1. In the competitive case with free entry into the industry, all firms equate their long-run marginal cost with average revenue, and therefore the industry output in the long run will be at an intersection of the industry's marginal cost (MC) and demand or average revenue function, $D = AR$; that is, at A. Output will be Q_c and price P_c. In the single-firm monopoly case, the monopolist will equate marginal cost (ΣMC) with marginal revenue (MR) at point B. Its output will be Q_m, which is smaller than Q_c, and its price will be P_m, which is higher than P_c. Finally, the consumer surplus of AKI under competition is larger than DKE under single-firm monopoly. Because competitors are free to enter the industry, competitive firms in the long run will not make any economic profit, at a time that the monopoly will make a profit.

This simplistic analysis neglects a number of major issues. Thus, for example, firms of different size tend to have different production and cost functions. Specifically there are often scale economies, and in their presence a monopoly price might be smaller than the competitive one. Moreover, firms who seek a monopoly position often have to engage in numerous activities, none of which tend to be costless. Instead, they incur major transaction costs, which may be so large as to persuade them to abandon their pursuit of a monopoly position. However, there can be little doubt that monopolists have more control over their own destiny than have competitive firms. Moreover, in a technologically sophisticated industry, scale economics tends to push firms to expand volume and thereby their market share. Thus, existing natural forces may lead to greater and greater monopoly power in industry.

The foregoing analysis of some of the effects of monopoly is very simplis-

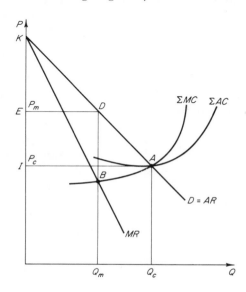

FIGURE 10-1 Profit-maximizing solutions of the single-firm monopolist and the competitive firm. (Key: MC, marginal cost function; AC, average cost; MR, marginal revenue function; $D = AR$, demand or average revenue function; P_m, price, and Q_m, output, of the monopolist; P_c, price, and Q_c, output, of the competitive firm.)

tic. In fact there is little agreement on the nature and magnitude of monopoly effects. For example, there is much disagreement about the relationship between concentration and profit rates. G. J. Stigler has shown that monopoly and concentration are positively correlated.[4] Demsetz, however, argues that profit rates may be less the result of concentration than of superior performance by firms. Moreover, he argues that since larger firms tend to earn a higher profit rate than smaller ones, Stigler's test should perhaps be modified by holding firm size constant. When firms are classified by asset size into five classes, standard deviations of profit rates tend to be greater for very large and very small firms than for moderate-size firms. Once firm size is controlled, no clear relationship between concentration and standard deviations emerges.[5]

Stigler has also argued that

> competitive industries will have a volatile pattern of rates of return, for the movements into high-profit industries and out of low-profit industries will . . . lead to a constantly changing (over time) hierarchy of rates of return. In the monopolistic industries, on the other hand, the unusually profitable industries will be able to observe their preferential position for considerable periods of time.[6]

Stigler tested this proposition by analyzing the stability and the time patterns of relative profit rates of different industries. Demsetz argues that the increased stability over time may be more the result of product diversification of large firms than concentration. Using data developed by J. F. Weston, Demsetz shows that large firms do exhibit greater persistence in relative profit positions, but industry concentration displays no significant or consistent relationship to the pattern of intertemporal stability of relative profit rates.[7]

WAYS TO MONOPOLIZE MARKETS: MANY ROADS LEAD TO ROME

Firms have traveled different roads toward enhanced monopoly power. Perhaps the single most direct one is consolidation, be it through merger or creation of conglomerates. Thus, for example, one study found that in 17 West German (four-digit) manufacturing industries, between 1958 and 1971, mergers were the single most important factor increasing market concentration. Internal growth was of secondary importance, and exit and

4. G. J. Stigler, *Capital and Rates of Return in Manufacturing Industries* (Princeton, N.J.: Princeton University Press, 1963), p. 78.

5. Demsetz, "Economics as a Guide," p. 377.

6. Stigler, *Capital and Rates of Return*, p. 70.

7. Demsetz, "Economics as a Guide," p. 380.

entry were relatively insignificant.[8] Mergers rarely if ever lead to a complete monopolization of the industry; more often they lead to oligopoly.

A second method often employed to monopolize markets involves various forms, often secret, of cooperation among competitors. The outstanding example is the cartel that engages in price fixing and/or market division.

Third, firms can engage in predatory price discrimination and fourthly in foreclosing entry through vertical integration and advertising. A fifth method involves such vertical restraints as exclusive vertical dealing arrangements, tie-in arrangements, reciprocal buying, and boycott. Finally, government can play a contributing role by inducing price fixing and foreclosure. A good example is occupational licensing.

A BRIEF OUTLINE OF ANTIMONOPOLY ACTS

Antimonopoly law, more commonly referred to as *antitrust law,* is derived from broad statutory guidelines provided mainly in the Sherman, Clayton, and Federal Trade Commission (FTC) acts.

Section 1 of the Sherman Act provides that every contract, combination, or conspiracy in restraint of trade among the several states is illegal. Section 2 outlaws single-firm monopolization. Thus, Sherman Act standards parallel Mason's legal definition of monopoly, cited earlier in the chapter. There is wide agreement that a per se approach toward conspiratorial conduct is justified. To the extent that conspiracies are effective, the chance of vigorous price competition is reduced.

The Clayton Act limits undertakings that tend to lessen competition substantially or create a monopoly. Horizontal mergers have been judged on almost a purely structural basis and have been found illegal whenever an increase in the centralization of market power is a probable result. The test for vertical mergers has been the degree to which customers or suppliers would be foreclosed from the part of the market represented by one of the merging firms. (On the basis of *FTC* v. *Proctor and Gamble Co.,*[9] courts find anticompetitive implications in overall firm size as well as in relative size in a given market.)

Section 2, amended by the Robinson–Patman Act, prohibits price discrimination.[10] This currently contested provision, which can prohibit the lowering of prices, has led to the businessman's lament that he cannot lower

8. J. Müller and R. Hochreiter, "Auswirkungen der Unterehmungskonzentration und deren mogliche Kontrolle durch ein Fusionsverbot," *Jahrbuch der National Ökonomie und Statistik* 190 (October 1976): 48–50.

9. *FTC* v. *Proctor and Gamble Co.* 386 U.S. 568 (1967).

10. 15 U.S.C. § 13.

prices, "administer" prices by keeping them constant, or raise prices without violating some antitrust law.[11] Section 3 makes tie-in arrangements illegal. These are sales or leases of products on condition not to buy from competitors. Section 7, amended by the Celler–Kefauver Act of 1950, renders corporate mergers and acquisitions illegal if they substantially lessen competition.[12] Finally, Section 8 prohibits individuals from being board members of competitors.[13]

The FTC Act gives the Federal Trade Commission jurisdiction over Sections 1 and 2 of the Sherman Act and over some provisions of the Clayton Act.[14] In addition, Section 5 of the FTC Act forbids "unfair methods of competition" and in some cases this includes violation under any other antitrust provision.

Also, states have passed antimonopoly laws. In 1975, 16 states budgeted over $100,000 each for antimonopoly enforcement, 14 employing full-time investigators. Among the most active states in 1975 were Wisconsin (35 suits), New York (7 suits), Ohio (6 suits), and Maryland (4 suits). Since 1976, state antimonopoly programs have expanded because of federal grants available to States under the Antitrust Improvements Act of 1976, $11 million in the first year.[15] Furthermore, the 1976 amendment to federal antitrust laws authorized state attorney generals to sue businesses in federal court for damages incurred by citizens of their states caused by Sherman Act violations.[16]

HORIZONTAL MERGERS AND JOINT OPERATING AGREEMENTS

Mergers result when one firm takes over one or more firms, often in the same industry. When the takeover comprises firms on a single level of the production–distribution systems, we talk about *horizontal mergers*. The United States has gone through three major merger waves—1897–1902, 1924–1930, and 1965–1970. During 1968 alone, 4400 business corporations disappeared by merger, with $43 billion in securities exchanged—less than 4% of the market value of corporate securities.[17]

11. 15 U.S.C. § 13, 15 U.S.C. § 1, 15 U.S.C. § 130.
12. 15. U.S.C. § 18.
13. 15 U.S.C. § 19.
14. 15 U.S.C. § 41–58.
15. M. Kwitny, "State Enforcement of Antitrust Law Can Be a Rude Shock," *Wall Street Journal*, January 23, 1978, p. 12.
16. 15 U.S.C. § 15C.
17. N. Jacoby, "The Conglomerate Corporation," *Financial Analysts Journal*, May–June 1950, pp. 2–3.

Figure 10-1 can also be applied to represent the horizontal merging of a number of competitive firms into a single-firm monopolist under the most simplified assumptions. Accordingly, creation of a single-firm monopoly leads to price and profit increases, and quantity and consumer surplus declines. A welfare loss to the public has occurred, since the output formerly produced and desired by consumers under competitive conditions is no longer being produced under monopoly conditions. Under these simplified assumptions, horizontal mergers are inefficient and therefore undesirable.

However, the merged firm might incur scale economies and obtain some input factors below the price paid before the merger. Lower cost functions then will result. Although under these conditions there will be monopoly profits, consumers may benefit from lower prices.

Many mergers, although mainly horizontal, do not combine exclusively identical activities and products on a single production or distribution level. Conglomerate mergers bring together two or more enterprises engaged in unrelated lines of business, in terms of either activities or products. In this connection it is particularly helpful to recognize that markets and firms are alternative instruments to complete related transactions. On a priori grounds it is not clear which alternative is more efficient. Much depends on the costs of writing and executing complex contracts across a market compared to costs incurred when the transactions are carried out within a single firm.

O. E. Williamson, by taking into consideration a number of important transaction costs, has concluded that

> the broadside attack . . . against conglomerates appears to be overdrawn. . . . Absent capital market frictions impeding takeover or proclivities of incumbent managements to reinvest earnings . . . , the conglomerate appears to lack compelling economic purpose of a socially redeeming kind. . . . Once such frictions are admitted, however, there is plainly a case for encouraging, or at least not impeding organizational innovations which have the potential to attenuate internal organizational distortions of a managerial discretion kind. Subject to the qualifications about organizational form . . . , the conglomerate has attractive properties both because it makes the market for corporate control more credible thereby inducing self-policing among otherwise opportunistic managements, and because it promotes the reallocation of resources to high yield users. Except therefore, among giant sized firms, where the risk of offsetting political distortions is seriously posed, a more sympathetic posture . . . towards conglomerates would seem warranted.[18]

For these reasons, Williamson suggests that antimonopoly policy with respect to conglomerate acquisitions focus on those mergers that impair

18. O. E. Williamson, "The Economics of Antitrust: Transaction Cost Considerations," *University of Pennsylvania Law Review* 122 (June 1974): 1446.

potential competition and those involving giant firms that do not dispose of comparable assets at the time of their acquisition.[19]

However, it must be realized that mergers into a single-firm monopoly are extremely rare. Most mergers lead to oligopoly positions, and the behavior of oligopoly markets is substantially less clear than that of single-firm monopolists. Thus, whatever limited analytical conclusions were drawn concerning the behavior of mergers into single-firm monopolies become even less clear in relation to oligopoly. Nevertheless, the 1950 amendment of Section 7 of the Clayton Act, which seems to place exceedingly stringent limitations on mergers between competitors, tends to be defended as necessary to prevent further increases in oligopoly.[20]

In this connection *FTC* v. *Procter and Gamble Co.*,[21] a product-extension merger that was ruled illegal, is of interest. Procter and Gamble sought to expand into the household liquid bleach market by acquiring the assets of Clorox, the leading producer of liquid bleach. Since this was not a merger of a firm producing the same good it was not a horizontal merger; and it was not a vertical merger since it was not between different levels of an industry. The merger, it was argued by the defendant, created efficiencies since it was an integration of Clorox into the larger capital market of Procter and Gamble, which reduced the transaction costs of obtaining capital in the market. It also created advertising efficiencies. The Supreme Court, in ruling the merger illegal, ignored these arguments as well as the existence of 200 small firms that produced 20% of the output of bleach.

One argument by the Court was that Procter and Gamble was a potential entrant in the market and knowledge of this fact kept the price competitive in the industry. The Court also felt that Procter and Gamble's huge assets gave it unwarranted leverage in the market and the power of predatory pricing. However, it could be argued that efficiencies in other markets are separate from each other. Therefore, Procter and Gamble may have already obtained the best deal possible in its other markets and may have been unable to gain a further advantage with Clorox unless it gave up other advantages.

Often firms seek to engage in less than a full merger, and they enter into joint operating agreements. Such agreements resemble to some extent horizontal contractual agreements, or cartels, which will be discussed later. Joint operating agreements tend to receive more favorable treatment from the courts than do cartels, because they entail more efficient resource use than do horizontal contractual agreements.

In *United States* v. *Penn–Olin Chemical Co.*,[22] Penn and Olin decided to form a joint venture in order to compete in the production of sodium

19. *Ibid.*, p. 1491.
20. R. Posner, *Economic Analysis of Law*, 2nd ed. (Boston: Little, Brown, 1977), p. 220,
21. *FTC* v. *Procter and Gamble Co.*, 386 U.S. 568 (1967).
22. *United States* v. *Penn–Olin Chemical Co.*, 378 U.S. 158 (1964).

chlorate. Section 7 of the Clayton Act, prohibiting anticompetitive mergers, was applied instead of Section 1 of the Sherman Act. The Supreme Court stated that it was probable that one but not both of the companies would have entered the market separately, hence there would appear to be no competitive loss. However, the other firm would have remained at the edge of the market as a potential competitor, exerting downward pressure on price; hence the merger had anticompetitive effects. The efficiencies gained from the integration of productive facilities were apparently completely ignored by the Court.

In *Citizen Publishing Co.* v. *United States,* [23] the two major Tucson newspapers formed a joint operating agreement. By most economic tests the agreement created productive efficiencies and was ancillary to the creation of these efficiencies, since it went no further than a merger. At the same time, it also would eliminate some competition, since the effect would have been a reduction in the number of independent newspapers from two to one in Tucson. However, one of the papers was in bad financial shape. Under the failing-company doctrine, an exception could be made if failure was imminent. Without the merger there would be only one paper. However, the Supreme Court did not accept this argument.

In summary, economic analysis of horizontal merger cases raises some serious questions about the 1950 amendment of Section 7 of the Clayton Act and key court decisions. More careful attention should be given to ascertaining the efficiency increases resulting from specific mergers. Their estimates should be carefully balanced against the potential ill effects of greater size, possibly leading to increased oligopoly power. In short, some horizontal mergers that result in large efficiency increases on balance may deserve to be tolerated.

CARTELS

Agreements to cooperate among competitors, either in terms of fixing prices or dividing markets, are referred to as *cartels*. These agreements are usually entered into without a formal contract. Cartel agreements are consummated like any other contract, because they appear to be beneficial to those who enter into them. At the same time, those who are not party to the agreement, all too often consumers, may be injured.

One major difference between a merger and a cartel relates to their effects on costs. Since cartels, unlike mergers, do not integrate productive facilities, there is little likelihood that production efficiencies will result from cartels.

---

23. *Citizen Publishing Co.* v. *United States,* 394 U.S. 131 (1969).

Cartels tend to engage in two major activities of concern to antimonopoly policymakers—horizontal price fixing and horizontal market division. The two activities will be taken up in turn.

HORIZONTAL PRICE FIXING

Entering an agreement to fix the price is unlikely to lower the cost functions of the colluding firms. Most likely, substantial transaction costs of monitoring and policing the behavior of cartel members will result. Costs may therefore be higher than before.

In the first important antitrust case, *United States* v. *Addyston Pipe and Steel Co.,*[24] involving cartelization and price fixing, a group of producers of cast iron cartelized, with all business being referred to a central authority that decided the price for the work. Members of the cartel then bid internally for the job and the central authority divided up the profits. Judge Taft noticed that no economies of scale or other productive efficiencies were involved in the cartel and therefore ruled it illegal. More important, for purposes of the Sherman Act horizontal price fixing and horizontal market division are identical and illegal per se. Additionally, Judge Taft formulated the doctrine of *ancillary restraints*. He stated that agreements that are ancillary to the purpose of the contract and no wider than necessary to create efficiency should be held valid. These valid common-law agreements include agreements by retiring partners not to compete with the firm, agreements by a partner not to compete with a pending partnership, contracts by a seller of a business not to compete with the buyer in derogation of the purchase price, and others.

Another doctrine formulated shortly thereafter is the *rule of reason*. After determining that a contract creates efficiencies and that the restriction is ancillary to the contract, the court looks into the purpose and effect of the agreement. In *United States* v. *Chicago Board of Trade,*[25] Justice Brandeis determined that a call rule, limiting the hours that differing bids could be made, was permissible. The rule created efficiencies and was ancillary to the purpose to enhance noneconomic values. Therefore, Justice Brandeis concluded that the purpose and effect of the rule was not significantly anticompetitive. This rule has economic rationale since presumably the anticompetitive effect of a contract between two firms, with, for example, 1% of the market, will be minimal. Those firms would be trying to expand their output, not restrict it. The purpose part of the test may not be so valuable. Presumably, any businessman would seek to restrain output and gain monopoly profits if he could; therefore, almost all activities of firms will have, as one important purpose, the enhancing of profits.

24. *United States* v. *Addyston Pipe and Steel Co.,* 85 Fed. 271 (6th Cir. 1898).
25. *United States* v. *Chicago Board of Trade* 246 U.S. 231 (1918).

United States v. *Socony Vacuum Oil Co.* represented the next major legal development.[26] The major oil companies tried to restrict the output of "hot" oil from Texas by contracting with small producers in an effort to keep the price up. There was no integration of productive facilities and no efficiencies were created; hence the agreement should have been ruled invalid as it was. However, the Supreme Court went further, declaring that all price-fixing agreements are per se illegal, regardless of whatever efficiencies might have been created. Here the investigation of agreements centered around the question of whether the particular contract fit within the per se rule, not whether it was economically efficient. This by and large is the state of the law today with respect to horizontal price fixing agreements.

HORIZONTAL MARKET DIVISION

Horizontal market divisions, which cut up the market among competitors, were also ruled illegal per se in *United States* v. *Sealy, Inc.*[27] Sealy was a trade-name combine that advertised nationally for a group of regional mattress producers. In order to increase local sales efforts, a market division arrangement, which prevented the producers from selling in neighboring territories, was part of the agreement. A price fix was also imposed to enforce the market division and reduce the incentive to shift the mattresses to neighboring areas. Since the price restriction was only on Sealy mattresses—a very small part of the market—there was no attempt to fix the price of mattresses in general. The real purpose of the market division was to eliminate free rides by nonadvertising sellers. Local advertising would suffer, it was argued, if some retailers could obtain the benefits of advertising paid for by the participating retailers. The Supreme Court held both the price fixing and market division per se illegal despite the creation of advertising efficiencies. The creation of a property right in information about Sealy and its enforcement through trademark advertising was destroyed.

The Supreme Court, in *United States* v. *Topco Associates, Inc.*, probably contributed to inefficiency.[28] Several small grocery chains formed a voluntary contract association in order to get volume discounts from wholesalers. Although no restriction of output by these small retailers was possible, the Court called the arrangement a naked restrain of trade. The Court most likely confused intrabrand and interbrand competition. Clearly, intrabrand restrictions such as Topco imposed here on its own retailers (or as Safeway does on its stores to prevent their competing with each other) have minimal impact on competition and are common practice. Horizontal interbrand

26. *United States* v. *Socony Vacuum Oil Co.*, 310 U.S. 150 (1940).
27. *United States* v. *Sealy, Inc.*, 388 U.S. 350 (1967).
28. *United States* v. *Topco Associates, Inc.*, 405 U.S. 596 (1972).

restrictions are clearly suspect, but none were present here since only one association was involved. The efficiencies of Topco were created to increase output, not restrict output, as the Court itself noted. Still, the territorial restrictions on the use of the Topco trademark were found to be horizontal in nature and illegal per se.

In summary, cartel arrangements are often anticompetitive and lack redeeming virtue that would justify their existence.

PRICE DISCRIMINATION

In addition to a firm increasing its monopoly power through merger and various forms of cooperation among competitors, it can attain the same objective by easing out competitors and keeping out potential new ones. One of the most potent strategies open to firms seeking to eliminate competitors is to engage in predatory price discrimination. I should hasten to point out, however, that not all price discrimination is predatory, such that the firm sells at a very low price in some markets, possibly below cost, in order to drive out competitors, and once this is accomplished it will set a monopoly price. Instead some price discrimination, at least in theory, can lead to an equilibrium position that is socially desirable in the sense that output approximates competitive output.

Williamson has shown that welfare assessment is quite complicated.[29] I will attempt to reproduce the Williamson argument here. Figure 10-2 assumes large-scale economies in relation to the size of the market; the average cost curve falls precipitously over a considerable output range. The unregulated, profit-maximizing monopolist who charges the uniform price to all customers will restrict output to Q_m, well below the social optimum of Q^*. The monopolist who segregates his market so that each customer pays his full valuation (given by the demand function) for each unit of output is inclined to add successive units of output until the price paid for the last unit equals marginal cost. The fully discriminating monopolist will thus favor the social optimum Q^*. At the same time, undesirable income redistribution is likely to take place.

So far zero transaction costs to achieve discrimination are assumed. However, in most cases, price discrimination will require substantial expenditures to reveal customers' true preferences and to prevent resale by those who paid little to those who are forced to pay dearly. Thus, the firm that seeks to engage in price discrimination, although possibly benefiting from scale economies, may incur major costs in connection with its price-discriminating schemes. Clearly there can be both types of cases, those

29. Williamson, "Economics of Antitrust," pp. 1447–1449.

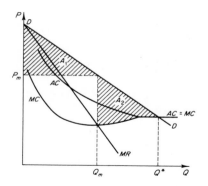

FIGURE 10-2 Effects of price discrimination on output; Q^* is the socially optimal output. (See key to Figure 10-1 for definitions of variables.)

where the transaction costs are smaller than the savings due to scale economies, and vice versa.

So much for a static analysis. However, predatory price discrimination, as has been mentioned, is a strategy designed to reduce competition by easing out competitors. Once this is accomplished, the monopolist thus strengthened may raise prices and reduce output in a socially undesirable manner. This part of the analysis is similar to that presented earlier regarding monopolization through merger.

The attitude of the courts has been influenced mainly by the Robinson–Patman Act, which prohibits discrimination only when the effect may be to substantially lessen competition. Rather than inquiring into the competitive implications of price discrimination, the courts tend to take the position that if differentials in price give some competitors an advantage over others, harm to competition is implied.[30] Thus, price differentials hurting one or more competitors are assumed to hurt competition by presumably contributing to the easing out of competitors. For example, in *Corn Products Refining Co.* v. *Federal Trade Commission*,[31] and in *Federal Trade Commission* v. *A. E. Stealey Mfg. Co.*,[32] the Supreme Court presumed that a disadvantage occurred to customers who were distant from the basing point. In both of these basing-point decisions, thus, harm to competition was presumed. In *Federal Trade Commission* v. *Morton Salt Co.*[33] the Court's presumption was that competition was lessened by the higher charge to smaller buyers.

Altogether, price discrimination can be used for deliberate predation designed to drive rivals from the market. Such acts clearly deserve to be declared illegal in the public interest. But it is important to distinguish between such predatory price discrimination and discrimination devoid of predation.

30. Peter Asch, *Economic Theory and the Antitrust Dilemma* (New York: Wiley, 1970), p. 344.
31. *Corn Products Refining Co.* v. *Federal Trade Commission,* 324 U.S. 726 (1945).
32. *Federal Trade Commission* v. *A. E. Stealey Mfg. Co.,* 324 U.S. 746 (1945).
33. *Federal Trade Commission* v. *Morton Salt Co.,* 334 U.S. 37 (1948).

FORECLOSING ENTRY THROUGH VERTICAL INTEGRATION AND ADVERTISING

A number of techniques have been used that may, to varying degrees, bar firms from entering an industry. Two such techniques, which also allegedly can ease out competition, will be considered—vertical integration and advertising.

VERTICAL INTEGRATION

A vertically integrated firm controls a number of successive stages of the production–delivery process. A firm may select such an internal organization in preference to market exchange, because the former has a number of attractive properties. Specifically, vertical arrangements can reduce transaction costs as well as other costs. Clearly, to the extent that vertical integration takes place solely for the purpose of reducing costs, such arrangements can be beneficial.

However, a vertically integrated firm can make it increasingly difficult for other firms to enter the industry. A prospective new entrant will not only need larger financing than if the industry were not integrated, but more important, he lacks prior experience. Thus, those who seek to enter a vertically integrated industry can seldom point to a reputation of success. Consequently, they tend to be forced to pay higher interest rates than they otherwise would. The potential entrant's high financing costs can constitute an effective barrier of entry into the industry.

Williamson has pointed to two situations in which a substantial disadvantage to potential entrants may arise.[34] One is the presence of a dominant firm or of otherwise strong concentration in the industry. The second involves moderately concentrated industries in which collusion has been successfully effected.

But even in concentrated industries, vertical integration is not to be condemned per se. It is objectionable, for example, where stage II would be competitively organized but for the vertical integration by the dominant firm in stage I of the industry. As a result, the residual, nonintegrated sector of the stage II market may be so small that only a few firms of efficient size can serve the stage II market. Firms that would otherwise be prepared to enter stage I would therefore be discouraged for fear "of having to engage in small numbers bargaining, with all the hazards that this entails, with these few nonintegrated stage II firms."[35] Additionally, entering into a vertically integrated industry may be unattractive if potential entrants lack stage II–related experience and therefore would incur high

---

34. Williamson, "Economics of Antitrust," pp. 1461–1462.
35. *Ibid.*, p. 1462.

capital costs. For this reason, Williamson concludes that permitting leading firms to integrate stages I and II is anticompetitive, in entry aspects at least.

The situation is quite different where scale economies at both stages are known to be large in relation to the size of the total market. Severing vertical connections then will not deter those contemplating entry into one of the stages, since entrants will not have to incur the adverse capital costs attached to entry at an unfamiliar stage.

Vertical integration in industries with low to moderate degrees of concentration often has few disadvantages. Under such conditions firms entering either stage can expect to strike competitive bargains with firms in the other stage, since no single integrated firm enjoys a strategic advantage with respect to such transactions.

In *Brown Shoe Co. Inc.*, v. *United States*,[36] the Supreme Court held that a lessening of competition in a vertical merger arises "primarily from foreclosure."[37] Rather than holding that the size of the market share that was foreclosed in itself determined whether a merger was illegal, the Court found it necessary to look further into the historical and economic background of affected markets.

The Court noted that though the shoe industry was atomistic, Brown's share of the national manufacturing market was 5–6%, and Kinney's retail sales were 2%. Thus, vertical integration would not have produced an overwhelmingly large firm. Although the Court found the industry highly competitive, it held that retaining vigor in competition cannot immunize a merger if the trend in the industry is toward oligopoly. Since Congress had revised Section 7 to preserve competition and prevent the formation of oligopolies, the Court found the merger suspect. It concluded that "the trend towards vertical integration in the shoe industry, when combined with Brown's avowed policy of forcing its own shoes upon its retail subsidiaries, may foreclose competition from a substantial share of the markets . . . without producing any countervailing competitive, economic or social advantages."[38] The Court's reading of congressional intent led Chief Justice Warren to conclude,

> The retail outlets of integrated companies, by eliminating wholesalers and by increasing the volume of purchases from the manufacturing division of the enterprise, can market their own brands at prices below those of competing independent retailers. Of course, some of the results of large integrated or chain operations are beneficial to consumers. . . . But we cannot fail to recognize Congress' desire to promote competition through the protection of viable, small, locally owned businesses. Congress appreciated that occasional higher costs and prices might result from the maintenance of fragmented

36. *Brown Shoe Co., Inc.* v. *United States*, 370 U.S. 294 (1962).
37. *Ibid.*, p. 328.
38. *Ibid.*, p. 334.

industries and markets. It resolved these competing considerations in favor of decentralization. We must give effect to that decision.[39]

In the *Brown Shoe* decision, the Court was searching for standards under which a lessening of competition because of vertical integration could be inferred. It apparently judged the competitive effect of the vertical integration purely in terms of its effect on the structure of relevant markets. Therefore, P. Asch concluded that "if it were found to be anticompetitive on this basis not even an expectation of improved market performance could save it from Section 7 prohibition. This strict view was undoubtedly influenced strongly by the Court's reading of Congressional intent."[40]

ADVERTISING

Advertising also has been pointed to as a method to increase monopoly power, mainly by establishing barriers to entry into the industry. It is argued that advertising makes possible effective product differentiation and prevents potential competitors from entering the industry. Before developing the latter argument in detail, it should be pointed out, however, that advertising can have distinctly positive effects. For example, by providing information, advertising can serve an important requirement of competition.

A theoretical argument tying advertising to entry barriers has been advanced by Comanor and Wilson.[41] They argue that new firms have higher costs than established firms at every level of output. Firms new to the industry, in addition to the production costs and advertising costs incurred by all firms, must also spend money on advertising to gain market penetration.

Comanor and Wilson tested their hypothesis indirectly. Assuming that large-scale advertising, by foreclosing entry, would increase profits, they engaged in empirical analyses of the relationship between rates of return and advertising intensity as measured by firms' advertising-to-sales ratios. Comanor and Wilson and a number of other studies treating advertising as a current expense found a strong positive relationship between advertising and profits.[42] However, there are two studies that treat advertising as an investment. One, by Weiss, confirms the earlier results of a strong positive relationship between advertising intensity and profits.[43] A study by Ayanian

39. *Ibid.*, p. 344.

40. Asch, *Economic Theory*, p. 300.

41. W. S. Comanor and T. S. Wilson, "Advertising, Market Structure and Performance," *Review of Economics and Statistics* 49 (November 1967): 423–440.

42. L. S. Esposito and F. F. W. Esposito, "Foreign Competition and Domestic Industry Profitability," *Review of Economics and Statistics* 53 (November 1971): 343–353; W. G. Shepherd, "The Elements of Market Structure," *Review of Economics and Statistics* 54 (February 1972): 25–37.

43. L. W. Weiss, "Advertising, Profit, and Corporate Taxes," *Review of Economics and Statistics* 51 (November 1969): 421–430.

employs a set of advertising depreciation rates to recalculate rates of return for a group of heavy advertisers by capitalizing their past advertising expenditures. Ayanian does not find a statistically significant relation between these corrected rates of return and firms' advertising intensities.[44]

An earlier study by Telser sought to test the relationship between advertising intensity and concentration.[45] A positive though not statistically significant relationship was found.

Although the empirical information is not entirely unequivocal, D. F. Turner, the former assistant attorney general in charge of the Department of Justice Antitrust Division, was convinced intuitively that heavy advertising promotes industry concentration and may thus harm competition.[46] However, this position should be somewhat modified in those industries in which advertising by the original firms in the market has created public acceptance for the product and thus gives the new entrants a "free ride."

In conclusion, firms who vertically integrate activities and/or advertise may or may not reduce competition in their industry. Careful economic analysis must be applied, on a case-by-case basis, in order to judge the social desirability of such activities.

OTHER VERTICAL RESTRAINTS

A number of vertical restraints are available to firms who do not undertake full vertical integration. Although exclusive dealing arrangements, tie-in arrangements, reciprocal buying, and boycotts differ, under certain circumstances all can ease out competitors. In some instances these instruments may also act as barriers to entry into the industry.

Under exclusive dealing and tie-in arrangements, as well as reciprocal buying, the seller makes the sale of a product contingent on specified customer behavior toward another product or products. Thus in an exclusive dealing arrangement a manufacturer will sell to a retailer only if the latter agrees not to carry products produced by a competitor. To the extent that the manufacturer succeeds in having many retailers sign an exclusive dealing arrangement, his demand will rise and his monopoly position will be enhanced. A tie-in arrangement provides that the buyer can purchase one product—the tying good—from the seller only if he agrees to purchase a tied good as well. Reciprocal buying relies on an explicit quid pro quo

44. R. Ayanian, "Advertising and Rate of Return," *Journal of Law and Economics* 18 (October 1975): 479–506.

45. L. G. Telser, "Advertising and Competition," *Journal of Political Economy* 72 (December 1964): 537–562.

46. D. F. Turner, "Advertising and Competition" (Address delivered before the Briefing Conference of Federal Controls of Advertising and Promotion, June 1966, mimeographed).

arrangement between the buyer and the seller. A boycott involves a concerted, collective refusal to have dealings with a party.

EXCLUSIVE VERTICAL DEALING ARRANGEMENTS

Let us begin with a review of some early court decisions involving exclusive dealing arrangements. The Standard Oil Company of California had entered into exclusive supply contracts with 5937 independent service stations binding them to fill their entire requirement from the company. It was the largest seller of petroleum products in the area and the service stations involved in the exclusive contract comprised 16% of total area outlets. Standard's competitors practiced similar dealings and only 1.6% of the area service stations were supplied by more than one company. In *Standard Oil of California and Standard Stations, Inc.* v. *United States*,[47] the Supreme Court ruled that the exclusive requirement contracts created a "potential clog on competition,"[48] and were in violation of Section 3 of the Clayton Act. The Court stated that exclusive requirement contracts— unlike tying arrangements—might prove to be desirable. Yet because of serious difficulties encountered in applying the necessary tests, a presumption was made against contracts involving a substantial volume of business. Though the Court seemed to argue for a rule-of-reason approach, it actually applied a per se test modified by the significance of commerce affected.[49]

In *Tampa Electric Co.* v. *Nashville Coal Co.*,[50] the Tampa Electric Company and the Nashville Coal Company had entered into a contract in which the former agreed to fill its entire coal requirements from the latter for a period of 20 years. The Supreme Court in 1961 did not find the requirement contract in violation of Section 3. Although the Court held the contract to amount to exclusive dealing, it decided such contracts were not illegal per se. The sum of the contract amounted to less than 1% of the relevant market, and this was not considered sufficient to imply a Section 3 violation. Thus, the Court did not rule out that exclusive dealing arrangements could have positive benefits, and for this reason such arrangements should be judged under a rule-of-reason approach.

If the Court's view of exclusive dealing arrangements was unclear in 1961, matters did not get much better after that date. In *White Motor Co.* v. *United States*,[51] the company was accused of employing written dealer agreements that limited dealer resales to specified geographical areas and reserved all sales to government to White alone. The Supreme Court

47. *Standard Oil of California and Standard Stations, Inc.* v. *United States*, 337 U.S. 293 (1949).
48. *Ibid.*, p. 314.
49. Asch, *Economic Theory*, pp. 351–352.
50. *Tampa Electric Co.* v. *Nashville Coal Co.*, 365 U.S. 320 (1961).
51. *White Motor Co.* v. *United States*, 372 U.S. 253 (1963).

reversed the summary judgment for the government and remanded for trial. The majority felt it had insufficient information to know whether the elimination of rivalry restricted output, as a cartel would, or created efficiency and therefore might be permissible. Unfortunately, an out-of-court settlement prevented a final judicial determination that might have recognized that, depending on the forms taken by vertical restraint or market division, efficiencies might result and make the per se rule inappropriate.

In *United States* v. *Arnold, Schwinn and Co.*,[52] the following were the facts: Arnold, Schwinn and Co. sold bicycles it manufactured in a variety of ways but always insisted that its wholesalers sell only within assigned territories and only to retailers franchised by Schwinn, and that its retailers sell only to ultimate consumers. The decisions to adopt this exclusive vertical dealing arrangement was taken when Schwinn was the industry leader with a 22.5% market share.

The Supreme Court held that "the antitrust outcome does not turn merely on the presence of sound business reason or motive," but upon the question whether "the effect upon competition in the marketplace is substantially adverse."[53]

As Bork has observed,

One might have thought the two questions closely related, if not identical. . . . the opinion did not answer either the question of efficiency . . . or the question of restriction of output. Instead, it offered a rule that turned upon no conventional antitrust or economic criteria but . . . upon the passage of titles.[54]

Specifically, the Court ruled,

We conclude that the proper application of § 1 of the Sherman Act to this problem requires differentiation between the situation where the manufacturer parts with title, dominion, or risk with respect to the article, and where he completely retains ownership and risk of loss. . . . [We] are not prepared to introduce the inflexibility which *per se* rule might bring if it were applied to prohibit all vertical restrictions of territory and all franchising. . . . But to allow this freedom where the manufacturer has parted with dominion over the goods—the usual marketing situation—would violate the ancient rule against restraints on alienation and open the door to exclusivity of outlets and limitation of territory further than prudence permits.[55]

The concern of the Court was that Schwinn had achieved vertical market division by a territorial as well as a customer clause. Location clauses were

---

52. *United States* v. *Arnold, Schwinn and Co.*, 388 U.S. 365 (1967).
53. *Ibid.*, p. 378.
54. Bork, "Vertical Constraints," pp. 178–179.
55. 388 U.S. 378–380.

declared per se illegal. In *Continental TV* v. *GTE Sylvania, Inc.*,[56] the Court broke new ground. Sylvania's position in the color television market had deteriorated until by 1960 its share had fallen to 1–2%. In 1962, a new marketing strategy was adopted. Sylvania decided to sell directly to retailers, few in number, and adopt a dealer "elbow room" policy; in order to limit competition between resellers of Sylvania products, it spaced its franchisees. To protect dealers, Sylvania would not add dealers if the dealer in the area performed well. To prevent encroachment by another dealer, Sylvania representatives made it clear orally that a franchise was for a specified location only.

By 1965 Sylvania's national market share had grown to 5%—eighth in the industry. In that year, Continental TV of San Francisco, one of its most successful dealers, opened a shop in Sacramento, where it had no franchise, and moved Sylvania sets from franchised locations to Sacramento. There it infringed on Handy Andy, a very successful Sacramento franchisee. When Continental did not withdraw its Sylvania sets from Sacramento, its franchises everywhere were canceled. Continental then filed suit against Sylvania claiming violation of Section 1 of the Sherman Act.

The Supreme Court upheld an appeals court opinion that the location clause used by Sylvania was not per se unreasonable. Mr. Justice Powell, writing for the five members of the majority, declared, "*Per se* rules of illegality are appropriate only when they relate to conduct that is manifestly anti-competitive,"[57] or, as the language he quoted from the *Northern Pacific* opinion put it, when a practice or agreement displays a "pernicious effect on competition and lack of any redeeming virtue."[58] But the "market impact of vertical restrictions is complex because of their potential for a simultaneous reduction of intrabrand competition and stimulation of interbrand competition."[59] Mr. Justice Powell cited examples of distributive efficiencies that must be considered "redeeming virtues." Manufacturers may then use them, for example, to induce retailers to engage in promotional activities or to provide service and repair facilities necessary to the efficient marketing of their products. Here he referred to the "free-rider" phenomenon.

Turning to the question of whether to extend the *Schwinn* per se rule to nonsale transactions, Mr. Justice Powell adverted to the test stated in *Northern Pacific*. He noted that vertical restrictions of a nonprice variety did not meet the standard for per se illegality:

Such restrictions, in varying forms, are widely used in our free market economy. . . . [There] is substantial scholarly and judicial authority support-

56. *Continental TV* v. *GTE Sylvania, Inc.*, 97 S. Ct. 2549.
57. *Ibid.*, p. 2558.
58. *Northern Pacific Ry. Co.* v. *United States*, 356 U.S. 1, 5 (1958).
59. *Continental TV* v. *GTE Sylvania, Inc.*, 97 S. Ct. 2558–2561.

ing their economic utility. There is relatively little authority to the contrary. Certainly, there has been no showing in this case, either generally or with respect to Sylvania's agreements, that vertical restrictions have or are likely to have a "pernicious effect on competition" or that they "lack . . . any redeeming virtue." . . . Accordingly, we conclude that the *per se* ruled stated in *Schwinn* must be overruled.[60]

In summary, *Sylvania* can be a guide for an assessment of the legality of exclusive vertical dealing arrangements—exclusive dealings must be carefully checked for their effects on efficiency. The per se rule should not be applied. But how can one determine that substantial efficiencies result from such arrangements and conduct is not anticompetitive? In this connection, the status and future of the interbrand competition must be considered. If, for example, exclusive constraints increase a company's volume substantially, and, in the presence of a declining average cost curve, reduce the manufacturer's cost, the question remains whether much of these savings will be passed on to consumers. If the firm that introduces exclusive vertical constraints has a small share of a market that benefits from aggressive interbrand competition or seeks to enter such a market, both increases in efficiency and interbrand competition are likely to result. Declaring an exclusive vertical restraint illegal under these circumstances would not serve a social purpose.

TIE-IN ARRANGEMENTS

Section 3 of the Clayton Act declares it to be illegal for a person to lease or sell commodities "on the condition, agreement or understanding that the lessee or purchaser thereof shall not use or deal in the goods . . . of a competitor or competitors of the lessor or seller, where the effect . . . may be to substantially lessen competition or tend to create a monopoly in any line of commerce."[61] This section is directly applicable to tie-in arrangements. However, the legal position toward tie-in arrangements is somewhat clouded by the fact that under Section 5 of the FTC Act, the arrangement, to be illegal, must merely be unfair to competitors. Hence under the FTC Act standard, almost any agreement can be unfair.

Several important court cases have involved tie-in arrangements. In *Federal Trade Commission v. Brown Shoe Co.*, the defendant agreed to provide certain services if the dealer would agree to buy its shoes.[62] Clearly, Brown did not want the dealer buying another company's shoes, to take a free ride on the services Brown provided. Possibly, the dealer preferred this arrangement to any other since he entered into it voluntarily. The Supreme

---

60. *Ibid.*, p. 2562.
61. 15 U.S.C. § 14.
62. *Federal Trade Commission* v. *Brown Shoe Co.*, 384 U.S. 316 (1966).

Court, however, was somewhat confused by this nonprice competition; it voided the arrangement, giving the FTC under the FTC Act wide latitude to attack these *de minimis* arrangements in their incipiency.

Another case is *Fortner Enterprises* v. *United States Steel Co.*[63] United States Steel provided Fortner with cheap 100% financing in its contruction of prefabricated homes. Fortner was then obligated to buy the products of United States Steel for the production of the homes. Presumably, Fortner would not have obtained the financing without the latter agreement. The Supreme Court stated that a tie-in is "unreasonable . . . whenever a party has sufficient economic power with respect to the tying product to restrain competition in the market for the tied product, and interstate commerce is affected."[64] The Court reversed a summary judgment for United States Steel and remanded, asking the lower court to determine whether the defendant had sufficient market power in the credit market for the tie-in arrangement to be a per se violation as an extension of monopoly power.

The case eventually returned to the U.S. Supreme Court and the Court reversed a judgment for Fortner Enterprises. Justice Stevens concluded that United States Steel had no monopoly over money and that Fortner would not have agreed to accept a higher price for houses if they were not getting a lower price for credit. Clearly, a firm with a cost advantage can either lower the price for the product and impose a tie-in, or keep the price the same with no tie-in. Why United States Steel selected the first route is unclear.

Tie-in arrangements can also be viewed as a price discrimination or cartel reinforcement device. In *IBM* v. *United States,* IBM charged a single price for a given computer but required the purchase of its cards used by the machine.[65] For cards it charged a varying price based on the quantity purchased. This arrangement could be viewed as an attempt to capture the consumer surplus.

However, IBM did not have a monopoly. Remington was a major competitor. Thus, IBM and Remington entered into an arrangement whereby neither sold to the other's lessees. Therefore, the tie-in exclusive dealing arrangement was a horizontal cartel reinforcement device.

By and large, the Court has applied a harsher standard to tie-in than to exclusive requirement arrangements. Although the Court has declared on several occasions that tying is per se illegal, a rather loose definition of per se has often been applied. Actually tie-ins have been found illegal only when monopolistic power in the market for the tying good or substantial

---

63. *Fortner Enterprises* v. *United States Steel Co.,* 394 U.S. 495 (1969), and 51 L. Ed. 2d 80 (1977).

64. 394 U.S. 495, 499 (1969), quoting *Northern Pacific Ry. Co.* v. *United States,* 356 U.S. 1, 5–6 (1958).

65. *IBM* v. *United States,* 298 U.S. 131 (1936).

market foreclosure in the tied good existed.[66] Altogether the Court's position has not been consistent.[67]

Economic analysis indicates that tie-in arrangements can under certain circumstances foster price competition, particularly when direct price cuts are considered undesirable. For this reason a per se standard seems inappropriate.

RECIPROCAL BUYING

Another arrangement that can reduce present and potential competition is reciprocal buying. Reciprocal buying is conditional in that A buys from B on condition that B buys something from A. Often this is used as a secret price-cutting device.[68] Instead of openly cutting the price of a good that A manufactures, he may sell in exchange for some good from B at a price lower than that normally charged. This arrangement enables the producer to cut prices discriminatorily and has the advantage of being difficult to detect by a competitor.

Reciprocal agreements can lead to the downfall of cartels. The secret price cut introduces uncertainty into the cartel, and often causes the other parties to respond with more competitive behavior as they see their market shares decline. Thus, reciprocal buying need not reduce competition, unless the dominant firm already has a strong monopoly position in the industry.

BOYCOTTS

Finally, there are boycotts—for example, agreements among a group of retailers not to buy from a supplier who enters into the retail business in competition with the members of the retail group. This was the case in *Eastern States Retail Lumber Dealers Association* v. *United States*.[69] However, here the question is why retailers with strong monopsony power would not exercise it directly by reducing business volume below the competitive level rather than by using an indirect boycott method.

GOVERNMENT-INDUCED PRICE FIXING AND FORECLOSURE

Various statutes have injected government into a situation where its activities clearly interfere with the competitive behavior of markets. Retail

---

66. Asch, *Economic Theory,* pp. 357–358.

67. For example, in *United States* v. *Jerrold Electronics*, 187 F. Supp. 545 (E.C. Pa., 1960), the court agreed to tie service contracts to community antennae television systems for a limited period in order to ensure satisfactory performance of the equipment and to facilitate Jerrold's innovative business.

68. See S. Liebeler, "The Emperor's New Clothes: Why Is Reciprocity Anticompetitive?" *St. John's Law Review* 44 (1970): 543.

69. *Eastern States Retail Lumber Dealers Association* v. *United States,* 234 U.S. 600 (1914).

sales maintenance laws will be discussed as an example of government-induced price fixing and occupational licensing as an example of steps to bar entry into certain professions.

It should be noted that government engages in many other activities of a similar nature. For example, there are the minimum wage laws, which have particularly far-reaching effects on the employment of the young. When those who are employed are assured a minimum wage that is higher than it otherwise would be, employers find it unprofitable to fill jobs that do not warrant such a wage. Public utility regulation is another area of intervention where government establishes prices and stipulates performance. Here in addition to the question of regulation in general is the issue of the specific rate that is being set by government. Changes in government attitude toward airline regulation, for example, indicate that previous governmental policies toward this industry might indeed have been erroneous. Specifically, past pricing policies appear to have resulted in greatly reduced demand for the industry's services and lower profitability, as was revealed when various types of airline services became available at lower prices.

A further interesting part of government's role in antimonopoly laws relates to exceptions. Thus Section 6 of the Clayton Act provides that

> nothing contained in the antitrust laws shall be construed to forbid the existence and operation of labor, agricultural or horticultural organizations, instituted for the purpose of mutual help . . . ; nor such organizations, or members thereof, be held or construed to be illegal combinations or conspiracies in restraint of trade under the antitrust laws.[70]

This provision has been declared by Asch as "the clearest departures from the procompetitive orientation of the antitrust laws."[71] Yet the provision covers a significant part of the American economy. In 1977, for example, about 27% of all farm products were sold by agricultural cooperatives operating under antitrust exception.[72]

RETAIL SALES MAINTENANCE LAWS

Since the early 1900s, the legal attitude toward artificial resale price fixing has changed a number of times. When, soon after the turn of the century, a drug manufacturer sought to establish a resale price below which no retailer was permitted to resell the product, the Supreme Court declared resale price maintenance illegal. Thus in 1911 the Court held in *Dr. Miles Medical Co.* v. *John D. Park and Sons Co.*[73] that since the result of this

---

70. 15 U.S.C. § 617.
71. Asch, *Economic Theory*, p. 373.
72. R. Smith, "Are Ag. Co-ops Overly Healthy," *Los Angeles Times,* December 18, 1977.
73. *Dr. Miles Medical Co.* v. *John D. Park and Sons Co.,* 220 U.S. 373 (1911).

practice was the same as if the retailers had gotten together and agreed what price to charge, which would be illegal price fixing, resale price maintenance, too, was illegal per se. But in 1931, California passed the first statute exempting resale-price-maintenance agreements from prosecution under state antitrust laws. The statute allowed manufacturers to set a retail price below which no resale of their product could be made. When some retailers who declined to sign price-maintenance agreements ignored the price specification of the manufacturer, California added a nonsigner provision in 1933. As a result all resellers had to adhere to the resale price established by the manufacturer as long as one reseller within the state had signed a price-maintenance contract. Other states rapidly passed similar legislation, which was upheld in 1939 by the Supreme Court.[74] According to the Court, a manufacturer's right to protect his "goodwill" justified this so-called "fair-trade" legislation. The Miller–Tydings Acts, an amendment to the Sherman Act, exempted from prosecution resale-price-maintenance contracts in interstate commerce, whenever such contracts were permitted in the reseller's state.

When in 1951 the Supreme Court in *Schwegmann Bros.* v. *Calvert Distillers Corporation*[75] weakened resale price maintenance, Congress in 1952 passed the McGuire–Keough Act as an amendment to Section 5 of the FTC Act. Under this act, resale-price-maintenance contracts in interstate commerce are permissible when legal under state law; such contracts may be enforced against nonsigning retailers whenever one retailer in the state signs and the rest are notified.

Major loopholes to fair-trade legislation began to appear in 1957 when the Supreme Court allowed undercutting a manufacturer's specified price by shipping from a non-fair-trade state or district.[76] Public Law 94-145 of 1975 ended fair-trade-law provisions and eliminated the authority of the states to enforce their own fair-trade laws.

The argument against fair-trade laws is that such agreements legalize price fixing and restrict competition. As a result, retail prices tend to be higher than they otherwise would be. Repeal of the fair-trade provisions thus would result in lower prices to consumers.

Small producers appear to have favored the repeal, whereas large producers opposed it. However, it is not quite clear why large manufacturers should favor fair trade. If consumers associate quality with price, manufacturers might feel that active price competition could hurt the reputation of their products and future marketability. Moreover, in the presence of active price competition, profit margins of retailers might be driven down. As a result, retailers might be less willing to find space for such items on

---

74. *Old Dearborn Distilling Co.* v. *Seagram Distillers Corp.*, 299 U.S. 183 (1936).

75. *Schwegmann Bros.* v. *Calvert Distillers Corp.*, 340 U.S. 928 (1951).

76. *General Electric Co.* v. *Masters Mail Order Co.*, 244 F. 2d 681, *cert. denied* 355 U.S. 824 (1957).

their shelves. On the other hand, it can be argued that manufacturers should favor active competition, in the hope that retailers would lower prices and increase sales.[77]

It is clearer why small retailers favor fair-trade laws. Price competition, especially in the presence of large discount houses, is threatening to small retailers. This fact in turn makes it clear why large retailers favored abolition of fair trade.

OCCUPATIONAL LICENSING

The states have long exercised their police power to provide for occupational licensing of law and medicine. During the latter part of the 1890s, states began to extend licensing control over more and more occupations. Today all 50 states and the District of Columbia have such occupational licensing boards, about 1500 all told.[78]

Licensing legislation is usually initiated by the occupational groups themselves rather than by the public. They argue that professional licensing is needed to protect an unwary public from unscrupulous and unethical practices. Only competent individuals should be permitted to engage in a particular practice. Opposition has usually come from other occupational groups, which feel that such licensing may jeopardize their own interests.

Following Rottenburg, many economists have looked upon occupational licensing as limiting the supply of trained labor to the market.[79] Infractions of the supply limitations are remedied by the police power. In order to restrict supply, entry costs into the market are increased, be it by additional required schooling, lower pass rates on licensing examinations, citizenship requirements, training quotas, prior experience requirements, residency requirements, age limits, character qualifications, or other restrictions. Each restrictive device reduces the supply of trained practitioners and tends to raise the costs to consumers of employing licensed professionals. An income redistribution takes place from consumers to those possessing a license. The result is an excess of persons seeking entry into the occupation, encouraging illegal markets and often unequal returns between practitioners depending upon their pre- or postrestrictiveness entry to the occupation.

The purpose of occupational licensing, as mentioned earlier, is allegedly to increase labor quality and thereby protect consumers from unethical,

77. L. G. Telser, "Why Should Manufacturers Want Fair Trade?" *Journal of Law and Economics* 3 (October 1960): 86–105.

78. For example, at the end of 1976, California had 38 such boards to regulate every licensed profession in the state, except law and real estate. The boards affected about 1 million practitioners, including 71,163 licensed physicians, 180,000 registered nurses, 15,500 dentists, 5460 dental hygienists, 4019 optometrists, 113,750 contractors, and 48,800 engineers.

79. S. Rottenburg, "The Economics of Occupational Licensing," in *Aspects of Labor Economics,* New York: National Bureau of Economic Research, 1962.

incompetent, or low-quality suppliers. But it is not entirely clear which quality is supposedly increased. If only those who are licensed are considered, then the effect of occupational licensing would be to raise the average quality assuming that proper entry requirements were selected. However, if a broader view of quality is taken and the quality of service received by all consumers from all sources is considered, then licensing does not necessarily raise quality. The quality of services received by consumers may decline because of the substitution incentives that licensing creates for consumers. These incentives stem from licensing restrictiveness that raises prices and lowers the quantity of services available. Consumers react to these influences by substituting self-service or no service for professional services. Moreover, the quality may also decline because licensed practitioners are so few that they can afford to deliver shoddy service. The question of whether occupational licensing raises quality and is in the public interest is thus an empirical question. Therefore, a number of studies will be presented in this connection.

In a detailed study of licensing in dentistry, Arlene Holen identifies four major benefits consumers might realize from licensing of dentists: reduced risk of adverse outcomes, reduced costs of acquiring information, placebo effects, and administrative recourse in the event of an adverse outcome.[80] Careful empirical analyses lead to the conclusion that licensing in dentistry appears to increase the quality of service. Higher licensing standards are found to reduce the probability of adverse outcomes, giving rise to benefits through reduced risk and uncertainty. The effect of stricter licensing on dental health status is not entirely clear. Using data on a sample of naval recruits, more stringent licensing reduced dental neglect measured as untreated dental disease relative to total dental disease treated and untreated. However, when neglect was measured as lack of all teeth, no statistical connection was found. Thus Holen concludes that "even allowing for restriction of entry, licensing appears to be beneficial. Further evidence that licensing benefits consumers is provided by their willingness to pay higher prices when standards are high."[81]

A second study, by Carroll and Gaston, reached somewhat different conclusions.[82] Their empirical studies covered real estate brokers, attorneys, sanitarians, electricians, optometrists, veterinarians, plumbers, and pharmacists. The results for the last four groups were entirely inconclusive. Somewhat better results were obtained for the first four occupations. The results are summarized as follows:

80. Arlene Holen, *The Economics of Dental Licensing* (Washington, D.C.: Public Research Institute of the Center for Naval Analyses, October 1977).

81. *Ibid.,* p. 67.

82. S. L. Carroll and Robert J. Gaston, *Occupational Licensing,* mimeographed (Knoxville: University of Tennessee, 1977).

. . . there existed a strong negative association between per capita numbers of an occupation and per capita service received. Further, almost as consistently restrictive licensing appeared to significantly lower the stocks of licensees. There is, then, evidence from several professions and trades that indicates that restrictive licensing may lower service quality.[83]

The federal courts have been largely unsympathetic to constitutional challenges to licensing legislation. For the most part they have been unwilling to pass judgment on the reasonableness of state economic regulations. For example, in *Ferguson* v. *Skrupa* the Supreme Court stated, "It is now settled that states have the power to legislate against what are found to be injurious practices in their internal and business affairs, so long as their laws do not run afoul of some specific federal constitutional prohibition, or of some valid federal law."[84] Neither have state courts halted the expansion of occupational licensing.

The federal antitrust agencies have been moving more boldly in attacking occupational licensing boards. The Antitrust Division of the Department of Justice has filed suits against the American Bar Association, the National Society of Professional Engineers, the American Institute of Certified Public Accountants, the American Institute of Architects, and the American Society of Anesthesiologists. By late 1977 the Federal Trade Commission was looking at practices of as many as 20 professions. The questions raised include the legality of restricting advertising, limiting licenses, and dictating educational requirements for members. Those under scrutiny include physicians, accountants, tour operators, and veterinarians.

Moreover, some states have also taken action. For example, state agencies have taken to court the Alabama Optometric Assocation and the Virginia State Board of Pharmacists. Civil suits have been filed against accountants in Arizona and architects in Ohio. California in 1976 passed the Public Members Act, which requires all professional and occupational boards other than those of the healing arts and accountancy to have a majority of public members.[85]

REMEDIES

Clearly as long as monopoly means something distinctly different to lawyers and economists, as mentioned in 1937 by Mason, and it is treated primarily as a phenomenon of conduct under the Sherman Act and as a

83. *Ibid.*, p. 41.
84. *Ferguson* v. *Skrupa*, 372 U.S. 726 (1963).
85. California S.B. 21-13 and California A.B. 41-32.

phenomenon of structure under the Clayton Act, consistent remedies are difficult to come by.[86] Various sanctions have been imposed once a violation of law has been established. Matters are complicated because the economic problem posed by monopoly is often independent of business conduct in any particular situation. Thus, resource misallocation and increased prices appear to stem more from the power of monopolists than from specific business strategies they may pursue. One might therefore argue that criminal fines, imprisonment, and treble damages in private suits are often inappropriate. Divestiture, instead, would deal with the more basic structural problems of the industry.

Thus in criminal cases, frequently involving conspiracy, those who are found guilty can be fined or even incarcerated. Fines are usually small in comparison to the wealth of the firm, and prison sentences are infrequent.

Once an illegal act has been found to have taken place, the court often issues an injunction to discontinue the practice in question. Such a restriction, even if combined with positive conduct requirements, is frequently insufficient. Moreover, there is no mechanism for policing the firm to see whether the court ruling is indeed consistently and fully implemented. Therefore, rather than insisting on divestiture, courts have in some cases threatened divestiture within a given time period unless satisfactory structural changes are carried out. For example, in *United States* v. *Eastman Kodak Co.*,[87] consent decrees were entered requiring that the company split the tie-in between its color film and color-film-processing activities. Eastman Kodak was to divest itself in 7 years of any processing facilities in excess of 50% of national capacity, but divestiture would *not* be required if in 6 years it was shown that purchasers of Eastman color film had easy access to processors other than Eastman. When in 1961 the government and the company agreed that independent processors had captured more than 50% of the market, divestiture was set aside.

Class action has been permitted in those cases where the effects of violation are so widely diffused among consumers that none has an incentive to bear the costs of a suit. Class action permits persons who would be affected by a decree, but are so numerous that it would be impossible or at least impracticable to bring them all in as parties, to seek judgment as a "class"; though only some members of the class may be parties to the suit, the judicial opinion may bind all members of that class. Class action provides economies of scale as well as enhanced power to plaintiffs. But class action can also lead to frivolous harassment of defendants. The importance of class actions has been rapidly increasing, though admittedly only some cases relate to antimonopoly action. For example, between 1967 and 1971 in the Southern District of New York the number of class actions filed

86. Mason, "Monopoly," pp. 34–49.
87. Trade Cas. Par. 67, 920 (W.D. N.Y., 1954).

increased from 118 to 410, with their percentage of all civil actions also increasing more than threefold, from 2.2 to 6.8%.[88]

A further remedy is to bring about more equal knowledge available to buyer and seller. The central purpose of the provision of the Federal Trade Commission Act prohibiting false advertising is to abolish the rule of caveat emptor and give consumers the right to rely on the representations of fact as truths.[89] The Fair Packaging and Labeling Program makes it unlawful to distribute commodities that fail to conform to the act's provisions.[90] Conspicuously visible labels must specify the identity of the commodity, the name and place of business of the manufacturer, packer, or distributor, and the net quantity of content, which should be separately and accurately stated in a uniform location on the label.

CONCLUSION

Economists have worked with lawyers in antimonopoly matters for longer than in any other legal field, but one would be wrong to assume that antimonopoly law is therefore clear and implemented in an unambiguous manner. Dissatisfaction with the status of antimonopoly law is widespread. In part this stems from major disagreements about the purposes of antimonopoly laws. As seen, for example, by Chief Justice Warren, the congressional mandate often is to promote competition by protecting "viable, small, locally owned businesses," and it is the court's duty to implement this mandate.[91] Others see the purpose of antimonopoly laws to be the promotion of consumer welfare. Still others blame a mismatch between the time when courts began to act and the time when thoughtful analysis became available to interpret the economic effects for the court—a view eloquently expressed by Bork:

> The trouble with the correct analysis of vertical restraints is that it appeared in the literature long after the law had to deal with the phenomenon, so that now the courts are asked to rethink and abandon an entire body of doctrine of many years standing.[92]

But mere dissatisfaction with our antimonopoly laws is far from universal, even if we do not count members of the Justice Department's Antitrust

88. American College of Trial Lawyers, *Report and Recommendations of the Special Committee on Rule 23 of the Federal Rules of Civil Procedure* (1972), p. 13; and *Annual Report of the Director of the Administrative Office of the U.S. Courts* (Washington, D.C.: U.S. Government Printing Office, 1972).

89. 15 U.S.C. § 52.

90. 15 U.S.C. § 1451 *et seq.*

91. *Brown Shoe Co., Inc.,* v. *United States,* 370 U.S. 294, 344 (1962).

92. Bork, "Vertical Constraints," p. 192.

Division. Thus, S. Whitney concludes and N. Jacoby, among others, concurs that "historically antitrust has contributed importantly to the maintenance of effective competition."[93] Thus, unhappiness with antimonopoly efforts stems more from desultoriness than from the limits of economic analysis.

93. Cited by N. Jacoby in "Antitrust or Pro-competition," *California Management Review* 16 (Summer 1974): 54, from S. Whitney, "Antitrust-Costs and Benefits," in *Business Problems of the Seventies,* ed. Jules Zackman (New York: New York University Press, 1973).

INDEX

269